THE CHORAL TRADITION

THE
CHORAL
TRADITION

An historical and analytical survey
from the sixteenth century
to the present day

PERCY M. YOUNG
M.A., Mus. D.

'*All waits for the right voice*'
WALT WHITMAN

HUTCHINSON & CO. *(Publishers)* LTD

178–202 Great Portland Street, London, W.1

London Melbourne Sydney
Auckland Bombay Toronto
Johannesburg New York

First published 1962
Second impression 1963
Third impression 1966

Reproduced and printed offset litho
in Great Britain by The Hollen Street Press Ltd.
Slough, Bucks.

Permission to include musical quotations is gratefully acknowledged in the following cases:

'Westron Wynde' Mass (Taverner), J. W. Chester Ltd., London.

Stabat Mater (Pergolesi, ed. C. Kennedy Scott), The Rio Grande (Constant Lambert), Oxford University Press, London.

The Dream of Gerontius (Elgar), Novello & Co., Ltd., London.

Requiem (Fauré), Mm. Hamelle & Cie, Paris.

Stabat Mater (Szymanowski), Golgotha (Martin), Drei Satiren (Schoenberg), Magnificat (Kamsinski), Universal Edition (Alfred A. Kalmus Ltd.), Vienna and London.

Mass in G Minor and Sancta Civitas (Vaughan Williams), J. Curwen & Sons, Ltd., London.

The Hymn of Jesus (Holst), Stainer & Bell Ltd., London.

Symphony of Psalms (Stravinsky), Spring Symphony (Britten), Boosey & Hawkes Ltd., London.

Sacred Service (Bloch), Summy-Birchard Company, Evanston, Illinois.

A Psalm of David (Dello Joio), Carl Fischer Inc., New York.

Contents

CONTENTS

Introduction

I HAVE HAD MUCH pleasure in and understanding from choral music. From long experience in it I have, I think, learned more about the nature and purpose of music as a whole than in any other way. I have, too, learned a great deal about people. As it happens I regard people, as individuals, as more significant than any form of art which may be said to exist 'for art's sake'. I can, therefore, rarely see a picture without, at the same time, seeing with some conviction of reality the working hand of the painter; nor the play without the presence of the playwright. I can never hear a work by Bach without realizing also his circumstances in Leipzig; without hearing the background of domestic, ecclesiastical and civic activity against which he composed; without feeling the impulses of time and place which caused the accent and intonation of his style. So there is such companionship with the past that the past, as such, ceases to exist.

Neither can I escape the other agreeable realities: the liveliness of those choirs of children who have so often sung great music for me whether at home or abroad; the gaiety of Austrian choirs, the sweetness of Spanish choirs, the gravity of Roman choirs, the fervour of Welsh choirs, the thoroughness and enthusiasm of American choirs I have heard, and whose members I have met; the humility of those who have been nearly associated with me in great enterprises in Bach or Handel. I am with Jean Jacques Rousseau in one aspect of musical appreciation:

> '. . . I vividly recollect the time, the place, the persons, and even the temperature and odour of the air, while the lively idea of a certain local impression peculiar to those times transports me back again to the very spot; for example, all that was repeated at our meetings, all that was sung in the choir, everything that passed then —the beautiful and noble vestments of the canons, the chasubles of the priests, the mitres of the singers, the persons of the musicians, an old lame carpenter who played the double-bass, a little fair abbé who performed on the violin, the ragged cassock which M. le

Maître (after taking off his sword) used to put over his secular habit, and the fine surplice with which he covered the rags of the former when he went to the choir, the pride with which I bore my little flute, and seated myself in the orchestra . . . the good dinner that afterwards awaited us, and the good appetites we carried to it. This concourse of objects, strongly retraced in my memory, has charmed me a hundred times as much, or perhaps more, than ever the reality had done.'

There is hardly one of us who has been concerned with choral music and has not met the counterpart of Rousseau's old lame carpenter. For choral music—today, at all events—is largely a concern of amateur musicians—volunteers; those who are, more often than not, conscious of their limitations rather than their virtues. And even when, as in famous religious foundations, the singing is on a professional basis the personality of the singer (who has to work with other singers day after day, year after year) is necessarily evident—more than, for instance, in the case of a trombonist or a flutist who is not, but is behind, an instrument. I will not press this too far, for I have great affection for orchestral players, but merely state that when the person becomes an intimate and essential part of music then the atmosphere of the music is affected in a particular way.

It is, of course, a two-way operation. You and I singing the bass line of the 'Sanctus' in the *Mass in B Minor* make our temporary impress on the movement—but we are, all the time, being secretly moulded by the hand of Bach. To what end?

We are guided in opinion by the words we sing and by the manner in which we are made to sing them. Words: herein lies another significance. Music which is sung is significant because it is sung, because it extends a natural function. Words expand into melodies, harmonies, and musical rhythms, and as they expand they afford deeper insight into their own symbolism. A composer sees a word and interprets the idea which underlies the word. To show how composers have symbolized word-concepts in various ways at various times is one part of my purpose in this book. What is here important is the realization that choral music has its roots in what is familiar: familiar, that is, in relation to the general origins of instrumental and 'abstract' music.

Choral music has its practical value in society, as any mayor or minister will—even though reluctantly—agree. In religion choral music can often assist a point of view—even a doctrine. In philosophy its nature is not negligible: thus the music of Bach may be felt as a particular exposition of the spirit of Lutheranism, as that of Delius sometimes is of Nietzsche. Such considerations of practical or philosophical fitness may produce works which must be placed among the greatest works of art (there is an analogy here with architecture). On the other hand, awareness of immediate purpose—as of a liturgy—or devotion to a philosophical (which may in these days be even political) cause may have the reverse affect. Accordingly listeners to, and performers of, choral music need particular standards of judgement. Since evaluation of choral music is affected by considerations which lie without the narrower field of 'abstract' music it would appear that this form of art is our ideal introduction to music in general. In a sense no one is ignorant of the material from which choral music springs. For this material is, in large measure, the epitomized thought, feeling, aspiration of a community rather than an individual.

As the great choral works lie midway between the actual and the ideal so do they form the connecting link between the two aspects of music defined in 'song' and 'symphony'. No music, I suggest, can be more classical—in poise, serenity, proportion and determination—than that of Palestrina; and no music can more richly secure the essential feeling of Romanticism than the great *Requiem* of Verdi.

Yet a large part of the company of music-lovers who do not sing in choral societies is almost entirely oblivious of the great tradition of choral music. It is very many years since a general book on the subject was published (which is my excuse for providing this); yet works discussing orchestral music, pianoforte music, songs, chamber music, opera and ballet fly off the presses at an alarming rate. I am old-fashioned enough to believe that understanding of all music comes through a relation of sounds heard to the personal ability to create ordered sound. Handel's acquaintance, Johann Mattheson, stated as a premise that the foundation of all music was singing. I believe him to have been psychologically correct.

It will be to the general benefit of music when audiences respond again to choral performances with enthusiasm and discrimination. The understanding of the individual will be increased; composers will be pulled back from the extremes of intellectual esotericism which sometimes lead them to compose merely for one another; and standards in choral performance will improve. There are limits to what can be done with voices but—as Stravinsky, among contemporaries, shows—these do not need to impede either originality or largeness of idea.

Those who sing chorally are sometimes victims of fallacious ideas. They too often imbue all that they sing with a specialized all-purpose tone which, when affected by lack of rhythmic awareness, may exhibit the quintessence of musical dulness. This frequent, characteristic tone is known to have two dynamic levels—loud and very loud. And what goes for Mendelssohn goes, as a matter of course, for Handel and Haydn and (if he is ever reached) for Palestrina too. Choral music covers many centuries and many countries, and in interpretation and appreciation it is necessary to be aware of distinctions in style and intention.

What has been stated determines the shape of this book.

The greater works—those which are in the general repertoire—are discussed in some detail but also set in their environment so that we have in effect a history of choral music since the sixteenth century. Beyond that I did not feel obliged to go in a work which has in view the general rather than the particular reader. Thus I would hesitate, despite the recent and distinguished researches into medieval music, to increase the proportion of unfamiliar to familiar works and the analysis of such works.

As it is we are faced with numerous difficulties. In the end the listener will be assisted if he is aware of some interpretative problems which especially assail the choral conductor. It is always desirable to present a work as the composer would have had it. But we cannot always tell from the available evidence how the composer would have had it. There is, in music earlier than the nineteenth century, doubt (despite all the factors reproduced by modern musicology) as to correct *tempi*. Here we must first be guided by the impression that pre-Romantic *tempi* were generally deliberate; and that the texture of music was in itself emotionally affective. We should aim at clarity, but not by 'bringing-out' the inner parts. We should regard the music in relation to the building in which it is performed and adjust *tempi* accordingly.

It is sometimes suggested that to sing *a cappella* is essential in all sixteenth-century music—and also in those Bach motets which we now know to have been originally accompanied. Now *a cappella* singing can be exquisite: under a burden of intonational inaccuracies, however, it can be the reverse. Our sixteenth-century musicians were a practical lot. They sang *a cappella* more often than not, but they were not above putting in an organ part or even a supporting group of whatever suitable instruments were available in order to achieve security or to explore the forbidden delights of variegated timbres. Rather than not sing the *Missa Papae Marcelli* I would use organ diapason stops to support my choir (supposing its enthusiasm was in advance of its technical accomplishment). In so doing I should consider the practice in accordance with what Palestrina would have done under similar conditions. One must be discreet though. For instance, it would be unpardonable to use either the vulgar mellifluity of the *voix céleste* or the arrogant pomp of a sola tuba stop for such instrumental support.

With madrigals I often feel that an admixture of strings with voices might be enchanting. I know that *The Silver Swan* sung by one voice above string quartet is enchanting. Would Gibbons have done this? Certainly, if he had one day found himself with these forces available. Often we have the permissive phrase 'apt for viols or voices', which shows how the sixteenth-century composer had in mind the varying conditions under which his music was likely to be performed.

In the eighteenth century music was not, on the whole, deliberately composed at posterity. It was composed for a particular day and time. If a church cantata were repeated on a subsequent occasion and if the original instruments were not to be found then Bach revised his scoring accordingly. In Handel's experience male sopranos and male altos were available (in limited quantities). In listing his oratorios for performance it is practically valueless to propose the impossible. Accordingly the solo parts are set down as for the voices which may now be expected to be employed.

To present the spirit of a particular work depends on an understanding of the purpose of the composer and the general means adopted to achieve his purpose rather than on a too acute devotion to musicological minutiae. For if we go too far along the road of purism we must inevitably conclude that to perform a work by Bach adequately we should play it out of tune on the grounds that in his day out-of-tune playing was much more common than it is today. We should observe the proportions of the music, we should retain the type of tone colouring; we should regard the music from the standpoint of its own age rather than of that of a succeeding age. Within these limits we shall make the music more impressive to a contemporary audience

—because the manipulation of the sounds will seem striking and novel
—than if we try to bring it 'up to date'.

There is a recording of the *Mass in B Minor* which turns the work
out of the eighteenth into the nineteenth century by reason of ex-
aggerated nuances and sentimental misapplication of rubato. The
intention apparently was to make the work 'beautiful'. Handel's
Messiah is made to sound like an overgrown anthem on many occasions
of its performance. It was conceived as for a theatre and the whole
nature of the music is theatrical. It is only when it is set out with this
in mind that its true spiritual virtues appear.

The end of this is that I would have choral singers flexible and
adaptable to all kinds of music—from Hassler to Harris. Skill extends
with experience. So turn to the Appendix of Works to see only a small
part of what is available for the eager and the resolute. Choral music,
say the too exclusive orchestraphiles, is dull. Let them listen to what
there is. Then let them revise their opinions.

Occasionally I have made observations of a practical nature which
appear to me of some importance. The few remarks addressed to
conductors and singers are within square brackets. The 'listener' is not
obliged to read them but it will do him no harm if he does.

Since I have already placed on record my gratitude to those who
have sung so many works for me and, therefore, taught me so much
it is only left to acknowledge my further indebtedness to the following:
to the C. C. Birchard Co. (Boston), Carl Fischer, Inc. (New York),
G. Schirmer, Inc. (New York), Universal Edition A. G. (Vienna),
Boosey and Hawkes, Ltd. (London), for their generosity in gifts or
loans of music; to the library of the Barber Institute of Fine Arts in
Birmingham and the Henry Watson Library in Manchester, who have
borne my requests for assistance with exemplary patience; to my
assistants Miss Kathleen Sims (who alone can transcribe my manuscript)
and Miss Hilda Hunter; and finally to my son Julian who has (he points
out) carried a lot of books from one place to another on my account.

                                             PERCY M. YOUNG

I

The Sixteenth Century

THE NATURE AND PURPOSE OF SIXTEENTH-CENTURY MUSIC

THERE are two ways towards an appreciation of music: one is the way of pleasure, the other of duty. I notice that most music-lovers (and musicians too, if the distinction will not give offence) take the first way in regard to, say, Tchaikovsky and Haydn, but the second if and when they come across music that is either much older or much more recent.

It is partly a matter of familiarity—the feeling that Tchaikovsky and Haydn speak an intelligible, established language, of which terms and definitions are commonly used and understood: whereas the extremes of ancient and modern have significance only for the select. Further, pleasure in Palestrina seems to savour of *lèse majesté*. It is often conceived as a duty to listen to the works of Palestrina: it is a duty to listen with ears attuned to the gravity of the style: it is a duty to feel that in such style lies the ultimate of other-worldliness and of contrapuntal mystery: it is a duty to recognize that *a cappella* (literally, for reasons which will appear, 'in the chapel') spells highbrow.

Let us start with a clean sheet.

The sixteenth century is the first great climax in the development of music. In this age choral music, for the last time, ranks as superior to instrumental. It is the age in which wealth, learning, feeling and a sense of purpose unite—for a brief period—to demand fine music.

Sixteenth-century music on the largest scale is largely choral. It was generally conceived as belonging to a particular environment. That is to say it belonged to a Latin liturgy proper to cathedral or collegiate churches. It was constructed according to ancient modal principles, based on subtle and varied rhythmic formulae and modest in harmonic coloration. Partly because of these circumstances it may now often appear to be curiously unimpassioned.

B

It is the purposefulness of the music—a guarantee of one aspect of philosophic beauty—which makes the period intensely rewarding. The purpose may briefly be epitomized in the commanding phrase *ad majorem Dei gloriam*—'to the greater glory of God'. It was not for nothing that so many masters of the eighteenth and subsequent centuries reverenced those of the sixteenth: it was because poetic and spiritual truths were then expressed in a high degree of perfection and in a form which expressed the whole outlook of contemporary life.

'At times,' wrote Schumann to Karl Franz Brendel, his successor as editor of the *Neue Zeitschrift für Musik*, 'it really sounds like the music of the spheres, and then, what art! I verily believe he is the greatest musical genius ever produced by Italy.' That was of Palestrina.

THE INFLUENCE OF THE CHURCH

The greater works of the period were written for performance in church,[1] and, since the greatest composers were employed by the wealthiest churches, then we may generally bear in mind a great resonant building which will add its own atmosphere to the total effect of music. Motets and Masses and anthems were framed in a particular setting—just as is the case with opera. The listener must be prepared to put St. Peter's in Rome, St. Mark's in Venice, the Duomo in Florence into his imagination, just as Wagner or Verdi in the concert hall or on the radio make other demands on visual imagination.

For a thousand years before the period of which we write schools of singing had flourished under the direction of the Church. It is said that a *schola cantorum* existed in Rome during the reign of Pope Silvester (A.D. 314–336). During this time instrumental music had been deliberately restrained by the Church because of suspected pagan associations. Thus by the end of the Middle Ages the best singing reached a remarkable standard.

Ease in performance stimulates invention, for the composer is encouraged to experiment with the forces at his disposal. So, while much music was conveniently disposed for four parts, polyphony in

---

[1] 'In church' may be interpreted with a little freedom. Palestrina, for example, composed a *Vexilla Regis* and other music for the erection, and blessing by Sixtus V, of the obelisk brought from Egypt by Caligula and set up in the piazza of St. Peter's, Rome, in 1585. Zarlino composed the pageant music to celebrate the victory of Lepanto (1571). Willaert essayed a series of motets on the story of Susanna. And so on.

any number of parts from two to twenty[1] abounded. Many works demanded double choir. This was a natural development from a long tradition of antiphonal singing.

SOME ASPECTS OF TECHNIQUE

Musica ficta (i.e. 'pretended music') was a convention whereby certain details in notation were, actually and intentionally, differently represented in performance. Thus: G F G in a cadence would become G F# G, giving the essential 'leading-tone' effect which was to play an important part in music of the classical period; C B A would be softened and 'modernized' to C B♭ A, the flattened seventh degree of the scale preparing for a future field of exploration on the subdominant side: F B A would become F B♭ A, avoiding one difficult and unpleasant interval, and B♭ E F would similarly change to B♭ E♭ F for the avoidance of another. These conventions were encouraged, we may believe, by the laws of acoustics, but also by much knowledge of the natural capacity of singers. The sixteenth century was the one age in which singers were discouraged from singing difficult intervals —in church at any rate, where the individual voice was subordinated to the needs of the ritual.

All sixteenth-century composers were supposed to respect the modal schematization which, though modified later, dated from the time of Pope Gregory I and was called Gregorian. Taking a diatonic octave the Modes, for practical purposes, were:

D – d	(Dorian)	G – g	(Mixolydian)
E – e	(Phrygian)	A – a	(Aeolian)
F – f	(Lydian)	C – c	(Ionian)

It will be seen that one of these is, in fact, what we now call a major scale and that another (Aeolian) is almost (quite, with a little *musica ficta*) a minor scale. By the beginning of the seventeenth century these two modes had virtually put the rest out of court. It is as well to accustom oneself to the sound of the 'ecclesiastical' modes if only because they appear not infrequently in modern music.

---

[1] A classic work, in forty parts, is the motet *Spem in alium nunquam habui* by Thomas Tallis. At the end of the polyphonic era in Italy very many composers were expanding their works for numerous voices in an attempt to counter the thesis that emotion could only come through monody.

Throughout the sixteenth century ecclesiastical officers imagined that they were keeping composers in their places. Music was for a specific purpose. It was composed to accompany and illuminate the liturgy. Therefore, settings of the service of the Mass were the largest scale works then known. There were also motets—often extensive—which coloured the various seasons of the liturgical year with settings of apposite texts. There were varied settings of canticles (which usually included alternate verses delivered in the traditional, unison, plainchant), and hymns for the services of vespers, compline and matins. In the Reformed Church in England there were anthems—these to texts in the vernacular—of the same order as motets. In all Reformed Churches there were psalm settings of great simplicity, but great power. A number of psalm tunes are still in use in the Protestant churches and may well serve as a first introduction to the music of the period. Whether Catholic or Reformed the aim was the same: to serve God through text and liturgy.

Latin was used because it was a universal language. To some extent it assisted in creating a musical style that was universal. To some extent it still does. For Stravinsky and Kodály, Vaughan Williams and Pizzetti have all found the words of the Latin liturgy a vehicle for expressing some of their most profound conclusions. To my mind there is no better way of understanding the differing qualities of spiritual awareness than in looking through the ages at settings of the one word *Sanctus* ('Holy'). In comparing Bach and Berlioz, for example, it will soon be seen how the word itself stimulates the musical imagination.

It is a truism that perfect freedom exists only under discipline. We discover that the sixteenth-century composer is disciplined by the physical and spiritual character of the Church, and further by the texts which he was obliged to set. Yet the very fact that words were, officially at all events, the dominating partner in sacred music admitted greater rhythmic freedom than is possible when, for instance, music is intended for the dance. The freedom from the tyranny of the bar line (bar lines found in music of this period are inserted by helpful editors) is the factor in early music most envied by contemporary composers who often stand on their heads in an endeavour to achieve freedom.

This is how Palestrina, in a characteristic phrase, would draw a melodic contour, sure in rhythmic balance but fluid and quite unhampered by the inexorability of regular stress.

Ex. 1

Ex - al - ta-bo te_____ Do - - - - - - mi - ne_____

It may be as well here to state that the nature of 'melody' changes from age to age. The sixteenth century was not less tuneful than the eighteenth (although it was the latter which taught us to recognize a hierarchy of 'subjects' in symphonic music). In one sense it was more tuneful. A casual glance at one of *The Triumphs of Oriana* shows not less than a dozen separate melodic ideas. They cross the score as part follows part so that the total effect is not so much of a sequence of defined tunes as of a musical mosaic wherein the fragments blend into a wonderful and coloured unity.

Under ideal conditions, the polyphonic masters gave everybody, and not only the top line, tuneful parts. Thus, the listener must learn to cast his ear far and wide, while the conductor must always be on the look-out for inner stresses and climaxes.

MANNER OF PERFORMANCE

It is always possible to idealize performances of the past. Thus a false aura of respectability often sits over Palestrina and his contemporaries. We imagine pure-throated choristers, hands clasped in sanctimony, delivering motets and masses in impeccable style and perfect in intonation—though free from the grosser noises of instrumental music. Unfortunately, false idealism often prevents our contemporary attempts at re-creation of this music. But Palestrina was too great a composer not to know that his singers in the Sistine Chapel expected (for their part) to enjoy their singing; and enjoyment in singing is intimately related to expression.

There is a good deal of internal evidence relating to expression in sixteenth-century music. Equally there is evidence that instruments— sometimes organ, sometimes brass instruments, sometimes strings, sometimes all—were called upon at times to support the voices.[1] In short, choral singing was *a cappella* when it was found possible, but accompanied when expediency suggested. Some composers were more interested in the possibilities of choral/orchestral development than others. Particularly was this the case in Venice, where at an early date Giovanni Gabrieli was using all the resources of late-sixteenth-century music (see the Davison–Apel *Historical Anthology of Music*, Vol. I, No. 157), while in England both Byrd and Gibbons[2] were well advanced in the technique of the 'verse anthem'—a rudimentary cantata.

Earlier ages had been uncompromising in regard to what constituted sacred music. Instruments were not favoured because they too easily provoked memories of secular orgies. That, at any rate, was a theory promoted by the Early Fathers and constantly kept alive by the more diligent among Church dignitaries. We have already mentioned that the age of Palestrina's music—music which in so many ways was so truly medieval—was that in which the ideals of the Renaissance were in full swing. We have allowed that the grace and fluidity of the sixteenth century symbolized one part of the Renaissance outlook. That instrumental music began to take its place in church symbolized another. The frontiers between sacred and secular, never very clear, began to collapse. On the one hand cynical churchmen considered their own pleasure and were prepared to turn the Church into a picture gallery, or a concert room. On the other, there were those like St. Philip Neri, friend and patron of many musicians, who saw in fine art an opportunity for spiritual reclamation. Thus it was that St. Philip drew the pattern of what was later to become oratorio.

A minority of privileged persons in all countries were able to cultivate refinement in their own homes, again in accordance with Renaissance philosophy. So we discover Palestrina encouraged secularly by the Duke Guglielmo Gonzaga of Mantua, John Wilbye finding exclusive employment in an English country house, and Prince Carlo Gesualdo combining all the qualities—both attractive and unattractive—of a Renaissance idealist by writing music with one hand

---

[1] In 1526 Erasmus had complained of noisy accompaniments to the *Sanctus*, while Giovanni Gabrieli's experiments with voices and orchestra at St. Mark's, Venice, were milestones on the way to Monteverdi and Schütz. In 1592 Friedrich, Duke of Würtemberg, visited Windsor and enjoyed the organ, together with cornets, flutes, fifes and other instruments—and 'a little boy who sang so sweetly amongst it all . . .' The motets of Lassus were described as for instrumental accompaniment, and the Munich court employed a fine team of 30 instrumentalists.

[2] See Byrd's *From Virgin's Womb this day did spring, An earthly tree a heavenly fruit it bore*, and Orlando Gibbons's *This is the record of John*.

and assassinating his enemies with the other. Both, so it is said, out of love. Side by side with mass and motet we have, therefore, madrigal and ballet. The outward forms of motet and madrigal were much the same. The ballet, lighter in conception, brought to choral music the verve of the dance.

So as we sing Morley's, or Gastoldi's, or Festa's or Costeley's frivolities we should bear in mind the not-very-distant snap of the castanet or twang of the fiddle. One quality of the sixteenth century, much respected by those of the literary who are deficient in it, is wit. Those who sing madrigals gravely, unaware of the reserves of humour contained in them, should be debarred from musical performance.

We may summarize this introduction to the sixteenth century by underlining the opportunities then open to composers. Both church and palace kept them in full production—and there was something of an export market too. Further to encourage abundance occasions of State demanded new music. Stylistic efficiency and fluency were more desirable than mere innovation. (It is striking that within the period 1550–1620 the mass of polyphonic music changed its general outlook very little.) There was one style which incorporated both sacred and secular. And above all there was a sense of purpose. Making allowance for all conventions in formal address we may believe that when William Byrd wrote his 'Epistle to the Reader' in his *Psalmes, Sonets and Songs of Sadness and Piety* (1588) he meant what he said:

'If thou finde any thing here worthy of lykeing and commendation, give prayse unto God, from whome (as a most pure and plentiful fountaine) all good gifts of Scyence doe flow: whose name be glorified for ever.'

'THE WESTRON (OR WESTERN) WYNDE' MASS BY JOHN TAVERNER (1495(?)-1545)

John Taverner was probably a native of Boston, in Lincolnshire, where he was buried under the famous 'Stump'—one of the glories of English church architecture. In 1526 he was appointed as 'Informator' (or superintendent) of the choirboys at Cardinal Wolsey's new college in Oxford (later Christ Church). Three and a half years later Taverner, who had been accused of, and temporarily imprisoned for, heresy, resigned this appointment. Cardinal College was a notorious centre of Lutheranism and there seems little doubt but that Taverner became sincerely and fanatically affected by his environment; so that he retired from the profession of music to put himself at the disposal of the government as a zealous administrator at the time of Henry VIII's Dissolution of the Monasteries.

Taverner's music was composed before the year 1530. Therefore he belongs to the group of composers—Fayrfax, Aston and Ludford—who first began to emancipate English music from the academic stringency of the powerful Flemish school. He left eight Masses, some other Latin Service music, and a number of motets. Of this music 'The Westron Wynde' Mass is the best known.

At various times during the Middle Ages composers attempted to humanize ecclesiastical music by introducing secular melodies in the place of those which were sacred. (Not infrequently restrictions were issued by the authorities condemning this practice.) To base a work on a known melody, or *cantus firmus*, was not a sign of deficient imagination. Melodies, especially those with a liturgical history, aroused associations. When Bach used chorale melodies in his extended works he followed medieval principle. A celebrated continental folk melody was 'L'homme armé'.[1] The English favourite was 'The Westron Wynde', a melody found also in Masses by Christopher Tye and John Shepherd. Taverner sets the melody in each movement of his Mass, thus we have, in fact, a set of variations on a given theme.

The work of Taverner shows affinities with the style of des Prés and Ockeghem in that canonic and fugal rigour (in both canon and fugue the several parts imitate each other in the delivery of one theme) give shape and direction to the layout of the music, and the rhythmic detail is based on Flemish scholasticism (some of the rhythmic exercises of the more academic Flemings were as intellectually fascinating and as musically uninspiring as some essays of contemporary writers of the twelve-tone school); while there were recent precedents for basing church music on secular melodies in Dufay and des Prés.

THE NATURE OF THE MASS

The service of the Mass must be understood with all its ancient significance. The Mass was the central activity of the Church and every attribute of art was brought into play to increase its significance: the

[1] Busnois and Dufay were among the first to use this melody as *cantus firmus*; Carissimi was the last.

sanctuary was designed as a stage for the better exhibition of the sacred rites; altar furnishings were richly designed and not infrequently enhanced by the presence of priceless works of art and by the serene light filtered through the stained windows of the clerestory; priests and deacons, sub-deacons and acolytes were the actors in the drama; churches themselves, with aisles and ambulatories and side chapels, were designed around the motiv of the Mass. If it is suggested that the total effect was theatrical the intention is to dignify the theatrical and not to denigrate the religious. We must see the Mass as the social, philosophic and artistic hub of the life of Europe for a long period in its history. Such consideration brings the music that was composed for the Mass into closer contact with the ordinary parts of human behaviour than merely academic observation often seems to indicate. John Taverner must have been very well aware of the necessity for keeping sacred music within the limits of Tudor appreciation for, before going to Oxford, he had been employed in a smaller collegiate church establishment at Tattershall, in Lincolnshire.

It is always a matter for wonderment that in olden times people were content to stay in church for so long. Yet the truth is that (and part of the reason is detailed above) people enjoyed church-going. It will be discovered that Taverner, like his contemporary Christopher Tye, was inclined to compose at considerable length.

Those sections of the Mass obligatory on composers are the 'Kyrie': the 'Gloria': the 'Credo': the 'Sanctus' (with the 'Benedictus'): the 'Agnus Dei'. The 'Kyrie' is an introductory prayer, the 'Gloria' a hymn of praise, the 'Credo' a declaration of faith and an expression of dogma: the remaining sections are felt as more reflective and more poetic. Collectively these sections are known as the *Ordinarium* (or Ordinary) of the Mass. Those parts of the Mass subject to alteration according to the significance of the day comprise the *Proprium* (or Proper) ('Introit': 'Gradual': 'Alleluia': 'Offertory': 'Communion'). At all times the Mass has retained some connection with its plainsong ancestry. Thus the introductory words of 'Gloria' and 'Credo' are invariably meant to be intoned by the priest to the traditional motivs. In English Masses of the Tudor period more plainsong was introduced than in Flemish or Italian Masses. Taverner and most of his contemporaries normally did not set the 'Kyrie'—this being associated with a variable trope on the larger Festivals, and in the 'Credo' the clauses between 'Non erit finis' and 'Et exspecto' were omitted. This practice dated from the time of John Dunstable, who (in the Bologna MS.) had different parts singing different words at the same time. Dunstable's successors, apparently unaware of his methods in this respect and finding words missing in certain parts continued to leave them out, not always quite consistently.[1]

The textual form of the Mass and the dramatic activity which accompanied its presentation suggest that the imaginative composer must have viewed his task as did the eighteenth-century composer of a symphony: so many contrasted movements—and each with its own character. The 'Kyrie' (if set) was a slow introduction and the 'Gloria'— 'Glory to God'—obviously a quick movement: the 'Credo', with its long dogmatic clauses, an opportunity for purely musical development and the climax of the whole: the 'Sanctus' a solemnity (the 'Sanctus' feeling infuses the wonderful fourth movement of Schumann's 'Rhenish' Symphony, which movement is itself a tribute to the sixteenth century): the 'Agnus Dei' a mystical coda to the whole. Within these general lines of thought there are whole worlds for exploration. Taverner sets the Mass in one way: Beethoven in another. The difference between their works is not necessarily of excellence (for technical comparisons are impossible) but of perception.

The techniques available to Taverner were, by later standards, limited. But a simple vocabulary may encourage strength and direct-ness in utterance. This is the quality of 'The Westron Wynde' melody itself. With this as foundation Taverner designed a great monument, but a monument of granite rather than marble.

Taverner, as has been stated, wrote no 'Kyrie' setting for his Mass. In performance, however, it is now customary to employ the arrange-ment of 'Benedictus' music to the words of the 'Kyrie' prepared by H. B. Collins. In this edition the 'Westron Wynde' melody first appears in this 'Kyrie' in double time in the soprano. It is transferred to the tenor part for the 'Christe eleison' and the final 'Kyrie'. Mostly the melody is allotted to these two voices throughout the Mass (the altos are not allowed to sing it at all: being a practical man Taverner probably considered that its wide range was beyond the limits of those— necessarily male—altos he knew); but the bass twice announces it with

[1] This subject is dealt with by Dom Anselm Hughes in the Missa 'O quam suavis' (ed. H. B. Collins, Plainsong and Medieval Music Society, 1927), pp. XXXIII–XXXVI. Among the earliest complete settings of the Mass were those by Ludford and Mundy, while those of William Byrd were also complete, although not practicable in public in Elizabethen and Protestant England.

great effect. Once for the 'Crucifixus' and once for the 'Agnus Dei'. Thus Taverner suggests that at these moments it is right to submerge worldly instincts and feelings. Bach was a symbolist in one way, Taverner in another. Occasionally Taverner changes the rhythmic mode of the melody (students of Berlioz and Wagner and other practitioners of the *leit-motiv*—or 'motto-theme'—might glance at Taverner: writers sometimes suggest that Taverner was merely mechanical, but they are wrong)—as in the final section of his 'Gloria' where he whips up the tempo and sets all the bells ringing.

In the final 'Dona nobis pacem' the melody is set again in triple time, but a gentler flow of contrasting tunes in the lower voices introduces a spirit of tranquillity. Otherwise triple meter is used dramatically to catch the listener's attention at 'Et exspecto resurrectionem'—'And I expect the resurrection of the dead'.

Rhythmic alteration is one way to catch attention. Melodic alteration is another. A third is textural. Taverner varies the number of parts in action with great skill. Thus there is two-part counterpoint (soprano and tenor) at 'gratias agimus', and again, with beatific intention, at the opening of the 'Benedictus' (to which the dual entry of tenor and bass at 'qui venit' is highly picturesque); and three-part counterpoint to emphasize the grave 'et incarnatus est' and, later, 'qui tollis peccata'. Elsewhere three-part writing is used as a foil to four parts so that, by contrast, the four parts may sound innumerable. The 'Sanctus' (note the rising bass) is a movement which exemplifies this. The first measures of this movement are immense and by suggestive use as of the combined voices of angels and archangels and the communion of the faithful:

Ex. 2

The crisis in any Mass lies in the treatment of the crucifixion. Here is Taverner's picture:

This plangent passage shows how artistic perception makes a mockery of ancient and modern. In certain later medieval music long phrases had been broken—apparently arbitrarily and certainly without regard to the accommodation of the words—by rests. Such a device had been termed *ochetus* (hocket—'hiccough'). Here Taverner remembers the practice, but makes of it a virtue. The word 'sepultus'—'buried' —is broken tragically. The colouring of the music by the omission of the top part and the descent of the bass (which is, of course, 'The Westron Wynde' melody) is likewise contributory to a most moving crisis in the affairs of the music.

Strangely remote—for Taverner was not, even at Oxford, in the centre of musical affairs—this Mass commands attention by its simplicity, its strength and its sincerity.

'MISSA PAPAE MARCELLI' AND 'STABAT MATER' BY GIOVANNI PIERLUIGI DA PALESTRINA (1525-1595)

Palestrina is the composer, accepted throughout three centuries and more, as the first of his age. Perhaps this ascription of pre-eminence has been in some measure due to the erroneous impression that sixteenth-century music was exclusively ecclesiastical. Palestrina worked in the ecclesiastical capital of the world, was approved by Popes, was connected intimately with the reforms called for by the Council of Trent and left a vast corpus of music. He was favoured by environment. But the quality of his music is such that criticism is almost impertinent. He may be regarded as the archetype of the classical ideal in music. Before Palestrina Dr. Charles Burney, the eighteenth-century English musical historian, held his breath (and his tongue, which sometimes wagged maliciously over the solecisms of the 'Gothic' composers of the sixteenth century): 'In a general *History of Ancient Poetry*, Homer would doubtless occupy the most ample and honourable place; and Palestrina, the Homer of the most *Ancient Music* that has been preserved, merits all the reverence and attention which it is in a musical historian's power to bestow.'

The unique quality of Palestrina lies in his perfection of balance and proportion, in his intellectual stamina which can dispose of all problems with sublime ease of manner and integrity of judgement, in his consummate sense of appropriateness; above all in his calm.

PALESTRINA'S CAREER

So far as we may judge Palestrina was—as the world reckons—a successful man. He twice married—once profitably. He engaged in trade: clothing, horses and wine. He came from modest, though not impoverished, provincial surroundings and had the good fortune to gain the patronage of the influential. Thus the Bishop of the town of Palestrina, becoming arch-priest at S. Maria Maggiore, in Rome, there arranged for the boy's education. After this his first appointment was as organist in the cathedral at Palestrina.

At that time (1544) the Bishop was Cardinal Giovanni del Monte, who became, in 1550, Pope Julius III. A year after the accession of the pontiff Palestrina was appointed *maestro di cappella* ('master of the chapel', viz. director of the choir) of the Julian Choir (founded by Julius II in 1513) at St. Peter's. Four years afterwards Palestrina became a member of the Papal Choir. This body of singers, with which he was connected for the greater part of his life, was the Pope's personal choir and sang in the Sistine Chapel. Numerous intrigues, changes consequent on new administrations and political and personal calamities gave Palestrina much cause for anxiety. But his reputation was such that he could take almost any musical appointment that might be vacant. Then, in 1555, he succeeded Orlandus Lassus as musical director of St. John Lateran; in 1561 he became *maestro di cappella* of St. Mary the Great (S. Maria Maggiore); in 1565 he directed the musical education of students at the new Roman seminary; in 1570 he succeeded Giovanni Animuccia and became for the second time in his career director of the Julian choir.[1]

With all this—and more—Palestrina found time to compose nearly a hundred Masses, five hundred motets, numerous hymns, offertories, lamentations, litanies, psalms and madrigals. With Palestrina, as with Bach, we must select. Our objective should be variety. Two or three Masses, a handful of motets and specimens of other liturgical music will show us something of the vast range of Palestrina's beauty.

I would elect to hear the magnificent *Tu es Petrus*; the Christmas motet O *magnum mysterium*, tender and evocative; the great eight-part *Surge illuminare*; the serene four-part *Alma Redemptoris* which springs, with the freshness of Botticelli, from the lyrical idea of the 'star of the sea', or *stella maris*; the Pentecostal *Deum Complerentur*; and *Adoramus te Christe*—in which the humble believer is on his knees in simple prayer: the *Stabat Mater*, which Wagner regarded as the greatest work of its kind; the *Missa Aeterna Christi Munera* (a Mass based on the tune for the hymn 'The eternal gifts of Christ'), the *Missa brevis* ('Short' Mass) and the *Missa Papae Marcelli*—the Mass for Pope Marcellus.

These works reveal the superb appositeness of the music—so that with *Tu es Petrus*—'Thou art Peter'—one would be in the forecourt of St. Peter's on Easter Day to see the Pope and his entourage proceed to the door of the Basilica surrounded by the tumult of drums and trumpets and bells.

He hints at his own aesthetic principles in a letter (criticizing a ducal composition) to the Duke Guglielmo Gonzaga: 'I have marked a few places where the harmony would be clearer with fewer notes . . . some unisons in the fugue seem to give a forced movement to the parts—and at the *stretto* the words may be obscured, a fault to be found in second-rate work.' There are numerous great composers whose aim in revision is elimination of the superfluous. Palestrina was one of these.

---

[1] For a more detailed understanding of the place occupied by Palestrina's music at St. Peter's, the reader is referred to R. R. Terry's 'Some Sistine Chapel Traditions' in *A Forgotten Psalter* (London 1929). The number of singers in the Julian choir varied from twenty-four (seven soprano, seven contralto, four tenor, six bass) in the reign of Clement VII to thirty-six (1624).

Compared with 'The Westron Wynde' Mass there are certain differences in style. However, Palestrina's Mass is later in date by little more than a quarter of a century: it was composed at some time between 1555 and 1560.

The obvious point to notice first is that Palestrina does not rely on a *cantus firmus*. In many works Palestrina had used a basic theme. There were, for example, the *Ecce sacerdos magnus*, the *L'Homme Armé* and the 'Hexachord' Masses. The first is built on a hymn tune, the second on a secular song and the third on a motiv favoured by earlier masters of the 'academic' style. Later Masses—such as *Aeterna Christi Munera*, *Veni Creator* and *Assumpta est Maria*—were to use significant and familiar melodies (as Bach was later to use the chorale) to stimulate devotional concentration. That treatment is free and suggestive *Missa Papae Marcelli*, however, is independent of such adventitious aid.

Next notice the crystallization of the fugal manner. Taverner could manage imitation effectively at the octave, but Palestrina gives us the familiar intervals of imitation as in Bach. Thus the 'Kyrie'.

Ex. 4

This excerpt shows a development in tonal sense and, further, the suspended discords which were the most important feature of sixteenth-century dissonance. There is also evident a capacity for making music run fluently along by treating a cadence not only as a point of arrival but also of departure. This emphasizes the plasticity of the style in relation to melody (for each part is coequal in counterpoint and the lines may cross and recross), rhythm and phrase.

This Mass employs six voices. Palestrina would have noticed that his predecessors were aware of the colour potential of the choral unit. He anticipated, more than anything else, the seventeenth-century tradition of *concertino* and *concerto grosso* (i.e. the small group used in apposition to the larger group in instrumental ensembles), while surely carrying into choral style the familiar contrast between string and wind groups. With great dignity and simplicity—but entirely without sentimentality—Palestrina depicts Him who 'taketh away the sins of the world' and, spreading his melodic range and quickening the tempo, implores:

Ex. 5

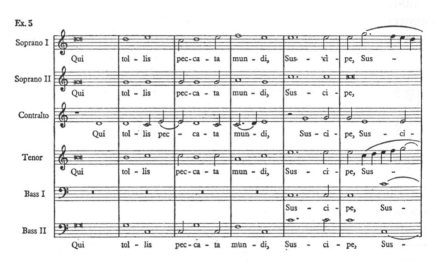

Here Palestrina makes great use of harmonic statement: the chords (we are limited to major, minor and diminished triads) become significant in themselves and in relation to the whole. Homophony—the use of chord blocks rather than of interweaving tunes—is used for emphasis. The chief doctrinal classes of the 'Credo' are stated in this way. So we recognize in Palestrina a harmonist as well as a contrapuntalist. In some ways one may compare Palestrina with Handel: for they were united by the same superb talent of precision.

An unfortunate friend of mine (since he has now some little eminence he shall be nameless) was once taunted by a dyspeptic examiner: 'And how many violin concertos did Palestrina write?' The answer was, of course, none. But if Palestrina had composed such a work it would surely have included

Ex. 6

for the soprano rises serenely over the alternations of tonic and dominant and carries aspiration beyond logic—otherwise one might quote the 'Sanctus' in support of Spinoza's proposition that 'the human mind has an adequate knowledge of the eternal and infinite essence of God'.

In itself the *Missa Papae Marcelli* is an absorbing aesthetic experience. It was intended as something more. In 1555 Pope Marcellus II, newly elected but destined only to reign for three weeks, addressed the Papal Choir on the need for a simpler form of church music 'so that everything could be both heard and understood properly'. Pope Marcellus was expressing opinions on church music which were also voiced at the Council of Trent, and, even more, by Protestant reformers. Whether Palestrina's Mass was heard and approved by the panel of Cardinals appointed to approve a suitable style for liturgical music is not known, although many fables have surrounded the known facts. It must suffice to say that Palestrina was asked to revise the liturgy as a result of a brief from Gregory XIII, that he was patronized by Sixtus V, and that he held pride of place, in his own day, among composers of church music. The 'Pope Marcellus' Mass may well stand as a symbol of counter-Reformation determination to improve standards of worship.

'STABAT MATER'

It is axiomatic that no composer is either wholly 'classical' or wholly 'romantic'. Palestrina was, we may say, on the classical side, but pity and wonder colour his vision. The *Stabat Mater* is not only a great work but a moving work: immediately moving. Insofar as the term can have any meaning in the sixteenth century it is profoundly romantic in impulse. This could hardly be otherwise, for the ancient poem of the *Stabat Mater*—written in the thirteenth century by Jacopone de Benedictis—is intensely emotional. It was one of the five *Sequences*, or hymns which developed an existence independently of the Mass of which they once formed part, allowed in the Church after the Council of Trent. It describes the scene of the Crucifixion with special focus on Mary, the Mother of Jesus, and naturally came to belong to the Good Friday rites; although Palestrina's setting was given in St. Peter's on Palm Sunday.

In 1880 the Societa Musicale Romana asked Wagner to contribute a work on the occasion of the unveiling of a bust of Palestrina. Wagner's response was to send the score of the *Stabat Mater*, the 'Sanctus' from *Aeterna Christi Munera* and a *Magnificat* of Palestrina. His interest in the *Stabat Mater* was of long standing, for he had edited the work for performance in Dresden in 1848.

The opening of the *Stabat Mater* is a classic quotation. The first choir (for the work is designed for double choir) sings

Ex. 7

Sta - bat   Ma - ter   do - lo - ro - sa

which may, for interest, be compared with the first phrase of Dvořák's *Stabat Mater*. The second choir repeats the same music but to the appositional phrase—'juxta crucem lacrymosa'. This first section establishes the atmosphere of the whole work—pity, and love, and wonder. The music opens to a climax at the words 'pertransivit

gladius'. By this time the listener will have found himself at home with
the tonality. Technically the music is cast in the Aeolian mode; but more
evident are the changes to D minor and to F major, with a final close
on a firm chord of D major.

The next section starts with (Ex. 8). The eight parts encompass the

love of the devout for the afflicted Saviour in wide-spaced triads,
within which rhythmic pulsation symbolizes the throb of anguish.
From this point the narrative runs, mostly homophonically and with the
choirs divided antiphonally, to (Ex. 9), where again concentration on

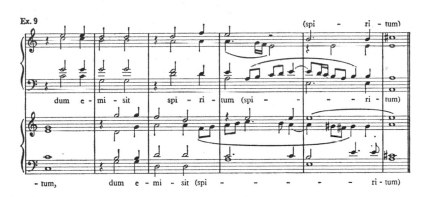

an isolated action—one of the central actions in human experience—
calls from the music lyrical extension of the counterpoint. (It is interesting to notice how Palestrina and Victoria—see the latter's *Tenebrae*—
beautify the death of Jesus by avoiding realism, whereas Pergolesi,
Verdi, Dvořák, aiming at realism, contract the vocal line into
imitative ejaculations.)

'Eja, mater' begins what is virtually a second movement. The music is less tense and runs in triple time, and to a climax with

'In amando Christum Deum
Ut sibi complaceam.'

The significant word is 'amando' and the sopranos sweep up a scale passage until a cadence in D is reached. This introduces the concluding section. The 'Sancta Mater' is set to an infinitely beautiful sequence of three chords: G major, C major and F major. It is noticeable that drama is avoided throughout and the most dramatic passages Palestrina leaves to be expressed through a clear exposition of the words.

[It was through Wagner that the *Stabat Mater* of Palestrina became part of the modern repertoire. A glance at his editorial method will show some problems in present performance and appreciation. However, Wagner's edition of the *Stabat Mater* is, like many nineteenth-century editions of earlier music, too generously marked with dynamics. The secret of impressive interpretation of Palestrina lies in dignity—which the Romans had as opposed to the greater picturesqueness of the Venetians, in controlled phrasing which can enhance the natural spaciousness of the style, in flexibility of rhythm, in abhorrence of all eccentricities. It will thus be found that 'interpretation' will come.

The coda of the *Stabat Mater* shows admirably the need of all the requisite qualities.]

'PENITENTIAL PSALMS' AND MOTETS BY ORLANDUS LASSUS (1532(?)-1594)

Palestrina succeeded Lassus in 1555 at the great Basilica of St. John Lateran. It would be instructive to know what the worshippers at St. John's thought of the change of musical direction; for if we indulge in the harmless game of comparison and contrast—Bach, Handel; Haydn, Mozart; Verdi, Wagner, etc.—we must set Palestrina, greatest of the Italians, against Lassus, last and greatest of the Flemish school. Lassus, writes Cecil Gray,

'closes an epoch and inaugurates another; he is at once a conclusion and a commencement, a lake into one end of which a river empties itself while from the other a new stream takes departure—one the stream of the Middle Ages, the other the stream of modern music. While Palestrina may be considered as the last flowering in music of the medieval spirit . . ., and Victoria the musical representative of the Catholic Revival or the Counter-Reformation, so Lassus is to a great extent the musical embodiment of the spirit of the Renaissance. Like Euphrosia, the offspring of the unison of Faust and Helen, the ancient and the modern world, Lassus is a dual personality in whom two opposite tendencies meet in perpetual conflict.'

1434074

CAREER AND CHARACTER OF LASSUS

The musical personality of Lassus is so powerful that, even after the passage of nearly four centuries, the soul of the man can be ascertained from the nature of his music. This is not true of Palestrina, whose personality remains inscrutable.

Palestrina spent the whole of his professional life in Rome. Since Rome was the centre of the Western world he could hardly be described as provincial: but he had a Roman mind and a Roman outlook. Lassus was different. His music indexes his many interests and opportunities. He had many secular opportunities and his range is from the courtly madrigal to part-music of a more popular-*cum*-experimental, order. So he composed madrigals and villanellas—his first set appeared in 1555, the same year in which Palestrina's first set were published; *chansons*; *Deutsche Liedlein* (lit. 'little German songs'); some Neapolitan character sketches (accompanied villanellas which may have been intended for action and therefore somewhere among the original sources of *opera buffa*); some instrumental music;[1] masses; motets; Passion music;[2] service music; and he even made arrangements of Lutheran melodies. In all Lassus left more than a thousand works. Some idea of his character may be gained from the fact that his Masses, except for the 'Sanctus', 'Benedictus' and 'Agnus' sections, are not of compelling interest; that his motets rise to strident intensity when the texts

[1] The 1577 set of *Cantiones* comprised twenty-four duets; twelve for voices and twelve for instruments. The latter were subsequently described as *fantasias* or *ricercari*.

[2] In the fourth volume of the *Patriocinium* (1575) appeared a *Passion according to St. Matthew*. The part of the Evangelist was to have been sung to the traditional plainsong. Lassus also composed Passion settings according to the other Evangelists.

call for melancholy or penitence; that his low-life music is also true-to-life.

Lassus, unlike Palestrina, was a copious letter writer. His correspondence with Duke William of Bavaria in an assortment of French, Latin, Italian and German reinforces the conclusions that may be drawn from the music. Lassus knew despair as he knew exuberant happiness. He was before his time in compounding his music of self-knowledge. In the end I am not sure that the sixteenth-century character is not as admirably summarized by Lassus as by any other artist of his time.

The circumstances of his life help to explain in some measure the richness of the music of Lassus. He was born at Mons, in Flanders, and at an early age, on account of the beauty of his voice, was taken into the retinue of Ferdinand Gonzaga, Viceroy of Sicily. Lassus spent his impressionable years of boyhood and adolescence in Sicily, Milan and Naples. Some part of his young manhood was spent in Rome and he was at St. John Lateran for about a year and a half until December 1544. He then entered the service of a Neapolitan nobleman who took him to England, to France and to Antwerp, where he lived for some years. His first madrigals were published in Antwerp and were remarkable for their adventures in chromatic harmony. In 1556 Lassus published his first book of motets, which was dedicated to the Bishop of Arras.

Probably through the influence of the Bishop, Lassus was appointed in 1556 to the court and chapel of Albert V, Duke of Bavaria. Lassus remained at Munich, in the employment of Duke Albert and, after his death in 1579, of his successor Duke William. The many acts of kindness shown by the ducal house and the freedom of activity permitted to the composer remind us of the good fortune of Haydn in respect of his patronage by the Esterházys. Both Albert and William took great pride in the work of Lassus and he was able to travel widely. He used to make frequent journeys to Italy to enrol new recruits for the musical establishment and kept abreast of all musical developments in that country. Otherwise he was held in high repute in France (he dedicated a book of *chansons*—hence the French title—to Charles IX and had other works published in Paris); he was ennobled by the Emperor Maximilian; he was decorated by Pope Gregory XIII, in the Papal Chapel, as Knight of the Golden Spur. The last years of Lassus' life were clouded by long periods of melancholia, and the thought of death—and of the Last Judgement—obsessed him.

This most remarkable artist must be accounted as one of the most

profound and searching of composers. His influence was long felt in
Germany so that we may even find a similarity of outlook, especially in
moods of deep perception, between Lassus and Bach, and Lassus and
Brahms.

A PERSONAL STYLE

Lassus had a superlative mastery of technique. He had the boldness and
scholarship of the Flemings together with the romantic awareness of
harmonic surprise exploited by Cipriano de Rore[1] and the dignity of
the Italians. More than any of his contemporaries he seems to examine
the significance and poetic background of every word that he sets.
Thus even in a conventional four-part *Magnificat*—in which the odd
verses are in the traditional, unison plainchant and the even verses in
parts—he must picture the hungry (Ex. 10) and the rich sent empty

Ex. 10

away (Ex. 11). In a short space *Lectio VIII* from the *Sacrae Lectiones*

Ex. 11

Novem ex Propheta Job (1567) displays a number of facets of style
(Ex. 12). The fine confidence of the opening, the almost Brahmsian
suspension of rhythmic interest and intensification of harmonic depth
in expectation of the 'novissimo die', the triumphant gesture of resurrection are magnificently personal: but also finely disciplined. Expectation is one characteristic of the visionary and another eminently sing-
able motet—*Exspectans Exspectavi*—from the *Sacrae Cantiones* of 1585

[1] De Rore was a Flemish composer who became *maestro di cappella* at St. Mark's, Venice, in
succession to Willaert. He was a notable exponent of chromatic harmony.

Ex. 12

shows Lassus waiting patiently for the Lord in quiet faith. This fugal point epitomizes the mood of the whole (Ex. 13).

Ex. 13

For choral orchestration turn to the great six-part *Salve Regina* of 1582. This, together with *Christus Resurgens* of the same year, represents the maturity of Lassus and is symbolic of the greater care taken of the religious establishment at Munich when Duke William—who was under considerable pressure from the Jesuits—came into his inheritance. In *Christus Resurgens*, an Easter anthem, we are aware of the court band in the background. The last Alleluias are punched out—as by brass—to repeated dominant and tonic chords; while in the motiv of the top part (Ex. 14), we descry a favourite germ in the equally vigorous, yet reflective style, of Vaughan Williams.

Ex. 14

The *Septem Psalmi Poenitentiales* (Seven Penitential Psalms) have generally been accepted as climactic works in the career of Lassus. It should be said at once that this is both true and untrue. If a *tour de force* is looked for the listener is certain to be disappointed. If, on the other hand, fitness to purpose is the intention, then it will be recognized that Lassus has here wrought finely. We may see the limitations. The psalms which comprise this sequence are Nos. 6, 32, 38, 51, 102, 130 and 143. The intention of the composer is to contemplate these grave poems and to admit of no more purely musical effect than is necessary to enable them to be sung. Therefore brilliance is lacking on the one hand and dramatic statement on the other. Each verse (sometimes long verses are divided) or half-verse is treated separately as a musical movement: therefore no prolongation of musical phrase—one of the great sixteenth-century means of allowing musical lyricism to spin its own web—is possible. Again consistent care for the words leads to homophony rather than polyphony. Thus interest in counterpoint is slender. The only place in which Lassus allows his musical technique free rein is in the second part of the 'Gloria' (*Sicut erat in principio . . .*). Each psalm maintains the same tonality throughout. In Psalm 130 the whole is further unified by introduction of the Gregorian Sixth Psalm Tone. This short and familiar chant acts as a *cantus firmus* throughout. The manner in which one psalm is treated will serve as a model for all.

Psalm 143 opens in five-part homophony, with slight alternations of rhythmic crisis in the lower voices. It will be discovered that Lassus employs subtle stresses of rhythm and melody to reinforce the associations of particular words: so, 'O Lord, hear my prayer' (Ex. 15) and

Ex. 15

Do - mi - ne ex - au - di___ o - ra - ti - o - nem me - - am

in the second verse (for the same voices) a compelling accent on 'Domine' (Ex. 16). The persecution of the enemy is depicted by the

Ex. 16

Et___ non in - tres in ju - di - ci - um cum ser-vo___ tu - o___ Do - mi - ne:___

two tenors and the bass in a fugato episode which has confusion in its cross-rhythmic development. All the voices enter to deliver the terrifying 'he hath laid me in the darkness, as the men that have been long dead'. The chordal sequence here is C major, B flat major, D minor, F major (first inversion), B flat major, E flat major, C minor, A flat major, B flat major, F major. It will be noticed that the harmonies are furthest from their starting point at the word 'mortuos' —'dead'. This is the conclusion of the first main section of the psalm.

With the remembrance of time past the music becomes plain and conventional. But immediately the genius of the composer catches at the pathetic beauty of 'I stretch forth my hands unto Thee: my soul goes forth unto Thee as a thirsty land.' The upper two voices speak (Ex. 17). The four voices enter, impetuous (Ex. 18): a telling rest

demonstrates the fainting spirit: a fugal point implores God to 'hide not Thy face' and a deep descent illustrates 'them that go down to the pit'. The next two verses sound a note of hope. Then hope vanishes and there is again a plea for deliverance, in a beautiful three-part passage for the middle voices. Four voices—the soprano is omitted so that an atmosphere of tranquillity is achieved—ask that the Holy Spirit shall 'lead me forth in the ways of righteousness'. Two short sections for all the voices bring the psalm to an end. Then, by way of coda, the 'Gloria', which opens at the 'sicut erat...' into a hymn of praise and hope.

The Psalms were composed between 1563 and 1570 and were undertaken at the special request of the Duke Albert, who considered them of such importance that he had them copied on parchment, illuminated with miniatures by the court painter, and handsomely bound. After 1563 the Jesuit mission in Bavaria encouraged a less lax attitude towards religion than had previously obtained in a community which contained many of Lutheran sympathy: the 'Penitential Psalms' were Lassus' response to the Tridentine postulates.

THE THREE MASSES OF WILLIAM BYRD
(1543–1623)

Probably Byrd is the greatest of all English composers. He may have been the greatest composer in Europe during the polyphonic period. He certainly would appear to be the most philosophic, the most single-minded and the most versatile. Consider his range: he excelled in Catholic church music; he wrote some of the finest of services and anthems for the Church of England; he was the virtual founder of the solo song (with string accompaniment) in England; his fantasias for viols must take a high place in the history of chamber music; he was a pioneer in keyboard music; he was important among madrigalists; he was even involved in the provision of dramatic music long before such music called for the attention of the distinguished. (In 1568 he contributed a wonderfully impressive song—'Come tread the path'—to Robert Wilmot's *Tancred and Gismonda* and in 1579 music to Thomas Legge's *Ricardus Tertius*.)

It is not Byrd's versatility which constitutes his greatness, but rather his strenuous idealism. It will be discovered that most of his music repays many hearings. He makes no concessions. His work stands on its own plane, indifferent to time or place, so that today we may hear him and wonder not at his antiquity of style, but at his integrity of thought. One feature distinguishes him from Palestrina and Lassus. He left, perhaps, less than half the number of works composed by either of them: further he was content to write works (like Bach) with no very immediate prospect of performance. Indeed it is in his Latin church music that his genius shines most brightly.

CHARACTER AND CAREER

There is something austere about this man who seems to have lived somewhat apart from his fellows, by whom he was held in awe even at the age of thirty: something corrective to the ebullience of the Elizabethan spirit. It is even possible that Byrd is the greatest English composer of the twentieth century, for it is from him that strength and independence of spirit has issued to revitalize modern British musical thought.

The determination which belongs to the music was also the chief characteristic of the man. He went to law quicker than most of us when he felt his rights as a citizen were being infringed. He remained, at some personal inconvenience, a Catholic. That he was generally unmolested while protesting this faith is a tribute to the government of the day and to Queen Elizabeth, who was, of course, no mean judge of men and musicians. Not only was he unhindered in his private beliefs: he was promoted to high official position.

He was a Lincolnshire man by birth, from which county John Taverner came. He was, probably, a chorister in the Chapel Royal under Thomas Tallis (c. 1505–1585). He became organist of Lincoln Cathedral at the age of twenty. In 1570 he succeeded to the place of Robert Parsons, also a composer of note, as a gentleman of the Chapel Royal. Two years later he became joint organist of the Chapel Royal with Tallis. Although he worked in London Byrd anticipated later habits of life by living in the country, in Essex, as a country gentleman. In 1575 Tallis and Byrd were granted a Licence (which amounted to a monopoly) for the printing and selling of music. At the end of twenty-one years this Licence passed to Byrd's pupil Thomas Morley. Byrd's life is, thus, a brief list of facts. We know, on the whole, singularly little about him.

The choral works by which we know Byrd are the motets contained in *Cantiones Sacrae* (1575)—which was the joint work of Tallis and Byrd—and in two volumes, under the same title but exclusively by Byrd, issued in 1589 and 1591; in the two books of *Gradualia* (1605 and 1607); and some which remained in manuscript: the English liturgical music, in which the peak was reached in the 'Great Service'; the madrigals in *Psalmes, Sonets and Songs* (1588), *Songs of Sundrie Natures* (1589) and the *Psalmes, Songs and Sonnets* (1611); and the Masses in three, four and five parts respectively.

It is not known why Byrd lavished such care over settings of the Mass which, if performed at all, could only be performed out of England. Nor is the actual date of composition known, although the text of the three-part Mass transcribed by John Baldwin is dated 1603. It would appear that Byrd had noted Italian changes consequent on the recommendations of the Council of Trent, for he set those sections which previously had not been set by English composers and he avoided the formerly conventional *cantus firmus*.

The three-part Mass is distinguished by elegance in counterpoint, by simplicity—the separate statements of 'Gloria' and 'Credo' being carefully defined by parenthetic rests. The Mass rises to ecstasy, but a restrained ecstasy, in the 'Sanctus' where long lines of melody intertwine in a radiant setting.

The four-part Mass is a grave work, possessing a Romanesque severity. Yet its gravity engenders its own beauty. 'There is,' Byrd wrote in the Preface to his 1605 *Gradualia*, 'a certain hidden power in the thoughts underlying the words themselves, so that as one meditates upon the sacred words and constantly and seriously considers them, the right notes, in some inexplicable fashion, suggest themselves quite spontaneously.'

One passage from the 'Gloria' may be taken to illustrate this sentiment, and also to epitomize the character of the work as a whole (Ex. 19). Here are the fully developed contrapuntal style: a poetic use

Ex. 19

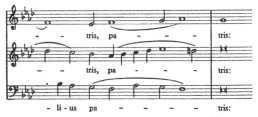

of ornamental passages or *melismata*; sensitive and free rhythm; choral orchestration exemplified in the holding back of the soprano line.

Besides the more general unifying features in this Mass Byrd tentatively places certain melodic formulae in significant situations. The descending group of notes for 'miserere', for instance, catches the supplicating phrase given to the 'Christe eleison' and anticipates the more extended treatment of the same idea in the 'Agnus Dei'; while the genuflecting fall of the fourth at 'Domine Deus' recalls, by its pattern, that which opens the 'Kyrie' and the 'Agnus Dei'. This last movement begins exactly as the 'Gloria'. The soprano and alto (every movement but the 'Sanctus' begins with these two voices) 'meditate upon the sacred words'. Comparing the opening of 'Gloria' and 'Agnus' it is instructive to see what different directions the same fundamental idea may suggest. It is also salutary to notice what depth of feeling may be touched by such simple means (Ex. 20). It is doubtful whether

Lassus, who was a master of two-part counterpoint, ever wrote a passage of greater intensity for the same medium.

The five-part Mass also has great gravity, but a greater intellectual power than its predecessor (that is if, as Dr. Edmund H. Fellowes suggests, it is later in date). It is, on the whole, more modal in flavour, each movement but the 'Sanctus' commencing (Ex. 21), the 'Et

incarnatus est' reposing serenely thus (Ex. 22), and the Holy Spirit

(Ex. 23). The second of these units is the classical motto that Mozart

introduced into his 'Jupiter' Symphony. It has certain rhythmic traits
which seem to belong to a more sophisticated age (Ex. 24), and which

are pitfalls to the unwary singer. Although there are many sections
treated in emphatic homophony there are few finalizing cadences; thus
the work proceeds with greater musical resolution. Yet, should it be felt
that this intellectual concentration should bear too much in one direction Byrd humanizes his score with numerous touches of definitive
realism. The words 'coelis', 'resurrexit', 'ascendit', 'venit' and so on,
call forth fragments of picturesque melodic shape; while the rhythm
changes, with subtlety, from mood to mood.

MOTETS

While these three Masses represent landmarks in European music, they
do not express, by any means, the whole of Byrd. He reserves his
greater daring and his more ready emotional reactions for his motets.
Consider the opening of the 'Ave Verum' from the second book of
Gradualia (Ex. 25) (somewhere in the middle of this motet, for those

particularly interested in such things, a dominant seventh chord, naked
and unashamed, rears its naughty head without the proper pre-
liminaries). Next consider the lovely delineation in 'Senex puerum
portabat' (Ex. 26) (*Gradualia I*) and then turn to the final 'adoravit'
(Ex. 27).

Ex. 27

Henry Peacham, who extolled Byrd in his *Compleat Gentleman* (1622) described his motets as 'angelicall and divine'. This is the sort of passage which, no doubt, carried him away. We may note, in passing, that all Byrd's cadences are full of expression and original beauty. Compare this cadence with that which terminates 'Civitas sancti tui' (*Cantiones Sacrae*, 1589) (Ex. 28). Here Byrd exploits his love of the

Ex. 28

unexpected discord and turns a conventional figure—the so-called *nota cambiata*—into a feature of the emotional quality of the work. This motet is throughout a masterpiece of tonal contrast. If you would see Byrd vying with de Rore and Lassus look at the chromatic opening of *O quam suavis* (Ex. 29), far removed from the exultant spirit and

Ex. 29

pageantry of 'Laudibus in Sanctis' (*Cantiones Sacrae*, 1591) in which he 'foreshadows some of the great motets of Bach, with a passage broadened out in long notes'. He thus gives massive dignity to the final phrase 'Tempus in omne Deo'. In his English settings Byrd had rivals. Indeed his anthems and his madrigals are sometimes more worthy of respect than affection. But one work of rare beauty must be quoted. The 'Lullaby, my sweet little baby' (*Psalmes, Sonets and Songs*), 1588 is a wonderfully evocative cradle-song (even though it is, on account of its wide spacing of voices and high soprano line, very difficult). The cadence shows a favourite Byrd device. What this 'means' must be determined by the listener (Ex. 30). But it is a measure of Byrd's

Ex. 30

ba - by, ba - - - - - by.

intention to go his own way. In his *Epistle to the Reader* Byrd makes himself plain: 'In the expressing of these songs, either by voices or instruments, if there happens to be any jarre or disonance, blame not the Printer, who (I doe assure thee) through his great paines and diligence doth heer deliver to thee a perfect and true Coppie.'

MOTETS BY TOMÁS LUIS DE VICTORIA (c. 1535/40–1611), JACOB HANDL (1550–1591), JAN PIETERSZOON SWEELINCK (1562–1621), PETER PHILIPS (d. 1634)

Palestrina, Lassus and Byrd are, perhaps, the most universal among composers of the sixteenth century: the first was pre-eminent in style, the second in humane feeling, the third in intellectual curiosity. But there is a great number of other composers who wrote music which is rich and full of character. There remains a still greater number whose competence was high but stopped short of distinction. These latter must be taken on trust. Here we must remain content with brief excursions to parts of Europe which we have hitherto not visited.

VICTORIA

Sixteenth-century Spain evokes memories of Philip II—possibly the most concentrated religious character ever to reign over a great empire. Philip II symbolizes exclusive devotion to the faith. It is fitting, then, that the chief Spanish composer of his reign—Victoria should also display singleness of purpose. Victoria was a native of Avila, birthplace of St. Teresa; he was an ordained priest; he wrote no other music than for the Church. He studied in Rome. He was on the staff of the Collegium Germanicum, which had been founded by St. Ignatius Loyola and enjoyed powerful Spanish influence, for some years. The greater part of his life, however, was spent in Madrid, as chaplain to

D

the Empress Maria (aunt of King Philip II) and as choirmaster to the
Chapel of the Descalzas Reales. Victoria composed no more than 180
works; but all are distinguished by suavity in craftsmanship, born of
much study of Palestrina, and an exquisite ardour. The peculiar
temperament of Victoria's music is defined by the great German editor
Karl Proske[1] in respect of the 'Quarti toni' Mass. 'Every note betrays
the master who in devout contemplation served the sanctuary and
among all the Roman contemporaries of Palestrina stood next to him
in spiritual nobility. Work and prayer, genius and humility are here
blended in perfect harmony.'

Victoria was more emotional than Palestrina. He depends to a considerable extent on harmonic injections into the system. When
qualities such as Proske defines are combined with a style which favours
mellifluous chromaticism the result may often be termed sentimental.
I should say that, judged by the highest standards of his age, Victoria
is sentimental. This may be a recommendation to those singers who
may feel that the music of long-ago is deficient in the quality which
ranks first with them. Compare the languorous charm of grief encompassed in the final section of the motet *O vos omnes qui transitis per
viam* (Ex. 31) with the cold desolation of Byrd's *Civitas sancti tui*. At

the same time notice that Victoria makes great use (a feature not
usually found in the strict school) of repeated notes. This motet gives
great *pleasure* in performance and we may note how, occasionally,
Victoria goes out of his way to imbue his music with the naive adoration of the untutored, but passionate worshipper. Thus in an extremely
beautiful *Ave Maria* (Ex. 32). A work to be sung with relative ease and

---

[1] Karl Proske, priest and musician, was one of the most notable scholars of the nineteenth
century. A great variety of the masterpieces of the polyphonic period were published by him in
his *Musica Divina* (Ratisbon 1855–61).

great delight is *Duo Seraphim*, a motet for four equal voices, for Trinity Sunday. I have no doubt that angels, if at all human, enjoy rehearsing (Ex. 33).

HANDL

Jacob Handl (who was sometimes latinized as Gallus) is a comfortable composer. He was an Austrian and became Kapellmeister (*c.* 1579) to the Bishop of Olmütz, after which he was employed as cantor at the church of St. John in Prague. His style is warm and he, no doubt, had as much pleasure in composing his music as we should in singing it. He possesses simplicity but is not deficient in grandeur, for he took much pleasure in composing for large forces (indeed, in the late eighteenth century his fame was kept alive by the fact that he had written a motet in twenty-four parts): he is neither precocious nor precious. There is a fine *Adoramus Te, Jesu Christe*, for double choir, which represents him with great dignity. This motet is a perfect example of ternary form. One other work to perform is his *Ecce, quomodo moritur justus*. No passage in music is more compelling than (Ex. 34). This motet was approved by a higher authority on these

matters, for Handel (George Frideric, that is) adapted it for his *Funeral Anthem for Queen Caroline*. He had found it among the traditional part of the *Passion* music of the Lutheran church (see pp. 128–9).

SWEELINCK

Sweelinck was an organist and one of the first effective composers in the variation form for keyboard. His reputation as organist was very great and since practically all German organists of the next generation were indebted to him for tuition there is a direct link between him and Bach. But he was also a student of the Venetian school and translated the *Instutioni harmoniche* of Zarlino. His choral works—*Cantiones Sacrae*, 1619, four books of Psalms and *Rimes françaises et italiennes*—are within the general style of the sixteenth century and show something of the colour and vivaciousness of the forward-looking school of Gabrieli. Sweelinck was one of the last of the polyphonic school (and his interests were divided between what was expected by his own contemporaries and what might be expected by his grandchildren) so that we may discern even in the music that pleases us most—in the joyous carolling of *Hodie Christus natus est* or the ringing alleluia at the end of *O Sacrum Convivium*—a certain regard for effect for effect's sake.

PHILIPS

An interest in effect also marks the *Cantiones Sacrae* of Peter Philips. He was one of the not inconsiderable company of English Catholics who found sanctuary in the Netherlands towards the end of the reign of Queen Elizabeth. Philips (and also his compatriot Richard Dering) shows a good deal of the spiritual intensity of such Catholic poets as Francis Quarles and Thomas Traherne and, like them, is—if music allows such classification—a metaphysical. Among his motets *O virum mirabilem* may be isolated for its charm, a quality not frequently to be encountered in the period. In an intimate manner—and much of

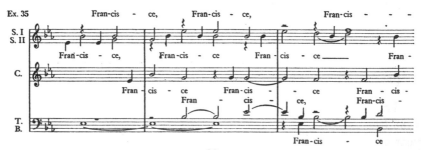

Philips's work sounds intimate—he calls across the centuries to St. Francis of Assisi (Ex 35) There are nearly a hundred years between Taverner and Philips. To turn from the one to the other is to see the extreme limits of sixteenth-century polyphony.

'THE TRIUMPHS OF ORIANA' (1601)

The composition of madrigals and such near allies as balletti, villanelle and frottole flourished, in Italy and where, in Europe, the Italian writ ran, throughout the sixteenth century. But nowhere did the idea take more entertaining shape than in England, when growing prosperity and the promise of peace at last, and enthusiasm for Italianate novelties crossed with delight in lyrical verse inspired the middle-class (and upper-class) gentry who were the solid core of Elizabethan society to take their recreation in the cultivation of domestic harmony in more ways than one. The English madrigal is music for the home. Thus the contemporary listener must train himself to listen, as it were, from the inside, otherwise the effluent wit and rapid transitions of mood will pass him by. 'I cannot hear the words' is what some will say. To be truthful you are not really meant to: they are there for singing.

In 1588 Nicolas Yonge, who was probably a chorister at St. Paul's Cathedral, published *Musica Transalpina*—a collection of fifty-seven madrigals. With the exception of William Byrd (whose *La Virginella* was to a text of Ariosto) the authors were Italian (or Flemish–Italian) and included Alfonso Ferrabosco I, Marenzio, Palestrina and Lassus. This book—and the reports of travellers—stimulated great activity in England. Yonge indicates the strength of the fashion:

> 'Since I first began to keep house in this City a great number of gentlemen and merchants of good account (as well of this realm as of foreign nations) have taken in good part such entertainment of pleasure, as my poor ability was able to afford them, both by the exercise of music daily used in my house, and by furnishing them with books of that kind yearly sent to me out of Italy and other places.'

The fertility of English composers, in madrigals alone, between 1588 (the year of the departure of the Spanish Armada) and 1625 (the year of the accession of Charles I) was prodigal. Music—apt for voices or viols and sometimes for both at the same time—poured out of organ lofts, schools, country houses, parsonages, in all parts of the land; and many gentlemen who had a little honour in their own day are remembered by posterity simply because they were the dedicatees of a set of madrigals.

The English madrigal touched life at many points: sometimes, like John Ward's elegy for Prince Henry—'Weep forth your tears', it was commemorative; sometimes, as in Michael East's 'Quick, quick away, despatch', it was an epithalamium; sometimes it was proper to a country pageant as in Weelkes's frivolous 'Tan ta ra cries Mars'; sometimes it expressed contemplation as in Orlando Gibbons's setting of Sir Walter Raleigh's 'What is our life?'; sometimes it went to town— as in Weelkes's vivid 'Thule, the period of cosmography'; and often and often to the country.

The division of voices was often caused by the nature of a family ensemble. Wit abounded, and pretty conceits in word play were matched with equal dexterity in melody, harmony and counterpoint. During those years English music was touched by a fairy's wand. Handel, as a naturalized Englishman, was proud enough of the English past to acknowledge it both by quotation—compare (Ex. 36)

Ex. 36

Heigh ho, for love I die,

from Mundy's 'Heigh ho! "chill go to plough no more"' with 'Lowly the matron bowed' from *Theodora*—and by imitation, for the 'Nightingale' chorus, so suggestive of atmosphere, of *Solomon* is but a sixteenth-century madrigal writ large.

The Triumphs of Oriana, designed honorifically after the Italian pattern of *Il Trionfo di Dori*, serve to set a sort of official seal on the whole school of madrigal composition. Queen Elizabeth deserved the intended gesture of respect implied in the gratulatory nature of the verses and the—sometimes self-conscious—brilliant dignity of the anthem-like finales. And the composers represented deserved their place in the nearest approach to a national Pantheon that English music ever produced. Many of them had enriched English music immeasurably in all branches. The editor was Thomas Morley, organist of St. Paul's Cathedral and a pupil of Byrd (who is, curiously, not in the anthology).

In addition to Morley these were the contributors: Michael East, organist of Lichfield Cathedral; Daniel Norcombe, a minor canon of St. George's Chapel, Windsor; John Mundy, organist of Eton College and later of St. George's, Windsor; Ellis Gibbons, brother of Orlando; John Bennet, a provincial musician from Cheshire; John Hilton, organist of Trinity College, Cambridge; George Marson, organist of Canterbury Cathedral; Richard Carlton, a Norfolk clergyman; John Holmes, organist of Winchester and Salisbury cathedrals; Richard Nicholson, an organist and lecturer in Oxford; Thomas Tomkins, organist of Worcester Cathedral and the Chapel Royal, and one of Byrd's most distinguished pupils; Michael Cavendish, member of an aristocratic Suffolk family; William Cobbold, organist of Norwich Cathedral; John Farmer, a somewhat disorderly organist of St. Patrick's Cathedral in Dublin; John Wilbye, a musician in private employment in Suffolk and one of the greatest of madrigalists; Thomas Hunt, organist of Wells Cathedral; Thomas Weelkes, of Winchester College and Chichester Cathedral, who shared the pinnacle of madrigalian fame with Wilbye; John Milton, father of the poet; George Kirbye, another musician in private service; Robert Jones, a witty Welsh lutenist; John Lisley; and Edward Johnson, who had written a work for the visit of Queen Elizabeth to the Earl of Hertford in 1598.

One madrigal—of great and deserved fame—shall summarize the Oriana set and the brilliance of the period—Weelkes's 'As Vesta was from Latmos hill descending', in six parts.

The four highest voices see Vesta in C major. Her descent is depicted in a faithful downward-tripping scale. She, in turn, sees 'a maiden Queen' going up the hill—in G major. A homophonic episode shows attendant shepherds 'to whom Diana's darlings' (Ex. 37).

Ex. 37

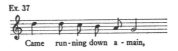

Came   run-ning down   a - main,

They take a considerable time to execute this measure, for not only do they come running down again, but (Ex. 38), (Ex. 39).

Ex. 38

First   two   by   two

Ex. 39

Then   three   by   three

They mingle with the shepherds in six-part harmony and build up the final paean of loyalty and affection. They weave brilliant counterpoint out of (Ex. 40) and the basses have two bouts of augmentation—

Ex. 40

Long live fair O - ri - a - na

wherein melody notes are greatly lengthened and dignity added—before the whole work lights up every candle in the sky.

2

The Seventeenth Century

NEW STYLES

THE seventeenth century was a revolutionary epoch. In one way or another, of course, all ages are revolutionary; but the seventeenth century with its spate of philosophers, with all its religious and political disturbance—absolutism in monarchic government here, republicanism there and regicides elsewhere—was exceptional. One characteristic of the seventeenth century which goes some way to explain the great social upheavals was a zest for experiment. And this in turn led to the dominant mode of seventeenth-century expression— precision. Galileo (whose father was a not unimportant Florentine composer), Bacon, Newton, Descartes, Spinoza, Leibniz (who knew Handel at Hanover) signify this quality within science and philosophy. Literature was the dominant art—especially in France—and the other arts became, for a time, subordinate. The artist fights for survival. Therefore it is exhilarating to watch the process of musical acclimatization to the new tendencies of general thought.

Choral music is especially interesting; first, because of its natural contiguity to words, and second, because of its natural function as some sort of communal symbol. About the year 1600 the world was plagued by young men with progressive ideas. As is often the case some of these young men were young only in spirit: otherwise somewhat past middle age. Musically the most notable were the Florentine group headed by Count Giovanni Bardi, the principal pioneer of the 'new music'—*nuove musiche*. Bardi indicates the advanced opinions of Florentine criticism in one essay addressed to Giulio Caccini. It will be noticed that the style of choral writing that was formerly general there comes in for as much adverse criticism as any of our own day, which may be thought to resemble, say, Brahms.

'Nowadays,' he wrote, 'music falls into two main divisions; one belongs to counterpoint. The other should be called *arte di ben cantare*.' He disliked madrigals in particular, because—

55

'our composers would consider it a deadly sin if they happened to hear the voices at the same moment on the same syllable of the text and on notes of the same rhythmical value. The more they bring the parts into motion the more gifted they consider themselves . . . we want at least to try to make a little light for poor music, for, since her decline up to the present day she has not found, in so many centuries, one composer who thinks about her needs, who does not rather force her into the ways of her mortal enemy—counterpoint.'

Counterpoint could, no doubt, have withstood a single attack. (There are always anti-contrapuntal tractarians whose justification is often that they are not very good at it.) But there was the zeal of Reformers on one hand (who were all for psalms and simplicity), the equal zeal of Counter-Reformers on the other (see under Council of Trent *supra*); and a large number of 'expressionists' who began to place instrumental colour before vocal texture. The outcome was, of course, that counterpoint survived to enjoy in the music of Bach and Handel the fruits of experiment in every conceivable direction. And after that the trouble started all over again!

During the seventeenth century significant names in choral music were Monteverdi and Cavalli, of Venice; Giacomo Carissimi, of Rome; Alessandro Scarlatti, of Naples; Heinrich Schütz, of Saxony; Dietrich Buxtehude, a Swede whose reputation is generally associated with Lübeck; Friedrich Zachau, Handel's first teacher at Halle; Jean Baptiste Lully, François Couperin, and Michel de Lalande, of the royal music in Versailles; John Blow and Henry Purcell, of London. (We must except those who like Prince Carlo Gesualdo, Girolamo Frescobaldi and Orazio Vecchi belonged to the polyphonic period, although to some extent impatient of the limitations of its technique.)

IDEAS AND OPPORTUNITIES

Among these composers there are few who were not expert in the ancient *a cappella* style. Likewise there are none who were not fully conversant with the demands of the 'new music'. Indeed, in one way or another, they tumbled over themselves to assimilate novelty in the vocabulary and the design of music. Choral technique, then, branched out and we find a growing delight in virtuosity. The runs and flourishes of solo song and the divisions of string style, which was also developing greatly at this time, infected Monteverdi. Realism inspired Purcell, Cavalli and Schütz. The lightness of the dance urged the French school to delicious choral interpolations of characteristic charm within operas and ballets. The severity and ethical function of chorale restrained the Germans to a gravity of purpose which often anticipates Brahms.

During the seventeenth century motets and anthems, services and Masses continued to engage the attention of composers. But wider opportunities in choral music were displayed as oratorio and cantata (and, to a certain extent, opera) grew into adolescence, and as great secular occasions demanded ample commemoration. Oratorio emerged on the Catholic side while the church cantata—of the sort that reached its climax in Bach—came through Lutheranism and the chorale.

The Oratory of St. Philip Neri flourished in the middle of the sixteenth century. The fraternity was founded to combat growing secularism and with special emphasis on prayer, hence 'Ora-tory'. St. Philip was one of the greatest, if not the greatest, saint of his age. He had a great concern for teaching and was willing to use all available means to make religious history and doctrine vivid and memorable. He had, equally, an affection for musicians, which brought many, including Palestrina, to him as father confessor. Thus it was that freer, more dramatic and more lyrical music (*Laudi*) was composed for the special use of the Oratory.[1] In 1575 the community of St. Philip was transferred to the great church of S. Maria at Valicella. The tradition of music which was established by the saint was continued so that in 1600 Emilio del Cavalieri's *La rappresentazione di anima e di corpo* was performed in S. Maria. This work carried into sacred music the main principles of contemporary Florentine opera. (If anything Cavalieri's work was rather more lively than what survives of Peri or Caccini and was diversified with an enchanting orchestra—or consort—and dances.) The choral remains show a marked rhythmic character and the impact of secularity. Oratorio spread all over Italy and churchmen developed an interest in a form of music in which they could either piously indulge their liking for a concert or by which they could instruct the faithful— or both. Subjects for oratorio sometimes flavoured of the medieval Morality or they challenged the fables turned into opera for dramatic intent: *Samson*, *Deborah*, *Susanna* and *Jephtha* foreshadowed Handel

[1] *The Oratorios of Handel*, Percy M. Young, p. 14 *et seq*.

while *St. Thomas of Canterbury* and *Mary, Queen of Scots* explored more recent hagiology.

Two composers stand out for necessary mention: Steffano Landi, who was a member of the Papal choir, explored the byways of harmonic expression in independent string passages, or *ritornelli* which featured consecutive fifths and octaves, and Domenico Mazzochi achieved historical fame by being the first to signify dynamic expressional nuance by < and >. Until we reach Carissimi, however, choral interest in oratorio, as in opera, was slight. With Carissimi we reach a point at which the oratorio form is sufficiently mature to bear occasional performance today.

GIACOMO CARISSIMI (1605-1674): ORATORIOS

Carissimi was the first Italian composer to recognize the possible function of the chorus within an extended work which, while relying on the technical developments of opera—in recitative, aria (albeit still somewhat rudimentary) and orchestration—must be performed without the representational assistance of dress and scenery. Many composers had previously indicated realism in *a cappella* writing; but Carissimi began to show how large backcloths could be designed to influence the whole atmosphere of a scene or a work. Thus the double choirs of *Jonah* indicate vastness and upheaval: as sea music the choruses are even now convincing. In *Jephtha* the skirmishing voices can give a battlefield effect which, within its context, is sufficiently memorable. Or Carissimi can give great utterances to his chorus in a sort of intensified recitative. It is small wonder that Handel was a student of this style of composition. A testimony to the influence of Carissimi lies in the fact that Handel transferred the chorus 'Plorate, filiae Israel' to *Samson*, where it became 'Hear, Jacob's God.'

Carissimi was a Roman and in his spaciousness and dignity are continuation of traditional Roman—as opposed to Venetian—qualities. He was exclusively a church composer. After a brief period at Assisi he became, in 1628, *maestro di cappella* at the church of St. Apollinare, which was attached to the German College. His reputation in the city was very great and Pietro della Valle, a Roman writer, describes a Christmas Eve service which he attended (and for which he had to stand as the result of arriving late). The music he detailed, somewhat rhapsodically, as more exquisite than words could describe. One of the factors which leads to the exquisite is simplicity and Carissimi had the rare ability to express new ideas without recourse to the recondite.

His harmony—although in his cantatas he explored more expressive possibilities—was invariably simple, but it made its points by skilful rhythmic management. He gave momentum to melody by setting it over a moving bass[1] (his predecessors in the *nuove musiche* had been often oblivious of the fact that a stagnant bass part is worse than no bass part). Likewise he gave musical purposefulness to melody by making it self-sufficient yet flexible to verbal intention, and made of recitative a vehicle of emotion as well as an instrument of narration. He was virtually the creator of the church cantata, as developed by Alessandro Scarlatti.

Scarlatti, indeed, was a pupil of Carissimi, as were Cesti, Bassani and Johann Caspar Kerll, who was sent to Carissimi for instruction by the Emperor. Carissimi was sufficiently widely known, although he never appears to have left Rome, to be respected by Charles II of England. (The greatest collection of Carissimi manuscripts was acquired by Dr. Aldrich, architect, scholar, musician and sometime Vice-Chancellor of Oxford University.)

Carissimi's oratorios were to Latin texts. Latin, the official language of the Church, distinguished the oratorios which won the particular approval of the dignitaries of the Church. He composed, in all, sixteen and all from the Old Testament. The two which have survived in performance are *Jonah* and *Jephtha*.

The weakest part of Carissimi's scores is the instrumental music, which, perfunctory and colourless, is restricted to two violins, 'cello and organ. It may be suspected that, even in the middle of the seventeenth century, conservative instincts were still strong among conscientious church musicians. However, he is by no means the only master of choral effect deficient in instrumental feeling. *Jonah* has its magnificent sea music to commend it and the great tempest chorus surely inspired (by way of Alessandro Stradella, for Handel was indebted also to him for ideas) the climactic 'Sing ye to the Lord' in *Israel in Egypt*. Apart from the manner in which the two composers throw ideas from chorus to chorus, with colossal abandon, there is the same percussive intensity of rhythm.

---

[1] He described the bass as 'the axis whereon a melody turns', and thus suggests one of the axioms of the mature seventeenth–eighteenth century method.

Jephtha is a more convincing narrative and an infinitely more varied setting. Hawkins recorded it 'for sweetness of melody, artful modulation, and original harmony . . . justly esteemed one of the finest efforts, of musical skill and genius that the world knows of'. Carissimi, indeed was in high favour with eighteenth-century writers in general, for he did chart the course for many writers of that age.

Jephtha is introduced by a narrator (*historicus*), who explains that Jephtha is fighting against the Ammonites. Jephtha (tenor) makes his vow—to sacrifice the first living creature to meet him on return from a victory—in plain recitative. Then the chorus (in six parts) take Jephtha to battle in a broad homophonic prelude of four bars. The battle begins to rage, and the pace quickens while the alleged confusion of counterpoint comes in aptly and pictorially: two sopranos illustrate the sounding trumpets: a bass puts the fear of God into the Ammonites by judicious 'divisions' e.g. (Ex. 1.): the movement concludes with a riot

Ex. 1

of reverberant rhythms already shown in the bass solo. The *historicus* tersely details the extent of the victory. The children of Ammon bewail their tragedy in a poignant chordal sequence (Ex. 2). Then a passage

Ex. 2

of recitative takes Jephtha home, touching the singing and dancing of his daughter with more figuration. She next sings an air, which is interrupted by a duet for soprano voices. This affects too many consecutive thirds (the mannerism of expressing jollity in eighth notes and in thirds flourished for a long time), but the easy brilliance of the device attracted general consideration during the growing pains of the 'new music'. The full chorus sings a hymn of praise. Then Jephtha recalls his vow and explains it to his daughter. The recitative which describes this scene is imaginatively conceived and shows its improvement at the hands of Carissimi, for by tonal contrasts and by climactic accent the two characters assume musical personality. With this should be compared the vivid characterization of the judgement scene in Carissimi's *Judicium Salomonis*. Jephtha's daughter (how sensible Handel was to have her christened Iphis!) is allowed two months in which to retire to the mountains. The chorus solemnly describe her passage. She sings her lament and her cadences are echoed by the high voices. Finally there is the chorus which took its place later in *Samson*.

This chorus was printed in Athanasius Kircher's *Musurgia Universalis* (1650), a work which, in translation, circulated widely in Germany.

CLAUDIO MONTEVERDI (1567-1643): MADRIGALS, VESPERS AND MASSES

The career of Claudio Monteverdi is one of the most interesting in the history of music. He is of particular significance at the present day when the art of composition, again standing at a point of crisis, awaits a similar genius in synthesis who may combine a feeling for the 'spirit of the age' with awareness of the hidden possibilities within the rival theories of style, a commanding technique and a supreme concern for the aural effect of music. Carissimi influenced music most considerably through his teaching. His own works have great dignity and sincerity. They are, nevertheless, characteristic of a gifted *maestro di cappella*. In the case of Monteverdi the music challenges attention, apart from any historical significance it may possess, by its originality. Although in point of time Monteverdi was an earlier composer than Carissimi his outlook is more conspicuously modern and his imagination more resourceful.

In studying Monteverdi one is aware of a definition of religion by the late Archbishop Temple: '. . . (it) is something that stands out, as meaning the outward expression of what is spiritual and emotionally vital, with science, as the impulse to ascertain truth'. Substitute music for religion; but recollect that Monteverdi was deeply moved by religious values. Thus his church music, his madrigals and his operas are equally concerned with the exploration of human thought.

MADRIGALS

Monteverdi's intentions are revealed in the preface to his *Fifth Book of Madrigals* (1605), when he replies to some of the criticisms of Giovanni

Maria Artusi—'the modern composer takes his stand on the foundations of truth, that is to say—of expressive realism'. The early operas (*Orfeo*, 1607; *Arianna*, 1608) stirred Monteverdi to recognize what the early Florentines tended to overlook in their feverish justification of theory; that expression is invalid unless there is an idea to express and unless the manner of the expression can impose sympathy on the listener. Dr. H. F. Redlich summarizes[1] the unique value of Monteverdi's first operas: '(his) inspiration to the composition of these and similar texts lay in the inherent possibilities they offered of moulding the original expression of the *human passions* in dramatic fashion by means of symbolical musical sounds'. In his search for 'symbolical musical sounds' Monteverdi was influenced on the one hand by the most affective of the Renaissance poets, Tasso, and by the progressive approximation of musical to verbal symbol shown in the madrigals of Luca Marenzio, Orazio Vecchi[2] and Carlo Gesualdo. Through the madrigal Monteverdi reached the high intensity (note that the composer himself regards the 'Lamento' of *Arianna* and 'Preghiera' of *Orfeo* as the 'psychological axes' of their respective dramas) of the great Laments. That from *Arianna*—'Lasciate mi morire'—was reset in five parts for the *Sixth Book of Madrigals* (1614). This excerpt displays consideration for the word, the new tendency to think harmonically, the power of chromatic and discordant departure from the norm (Ex. 3).

Ex. 3

In all, Monteverdi composed eight books of Madrigals (the last in 1638). The last four books carry the pattern of the madrigal so far forward that eventually we no longer recognize the prototype. For Monteverdi increases the co-operation of instruments (which was

[1] See *Claudio Monteverdi: Life and Works*, H. F. Redlich (London 1952), p. 40.
[2] Especially by such works as the dramatic madrigal sequence entitled *L'Amfiparnasso*.

always possible even in the mid-sixteenth century) so that by the Eighth Book polyphony is virtually abolished and the prime interest lies in melodic and rhythmic shape; in respect of symbolic significance, in the variegated orchestration—employing the opera-proved devices of the *tremolo* and *pizzicato*; and in the emergence of a lighter formal control of musical material. The attention of the reader is called to *Ohimè, se tanto amate* from the Fourth Book (1615) in which the ultimate of expressiveness within the old style is displayed, and to *Non schivar, non parar* from the setting of Tasso's *Il combattimento di Tancredi e Clorinda* from the eighth book, where are all the features of the *stile concitato*—the style first used by Monteverdi for the expression of agitated feelings.

The madrigal is the focal point of Monteverdi's music in two ways. On the one hand it was the form which he was most conspicuously expected to practise as a court musician: on the other it was that (as was true of Weelkes and Wilbye) which afforded the greatest opportunity for personal expression.

Monteverdi's life divides thus: from 1590 to 1612 he was employed at the court of the Gonzagas at Mantua as violist and later, as *maestro di cappella*: in 1612 he became *maestro di cappella* at St. Mark's, Venice: after 1637, when public opera was instituted in Venice, he composed his last great operas, although still a church musician and, since 1632, in holy orders.

MASSES

When Monteverdi was appointed to St. Mark's he was enjoined to restore the former glories of the church in respect of the Palestrina style, which was to be the approved style for a considerable time to come. In the sixteenth century the music had been directed by Willaert, de Rore, Andrea Gabrieli, his nephew Giovanni Gabrieli, and Zarlino. After Zarlino's death a series of lesser composers allowed the standard to deteriorate. Monteverdi had both the skill and the determination to arrest this tendency: moreover he had such single-mindedness that he could turn his back on the new style of musical composition (the *seconda prattica*) and show mastery in the older polyphonic manner (the *prima prattica*).

Three considerable Masses, which only of a larger number are

E

extant,[1] testify to Monteverdi's polyphonic accomplishment. But we may look back at works composed when he was fifteen which show the thoroughness of his training in the classical, *prima prattica*, manner —see the *Sacrae Cantiunculae* of 1582. The first Mass was composed in 1610, was dedicated to the Pope in the hope of gaining the Pope's assistance and was based on themes from a motet—*In illo tempore*— by Nicholas Gombert. This work is in six parts and has a figured bass accompaniment for organ. (Accompaniments for keyboard instruments in the seventeenth and eighteenth centuries were not written out in full. The bass was given and with it a set of figures which epitomized the essential harmonies: hence 'figured bass'.) The Masses of 1641 and 1651 are direct and impressive settings of the text with few concessions to the age in general, except when these were to the advantage of simplicity. The words are set syllabically, harmonic innovations are excluded and the counterpoint retains all the lucidity of the sixteenth century. Yet one recognizes a difference of atmosphere. The general rejection of melisma (except on such words as 'eleison', 'amen', 'sanctus') makes for terseness; but something is lost on the side of mysticism. The functional character of the figured bass looks to the conventions of the eighteenth century and proposes a certain earthiness. Nevertheless there are moments of great beauty. We may refer to the Mass of 1641. The 'Gloria' has two moments in which wreaths of sound enshrine the text: at 'propter magnam gloriam' (Ex. 4) and in the

concluding 'Amen' in which the Monteverdian affection for sequence as a stylistic device is amply illustrated. At the crisis of the 'Credo' the

---

[1] See Dr. Redlich's Preface to his edition of the *Messa a 4 voci* (pub. Eulenberg). Some of the lost Masses were evidently in the *seconda prattica* style.

interfusion of madrigal and Mass is apparent (Ex. 5), while the succeed-

ing depiction of the Resurrection in three-four time—anticipating somewhat the clear-eyed cheerfulness of Haydn—catches the spirit of French music with which Monteverdi became acquainted in 1607. The Mass is organized about this descending figure (Ex. 6), or its inversion.

This Spanish 'Malaguena', or folksong theme, is the *ostinato* (i.e. 'obstinate', as applied to a recurring figure in the bass) of the *Lamento della Ninfa* (Book VIII of Madrigals). Of all the Monteverdi works which are available this is perhaps the most commendable to choralists. It is difficult vocally, but not unfamiliar in feeling. And in recognizing this sense of familiarity the choral singer will begin to appreciate why Monteverdi is sometimes described as the 'first modern composer'. (A somewhat arbitrary definition from which, in general, we should dissent.) In considering (Ex. 7) we notice the organization of the

melody, which is in all ways helpful to the performer; but do we not also notice a decline in contemplative reverence from the days of Palestrina? It is instructive to compare a twentieth-century Italian work, based on the ancient style—the *Requiem* of Ildebrando Pizzetti—with Monteverdi's evocation of the same period. Do we not see Monteverd, too close to Palestrina to recognize the essential ethos of Palestrina's art?

Throughout his career as church musician Monteverdi was excited by those impulses found in all artists of the Counter-Reformation. To appreciate the romantic ardour which is in the *seconda prattica* church music of Monteverdi one should read the life of St. Ignatius Loyola, or the poetry of Richard Crashaw and Thomas Traherne. One should recognize an intention to renew the faith through moving the heart of the sceptic or the merely conventional. But the Counter-Reformation was a movement in which discipline was all-important. Monteverdi was a rigorous disciplinarian: episodes in his life reveal one aspect of this; the formal conditioning of his music another.

We may take as an example the Psalm *Laetatus sum*, published posthumously in 1650 in the *Messa a quattro voci e salmi a 1, 2, 3, 4, 5, 6, 7 e 8 voci, concertati, a parte da cappella*. In this magnificent and exciting work for seven voices, strings, bassoon (which has attractive solo passages), two trombones and organ there is a splendid torrent of sound which spreads from the titular phrase. Every device of figuration—and the coloratura moves with an almost Handelian assurance of contrast of timbres and rhythms, of variation in texture is employed to ensure a wealth of colour and a continual vivacity. But the whole is unified by a basso ostinato (Ex. 8) of such persistence that the Italian composer

Ex. 8

Alfredo Casella can compare the work with Ravel's *Bolero*.

VESPERS

Somewhere between the austerity of the Masses and the finely polished romanticism of this Psalm is the work—or, rather, sequence of related works—which many now claim as Monteverdi's greatest: the so-called *Vespers of the Virgin Mary*.

In 1610 Monteverdi put into one volume a number of miscellaneous works—the Mass *In illo tempore*, a number of motet-style movements and two *Magnificats*—with which he wished to obtain papal patronage. In fact the mission to Rome was unsatisfactory, perhaps because the works designated *Sanctissimi Virginis Missa senis vocibus ad Ecclesiarum choros ac Vesperae pluribus decantandae cum nonnullis concentibus* had been published in Venice.

The Vespers are based on the opening of the Ordinary of the Ecclesiastical Hours (*Domine ad adiuvandum*), on Psalms 109, 112, 121, 126 and 147, on the hymn *Ave maris stella* and the *Magnificat*, all liturgically proper to the service of Vespers for the Feast of the Blessed Virgin Mary. These larger movements are interspersed with others in some editions which were printed in the original part-books. It is suggested by Monteverdi's Dedication that the whole sequence was hardly possible for liturgical performance but rather for private and princely chapel, or palace. The deviations from ecclesiastical propriety put us in mind of Bach's *Mass in B minor*.

As a whole the movements of the *Vespers* represent the *seconda prattica*—another term to define the 'new music'—but there are many links with the past. The movements are built on traditional plain-chant themes. Polyphony opulently enfolds the spacious 'Ave Maria Stella' for double choir. The orchestration (the actual disposition of the instruments was determined at the time of performance and any modern score, so far as the scoring is concerned, is editorial reconstruction)[1] carries forward the practice of Giovanni Gabrieli at St. Mark's, Venice, and stands at the end of the free and easy Renaissance tendency to recruit all available varieties of tone colour. On the other hand the orchestra asserts its independent function: thus against a full and hammered chord of D major with which the chorus begins 'Domine ad adiuvandum' the strings and brass play the toccata from the composer's *Orfeo*. Herein is the process, to culminate in Handel and for that matter Bach, which transmuted festive music fit for an earthly prince into that meet for a heavenly. In the 'Sonata sopra Sancta Maria' a purely instrumental movement is related to the liturgy solely by the solo soprano voice which announces the plainsong to 'Sancta Maria, ora pro nobis'.

The *Vespers* vary from the great movements which employ all the resources—the greatest being the vast 'Magnificat'[2]—to the chamber music of 'Nigra sum'—'Duo Seraphim' and 'Pulchra es'. Therefore the entire work is an index to almost every advanced practice of the early seventeenth century. There are devices and strokes of the imagination which, since the period and the style come fresh to contemporary

---

[1] The problems besetting a modern editor are clearly set out by Denis Stevens in his Preface to the *Vespers* (Novello). In this edition only those movements with liturgical warrant are given. For the purpose of this survey the extraneous sections often given in modern performances are included.

[2] Monteverdi appended another and simpler version of the *Magnificat* with organ accompaniment to the *Vespers*.

audiences, astonish today as much as they must have perplexed in the first case.

At the end of 'Domine ad adiuvandum' the harmony opens out from the long D major and the rhythm flings festively into triple time. In the 'Dixit Dominus' great use is made of characteristically *concitato* iteration of a single chord (the opening of Walton's *Belshazzar's Feast* is an extension of the system, as is the third part of Stravinsky's *Symphony of Psalms*). This practice is in contrast to the flowing tunes of more or less conventional counterpoint: note how the verbal rhythm and the solid mass of chordal tone throws the words right into the forefront. Monteverdi's interest in words often becomes an obsession: such is the case in 'Nigra sum', and in 'Pulchra es', where also may be seen Monteverdi's most emotional harmonic technique (Ex. 9) and, as in

Ex. 9

'Duo Seraphim', the extremes of vocal exploitation in trills and vibrato. The choral writing, leaving behind conservative method, often becomes highly poetic—as in the whimsical coloratura of 'Laetatus sum', where the musical feeling transcends any sense of mere service to the words—or the vigorous finality of instrumental gaiety, as in 'Lauda Jerusalem'.

One quality, however, is lacking in this work, and this may be attributed to the general restlessness of the age—tranquillity. One may compare Hans Leo Hassler's treatment of the same theme that serves Monteverdi in *Ave Maria Stella*. Hassler's setting, albeit simpler in general, has quietude of spirit: Monteverdi's must for ever be attentive to detail. In a sense one may regard the *Vespers* as the *Symphony of Psalms* of the seventeenth century.

HEINRICH SCHÜTZ (1585-1672)

Many of the earliest masters of German music had learned their technique in Italy and during the first part of the seventeenth century the influence of Venice was very strong. Composers such as Hassler, Gregor Aichinger, Christoph Straus (the Imperial *Kapellmeister* in Vienna 1616–1620) and Schütz were educated in Venice, while others like Johann Kaspar Kerll, who was a pupil of Carissimi in Rome, and Handl were well aware of the Venetian tradition. Certain works (and the same tendency is apparent among minor masters of the eighteenth century), indeed, surrender somewhat abjectly to the extravagance of Venetian *seconda prattica*. Thus Christoph Straus in his *Missa pro defunctis* introduces his work with a *symphonia ad imitationem campanae*—a 'symphony' in imitation of bells—and suggests trepidation in the 'Dies Irae' with effective *tremolo*. In other Masses his orchestration demands sometimes as many as seven trombones and a set of 'feldtrompeten'. There was, however, one great composer who could admire the achievement of the Italians and, at the same time, make technique subordinate to integrity of self-expression. This was Schütz.

Like many German composers (Schütz was a Saxon) he was broadly educated. He was a law student at the University of Marburg and did not finally decide to follow the vocation of music until 1614, in which year he became *Kapellmeister*—or chief musician, with authority over both secular and sacred music—at the Electoral Court of Dresden. He had been a pupil of Giovanni Gabrieli between 1609 and 1612 and returned to Venice, much respecting the works of Monteverdi, in 1628. He was connected with Dresden for the whole of his professional life, but, after the dislocation of court life by the Thirty Years' War, he obtained leave to visit Copenhagen, where he lived between 1633 and 1641. Schütz composed madrigals and (although the scores have been lost) operas[1] but his posthumous fame depended on his great corpus of church music.

In a period of experiment there are always composers who deserve attention by reason of originality of expression; those whose characteristic is depth of thought are less numerous. Schütz is often placed by the side of Bach (principally because both wrote Passion music). Insofar as both gave voice to the profound reflectiveness of German religion, to the overpowering sense of sympathy (in the real meaning of 'suffering with') which distinguishes the great tradition of German music, and to independence and tenacity in judgement this is just. But to regard Schütz merely as a forerunner of Bach is unjust. For Schütz was

[1] Among the works of Schütz which were destroyed by fire at Dresden in 1760 were the opera *Dafne* (1627), to a German text, and a ballet composed for the wedding of the Elector Johann Georg II, of Saxony, in 1638.

the end of a way of thought rather than a tentative explorer in new modes. Thus, despite his boldness in colouring and his affection for orchestral variety, he is a great polyphonist. At the end of his long life he went backwards rather than forwards and produced the great Passion music from which instruments were excluded. The severe nature of these works enhances their dignity (and relieves the modern conductor of many difficulties) and ensures that the listener is taken straight away to the heart of the matter. Schütz was inspired as was Monteverdi by the word, but, more than Monteverdi, he recognized that the meaning of a word is not always on the surface. Moreover he was less apt to regard the word in isolation.

The outstanding works of Schütz are the *Psalms of David* (26 in number) (1619), *The Resurrection Oratorio* (1623), the *Cantiones Sacrae* (1625), three sets of *Symphoniae Sacrae* (1629, 1647, 1650), the so-called *Christmas Oratorio* (1664), the *Seven Last Words* (c. 1645) and the four Passion settings (1665–6).

The *Psalms* display Venetian fashion in monodic and declamatory passages, in contrast between groups of voices, in contrast between instruments and voices and in richness of instrumental colouring; but the abiding impression is of great dignity and spiritual integrity. A noble example of Schütz's capacity for conserving the traditions of the past while enriching them with freshness of vision is Psalm VIII ('Herr unser Herrscher, wie herrlich ist dein Nam in allen Landen'). The opening statement by double choir, accompanied by three trumpets and two trombones, is a glorious invocation. (The early history of the trombone is one of great dignity. The instrument was highly regarded on account of its majestic tone and was accordingly much used in church music.) The imagery of the whole poem is implied by skilful and unobtrusive variations in texture, in timbre and in rhythm. In the 'Gloria' the bass part assumes great power and, with repeated melodic figures based on vigorous fourths and fifths, and percussive rhythm, reaches an ineluctable climax.

Among the *Cantiones Sacrae* (for four voices and organ) there is a similar intention to that evident in the Psalms—to imbue polyphony with a new atmosphere of dramatic expressiveness. In the *Cantiones Sacrae*, on the other hand, the possibilities of the solo voice are explored and, often, Schütz utilizes music as an aid to narrative. The first set of *Symphoniae Sacrae* followed Schütz's second visit to Venice where he noted considerable changes in music since his previous visit. These

works are landmarks in the history of style and represent the limit of
Schütz's capacity for experiment. In such a work as 'Wer betrübst du
dich, meine Seele' (Set II, 13) is to be noted a frequent use of the recur-
rent instrumental refrain, or *ritornello*; but the *ritornelli* are designed as
an essential part of the whole. Again there is much subtlety in melodic
organization, so that the symbolism is never allowed to obscure the
purely musical logic. And even in such a work as 'Saul, was verfolgst
du mich' the famous expostulations of the opening contribute to
musical thought as to dramatic expression.

There was a custom at Dresden of singing the story of the Resurrection at the service of Vespers on Easter Day. A celebrated Italian
(for many Italians were employed in the Dresden Court music)—
Antonio Scandello—had composed both Passion and Resurrection
music about 1561. Although Scandello's music continued to be performed during and even after Schütz's office at Dresden in 1623 it may
be presumed to have appeared old-fashioned. The major distinction
between Scandello's 'Resurrection' and that of Schütz is that the latter
is accompanied. Schütz's broad, motet-like opening chorus and the
final 'Gott sei dank', in 8 parts—with the voice of the Evangelist
ejaculating (Ex. 10) throughout—balance the choral movements of

Ex. 10

Vic - to - ri - a

Scandello (there is a brief middle chorus—'Der Herr ist wahrhaftig
auferstanden' which anticipates the 'crowd' music of the *St. Matthew*
Passion of Bach). The rest of the story is told by the Evangelist, whose
recitative, though largely liturgical, reaches out occasionally towards
a less impersonal mood (Ex. 11) and is accompanied by 'viola da

Ex. 11

und Pe - trus ver - wun - dert sich, wie es zu - ging.

gamba'—the instrument of the old viol family corresponding to the
more modern 'cello; and through the duets and trios which carry the
dramatis personae. By secular standards this transitional work is too
disparate for easy appreciation. But as an adjunct to the liturgy the
oratorio[1] should be recognized as a part of the liturgy and also as a
point of departure for German music.

[1] A loose, but convenient, connotation: see the title of the work.

After the 'Resurrection' oratorio it was nearly twenty years before Schütz composed another similar work. In this time he had made his second visit to Venice, had left Dresden for Copenhagen after the desolation wrought by the Thirty Years' War (1618–1648), and had returned in 1641, to find himself obliged to reconstitute the whole of the chapel music. Further he found himself increasingly out of sympathy with the outlook of Italian musicians practising at Dresden. Schütz—as is shown both by the nature of his music and by his literary remains—possessed a highly serious conception of his function and the effusive demonstrations of mere technical virtuosity in which the lesser Italians indulged found no place in his sympathy. The *Seven Last Words* of 1645, thus, is a protest against false standards and, at the same time, further token of the nobility of the composer.

The *Seven Last Words* are set within a choral and instrumental framework: the first and last choruses, polyphonic but not far distant from the character of chorale, are based on verses from the Passion chorale 'Da Jesus an dem Kreuze stand' and bring to the foot of the Cross the Christian believers. Thus we move one step nearer to the Passion style of Bach. After the first and before the last choral movements stands a 'Trauer-Symphonie' ('Grief-symphony') for five unspecified instruments (probably strings) in which the melodic shape is suggestive (Ex. 12). In earlier Passion music it had been the custom to

Ex. 12

set the words of Christ in four parts. Here Schütz retains four parts, but three are instrumental. Thus again we move in the direction of Bach. This excerpt (Ex. 13) shows beautifully the balance between the old

Ex. 13

motet style—for imitation remains as a structural principle—and the more modern expressive manner. The words of the Evangelist are given sometimes to a soloist and sometimes to a group of singers. Where the latter is the case, as at the Ninth Hour and as after the Last

Words have been uttered, the mood of the whole work is intensified. There are a few works of comparable length which are so suited to the rites of Passiontide.

In 1664, and at the suggestion of the Elector Johann Georg II, Schütz undertook a 'Christmas' Oratorio. Of all the works of Schütz this is the most fascinating in its colouring, the most joyful and the most charming. Were it not out of fashion to quote charm as a musical virtue one would be inclined to praise the composer for his introduction of this quality into seventeenth-century music. One may feel the whole work as an extended chorale and as an idealization of a childlike devotion to the fragrance of the Christmas narrative.

The work is set in eight scenes or *Intermedii*. Each is introduced by the Evangelist.

The first scene is of the appearance of the Angel to the Shepherds. The Angel, introduced by a bell figure, handles a descending phrase (cf. chorale 'In dir ist Freude') with playfulness and affection, and expands her song into something of a solo cantata. In the second scene the chorus of angels is exquisitely called from the sky (Ex. 14) and the

Ex. 14

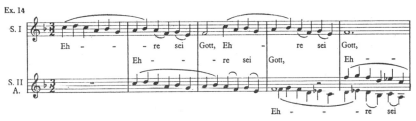

shepherds in Intermedium III set off for Bethlehem fugally, their occupation suggested in the accompanying pastoral texture of flutes and bassoon. Next come the Wise Men; after them, and for their benefit, the High Priests and learned men, who, in a pompous quartet for four basses—backed by trombones—say that the Child should be found in Bethlehem. A more complex aria, with two trumpets (instruments associated with royalty) in attendance, displays Herod and, in its way, the psychology of his character. The Angel tells Joseph to fly from the reach of Herod. A fine chorus joyfully phrased in an athletic dancing rhythm brings the story to an end with thanks to God.

The last works of Schütz were the four settings of the Passion.[1] In these the chorus is unaccompanied; but the rise to dramatic significance of the chorus is notable. The manner in which Schütz brings to life the

[1] The *St. Mark Passion* is not certainly by, but generally ascribed to, Schütz.

crowd who surround the Crucifixion is the outward symbol of the absorption within the 'motet style' of the expressiveness of the Italians. Here is the crowd, in the *St. Luke Passion*, demanding that Jesus should be crucified (Ex. 15); here the disciples, in *St. Matthew*, asking Jesus

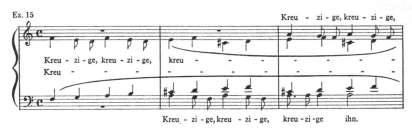

which should betray Him (Ex. 16); and here the congregation of

Christian believers recalling, in the final chorus of the *St. Matthew Passion*, the suffering of Jesus in the words 'der du littest Not . . .' (Ex. 17).

OTHER GERMAN COMPOSERS

Among non-Catholic communities the sixteenth and seventeenth centuries were remarkable for the development of a type of music suitable for the Reformed liturgies. Sometimes older material was adapted—so that numerous chorales were, in fact, harmonized plainsong. Where Calvinism prevailed, metrical versions of the Psalms were the custom (at the instigation of his Elector Schütz was, somewhat reluctantly, occupied at one time in setting the Psalter of Cornelius Becker, which it was hoped would replace the Calvinist Psalter in general use among Saxon Lutherans); but Lutheranism promoted a new conception of hymnody. Partly this was due to a long tradition of religious poetry in the vernacular, and partly to the especial concern of Luther himself. Luther wrote a number of poems which have become part of the heritage of Protestantism and he also composed a number of melodies for chorales. For two centuries there was a great output of Spiritual Songs—or *Geistliche Lieder*. Among composers and arrangers the most prominent were Johann Walther—a friend of Luther and director of the Court Chapel at Dresden; Heinrich Isaac, author of 'Innsbruck, ich muss dich lassen'; Hans Leo Hassler, who arranged this melody as a chorale; Michael Praetorius, who, as theoretician, was one of Monteverdi's most ardent champions; and Johann Crüger, whose *Praxis Pietatis Melica* (Berlin 1644) was the most widely used anthology of Lutheran hymns of the seventeenth and eighteenth centuries.

A great deal of German music must be approached by way of those spiritual songs which inspired such pride and devotion as is immortalized in Bach. Words and music together reflected the general character of the people who, in one way or another, made them.

'The Teutonic central part of Europe acquired a large collection of . . . poems, hymns and songs in the vernacular as well as in Latin; and with them were associated melodies which in many cases grew up with the words. Dancing was less associated with this singing here than among the Latin races; consequently the German melodies were not, as a rule, allied to dance rhythms, but rather to the descriptive and narrative spirit of folk-song, which relied for its attractiveness more on melodic grace and beauty than on rhythm.'[1]

Thus we notice that *expression* in music was considered from other angles than that of the Italians. And the independent, philosophical

[1] *Hymns Ancient and Modern, Historical Edition* (London 1912): see Introduction (p. lxvii) by W. H. Frere.

German approach is of equal importance in the development of music with the more flamboyant, more ideological attitude of the monodists. The influence of religion on German art is well epitomized in this summary of Paul Gerhardt, the hymn-writer.

'Religion in him went deeper than the level of individualistic piety, and fertilized a naturally mystic mind, so that as a writer of verse or prose he made his appeal not to the limited circle of his own confession, but to the great commonwealth of mystics that extends throughout all the various confessions of Christendom.'

It is this quality of mysticism which especially determined the future of German choral music.

Throughout the seventeenth century many composers endeavoured to make the chorale the focal point of sacred and choral music. Thus there were chorales treated in the style of motet. (See especially the *Cantiones Sacrae* of Samuel Scheidt.) In this respect there was much affinity with the development of the organ chorale prelude. On the other hand there were many attempts to assimilate the chorale into the *concertato* (or 'concerted') style familiar in the large choral movements of Bach. Two composers of great importance in this forward-looking tendency were Michael Praetorius (*Polyhymnia Caduceatrix*, 1619) and Johann Schein, one of the great German organists and a predecessor of Bach as cantor at the Thomasschule in Leipzig. Schein published his *Opella nova* or *Geistliche Konzerte* in two parts, in 1618 and 1626. He treated chorale melodies with considerable freedom, subjecting them to much decoration and to extensive harmonic glosses; by all available means he made the emotional detail of both words and music as effective as could be. A singularly beautiful and simple example of his style is the motet verson of *Vom Himmel hoch*. His expressiveness is exemplified in *Die mit Tränen säen* (Ex. 18). His influence was widespread. The most immediately significant of his followers was Franz Tunder.[1]

Tunder had been a pupil of Frescobaldi and became organist of St. Mary's Church in Lübeck, where he instituted the *Abendmusik* ('evening music'), or performances of (mainly sacred) music given in church, generally during the season of Advent. His successor and

---

[1] See *Historical Anthology of Music II*, no. 214.

Ex. 18

son-in-law was the Swedish Buxtehude, who worked in Lübeck from 1668 until his death in 1707.

DIETRICH BUXTEHUDE (1637-1707)

Buxtehude had exceptional opportunities at Lübeck for the composition of works of large scale. He seized his opportunities, was well supported by his fellow-citizens and made Lübeck so great a centre of music that, in 1705, J. S. Bach was among the many who made pilgrimage to the Marienkirche.[1] The impression made by Buxtehude's choral music (and there is a great deal available for performance) is of greatness in conception and certainty in execution. This body of music is not to be regarded merely as on the way to somewhere or other: it is a point of arrival—though, obviously, a point of arrival is also a point of departure.

Buxtehude was a famous organist and his development of chorale prelude, passacaglia, prelude and fugue, sonata and other purely instrumental forms was of considerable significance to his successors. In respect of his own work concentration on instrumental music

[1] Handel also went to Lübeck: for an account of his visit see *Handel*, Percy M. Young, pp. 12–13.

enabled him to achieve both plasticity and balance in those works which involved voices.

Buxtehude used every method of familiar chorale treatment in his cantatas (his works in this genre were variously entitled *Geistliche Symphonien*, *Geistliche Concerten* and *Geistliche Gespräche* before the classification 'cantata' was adopted). He was not averse from enlivening the *Abendmusik* with examples of southern brilliance and he took much delight in exploiting the solo voice in solo cantatas. He could also look over his shoulder at the classical polyphonic style in such works as the *Missa brevis*. The two movements which comprise this work ('Kyrie' and 'Gloria') are not so much imitations of an old style as essays in the spirit of the style within which such modernities of technique as are appropriate are allowed.

At the other extreme from the *Missa brevis* is the enormous motet *Benedicam Dominum*, all generously displayed in the Venetian manner for double choir; strings; cornets and bassoon; trumpets, and bombard; three trombones; and the usual accessories of organ and continuo (continuo = thorough bass = figured bass and defines, for practical purposes, the continuous harpsichord accompaniment devised by the player from his guiding figures). An exciting, if somewhat monotonous, sound. Between the two the *Magnificat* in D major which, while nicely varied as to solo, duet, chorus, instrumental (string) *ritornello* and so on has too stolid chordal writing and too many facile strings of thirds. It is in some of the chamber cantatas for three voices that Buxtehude is seen at his most thoughtful and revealing. In a most appealing, if fragmentary, *O Jesu mi dulcissime*, he evokes the sweet anguish of St. Bernard's text in exquisite and brief arioso passages and in such harmonic shifts as (Ex. 19). In cheerful contrast the Easter

Ex. 19

Surrexit Christus hodie starts, as Purcell or Handel might have done, with a flourish that needs no comment (Ex. 20)

Ex. 20

Sur - rex - it, Sur - rex - it, Sur - rex - it Chris - tus

ho - di - e hu - ma - no pro so - la - mi - ne hu - ma - - - -

- - - - - - - no pro so - la - mi - ne,

With all this variety of expression it is small wonder that the cantatas based on chorales were full of diversity. We may compare *Wachet auf* with works on the same theme by Tunder on one hand and Bach on the other. Three voices (two sopranos and bass), strings, bassoon and organ are employed. The *Sinfonia* is content to establish the festival key of D major in thirty-six measures of somewhat stereotyped tonic and dominant. The first verse is a decorated version of the melody, with interjected chords for the accompaniment. Verse 2 is a variation for bass voice. Verse 3 is a presentation by the whole group and we may be forgiven for reading the angelic spirit of Schütz into it. In *Jesu meine Freude* there is a more ambitious treatment of a chorale and Buxtehude succeeds here in allowing free melodic material to infiltrate, yet without destroying the unity of the whole. In feeling this work compares with Bach's motet variations on the same theme.

The plan of *Jesu meine Freude* is: 'Sonata' (*allegro: grave: allegro*) for instruments: verse 1-*tutti*, with a vigorous and rhythmic motiv developed independently in the *ritornello*; verse 2—soprano solo—in which no more than a hint of the contour of the chorale remains, but the concluding *ritornello* is that of verse 1; verse 3—a flashing bass solo in triple time—Buxtehude gave his bass singers much exercise in depiction and Hades demands (Ex. 21); a beautiful *ritornello*, which is

Ex. 21

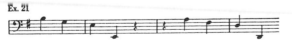

a variation of the melody; finally, a finely harmonized triple-time version of the melody and with some judicious cross rhythms; to which the same *ritornello* as for the previous verse is the coda.

The greater part of German religious verse, whether with or

F

without music, sprang from consideration either of Christmas or Passiontide. Among Buxtehude's Christmas music there is nothing that exemplifies the delicate, domestic significance of the Festival more beautifully than the tiny set of variations on the familiar carol theme *In dulci jubilo*.

MICHEL RICHARD DE LALANDE (1657–1726), 'DIXIT DOMINUS'

Michel de Lalande became the most distinguished church musician of his day in France more by accident than design. As a boy he was refused admission to Lully's band of violins and he determined, therefore, to specialize as organist. He became organist of three Paris churches, and at one of these—that of the Jesuits of the Maison Professe—he was commissioned to compose choruses and incidental music for dramatic performances. Through the Maréchal de Noailles he was recommended to Louis XIV to whom he became, successively, chamber musician and one of the superintendents of the Royal Chapel. He was connected with ecclesiastical music for more than forty years.

As a composer of church music his achievement was great, for he was able to unite the correct and fashionable styles of Italy and France, while imparting to them a gravity of feeling that distinguishes his motets (of which he wrote forty-two) from the too conventional, too secular works of most of his immediate predecessors and his contemporaries.

LULLY AND OTHER FRENCH COMPOSERS

The outstanding music of seventeenth-century France was that of Lully, who, of course, was primarily concerned with the development of opera. Within his operas, however, Lully made extensive use of the chorus and the manner in which he streamlined the form he had acquired from Carissimi gave to choral music the grace and neat refinement of the chanson on the one hand and the rhythmic verve of the ballet on the other. The vivacity of the 'Liberté' chorus, the *a cappella* chorus of Scythians for men's voices, the great pagan homophony of 'Aimons sans cesse' in *Isis* (1677); the cantata-like termination of the first act of *Armide* (1686), wherein solo ensembles and choral passages alternate in the manner of a rondo; the exhilarating response of trumpets and percussion to the hymn to the gods in *Psyche* (1678) are illustrations of the succinctness and relevance in Lully's treatment of the chorus. In (Ex. 22) we may see the individuality of the method.

Other attractive composers of the school of Lully were André Campra and Louis Marchand, both celebrated organists.

Lully composed motets—in effect cantatas for solo, chorus and orchestra, and therefore different in style from the sixteenth-century motet—and other church music, but it was left to Marc-Antoine Charpentier to introduce the oratorio form of Carissimi to France.

Charpentier (1634–1704) had been a pupil of Carissimi in Rome and we may note that among his oratorios were settings of subjects already treated by Carissimi—*Judicium Salomonis* is an outstanding example. Charpentier resembled Carissimi in his dramatic use of the chorus, in his finely organized coloratura and in his aptitude for chaconne basses. His instrumentation is richer than that of his master, his attitude to *bel canto*—the Italian style of singing—was affected by the necessity for embellishment by French ornaments and by the structural neatness of French song, and his harmonies could be both poignant and penetrating.

A third composer to be considered in relation to Lalande was Henri Dumont, a Fleming by birth, who was Lalande's predecessor at the Chapel Royal. Dumont composed in the old *a cappella* tradition all his life. At the same time he was the first Frenchman (see *Cantica Sacra* 1652) to make *basso continuo* obligatory and his solo cantatas have great merit. Dumont holds further interest in that he introduced plainsong motivs into his Masses, but inflected them rhythmically and harmonically so as to bring them within the ambit of 'modern music'.

Any composer of church music at the Court of Versailles, like any other artist at the Court of Versailles, was conditioned by the likes and dislikes of the king. Louis XIV expected music either to glorify the monarchy or to amuse him. Therefore, High Masses (a High Mass entailed a musical setting) gave way to Low Masses (in which the words were spoken, not sung), but Low Masses were made more palatable by the introduction of diversionary music without much—if any—religious significance. Hence the spirited quality of the motets. The *Dixit Dominus* of Lalande has spirit, but it also has a gravity of outlook that matches the more severe atmosphere of the last days of Louis XIV, when the glory of *le Roi Soleil* was dimmed by the reverses of the War of the Spanish Succession (1702–13).

LALANDE'S 'DIXIT DOMINUS'

The first four verses of the Psalm are bound together into one grand movement in C minor and C major; in this key contrast Lalande anticipates Handel, as indeed he often does in the explicitness of his counterpoint and the brilliance of his textures. An instrumental introduction forecasts the material with which soprano, and later tenor, soloist announce the first verse. The manner of the melody is characteristically French—clear, precise and then with an undercurrent of pensiveness (Ex. 23). The duet runs directly into an ensemble (the

Ex. 23

Dix - it   Do - mi - nus   Do - mi - ne   me - o: se - de,   se - de

varied use of the vocal resources is as in the operas of Lully) of six soloists and the rhythm changes to a sharp-edged pattern of eighth and quarter notes in which Lalande shows that the propensity of his school for declamatory exactness can apply to Latin as to French (Ex. 24). The

Ex. 24   Do - nec   po - nam   i - ni - mi - cos   tu - - - -

S. I
S. II   Do - nec   po - nam   i - ni -

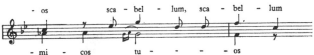

- os   sca - bel - lum,   sca - bel - lum
- mi - cos   tu - - - - os

full choir repeat what the soloists have delivered, but in extended form, and after soprano and mezzo-soprano have echoed the first section in a brief interlude. A long contralto section, which is somewhat tedious,

follows with the second verse of the psalm. This is succeeded by a
serene chorus in which the imaginative disposition of voices and
instruments exhales the spirit of the text—'the dew of thy birth is of
the womb of the morning'—without too much concern for literal
definition.

From the key centre of C we change to that of G and in the minor
mode, and against a commanding pulsation of strings, the pontifical
words 'Tu es sacerdos . . .' are given to a solo baritone. After this there
is one of the most purely beautiful passages in the whole of sacred
music. The mezzo-soprano, preceded by (Ex. 25), which belongs to

Ex. 25

the keyboard thought of Chambonnières, warns that not even kings
will be spared in the day of the wrath of the Lord. The warning is
repeated with exquisite melody and scoring by a trio of high voices.
At this moment Lalande is concerned with his musical texture and the
words disappear except as a support for melody: but a tremendous and
dramatic chorus—taken back to the minor—then comes in violent
contrast and in extreme climax. In his music for the judgement of the
heathen Lalande uses the most telling choral devices: expostulated
words isolated by long pauses; repetition of savage statements with
intensified dynamics; trumpet-calls in the voices in cumulative imitation
and against an idealized drum figure in the accompanying strings;
above all no technical interference with the enunciation of the words,
so that the mere sibillation of 'implebit ruinas' and 'conquassabit
capita' can inspire terror. The harmonic acridity of the conclusion is the
final vision of things to come (Ex. 26).

Ex. 26
S. I
A.
T.
B.

in   ter - ra mul - to   -   rum.

An elaborate soprano solo which runs into a choral extension
illustrates the keyword of 'He shall drink in the *brook* on the way' with
fluid quavers. The complementary part of this verse: 'therefore shall he

lift up his head' is set to an infinitely comforting phrase, in which
the contour, rhythm and harmony conspire to express a sublime
sympathy (Ex. 27). The simplicity and modesty of this movement,

Ex. 27

pro - te - re - a   ex - al - ta - bit   ca - put,

combined with the purity of the writing, suggests Fauré. Towards the
end of the verse 'exaltabit' flows more and more freely. The concluding 'Gloria' is a competent finale in the grand manner.

HENRY PURCELL (1658–1695)

Purcell has always been regarded as among the greatest names in
English music. The quality of his genius lies not in the fact that he
composed music which is narrowly English but that he could assimilate
the whole of European tradition and turn it to whatever purposes time
and place might demand. The English nature is empirical and this,
more than anything, distinguishes the Purcellian outlook. Purcell did
not in fact write many 'great works'—in the sense that greatness
indicates length and large resources—but he wrote a large number of
works, of infinite variety, which are stamped with the mark of
greatness.

Purcell was essentially an occasional composer—that is to say he
wrote music as and when he was required to do so. Since he was
organist of Westminster Abbey from 1679 until his death (his master
John Blow[1] is said to have resigned his appointment in Purcell's favour),
one of the organists of the Chapel Royal, a court musician on the
secular side with the modest title of 'composer in ordinary for the
violins', and much in demand as composer for the theatre his opportunities extended widely. He was fortunate in one way that the
Restoration of the Monarchy (in 1660) and the lively intelligence of
Charles II were encouraging to music in general. Less fortunate, perhaps, in that prevailing taste of the Court, and therefore of London,
was influenced by France.

[1] Good examples of Blow's style are the motet *Salvator mundi* and the *Ode for St. Cecilia*
of 1684.

Charles II had spent his years of exile at Versailles and one of his earliest gestures relating to music was to arrange for Pelham Humfrey, who taught Purcell as a choirboy at the Chapel Royal, to study composition in France and Italy. The chief consequences of the king's personal interest in English music were a development of orchestral music, a secularization of rhythm (Charles II was one of the class that likes a firm beat for which appreciation may be shown by time-keeping with a foot!) and a generous output of works calculated to reflect the happiness of the English people in having so noble, so good, so wise, and—above all—so cheerful a monarch.

Purcell composed many Welcome Songs, Birthday Odes, Odes for St. Cecilia (the 1692 Ode contains 'Soul of the World', one of Purcell's most inspired choral moments), for the Societies of Yorkshiremen and Irishmen, and in these he established the English secular cantata. He left models which Handel appreciated—as may be seen in the choral opening of the 1687 Welcome Song (this, of course, for James II who succeeded in 1685). Purcell's easy brilliance of orchestration, his telling interpolations of drums and trumpets, his recourse to D major, his supple use of the choral unit all strike a new note in English choral music. But much of this ceremonial music was ephemeral—largely on account of paltry texts.

The operas that Purcell wrote were for the most part not operas but plays with music. *Dido and Aeneas* is an exception, having no spoken dialogue; but this was, as it were, an unofficial work composed for a girls' school in Chelsea. None the less, these dramatic works do show Purcell's versatility as a choral composer more than almost any of his works. The Baroque idea of expressing the meaning of the word is most sensitively and subtly upheld. For Purcell both illuminates the literary quality of any text and enhances its visual significance. In the first scene of *The Fairy Queen* (a work based rather generally, and in accordance with the Restoration conclusion that Shakespeare needed much refurbishing, on *A Midsummer Night's Dream*) choral episodes, perfect in rhythmic reference and in verbal exposition, reach the eye through the ear.

In *Dido and Aeneas* we have choruses of courtiers, of witches, or sailors; and each class is easily distinguishable by the aptness of the music alone. In the same work the emotional range within the choruses, from the excitement of, say, 'Haste, haste to town' to the tender gravity of the final chorus is both a test for the imagination of

chorus singers and an exertion for the listener, whose mind must re-
orientate itself with speed. Again we must examine Handel's English
music, particularly the more picturesque choruses of *L'Allegro, Samson,
Belshazzar, Theodora, Susanna* and *Solomon* in the light of Purcell. And
behind Purcell the music of the Jacobean and Caroline court masques
(from which English opera stemmed) and the madrigalists.

There is a good deal of Lully in Purcell's style—for example, the
clear-cut rhythmic formulas of the homophonic choruses, the echo
effects, the dance music, the orchestration; much Italian influence in
the coloratura, the chromatic interest of such a work as *Blessed is he
that considereth the poor*, the frequent use of ground bass; something of
popular balladry—for Purcell was also an ale-house composer; but,
above all, there is continuity from the sixteenth century.

In his anthems Purcell, therefore, ranges from the gaiety of *Rejoice
in the Lord*, with its exhilarating *ritornelli* for strings, to the profundity
of the eight-part *Hear my Prayer*. In this work, as in the great Latin
motets—*Beati omnes qui timent Dominum* and *Jehovah quam multi sunt
hostes*—Purcell shows his affinity with Byrd and Bach in making
counterpoint the servant of emotional expression. Like these composers his use of discord and the unexpected dramatic inflection
shows an inflexible determination in musical logic. This passage
from *Hear my prayer* illustrates the composer's vigorous independence
(Ex. 28).

Hubert Parry observed that Purcell's church music was 'full of impertinence as well as noble moments'. There is the affinity with the best contemporary English choral music (in England Purcell is, in a sense, the chief composer of the twentieth as well as the seventeenth century), for Purcell was, above all, athletic; lithe, rhythmic, various in his colouring, unaware of binding convention, and quick to suit his forces to whatever engagement they were committed—whether in church, at court or in the theatre.

3

The Period of Bach and Handel

JOHANN SEBASTIAN BACH (1685-1750)

GEORGE FRIDERIC HANDEL (1685-1759)

IT MIGHT appear that Bach and Handel came to an agreement and that the one—both being Latin scholars—said to the other, 'Divide et impera.' For, as we look down the corridor of time, we see those two giants virtually to obscure everything and everybody else of the first half of the eighteenth century. Concerto—in all its forms; sonata; suite; fugue; opera; cantata—both sacred and secular; oratorio; mass; passion. In all these branches of music Bach and Handel were consummate masters. It should, however, be recognized that such realization comes after the considered judgements of two centuries; that in their own day both Bach and Handel had local rather than universal reputations (Handel, it is true, was better served in the matter of publicity and he was cosmopolitan in activity and outlook); that they had rivals who, in the eyes of the eighteenth century, appeared as at least of equal stature; that they were neither, in a general way, innovators but rather inheritors and guardians of certain traditions which each cherished; above all that they were practical music-makers observing the accepted convention of the time that a composer was not a special sort of musician but that every musician was a special sort of composer, obeying the needs of time and place. Because music belonged to eighteenth-century civilization and infected it at every point (note the contrast of the nineteenth and twentieth centuries wherein music is more often specialized and departmentalized) circumstances were very various: so, gratefully, we may find in Bach and Handel such music as will serve our present interests and requirements.

The facts of the biographies of Bach and Handel may briefly be reviewed. Set side by side they go some way towards explaining the great and ultimate divergence of style and viewpoint, but also a community of outlook that is sometimes unseen.

Handel (whose name at various times appeared as Haendel, Händel, Hendel, before settling—in England—on Handel) was born on February 23rd, 1685, in Halle in Saxony; Bach on March 21st, of the same year, in Eisenach in Thuringia. There was no musical tradition in Handel's family—his father was a prosperous surgeon who intended George Frideric for the Law and to that end entered him as a student in the University of Halle; on the other hand members of the Bach dynasty had been for generations conspicuous in musical affairs in Thuringia. The city of Halle, however, had its musical reputation, for Wolff Heintz, a friend of Luther, and Samuel Scheidt (see p. 76) had been organists there; while Handel, as a boy, was indebted to the sound tuition of the then organist of the Liebfrauenkirche—Friedrich Wilhelm Zachau (or Zachow), a composer of considerable stature. Eisenach, where Luther took refuge in 1521 and where he composed some of his hymns, had entertained Pachelbel as court organist in 1677; George Philipp Telemann was Kapellmeister between 1708 and 1712; but of long distinction in the musical history of the town was Bach's second cousin, Johann Christoph. He was senior organist in Eisenach for many years and his motets and organ chorale preludes were exemplars for Johann Sebastian. It remains to be said that Bach's father —Johann Ambrosius—was a violinist. Both Bach and Handel, then, were blessed in their environment; Bach also by heredity.

The general method of learning the technique of composition in the apprentice days of Bach and Handel was by making copies of all the works of acknowledged masters. Bach and Handel were studious copyists throughout their lives. Besides Johann Christoph Bach Johann Sebastian took as models the Italians, Frescobaldi, Corelli, Vivaldi, Lotti, Caldara, Legrenzi, Marcello; the French d'Anglebert, Couperin, Raison, Marchand; the Germans, Froberger, Kerll, Reinken, Buxtehude, Pachebel, Strungck, Telemann, Handel. Bach's special interests led to keyboard music, to violin music and to choral music. Handel, under Zachau, made an anthology of excerpts from Froberger, Kerll,

Strungck, Johann Krieger. During his later career he borrowed ideas (even whole movements) from numerous composers—including Alessandro Stradella, Giacomo Carissimi, Georg Muffatt, Karl Heinrich Graun, Giovanni Clari and even, through a harpist, from Welsh folk-song. The moral to be drawn is that no composer can afford to neglect the works of his contemporaries, of whatever styles, nor should he be ignorant of previous achievement. It is significant that neither Bach nor Handel were theoreticians and that their critics (see Johann Adolf Scheibe (1708–1776) who criticized Bach's conservatism in his *Der Critische Musikus* in 1737; and Charles Avison (1710–1770) who alluded to Handel's extravagance in *An Essay on Musical Expression*, 1753) were.

For a brief period Handel took the same path as Bach. He spent a year or so as organist at the Cathedral in Halle; but soon he sought wider fields of experience and opportunity in Hamburg and then, more significantly, in Italy. By this time he was a celebrated composer of opera and as such he came to London in 1710. By this year Bach, after his education as a chorister at Lüneburg, and organistships at Arnstadt and Mühlhausen, was at Weimar in the service of the duke as court organist and chamber musician. In youth as in age Bach and Handel shared a tendency to be obstinate or persevering—according to opinion. Familiar anecdotes are revealing and not without relevance to music as well as to character. Bach was in trouble at Arnstadt in 1706 because of his overlong and elaborate organ treatment of chorales (that he overstayed leave of absence when he went to hear Buxtehude in Lübeck did not help his reputation in the eyes of the church authorities). In 1708 at a performance in Rome of *Il trionfo del tempo e del disinganno* Handel remonstrated with the conservative Corelli for his inability to cope adequately with the overture. Bach, we may note, was brought to book for his thinking aloud; and by a petty local committee: Handel, in this instance, felt sure enough to criticize one of the greatest players (and composers) in Europe.

Bach looked inward: Handel outward. Partly through circumstance and tradition, partly through innate disposition, Bach considered the serious requirements of his offices and composed cantatas and organ music and, by genius and an aptitude for seeing the whole symbolism of words and doctrine, extended the character of his models. Handel, more fluent, more rhetorical, and a free agent with his way to make in the world seized the formalized patterns of entertainment music—in secular cantata, in oratorio (for to Roman audiences of the first decade of the eighteenth century an oratorio was but another concert), in opera, and in instrumental music—to assume, wherever he might go, a commanding position among the virtuoso composers.

The early extant music of the two composers is revealing. Handel's setting of *Dixit Dominus* (1707) shows its German origin in a persistent quasi-chorale motiv: its Italian association (for Zachau at Halle had cultivated the Italian fashions of figuration) in coloratura and in choral directness which recalls Carissimi—and, for that matter de Lalande. In moments of chromatic expression—which are rare—Handel displays a poignant expressiveness which may also be found in the exquisite solo cantata *Salve regina*. The feeling, however, is musical and dramatic rather than intellectual. Handel is moulding music, whereas in works of the same period Bach is constraining music to the purpose of his thought. Compare with Handel the intense inner energy of the solo cantata (189) *Meine Seele rühmt und preist* (in the first movement the melismata are characteristically unvocal) or the impressive extension of the chorale in the cantata (106) *Gottes Zeit ist die allerbeste Zeit*.

Had Handel remained in Italy he would, no doubt, have continued to supplement his opera output with numerous cantatas and oratorios such as were written by his contemporaries, Lotti, Vivaldi, Durante, Leo—to mention but a few. But he went to England.

MUSIC IN LONDON

In matters of music the English are incalculable: Handel, of course, quickly discovered this. Georgian England had music in the theatre so that the aristocracy could have some diversion to attend that would remind them of their Grand Tour: thus Italian Opera. But, according to the stalwart standards of native virility, foreign male singers were an insult to their sex. Therefore opera collapsed. *The Beggar's Opera* of 1728 helped it down and out—not, however, before Handel had composed a very large number of operas in the Italian style. In church there was a tradition of anthem writing, and, since the King was the head of the Church, there were frequent opportunities for composing extensive works which were expected to illuminate the pageantry of whatever occasion might arise. Therefore Handel, after careful study of Purcell, wrote a series of 'occasional' works—the *Utrecht Te Deum* (1713), the

Coronation Anthem (1727), the *Wedding Anthem* (1736), the *Funeral Anthem for Queen Caroline*[1] (1737), the *Dettingen Te Deum* (1743) as well as many other works—which precisely fitted their environment. Unlike Germany and Italy England was not blessed (or cursed) with petty princelings who could individually patronize the arts. (England has to its credit the invention of the 'committee' and so many committees of so many incompetent people were formed to encourage the development of Italian opera that failure was ensured on this account alone.) But there were two noblemen who had direct responsibility for Handel's progress. In his early days Handel wrote a series of anthems—the *Chandos Anthems* for the Duke of Chandos; while at Burlington House, under the patronage of the young Earl of Burlington, he met Gay and Pope and other men of letters through whom he began to turn his attention to English poetry on a larger scale. In 1719 he composed the pretty pastoral cantata *Acis and Galatea*[2] (the poem being by Gay) and a year later the masque (later to be called oratorio) *Haman and Mordecai* (or *Esther*). In 1732 *Esther* was revived. A notice in the *Daily Journal* at the beginning of April in that year is a landmark in English choral music:

> 'By his Majesty's command, at the King's Theatre in the Haymarket, on Tuesday the 2nd day of May, will be performed the sacred story of Esther; an oratorio in English, formerly composed by Mr. Handel, and now revised by him with several additions, and to be performed by a great number of voices and instruments. N.B. There will be no acting on the stage, but the house will be fitted up in a decent manner, for the audience. The Musick to be disposed after the manner of the coronation service. Tickets to be delivered at the usual prices.'

BACH'S APPOINTMENTS

On the whole, the pre-1732 works of Handel are unfamiliar and despite Handel's success in establishing himself as the principal

[1] In the *Funeral Anthem* Handel quotes directly, in the chorus 'But their name liveth evermore' Handl's motet *Ecce quomodo*. This motet, see p. 49, was a traditional part of Passion observances in Leipzig. There is no better example of Handel's apt use of quotation and the semantic properties accorded to music in the eighteenth century.

[2] Certain of the themes in *Acis and Galatea* (in the 'Polyphemus' chorus and the air 'O ruddier than the cherry') are taken from a cantata—*Das ist das ewige Leben*—by Zachau (see Vorwort to *Denkmäler Deutscher Tonkunst, Vol. XXI: Gesammelte Werke von Friedrich Wilhelm Zachau*).

English[1] composer), so far as we are concerned, his great works were yet to come. In contrast Bach's record included a vast number of cantatas—both secular and sacred—the *Brandenburg Concertos* (1721), the first book of *Das wohltemperirte Klavier* (1722), the *Magnificat, Jesu, meine Freude*, the *St. John Passion* (1723) and the *St. Matthew Passion* (1729). In 1732, indeed, we are within sight of the *Mass in B Minor*, for the 'Kyrie' and 'Gloria' were to be presented to the Elector of Saxony during the next year.

We left Bach at Weimar in 1708. His subsequent public career had its disappointments. Bach was regarded as a brilliant and exceptional organist and was frequently invited to give recitals; but the most congenial employment was difficult to obtain. No doubt that difficulty afflicts most men of genius. In 1713 he thought of succeeding Zachau at the Liebfrauenkirche in Halle, but the salary offered was too small (Bach's second son, Carl Philipp Emanuel, was born the next year). In 1717 he wished to accept appointment in the ducal establishment at Cöthen: for so wishing he was imprisoned by his Weimar patron. (He served his sentence philosophically and usefully by composing chorale preludes for the *Orgelbüchlein*.) In 1720 Bach, by now at Cöthen, visited Hamburg but refused an organistship there. In 1722 he applied for the cantorship at St. Thomas's, Leipzig, and was only appointed because Telemann and Christoph Graupner refused the vacancy. 'As the best are not available,' said the Mayor of Leipzig, 'I suppose we must take one of the second-rate men.' Leipzig had then to put up with this second-rate musician for the next twenty-seven years.

CRITICS

It has been suggested that Handel knew exactly how to adapt himself to the opinions, tastes, feelings and expectations of the society in which he lived. This, we must hasten to add, was without detriment to the originality and integrity of his ideas. Handel's music is often an expression of his friendly, sociable nature: of his proclivity for fitting-in with other people. Handel was a citizen of the world and much at home in the world. Bach, with his domestic commitments and his opportunity only to meet the great from a position of social inferiority, was inclined to let the world go hang. When Handel raged it was an

[1] Handel became a naturalized British subject in 1726.

occasion: princes and princesses blanched and the public applauded the old man's vagaries. But when Bach lost his temper—as he often did at Leipzig—there was no such effective presentation of his ire. What was wrong with Bach? His music was 'highbrow'. Scheibe put it very clearly in 1737.

> 'This great man would be the admiration of whole nations if he had more amenity, if he did not take away the natural elements in his pieces by giving them a turgid and confused style, and if he did not darken their beauty by an excess of art . . . Every ornament, every little grace, and everything that one thinks of as belonging to the method of playing, he expresses completely in notes; and this not only takes away from his pieces the beauty of harmony but completely covers the melody throughout. In short, he is in music what Mr. von Lohenstein was in poetry. Turgidity has led them both from the natural to the artificial, and from the lofty to the sombre; and in both one admires the onerous labour and unconscious effort—which, however, are vainly employed, since they conflict with Reason.'

Almost exactly at the same time as this criticism appeared Handel was suffering from his first severe breakdown in health. And, as it happened, he was also the victim of criticism. It was said that his oratorios were too noisy. Henry Carey, author of the farcical *Dragon of Wantley* epitomized a general opinion:

> 'Sing, sing and rorio
> An oratorio. . . .'

Bach was criticized because he was too intellectual and, paradoxically, because an excess of reason conflicted with the aesthetic precepts of the Age of Reason. Handel transgressed against the same set of principles, but from a different direction. Indeed it is possible to make a good case against Handel, assuming the premises of the period. Handel exceeded the conventional in the extras which he introduced into his orchestration to underline his dramatic appreciation of scene and situation.

In 1738 Charles Jennens, one of Handel's librettists, wrote to the Earl of Guernsey that he found in Handel's room 'a very queer instrument which he calls carillon (Anglice, a bell) and says some call it a

Tubalcain' That was for use in the triumphant opening of *Saul* (1738–9). For the same oratorio Handel borrowed kettle drums from the Tower of London and he employed the eeriness of three bassoons to raise the spirit of Samuel from the dead. 'Handel,' said Mozart, 'understands effect better than any of us—when he chooses, he strikes like a thunderbolt.' But on the whole audiences are slow to respond to novelty of expression, in whatever form it arrives. It is worth while realizing the easy division which puts Handel down as 'easy to understand' and Bach as 'difficult' is invalid: and the same goes for performance.

ENGLISH ORATORIO

From 1738 to 1752 Handel's great achievement was in the field of oratorio. After *Saul* and the overwhelming choral battery of *Israel in Egypt* (both were produced in the same year—1739) there followed *Messiah* and *Samson* (1742), *Joseph* and *Semele*, a secular oratorio (1744), *Belshazzar* and *Hercules*, another secular oratorio (1745), the *Occasional Oratorio* (1746), *Judas Maccabaeus* (1747), *Alexander Balus* and *Joshua* (1748), *Susanna* and *Solomon* (1749), *Theodora* (1750) and *Jephtha* (1752). Such was the prodigality of Handel's genius, until, in 1752, his eyesight failed.

A few general observations may be remarked. These oratorios were performed in the theatre and during Lent. They were substitutes for opera and were regarded by the public exactly as it regarded operas—as entertainment. The form of oratorio was that of opera—recitative, aria, concerted numbers and occasional instrumental interludes appearing in similar sequence and style—except that the chorus function was greatly increased. Therefore Handel seized plots which afforded dramatic exposition—excepting *Messiah*, *Susanna* and *Theodora*—from the Old Testament. As he made the form of oratorio his own Handel used it symbolically: *Messiah* is a firm token of the composer's invincible belief in the transcendence of the Christian faith and (this is where his vast dramatic skill is especially to be noticed) the divine humanity of Christ; *Belshazzar* and *Solomon* are monuments to the Court—the Lullian practice of apotheosizing kingship, conjoined with the earlier English sublimation of the Stuarts in the masque, came to Handel through Purcell; the *Occasional Oratorio* celebrates the defeat

G

and discomfiture of the Jacobites and the romantic fiasco of the '45—which was the last effort of the exiled Stuarts to oust the Hanoverian dynasty; *Judas Maccabaeus* and *Alexander Balus* are symptomatic of affection for Jewry, Handel having friends in the London Jewish community. However far Handel's ideas might range there was an abiding problem, which Bach did not have to face. The problem is a familiar one: the performances must be self-supporting. Handel was well aware of the fickleness of public taste. *Theodora*, a tale of martyrdom but also a tender study of young love, was his (and my) favourite oratorio. After philosophically reviewing one empty house and remarking, like Beecham on another occasion, that music sounded better without an audience he summed up the situation: 'The Jews will not come, because it is a Christian story, and the ladies will not come, because it is a virtuous one.'

Deep down in the English Handel old memories sometimes stirred. He was, in affluence, on one occasion notably generous to the widow of his old teacher, Zachau. Chance references to the music of Zachau from time to time serve to remind that at all times there was a common bond uniting Bach with Handel. The church cantatas of Zachau were a starting point for both. Handel quoted Zachau in *Acis and Galatea* in 1720. The air 'Rejoice greatly' in *Messiah* is shaped after the air 'Kommt jauchzet' in Zachau's fine *Lobe den Herrn, meine Seele*: while the chorus which graphically describes the fall of the walls of Jericho in *Joshua* is aware of an exciting choral climax in 'Lob und Preis' in the older master's *Ruhe, Friede, Freude und Wonne*. A further touching example of Handel's loyalty is in the coat of arms of the Foundling Hospital, of which Handel was a governor; for the arms of Halle are incorporated.

It would seem that Handel was as unacquainted with Bach the composer as were the majority of contemporary musicians. But Bach held Handel in high esteem. In 1716 Handel made a setting of Brockes' *Passion* for use in Hamburg, and Bach, with the aid of Anna Magdalena, made a copy—presumably for performance in Leipzig. (This work, except for some moving music for the Last Supper, is dull: but it obeys all the precepts laid down by Scheidt. This, no doubt, is why Telemann respected it highly and withheld his own music in its favour at the *Collegium Musicum* in Hamburg in 1722.) Twice Bach made determined efforts to meet Handel—in 1719 and in 1729. But both times he was unsuccessful.

Handel and Bach were afflicted in later days by near blindness. Some of the other obstacles in Handel's way have been suggested. In Leipzig Bach found no bed of roses. When he went to St. Thomas's the organization was appalling and it was not until he had roused many animosities, written numerous memorandums, and the death of the antagonistic Rector Ernesti and the appointment in his place of Gesner that matters began to mend. But some years later trouble again arose over matters of administration and this time Bach (who was adamant in claiming the rights and privileges of his official position) appealed to the Elector of Saxony, who supported him. Apart from petty wrangles in the Church and School there were contretemps between Bach and the University. Yet despite such hindrances and annoyances and a general lack of appreciation Bach continued, unremittingly, his creative activity. Church cantatas and secular cantatas and organ music flowed in abundance: the *Christmas Oratorio* (in itself a set of cantatas) was produced in 1734: the second part of *Das Wohltemperirte Klavier* was completed in 1744. In 1747 Bach received one rare recognition of his genius, from Frederick the Great, and thereafter came the *Musicalisches Opfer* and *Die Kunst der Fuge*.

In the last week of his life Handel attended *Messiah* at the Foundling Hospital. On his deathbed Bach dictated a chorale prelude on the theme 'Wenn wir in höchsten Nöten sein'. Thus the last thoughts of these composers were on the kind of music which they respectively took from their environment to transmute into the highest achievements of their ages and thus Professor Davison may justly sub-title his study of *Bach and Handel—The Consummation of the Baroque in Music*.

THE CONDITIONS OF CHORAL COMPOSITION

The great composer—for that matter any great creative artist—is essentially perceptive. So we may apply Tennyson to Bach and Handel:

'For I dipt into the future, far as human eye could see,
    Saw the vision of the world, and all the wonder that would be.'

But vision alone is not enough. Someone once asked Bach the secret of his greatness. He, sublime in modesty as in power, simply answered 'I worked hard'. To appreciate to the full the nature of his music, and also that of Handel, it is important to know something of the implications of hard work. In a sense the easiest part of musical composition is composition: witness the vast output of such composers as Purcell, Vivaldi, Handel, Bach, Mozart, Haydn. The hardest part (as any budding composer will ruefully testify) is achieving performance. This problem has two branches. There is the potential audience on the one hand—over which, for reasons already stated, Handel suffered more headaches than Bach: there are the available performers on the other—and here Bach, who dealt so frequently with amateurs, was more often at a disadvantage. It may safely be stated that, in general, performances were far from ideal.

One further factor should be borne in mind. Eighteenth-century music still retained a high degree of improvisation. Thus the important function of the harpsichord in binding together the ensemble was realized more or less extempore from a figured bass; vocal ornaments were added over and above the actual notation (Bach wrote out far more of his ornaments than Handel, whose texts leave many gaps originally filled by extemporized decorations); orchestration approximated as nearly to the composer's intentions as was practicable; in Handelian oratorio, and especially in the notable case of *Messiah*, what was sung by one voice in one place might be sung elsewhere by another —'But who may abide' was written for a bass voice, but on occasion sung by tenor (Mr. Lowe), contralto (Guadagni), and even soprano (Miss Young, Miss Brent, etc.). The fact was that works were composed, on the whole, for one performance and the presentation of a work, under the composer's direction, was an extension of the art of creation. Such is the great difference between music of that period and music of the present day.

Bach, in his choral music, was primarily concerned in satisfying the requirements of the Lutheran Church. We may then observe the particular influence of the Lutheran conception of worship on the development of music.

LUTHERAN AND CALVINIST INFLUENCES

In contrast with Calvinism Lutheranism found an honoured place for music, which is symbolized by the growth of the chorale. Among Lutherans, however, there was a vigorous minority of 'Pietists' who were intolerant of the early eighteenth-century tendency towards more elaboration in the musical part of the services. This desire to clip the wings of religious song is a familiar phenomenon at all times. In regard to Bach Pietist supremacy at Mühlhausen discouraged the composition of church cantatas for ritual use[1] and he felt obliged, after a short stay, to petition for his dismissal. He added the opinion to his petition that 'the people might in time have come to approve'.

Bach was a staunch Lutheran (Handel for his part was grandson of a Lutheran minister) and the greater part of his life was devoted to the service of the Church. But it should be remembered that at Cöthen he was in a Calvinist establishment, which accounts for concentration on music other than cantata. The prolific years of cantata production at Weimar were 1714–16. At the beginning of 1714 Bach was appointed Koncertmeister (a different title but with the same functions as a Kapellmeister) and the provision of a monthly cantata was a condition of his appointment. In fact a little less than thirty cantatas (Nos. 12, 18, 21, 31, 59, 61, 70, possibly 72, 88, 132, 142, 147, 152, 155, 158, 160, 161, 162, 163, possibly 164 and 168, 182, 185, and possibly 186) can with reasonable certainty be ascribed to Weimar. In regard to Nos. 21 and 70 it is interesting to note that they quote extracts from Handel's *Almira*[2] (1705), which Bach may well have seen when in Halle in 1713. That the devout Bach could in these instances introduce operatic music into his sacred works (elsewhere he raises considerable loans from his own secular music) emphasizes a point to be remembered even more in appreciation of Handel—music *per se* was not then (nor should it be now) divided into 'sacred' and 'secular' opposing styles; it was judged on its own merits and, when allied with words, its specific appropriateness to the immediate issue.

At Weimar Bach's musical establishment contained fifteen instrumentalists (he himself played the violin in addition to directing the

[1] Cantatas 71, 131, 196 certainly, and 106, 150 and 189 possibly, belong to the Mühlhausen period: Nos. 71 and 131 were for civic occasions, No. 106 for a funeral, No. 196 for a wedding; No. 150 probably was composed for a funeral and No. 189, being a solo cantata, properly more fitted private devotions than public ritual.

[2] See *Handel and his Orbit*, P. Robinson, pp. 189–96.

ensemble) and about the same number of singers. As well as musical duties these servants of the Duke undertook other tasks. In his cantatas Bach had the literary assistance of Salomon Franck (1659–1725), who was likewise an officer of the same court. Franck published texts of church cantatas just after Bach's appointment to Weimar and made him acquainted with the outstanding work of Erdmann Neumeister. Neumeister was a pastor in Hamburg and an 'orthodox' Lutheran (i.e. an opponent of 'Pietism'). Before Neumeister considered the literary form of the cantata, emphasis in church music had been on the biblical words (the term 'cantata' is inapplicable, except by courtesy, to much pre-Bach German church music—*concertato, symphonia sacra* or *motet* being more proper).[1] Neumeister saw the interpretative possibilities which might arise if the varied forms of recitative and aria could be incorporated. Neumeister's salient observation (which offended all Pietists but which made more likely the great works of Bach) was: 'In short, a cantata looks like a piece from an opera, composed of *stilo recitativo* and arias'. Thus, in a sense, Handel's oratorios and Bach's church cantatas were blood-relations, being the offspring of the ubiquitous Italian opera. The stylistic difference between the two may be set down thus: Bach communicated, through music, the symbolism of the Word and the significance of the Doctrine; Handel those elements in the personality and situation which sought musical definition. Bach was the true heir of the Middle Ages, Handel of the newer Humanism.

Bach's librettos, in which he took considerable personal interest, were directly related to the poetic outlook of his Church.[2] At Leipzig Bach especially used the hymn texts of the various available hymnals. Handel's librettos, whether by James Miller or Thomas Morell— ministers of the established Church, Samuel Humphreys—an indifferent playwright, Charles Jennens—a wealthy amateur, or any other collaborator were mere vehicles of narrative. Often they were highly efficient—nobler language appears when, as in *Samson*, the '*Occasional*' *Oratorio* and *Messiah*, either John Milton or the Authorized Version of the Bible is drawn on—but depth of feeling was entirely left to the composer. As it happened this worked very well and we may recollect that Handel, like Bach, took a great interest in the literary structure of his works.

---

[1] Bach designated only Cantatas 30, 54, 56, 173, 195, 197 as such: otherwise he used the term *Dialogus, Motetto, Stück, Stücklein.*

[2] Besides Erdmann Neumeister and Salomon Franck Bach had as librettists C. F. Henrici (1700–1764)—known as 'Picander'—Georg Lehms of Darmstadt and various clergymen.

An oratorio was entire in itself; it owed no duties to any ritual save that of the theatre. The cantata was essentially one part—however impressive that part might be—of a greater whole. It is imperative to bear in mind this background, at the same time commending gratefully the patient souls of those in Weimar and, more especially, Leipzig, who sat through the interminable period of the 'Hauptgottesdienst'— the principal service of Sundays and Holy Days. The English would have agitated against such impositions of devotion as Lutheranism entailed. Consequently their eighteenth-century ritual music went no further than the ten-minute average of the weekly 'anthem'.

We must envisage the cantata, then, within this context. The service of 'Hauptgottesdienst' commenced with the 'Kyrie' and 'Gloria', for this part of the ancient Mass (distinguished Lutheranly as the *Missa brevis*) was retained by Luther. After the 'Kyrie' and 'Gloria' came the reading of the epistle. Then a congregational hymn. Next the gospel for the day, the text of which frequently promoted the text of the cantata for the day. After this the 'Credo' was recited—in Latin. The cantata followed at this point and to underline its function as an extension of the Gospel the latter was generally read for a second time —now in German—before the commencement of the music. The centre part of the service was not ended by the cantata, for this was succeeded by the sermon. Towards midday Holy Communion was celebrated and the service therewith ended.

BACH: PERFORMERS

At Leipzig fifty-nine occasions were appointed throughout the ecclesiastical year for the performance of cantatas. The Cantor was responsible for the selection of the appropriate music and he was at liberty either to choose from works already in the possession of the church or to compose afresh.

Most German towns of any size in the eighteenth century regarded the maintenance of a musical establishment as a point of honour. Music was the centre of municipal and ecclesiastical activity: and it was also the hub of entertainment and recreation. In short, in such a city as Leipzig, music unified the whole of life and the Kapellmeister or Cantor who was responsible for such a variety of music was, artistically at least, in an enviable position. He could, as it were, see life in the round.

So Bach could range from *Phoebus and Pan* (a comic opera in all but name) to the 'Crucifixus' of the *B Minor Mass*, from the little pieces written for his children to the great *Passacaglia und Fugue* for organ, from the dance movements of the suites to the *Kunst der Fuge* without sacrificing either integrity or humour. It is this richness of observation, this breadth of vision, which must be placed beneath any attempt to re-create or understand Bach.

The material conditions in Leipzig were as follows. Bach, as Cantor of St. Thomas's, was a master (he taught Latin and Catechism as well as singing) in the school which provided choristers for the principal churches. At Leipzig these choristers were somewhat deficient in that angelic nature often ascribed to choristers by the idealistic. As Cantor Bach was (technically) supervisor of music—though not organist in any one—in all the town's churches and also (technically) Director of the University music. As has been stated his actual standing was on occasion the subject of considerable disagreement. Bach's orchestra was partly professional, partly amateur. The amateur element mostly came from among the *studiosi* of the University. It must not be supposed that this ensemble was remarkable in talent. The main choir, from which Bach drew his soloists, numbered about seventeen, the orchestra one or two less. Between them, no doubt, they frequently misrepresented Bach's intentions.

That eternally great music was created under such conditions is a token of the faith which inspired Bach. When men like Byrd and Lassus and Palestrina and Bach wrote, as they did, *ad majorem Dei gloriam* they meant precisely what they said. It is this magnificent immersion of self within a belief that was universal which links Bach with his illustrious predecessors.

In the fifteenth and sixteenth centuries composer and audience were held together by a common interest in familiar and evocative melodies —those of the plainsong heritage. Bach and his Leipzigers were similarly bound together by possession of the chorale. Even we, with experience of, say, the 'Passion' chorale can sense something of this community of interest and concentration of attention. When we consider Handel the case is different.

Handel was neither greater nor less great than Bach. Handel could not have written the *Mass in B Minor* but Bach could not have written *Saul*. Bach made religious philosophy infinitely more effective than it would have been without him (indeed we may, in the broadest sense, claim Bach as one of the greatest of all religious thinkers), but Handel made it possible for the irreligious, the negligent, the sceptical to be directed towards large issues through the vitality and originality of his treatment of a form of entertainment. Many, no doubt, ignored the large issues and remained content with the entertainment: but there were those who recognized the philosophical aspect. So, in his way too, Handel emphasized the essential one-ness of life and experience.

THE CONDITIONS OF ORATORIO

There are three sides of Handel's character which call for comment: his man-of-the-worldness; his contrasting love of quiet companionship; his charity. As a man of the world he was naturally at home in the theatre; so much so that his outward behaviour often appears as theatrical. His friend and erstwhile colleague in the opera house in Hamburg—Johann Mattheson— makes an observation in *Der Musikalische Patriot* which refers to the aesthetic outlook of the operatic composer of the eighteenth century in general, and, we may judge, of Handel in particular: 'All that produces an effect upon men is theatrical . . . the whole world is a gigantic theatre.' Beyond this, however, Handel possessed a serene lyrical imagination which he refreshed by communication with the English countryside (his excursions to Bath, to Salisbury, to Kent, to Staffordshire and—if a strong tradition is to be believed—to Wales are rarely given sufficient biographical prominence) and with English literature. His charity was shown to individuals and to institutions alike and, in the end, the fact that *Messiah* greatly increased the funds of the Foundling Hospital and continued to benefit almost every native corporation that relied on 'voluntary subscriptions' was, in one sense, a proper conclusion.

It has been shown that the church cantata of Germany was inevitable, as the consummation of generations of thought and effort. The church cantata would have existed without Bach even if in less glory. The English oratorio, however, would not have arrived without Handel and like everything that is English its arrival was fortuitous, unpremeditated, unwanted.

The effective centres of English music (which, after the lamented death of Purcell, was mainly supplied by foreign composers) during the periods of Queen Anne and the Georges were the theatres—the King's (or Queen's) Theatre, designed by John Vanbrugh, in the Haymarket and Covent Garden being the most celebrated. In 1732, a not very successful operatic year for Handel, his oratorio *Esther* was revived at the Haymarket Theatre. Prior to this it had been revived privately, as a birthday tribute to the composer, by Bernard Gates at his house in Westminster. Gates, who had taken part in the original performance of 1720 and was now Master of the Choristers of the Chapel Royal, employed his own choristers for the chorus parts. When the work was transferred to the theatre permission for the participation of the choristers was given by the Bishop of London, but there was to be no dressing-up and no action. The Bishop held conventional views on the morality of opera and opera singers and would countenance no obvious and visual admixture of the sacred and the profane.

By 1735 oratorio in Lent was firmly established, but by now at Covent Garden Theatre. The solo singers (grateful for employment during a normally unprofitable period) were from the opera; thus the recitatives and arias were designed to preserve the dramatic character which the singers understood and also to enable them to display their virtuosity. The orchestra was the theatre orchestra of perhaps twenty players, but the foundation tone of strings, oboes, bassoons, flutes, trumpets, drums, harpsichord was augmented as opportunity and imagination suggested. In the matter of orchestra Handel had the advantage of Bach in all ways. During the 1735 season Handel enlivened the oratorio performances by playing organ concertos between the Acts, by retaining which term in his scores Handel clearly showed the connection of oratorio with opera.

Dr. Burney notes of the 1735 season that Handel, with Niccola Porpora his rival in opera, 'as his capital singers were inferior in number and renown . . . very wisely discontinued the performance of opera for a considerable time, and rested his fame and fortune on his choral strength in the composition of oratorios'. It may be said here that Handel, having started a fashion in oratorio, had his imitators. Porpora, William Defesch—leader of the band at Marylebone Gardens—and Maurice Greene were all in the field in 1734-5.

Mrs. Pendarves (later Mrs. Delany), who was a close friend of Handel, gave an opinion of Porpora's *David*:

'It is a fine solemn piece of music, but I confess I think the subject too solemn for a theatre. To have words of piety made use of *only* to introduce good music, is *reversing* what it ought to be, and most of the people that hear the oratorio make no reflection on the meaning of the words, though God is addressed in the most solemn manner; some of the choruses and recitatives are extremely fine and touching, but they say it is not equal to Mr. Handel's oratorio of *Esther* or *Deborah*.'

'They say.' That is a crucial phrase. Opera was taken for granted. Opera was denounced. Singers were applauded, or vilified; but the nature of the opera, the significance of plot, the relevance of music was hardly ever discussed—except by the Burlington House intelligentsia. But oratorios in English were different. They touched more personal interest. Gradually the middle classes supplanted the aristocracy as Handel's principal supporters. So he is discussed in the pages of Fielding's novel *Amelia* and Richardson's *Sir Charles Grandison*, as also in the philosophic works of James Harris and the sermons of John Newton. That choral music formed a large part of his oratorios was a certain safeguard of propriety. Choral music suggested (particularly through the choristers employed by Handel) the church. From Handel's point of view the large-scale employment of the chorus introduced exciting possibilities of variety in tone colour. Far more promising than the opera where singers resented any music that diminished their glory and where choruses were regarded as unnecessary by audiences (as well as an expense to the production). It is sometimes stated that Handel's choruses came because of an English taste for choral music. That is rather less than a half-truth, for the statement has in implication the 'choral society'. And choral societies did not exist (as such) in the eighteenth century—nor did women take part in the oratorio chorus until after Handel's death. The English took to Handel's choralism because it decreed respectability. (English composers after Handel took respectability to be all that mattered and in pursuit of this decorous goal forgot to write music. Some Germans were similarly guilty. And the tradition persists to the present day in some American choral music.)

Paradoxically, the most choral of all the oratorios—*Israel in Egypt*— was a failure. In the *Daily Post* of April 13th, 1739, a correspondent referred to a performance two days earlier:

'I was not only pleased but also affected by it; for I never met with any musical performance in which the words and sentiments were so thoroughly studied, and so clearly understood; and as the words are taken from the Bible, they are perhaps some of the most sublime parts of it, I was indeed concerned that so excellent a work of so great a genius was neglected, for though it was a polite and attentive audience, it was not large enough, I doubt, to encourage him in any future attempt.'

The public took exception to the small amount of solo singing in this oratorio.

Messiah—performed first by the combined choirs[1] of St. Patrick's and Christchurch cathedrals, Dublin, in Neal's Music Hall in that city on April 13th, 1742—was ill-received when it came to London because it dealt with too sacred a subject. 'To be sure,' said one lady in 1745, 'the playhouse is an unfit place for such a solemn performance.'[2] On another occasion the same lady (Catherine Talbot, an adopted daughter of the Archbishop of Canterbury) expressed herself differently on the subject of oratorio. 'I really cannot help thinking this kind of entertainment must necessarily have some effect in correcting the levity of the age; and let an audience be ever so thoughtless, they can scarcely come away, I should think, without being the better for an evening so spent.'

Bach and his congregations together made possible his music. In a different but no less real way Handel and his audiences were artistic collaborators. There is a certain rough justice in the supposition that each country gets the music it deserves. The paradox here, of course, is that, taking the short view, neither Leipzig deserved Bach (whom it didn't want) nor London Handel.

Tradition, present purpose and opportunity, the composer's individual outlook: these affect the manner in which the composer disposes his musical material. These factors are of equal significance in the visual arts. See, for example, the contrasts of style, of symbolism, of feeling in such varied masterpieces as the mosaic *Good Shepherd* at Ravenna, *The Adoration of the Lamb* by the Van Eycks in Ghent, the Sistine Chapel masterpieces of Michelangelo. Bach and Handel had these principal patterns—cantata, anthem, mass, oratorio, passion. While no two works in any other genre follow precisely the same detail

---

[1] Not more than forty singers in all (including principals).
[2] I heard eminent critics who should have known better, say exactly the same of Vaughan Williams' *Pilgrim's Progress*, when it was put on at Covent Garden in 1951.

some generalizations will assist the listener to hear through the composer's mind and the performer to enter into the overall scheme.

CANTATA

Essentially the cantata is an offshoot of the seventeenth-century *nuove musiche* principles (see p. 55ff.). As developed by Carissimi and Alessandro Scarlatti in particular, it comprised contrasting passages of recitative and aria. Carissimi first applied this branch of chamber music to church use—hence the term *cantata da chiesa*. The solo numbers in Bach's cantatas, as also in his mass and passion music and in Handel's oratorios, show clearly their chamber-music origin. In a sense this gives a notably intimate quality even to the greatest works. Handel wrote many cantatas during his Italian period and, apart from text, there is no difference in the form and musical content of *camera* and *chiesa* specimens. The influence of Scarlatti is very strong, both in the graceful lines of melody and the easy brilliance of orchestration. It may be mentioned that both Scarlatti and Handel were affected by the atmosphere of Rome at the turn of the century; Innocent XII, being then Pope, discouraged opera but was favourable both to cantata and oratorio. (Roman oratorio of that period, exemplified in Handel's *La Resurrezione* and the little *St. John Passion* was but cantata writ large and with not very much chorus.)

ALESSANDRO SCARLATTI AND BACH'S CANTATAS

Scarlatti, faithful to Roman tradition, maintained the *a cappella* style in his masses, his motets (see his invigorating *Exultate Deo*), and his *Requiem* (1721). In following the traditional church style of the sixteenth century the composer often appears indifferent to the conventional words of the ritual. In the *Requiem* the music comes to life where the words evoke an immediate poetic response, principally in the opening introit and in the 'Sanctus' and 'Osanna'. Scarlatti enhanced religious experience when he was able to imbue sacred texts with lyrical commentary. His expansion of the aria into the familiar pattern enabled

him thus to dwell on such aspects of the Christian story. Oratorios and
cantatas were frequent at Christmas and the happiest, and most easily
available, work of Scarlatti—the 'Christmas' cantata—is a fine example
of his mature style and is directly related both to Bach and Handel. The
traditional Roman piper's tune which is imitated in the 'Pastoral
Symphony' of Handel's *Messiah* and, more gravely, in that of Bach's
Christmas Oratorio, is first met with in Scarlatti's *Senti che lieti intorno*.
Elsewhere the same musical device gives the title to Corelli's 'Christmas
Concerto'.

The Italian cantata flourished for a while after Scarlatti in the hands
of Domenico Scarlatti and Pergolesi; but main interest must centre in
Bach.

Bach composed cantatas for five complete cycles of the Church
year, nearly 300 in all; and about two-thirds of the whole have survived.
The range of these works is very great.

Cantata 82—*Ich habe genug*—is at one extreme. It is a solo cantata,
and therefore directly derived from the Italian prototypes. It was
composed for the Feast of the Purification about the year 1731. After
an orchestral introduction there are an aria; a recitative, briefly punctuated by two arioso (a style midway between recitative and aria) bars;
an aria; a recitative which dissolves practically into arioso at the words
'World! good night'; and a final and joyful aria (in *da capo* form) on
the theme of 'gladness'. The central aria carries all the sympathy of Bach
with the weary. The great Michaelmas Cantata (or, possibly, fragment
of a cantata) of *c.* 1740—*Nun ist das Heil* (No. 50)—a contrast in every
way to cantata 82—has the power of the Revelation of St. John
(Chapter XII, verse 10). The great apocalyptic vision of war in heaven
and the triumph of God demands double chorus, three oboes, three
trumpets, drums, strings, continuo, and is worked out in a mighty fugal
movement. In this the energy is limitless. But while this is proper
to the literary factor it is also released from mere matter-of-factness by
the virtue of the musical structure. Were one not to know a single
word of the text the 'meaning' of the music would be apparent so that
there would be complete agreement with Bach's biographer Philipp
Spitta: 'This gigantic work with its crushing weight and its savage cry
of triumph is an imperishable memorial of German art.' Perhaps this
countersubject sufficiently points the way to Bach's visionary power
(Ex. 1). Note the strong simplicity of the main theme; its sense of
movement; its purposeful direction: and in the counter-theme the

Ex. 1

urgency of the percussive (♫♩), and the equal urgency of the melodic range.

There is, clearly, a limit within a general work to what may be said of a particular detail. But the triumphant choruses of Bach must be underlined for the benefit of choral singers—for from inner experience of performance, there is no *catharsis* so complete as that effected by such works as that last mentioned; or the great chorus of cantata 31—*Der Himmel lacht, die Erde jubiliret*, in which heavenly laughter erupts into a universal detonation of joy and faith; or the vast *da capo* opening of cantata 149—*Man singet mit Freuden vom Sieg* (also for the Feast Day of St. Michael). This movement is cast in the cheerful triple time which Bach (but rarely Handel) adopted for choral exultation. Its orchestration is rich and demonstrative, with chorus of trumpets, oboes, timpani and strings. This full orchestra was obligatory for St. Michael's Day, the Civic Service, the Reformation Commemoration and the great Festivals. We may note, as we proceed, how everything in Bach is symbolic, yet, at the same time, also essential to the abstract musical texture. Sometimes one has a suspicion that the old catch phrase of music being the handmaid of religion has been invented in the factory of Bach's imagination. From which we may be inclined to deduce that music and religion are not two but one. Two facets of one whole and the whole only revealed to those of the calibre of Bach.

The same observation may arise from considering Bach's employment of the chorale. There were obvious reasons why he (and especially at Leipzig) centred his cantatas on chorales, but his variety of treatment often shows the composer reaching towards truth solely through the ineluctable shaping of musical logic. Bach the poet: Bach the mathematician. Variously has he been summed up at these opponent poles of definition. The truth is that poet and mathematician and, derivately, metaphysician are one.

The most complete exposition of this commentary is the great motet, *Jesu, meine Freude*, a set of chorale variations. The intense feeling of this highly romantic work can be experienced only by immediate contact. But the apparatus of romanticism is apparent (a) in the evocative use of harmony—see how, in anticipation of Beethoven, No. 5 starts out of key with a striking chord of the seventh (b) in rhythmic rhetoric—as in the commentary chorus No. 2 (c) in 'descriptive' melody shapes—in No. 2 the word 'walk' stimulates a picturesque if difficult episode; in No. 5 we 'rise' and 'soar' . . . (d) in demonstrative variety of timbre—see the two trio movements and the placing of voices within all the choruses. In the end, however, these references become merely incidental (there has been a violent reaction from the early estimates of Bach, and 'symbolism', thanks to Schweitzer and others, has returned to favour). Donald Tovey defines the notable characteristic of this motet.

'A glance at the list of movements in *Jesu, priceless treasure*, shows that they are arranged in a remarkable symmetry. Six verses of a chorale alternate with five passages from the eighth chapter of the Epistle to the Romans; the sixth chorale is set to the same music as the first; of the prose scriptural choruses the last resumes the music of the first, while the two scriptural numbers that are for three-part semi-chorus or solo voices (Bach gives no indication) are at equal distances the one from the beginning and the other from the end.'[1]

Jesu, meine Freude (written in 1723) is one of the six extant motets by Bach composed as funeral pieces, as the text of the magnificent eight-part *Komm, Jesu, Komm*, directly shows.

In contrast to these must be set the vast *Singet dem Herrn*, also in eight parts and for double choir. In this the relevant funeral chorale (*Nun lob, mein' 'Seel', den Herren*) forms the centrepiece of an immense

---

[1] *Jesu, meine Freude*, is normally considered *a cappella*. This and other Bach works treated in the same manner were most likely not sung unaccompanied. That would have been against the practice of the time. It should be remembered that music manuscript (especially orchestral parts) has a tendency to get lost easily. [Therefore, conductors should double the voice parts with strings (oboes and bassoons *ad libitum*) and add a discreet organ background. Singers will be grateful and the result will, in general, be more convincing.]

triptych. The chorale is stated by the second choir, while the first choir intersperses lyrical commentary between the phrases.

'Bach's motets display at its highest altitude of inspiration the genius for full-throated song he inherited from his Thuringian ancestry. Their massive virility gives them pre-eminence among their kind, and, alone of his vocal compositions, they were not shadowed by the eclipse that obscured him and his art in the century that followed his death.'

This is Tovey's remark. By its side may be placed one by Mozart, who heard *Singet dem Herrn* under Johann Friedrich Doles at the Thomaskirche in 1789. 'That,' said Mozart, 'is indeed something to take a lesson from!'

Before moving on to the 'greater' works (Bach would have been unconscionably great had no more than his cantatas survived) brief consideration should be given to the most chorale-infected of all the cantatas. *Wer nur den lieben Gott lässt walten* (No. 93, 1728) is designed as follows.

The opening chorus prefaces each phrase of the chorale with a fugato working out—one part following another in imitation—of the germ of the phrase in the voices. This, with the orchestra engaged in independent patterning, is an adaptation of one chorale-prelude method practised in organ music. The key is C minor. The second section (in G minor) is a curious admixture of chorale and recitative. Note the union (Ex. 3). A lesser aria follows in E flat major in which the chorale

Ex. 3   3rd line of Chorale   Recit.

We do but make our   cross - - of   cares   the har-der by our gloom-y mourn-ing

is turned into a pretty—if rather ineffectual—binary form, and which is based on a pattern of construction familiar in the keyboard suites. Next, back in C minor, a duet variant of the chorale for soprano and contralto. A lengthy recitative and chorale for tenor is chiefly remarkable for its harmonic fluctuations; each line of the chorale appearing in a different key. The soprano aria which succeeds is again cast in chorale-fantasia fashion, the melody line being at first stimulated by the original phrase pattern to paraphrase but gradually crystallizing into the actual notes of the last two lines of the chorale. Finally the chorale is stated in

H

plain form and at this point it is presumed that the congregation joined in. This cantata is interesting as showing the contagion which chorale enthusiasm could spread.

As I look around me I see the open scores of many more cantatas: of No. 60—*O Ewigkeit du Donnerwort*—with its opening dialogue (recalling a side of domestic musico-religious experience enjoyed during the Schütz period) between Fear and Hope, with the former announcing the chorale and being answered by a lyrical free melody— and all set against a fascinating accompaniment of horns, two *oboi d'amore* and strings; of Nos. 80 and 140—*Ein' feste Burg* and *Wachet auf*, in both of which the chorale projects notable development; of No. 56, *Ich will den Kreuzstab gerne tragen*, with an odd variant of the Neapolitan cantata form—aria, recitative, aria, recitative (chorale)— in which recitative comes in an unusual order, with *recitativo accompagnato* ('accompanied recitative'—one of Bach's most notable achievements), and with an almost Schönbergian dissolution of conventional tonal precepts;[1] of No. 18—*Gleich wie der Regen und Schnee* with its large descriptive *sinfonia* or overture (scored for two flutes, four violas, bassoon, 'cello, bass and continuo) and its histrionic choral outbursts of 'erhör uns, lieber Herr Gott'; of No. 81—*Jesus schläft, was soll ich hoffen*, wherein Christ stills the tempest. I see too the secular cantatas—the *Peasant Cantata* (1742) with its references to folk melody, its bucolic orchestration, its Saxon dialect; the *Coffee Cantata* (c. 1742), a domestic comedy; and *Phoebus and Pan* (1731), in which the critic Scheibe is satirized. The secular cantatas are perfectly complementary to the church cantatas and bear further evidence of the wholeness of Bach's outlook.

'CHRISTMAS ORATORIO'

The *Christmas Oratorio* (1734) is an obvious link with the secular cantatas; for of all the large-scale church works of Bach it is the most comfortably (if that is the right word) human. It is immediately notable that the beautiful lullaby (No. 19) of the Madonna is also used in *The Choice of Hercules* (1733). The *Christmas Oratorio* is not an oratorio

---

[1] 'Bach . . . enlarged [the Netherlanders' methods in combining melodies into counterpoint] to such an extent that they comprised all the twelve tones of the chromatic scale. Bach sometimes operated with the twelve tones in such a manner that one would be inclined to call him the first twelve-tone composer' (*Style and Idea*, A. Schoenberg, London 1951).

according to the accepted (Handelian) standards. It is a set of six cantatas[1]—for performance on Christmas Day and the two succeeding days, on the Feast of the Circumcision, the Sunday following and the Feast of the Epiphany. The only significant difference from the normal cantata form is in the narrative part of the Evangelist: it would seem that Bach may have introduced the term oratorio since the performance of oratorios was common in Dresden.

The keynote of the *Christmas Oratorio* is joyful exhilaration. And in expressing this mood the chorus has numerous opportunities, which may collectively be considered. Purcell, in the *Fairy Queen*, greets the god Phoebus with the solo timpani; so in the first chorus of the *Christmas Oratorio* Bach welcomes the infant Christ, in music which he adapted from *The Choice of Hercules*. He casts the music in triple time, a customary rhythm for such music. After a measure the two flutes enter in thirds and are followed after another measure by oboes in sixths; thus the regal and the pastoral are severally symbolized. The three trumpets enhance the former with a fanfare and the strings cut across this figure with a brilliant scalic flurry. After thirty-two bars, by which time the winds may feel that they have had enough thirty-second notes for the time being, the chorus enter in hard-hitting octaves—'Christians be joyful'. After four exultant outbursts, punctuated with rests and during which the orchestra recommences its preludial excitement, the voices settle down to work out their high cheer in contrasting passages of homophony and polyphony. Just before the *da capo* the music leaves the earth in an ecstasy of devotion. The next large chorus, not based on a chorale, is the 'Gloria', which is the climax of the second part of the oratorio.

In this movement (No. 21) it is imperative that choir and orchestra shall meet on equal terms, for the evocative rustic interplay between strings and a charming company of flutes oboi d'amore and oboi da caccia[2] is an entrancing foil to the somewhat intellectual hymn of the angels.

The scoring of this movement is full of humour and this should not be obscured. A graver mood, however, surrounds the cry for peace on earth. Towards the end of the chorus there is an excellent illustration of the way in which Bach demands to be heard with the

[1] The 'Easter' and 'Ascension' Oratorios (Bach—*Oratorium*) are, in fact, cantatas also. They show with the *Christmas Oratorio*, and were written about the same time, the life of Jesus.
[2] The compass of the oboe d'amore was a third below that of the oboe; the oboe da caccia—like the English horn by which it was superseded—a fifth lower.

understanding. His glorias rise, fourth piling on fourth (Ex. 4), the

disposition in vocal score being (Ex. 5)

The brief chorus which opens Part III brings back the festal atmosphere of the opening of Part I, rhythm and scoring being more or less the same and the voices are given individual tunes. Almost immediately the chorus turns from its independent role and participates directly within the action. 'Let us even now go to Bethlehem.' The way in which the voices enter, the one imitating the other, and the scoring of flutes and violins intends a realistic picture: but once again if the chorus is too strong the clarity of the picture is obscured and the movement becomes dull.

Part IV begins with a chorus which is almost the most graceful to sing among all the choruses of Bach and, for that reason, often taken from its context. 'Come and thank Him', again in triple time, is a warm, middle-register piece and the warmth of the music is increased by the use, for the first time in the oratorio, of horns.

Glory and thanksgiving dominate the introductory chorus to Part V. The key is A major and thirds and sixths are effectively used in the brilliant Italian manner; a fine fugal theme swings across the beat and stimulates further freedom in syncopation; the basses have wonderful passages which seem transferred from the pedals of the organ. This is a *da capo* chorus (a chorus, that is, in which the opening section is repeated after a contrasting passage as was also frequently the case in eighteenth-century aria), and the middle section is in the relative minor.

There is a brief chorus recalling the manner of Schütz and representing the Magi. It is interrupted by a theological aside from the contralto solo.

The last part of the work is full of power and the sense of victory. The full panoply of trumpets and drums accompany the first and last choruses, No. 54 (*Lord, when our haughty foes assail us*) is a fugal *tour de force*. As in all great fugues, the character is epitomized in the subject (Ex. 6a). The final chorus of the whole oratorio is a superb reconsidera-

Ex. 6a

Lord, when our haught-y foes___ as - sail

tion of the possibilities inherent in what elsewhere is called the 'Passion' chorale, 'O Haupt voll blut und wunden' or 'O Sacred Head'. The phrases of the chorale are delivered (and here one may bring in a thousand voices, or twenty thousand voices, for this is congregational, communal, universal) one by one with enormous power and dignity. They are each introduced by a superb and broad gesture by the trumpet.

And now we may return to see the treatment of the other chorales which run through the oratorio. Although the *Christmas Oratorio* is a collection of six independent works a feeling of unity is imposed first by the dominating, festive key centre of D; but secondly by the fact that the last, glorious realization of the 'Passion' chorale is the apotheosis of the first Advent presentation which succeeds—and in the same solemn key of A minor—the air 'Prepare thyself Zion' in Part I.

Sometimes in the *Christmas Oratorio* Bach leaves the chorales in great austere simplicity, the only comment on their significance arising from the semantics of his intense harmonic and contrapuntal thought. Otherwise, however, he admits lyrical commentary, which in this work serves to illuminate the tenderness with which Bach's imagination haloed the subject. No. 7 ('For us the earth He cometh poor' with Luther's melody) is set in dialogue form, the phrases being interrupted by passages of bass recitative, and the whole enwrapped in (Ex. 6b), which fragment is pastorally scored. The last chorale of Part I

Ex. 6b Oboe

Oboe d'amore

—to a melody also by Luther—is ennobled as a final (to the individual cantata) symbol of faith and joy. The setting is antiphonal, the chorus of voices being answered by the chorus of brass. The final chorus of Part II is a great hymn of praise. In this case the melody of No. 17 is again used (which assists in unifying the cantata) but the setting is a fourth higher. The method is antiphonal but on this occasion the contrasting chorus is of the woodwind ensemble, recalling the material employed in the Pastoral Symphony which announces Part II.

In Part III all the chorales are stated directly. In fact this portion of the work does not reach the highest level of inspiration: it will be noticed that the narrative stands still while numerous Pietist sentiments are uttered. The chorale 'Jesus, who didst even guide me' (this chorale, together with 'All darkness flies before Thy face', was probably Bach's own composition) is set against an independent, dance-like pattern developed by horns and strings. Part IV bears the impress of localized theological teaching—the only Biblical words are a single verse from St. Luke concerning the circumcision and naming of Jesus. The effect of sentimental sermonizing induces Bach to include the relatively erotic duet music of 'Immanuel, beloved Name' and ' 'Tis well! Thy Name, O Lord' and the old-fashioned echo device of 'Ah! My Saviour.'

Chorally the *Christmas Oratorio* is rewarding. In the recitatives it may be felt that Bach is sometimes (see, for instance, Nos. 34 and 58) straining for unnecessary effect and that in some of the other music there is not much more than a well-oiled mechanism at work. In fact the solo music of the highest quality is contained within the first two parts and all this music has secular associations.

[It is clear that the *Christmas Oratorio* should not be performed in its entirety on one occasion. One may elect, therefore, to follow the original plan (which is not very practicable) and produce the separate cantatas on separate days; one may use two days—the first for Parts I–III, the second for Parts IV–VI; one may make a selection of the music to contain within two hours. In cutting bear in mind the portions in Parts III and IV which had a more particular significance in 1734 than now. The numbers which may most easily be considered for excision are 15, 29, possibly 31 (beautiful but not entirely musically relevant), 38, 39, 40, 47, 51. And, of course, the number of the chorales may be reduced.]

'MESSIAH'

Since we have considered the Bachian oratorio and since Handel's *Messiah* is inseparable from the Christmas season we have an opportunity of seeing the two forms of musical expression in some close association. 'Nor can we hear,' wrote Charles Lamb, 'without particular emotion at this season [Christmas], that divine composition of Handel's with the recitative full of singleness of purpose and a truly pastoral simplicity. "There were shepherds abiding in the fields." ' It is this 'singleness of purpose' that we should consider.

Handel's conception of Christ, so far as we may judge, from what we may learn of his philosophy and from his musical and dramatic emphasis, was essentially humanistic: he was conscious of an heroic, noble, exemplar of all the recognizable human virtues. Now Handel, in opera and oratorio, was always directly concerned with the exposition of human problems and, with his supreme and economical dramatic style, he was able to make his audiences see with their ears.

We do not know whether Bach had particular opinions on the visual arts: of Handel we do know that he was a connoisseur and a collector. His music bears at all points the influence of this interest. So, in *Messiah*, we may actually feel that we see the angels and the shepherds, the suffering Christ, the risen Christ, and—with Handel[1]—the heavens opened and the great God upon his throne.

It is true that Bach is pictorial. It was, after all, the manner of the period to indulge in musical illustration. But Bach is not content with the simple gesture that stimulates visual perceptiveness. He adds a gloss on the literary or theological interpretation of the visual idea. So we have the paradox that although Handel gives us less to think about than Bach he invites us to think more. Within Handel there is much room for individual contemplation and imaginative exercise. This brings us back to the opinion that Bach was akin to the medievals, while Handel was a child of the Renaissance.

Immediately one may instance the libretto of *Messiah* as an achievement of the humanist viewpoint, for (although we do not forget that medieval religious drama was productive of great artistic and humanist expression) words from the Bible, arranged and occasionally edited for the better service of music by Jennens and Handel jointly, are set out as for a three-act opera. For the better understanding both of words and music it is imperative that in performance this division into three should be maintained. (Those who split the work after 'Lift up your heads' do so to accommodate the music to the conventions of the concert hall—

---

[1] 'I did think I did see all Heaven before me, and the great God himself'; Handel's comment as related by Dr. Allott to Miss Hawkins (*Anecdotes of G. F. Handel and J. C. Smith*, etc., W. Coxe, London 1799).

with coffee in the interval—or to enable patrons to catch convenient transport. Let all such be anathema!)

Part I deals with the expectation of and the coming of Christ. Part II tells of the suffering and sacrifice of Christ; yet the climactic 'Hallelujah' shows the victory of the sacrifice. Part III is a summary of Christian faith and hope. Each part is in itself a unity, yet a part of a greater unity.

I saw recently a televised play for children, based on the story of the Good Samaritan. I saw, and was fascinated by, the bringing-to-life of the characters of that story and by the simplicity of the production. It is neither here nor there that philosophy and theology were left implicit. What mattered was that simplicity of character-drawing and narrative presentation made the explicit lead to the implicit, the first and obvious 'reality' to the deeper and more positive reality. So I feel with *Messiah* and for that matter with the rest of Handel's oratorios.

Let us notice the main differences of musical treatment between Handel and Bach. Handel's style is more suave: his vocal and his instrumental lines are perfectly fitted to their musical purpose. His pictorialism leads to the scene or the character rather than to the word (even when his coloratura is imitative) or the gesture. His counterpoint is pellucid, even delicate (though choristers often obscure this by a perpetual *fortissimo*), and much more frequently than in Bach is in four parts. It is less ambitious in chord and modulation than that of Bach. Yet, in this connection, we may look at the harmonies of 'Glory to God', 'Surely He hath borne our griefs', 'Since by man came death': the placing and the rhythmic manipulation of chords is prodigiously telling. We may further consider the extraordinarily apt chromatics which at the beginning of 'The people that walked in darkness' leave us in bewilderment: 'the chromatic and indeterminate modulation,' says Burney, 'seems to delineate the uncertain footsteps of persons exploring their way in obscurity.' Professor A. T. Davison is perceptive in respect of Handel's harmonic originality:

'Hugo Leichtentritt has written of the care with which Handel, having in mind the particular character of a key, chose for example the appropriate tonality for each of his opera arias. How far Handel observed the effective nature of the different keys in setting his choruses I cannot say, but Handel being Handel, I suspect that his choice was dictated mainly by choral considerations. In any case, the diversity of keys is notably larger in *Messiah* than it is in either the *B Minor Mass* or the *Magnificat*. . . In *Messiah* D is the tonality for six of the twenty-one choruses; but in Bach's *B Minor Mass* the proportion is greater, being nine out of fifteen; and in the *Magnificat* of the five choruses four are in D.'[1]

Observe the key structure of *Messiah*. The overture, a French-type overture, of which the general pattern was—slow introduction, quick fugal movement, and minuet, but shorn of the final dance movement (which appears in other overtures—as for example in that of *Samson*) is in E minor. The arioso-recitative 'Comfort ye' and the air 'Every valley' are taken into the warmer atmosphere of E major. The chorus enter with a positive affirmation—'And the glory of the Lord shall be revealed': the key is A major, for which, therefore, everything that had gone before was a dominant preparation. A major leads eventually to D: but D minor serves—in 'Thus saith the Lord' and 'But who may abide' to evoke a judicial deity. Rhythm and details of sonority and decoration add to the key symbolism (the symbolism is aroused by the contrast of one key with another rather than by the independent associations surrounding a particular key centre) and we are aware of the sternness and righteous anger of the God-idea conveyed in the words of Haggai and Malachi. The chorus of purification is in G minor—still the dominant-tonic sequence is continued—and the theme of purification is lightly announced with the clarity of the highest voices.

But the prophetic words of Isaiah, in the warmth of the contralto and the apparent serenity of D major (this being the first appearance of this key), point to the coming birth of Jesus. The recitative 'Behold! a virgin shall conceive' is the quintessence of simplicity. Yet placed where it is it is not only adequate but inspired. The succeeding air and chorus dance their way towards the glory of the Lord. The music moves backwards with the text to see the benighted men of earth (B minor) but when 'the Lord shall arise' in D major anticipating 'For unto us a Child is born', there the key is G major and the light sinuous counterpoint is developed from an early secular cantata—*Nò, di voi non vo' fidarmi*.

The *Pastoral Symphony* or *Pifa*, recalling the popular Christmas music of Rome, is in C: it is enchantingly scored with the violins

[1] *Bach and Handel: The Consummation of the Baroque in Music*, pp. 16–17.

divided into three. These are no Italian bagpipers but an illusion of those which might be heard in heaven. Handel here shows how to practise restraint. The Christmas music glitters with soprano voice, starry sixteenth notes, and quick switches from C ('There were shepherds') to F ('And lo! the angel of the Lord') to D major and F sharp minor ('And the angel said unto them'), to D major ('And suddenly there was with the angel' running directly into 'Glory to God'). The last section of Part I has a new key centre—of B flat major: 'Rejoice greatly', of which there was an earlier version in twelve time and in which[1] Handel recalls Zachau, thus appears fresh and virginal. The contralto slips back to G major and A minor for the prophecies of healing. Soprano and contralto then picture the Good Shepherd in Handel's favourite *pastorale* figure and we note that the key of F major (which changes to B flat major) matches with 'All we like sheep'. 'His yoke is easy' is a chorus again of extreme delicacy and must be conceived as belonging to the pastoral atmosphere of this whole section of the oratorio. Once again Handel was in debt to himself, for the material is developed from a duet for two sopranos—*Quel fior che all' alba ride*—which was drawn on for 'And He shall purify'.

This first part of *Messiah* is one of the supreme examples of ethereal lightness in musical literature. Thus performance must be delicate, eager, but coloured and responsive to the shape of the melodic and rhythmic contours. There is a Madonna and Child by Botticelli in the Louvre which appears to me as a pictorial counterpart.

In Part II contrast is immediate. 'Behold the Lamb of God' (G minor) 'Surely He hath borne our griefs' (F minor) bear tragedy and conviction in the jagged percussions of rhythm: these figures were common in German music in such contexts. The two great choruses are linked by the sublime 'He was despised'. The poignancy of this air is enhanced by the use of a major key and we feel (as in the 'Dead March' in *Saul*) how striking is the effect of the major mood for the portrayal of grief. The middle part of this air, which should on no account be omitted, returns to the type of rhythmic figure which dominates the surrounding choruses. It must be mentioned in passing that the final 'from shame and spitting', to be sung almost *parlando* ('speaking'), is a sweeping condemnation of inhuman humanity in no more than five notes. The fugal chorus 'And with his stripes' is built on a German subject used by Bach and also by Mozart. This section of

[1] See *Vorwort, Denkmäler Deutscher Tonkunst*, Vol. XXI.

Messiah, German sentiment in opposition to the Italian modelling of the Christmas music, illustrates the great advantage to Handel of cosmopolitan experience.

'All we like sheep' fills the place of a scherzo and is based on the duet which provided the music for 'For unto us'. One may be forgiven for seeing somewhat irresponsible sheep in this entertaining chorus: but the entertainment is deliberate; the endpiece—'And the Lord hath laid on Him the iniquity of us all' is great tragedy again. The chorus ends in F minor. We pass to B flat minor—'All they that see Him'—and through E flat major to the contumelious 'He trusted in God' in C minor. 'Thy rebuke hath broken His heart' expresses the depths of despair in harmonic surprises: nothing is more illustrative of the fruitless search for consolation than the sequence of chords which starts with that of A flat major and ends with a perfect cadence in B major. From thence to E and eventual relief in the unsullied hope of 'But Thou didst not leave His soul in hell', in which the spirit is uplifted not only by the relative brightness of the key but also the initial rise in the melody. From now on there is gratitude and adoration in 'Lift up your heads O ye gates' and 'Let all the angels of God'—a masterly and lovely chorus in its deftness and its trails of floating thought.

The bass air 'Thou art gone up on high' is a fine, bold piece of chamber-music composition, mainly a dialogue between the sung melody and the vigorous counterpoint of the unison violins. This movement, admittedly long, is often omitted; when it is not omitted it is too heavily accompanied, for its true strength depends on the preservation of Handel's original intentions. This is in D minor, the succeeding chorus—'The Lord gave the word' is in B flat. In this chorus the spread of the Gospel is depicted; first by a unison declamation which in its strong simplicity bears the impress of divine authority, and secondly in a great mobility of sixteenth notes in which all four parts join. The continuation of the spread of the Gospel is in the pastoral air 'How beautiful are the feet' (G minor) and the authoritative homophony of 'Their sound is gone out' (E flat major). The sonorities of the last 16 bars of this chorus are a magnificent example of the broadest understanding by Handel of choral effect. The music is now called back to C major for the fire and fury of 'Why do the nations' and 'Let us break their bonds asunder'. A *da capo* in the air is not wanted (though often added), for the chorus is, in fact, the complement to the first two sections of the air. Coloratura and melodic contour together with rhythmic incisiveness raise this portion of the oratorio to a high dramatic level. The drama is maintained through the A minor recitative and air—in which Handel allows the words 'Thou shalt break them' to make their own effect unimpeded by any extravagant musical posturing. And so we come to God in His glory in the 'Hallelujah' chorus, in the triumphant key of D major.

It is abundantly clear that any music following immediately on this chorus would be but anticlimax. Therefore an interval is imperative. An interval equally benefits the serene beauty of 'I know that my Redeemer liveth', which must be allowed time to gather up its own background of reflective tenderness. The key of E major returns us to the tonal atmosphere of 'Comfort ye my people'. The four short choruses which commence with 'Since by man came death' are a theological summary of Christian faith. They are gravely based within A minor—though moving through C major, G minor and D minor— and the first of each pair is *a cappella*. Finally the great coda of praise, in which D major again triumphantly asserts itself and in which the trumpets (used with great discretion throughout the oratorio) crown the climax. [I normally cut the rather dull 'Then shall be brought to pass', 'O death where is thy sting' and 'But thanks be to God', leaving 'If God be for us' as insulator between 'The trumpet shall sound' and 'Worthy is the Lamb' and the concomitant 'Amen', in which Handel restates in his own terms the spirit of the sixteenth century.]

If the tonal structure of *Messiah* is revealing so also is the orchestration. There is a growing conviction that Handel knew what he was about when he omitted from the *Messiah* score a number of instruments *which he could have had and which he employed in other works*. He used no more than strings (but notice how effective they are when employed as in the *concerto grosso*—with a *concertino* section opposing the full ensemble), harpsichord, oboes and bassoons together with organ for the choruses, and trumpets and drums. We may turn to the use of the brass. Handel brings the trumpets into 'Glory to God' off-stage (*da lontano*—'at a distance'—is his own explicit marking) so as to give the effect of heavenly trumpets. Then there is a long wait until the outburst, with chorus, in 'Hallelujah'. There is a solo trumpet for obvious reasons in 'The trumpet shall sound' and the full brass in the final choruses. The thrill of these entries is gravely impaired when further, unauthorized, use of brass is allowed.

Messiah is dramatic, but not so patently histrionic as, say, *Saul*.

Handel deliberately kept his desires and private proclivities within bounds. Why? Part of the answer is in a remark reported to have been addressed by Handel to Lord Kinnoul. 'My Lord,' he said after the first London performance, 'I should be sorry if I only entertained them; I wished to make them better.' The vogue of *Messiah* in English-speaking countries has been extraordinary. But 'popularity' has sometimes played havoc with Handel's music, which has suffered much from two centuries' overlay of pious and impious philistinism.

'This great work,' wrote Dr. Burney after the mammoth Commemoration of Handel in Westminster Abbey in 1784,[1] 'has been heard in all parts of the kingdom with increasing reverence and delight; it has fed the hungry, clothed the naked, fostered the orphan, and enriched succeeding managers of oratorios more than any single musical production in this or any country.' The reverence attached to *Messiah* has destroyed its verve and brilliance, its Italian grace, and, thus, its meaning. In the long run, perhaps, Bach has come off better through having to wait for a century and more for a zealous interest in his music.

Dr. J. M. Coopersmith (whose excellent edition of *Messiah* is strongly recommended together with that of Watkins Shaw) feels

'that a complete performance of *Messiah*, at least once a year, not only is artistically feasible, but also would be musically rewarding. It is not uncommon for concert-goers to hear the complete *St. Matthew Passion* of Bach at regular intervals; but how many have ever heard a complete performance of *Messiah*? . . . Approached as a *musical* experience, a complete *Messiah* performance would do much to counteract the false traditions that have surrounded this work. . . . It should be emphasized that it is far better to perform one part in its entirety than to present a distorted conception of the whole work.'

Messiah is in accord with modern thought in its economy of statement and apparatus. It is, therefore, to be deplored when its presentation is guided by the outworn precepts of nineteenth-century romanticism. Exploration of the remaining oratorios will reveal

[1] 60 trebles; 48 countertenors; 83 tenors; 84 basses; 6 flutes; 26 oboes; 26 bassoons; 1 double bassoon; 12 horns; 12 trumpets; 6 trombones, or sackbuts ('These performers,' writes Burney, 'played on other instruments, when the sackbuts were not wanted'); 3 kettle drums and 1 'double kettle drum'; 48 first violins; 47 second violins; 26 'tenors' (violas); 21 'cellos; 15 double basses and organ.

surprising contrasts, and practice in the choral music of Handel will stimulate both the listening imagination and the adaptability which choirs should possess for full competence in performance.

OTHER ORATORIOS

It is unfortunate that *Judas Maccabaeus*, an occasional work, written together with the *Occasional Oratorio* in celebration of the defeat of the Jacobites at Culloden in 1745, has won considerable popularity. Possibly this is on account of the relative ease of the music from the performer's point of view. Certainly the 'popular' numbers—'Arm, arm, ye brave', 'Come, ever smiling liberty', 'From mighty kings', 'See the conquering hero comes', the jingoistic cheer of the majority of the choruses are effective; but they are relatively no more than competent. (The opening funeral choruses are a different matter, rising to the tragic grandeur of the nobler moods of *Israel in Egypt*.) Handel was not deficient in self-criticism. When a friend looked over the music of *Judas Maccabaeus* Handel commented 'Well, to be sure you have picked out the best songs, but you take no notice of that which is to get me all the money.'

We occasionally have glimpses of Handel at work. Dr. Thomas Morell who wrote the libretti of a number of the oratorios writes about the inception of *Judas*:

'As to myself, great lover as I am of music, I should never have thought of such an undertaking . . . had not Mr. Handel applied to me when at Kew in 1746, and added to his request the honour of a recommendation from Prince Frederick (Prince of Wales). Upon this I thought I could do as well as some who had gone before me, and within two or three days carried him the first act of *Judas Maccabaeus* which he approved of. "Well," says he, "and how are you to go on?" " Why, we are to suppose an engagement, and that the Israelites have conquered, and so begin with a chorus as 'Fallen is the foe', or something like it." "No, I will have this," and began working it, as it is, upon the harpsichord. "Well, go on." "I will bring you more tomorrow." "No, something now." "So fall thy foes, O Lord—" "That will do," and immediately carried on the composition as we have it in that most admirable chorus. That

incomparable air, "Wise men, flattering, may deceive us" (which
was his last chorus) was designed for *Belshazzar* but that not being
performed, we happily flung it into *Judas Maccabaeus*. N.B. The
plan of *Judas Maccabaeus* was designed as a compliment to the Duke
of Cumberland, upon his returning victorious from Scotland. I had
introduced several incidents more apropos, but it was thought
they would make it too long, and they were therefore omitted.
The Duke, however, made me a handsome present. . . . The success
of the oratorio was very great, and I have often wished that at first
I had asked in jest for the benefit of the 30th night instead of a 3rd.
I am sure he would have given it to me: on which night there was
above £400 in the house. He left me a legacy, however, of £200.'

We may read between the lines and discover something of Morell's
character and taste, something of Handel's preferences and generosity,
of the working relationship between the two, of the interest of the
Court, of the circumstances which made for popular acclaim. But as
Handel was able to distinguish between his works so should we and
in the process of discrimination we shall learn to acquire something of
his critical judgement.

Some sort of summary must be attempted sufficient to set the eager
reader turning the pages of one score after another. *Israel in Egypt*,
based on many Italian models, is a prodigious choral work. This is the
story of a people and as individuals are absorbed into the mass so
recitative and arias form a very small part of the whole. In the solidity
of the work the example of Carissimi may be descried. The descriptive
choruses, exciting to sing, are incidental to the main theme—the
progress of a people from subjugation and despair to liberation and

Ex. 7a

He sent a thick dark - ness o - ver all the land, o - ver

all the land, e - ven dark - ness which might be felt

victory. The first and last choruses are the measure of Handel's epic genius, just as the 'darkness' chorus is an introduction to his visual opportunism. No chromatic harmony can outbid Ex. 7a). *Saul,* composed at the same time as *Israel in Egypt,* is a psychological study. The character of Saul fascinated Handel who here shows his forward-looking sense of character analysis through music. We would quote the disturbed chorus which shows the decline of Saul's mental condition (Ex. 7b). This is not what the age was accustomed to.

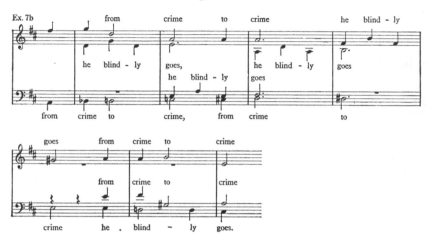

Ex. 7b

Works which similarly display a keen appreciation of human power and human weakness are *Samson,* where the choral writing throughout is on the peak of Handel's greatness; *Jephtha,* a study of obedience to the will of God, which some hold as the composer's greatest monument; and *Hercules* (1745), a non-religious work based on a text derived from Sophocles' *Women of Trachis* and a profound study of jealousy. Then there are the glittering works which show barbaric splendour in music which is operatic, but which is greater than any opera known in the eighteenth century, where drama was often but a side-issue.

Belshazzar depicts the splendid debauchery of one court, *Solomon* the might and wealth of another (for King Solomon one can read King George II, for there is no doubt that Handel employed the mode of apotheosis which had been cultivated by Lully in respect of Louis XIV). *Susanna* is a novel in terms of music, *Alexander Balus* another; and both moral in their celebration of chastity on the one hand and matrimonial fidelity on the other. *Theodora,* the most charming and tender of oratorios, is to Handel as *Romeo and Juliet* to Shakespeare, a depiction of youth and love and the tragedy and beauty and mortality of all things young and lovely. It is possible to consider that an impetus was given to oratorios dealing with virtuous women such as Susanna and Theodora by the novels of Samuel Richardson.

The quality of Handel lies not so much in the nature of his style as in his application. See the grace of this invocation in *Theodora* (Ex. 8),

Ex. 8

Come, might-y Fa - ther,   might - y Lord,

the bejewelled serenity of this scene in *Solomon* (Ex. 9), the harshness

Ex. 9

While night-in - gales lull — them to   sleep   to — sleep with their song.

of the 'calumny' chorus from *Alexander Balus* over its inexorable ground (Ex. 10). Of all great composers he is the least known, for,

Ex. 10

dark . - ness e - - - - - ver lie

(Vlas. and Vlns. 8va higher)

despite general opinion, he is never without surprise.

Now Handel is an adorable composer because of his humanity. He was for ever making mistakes. He overworked. He sometimes lost interest. As it happens what is nearly his worst work brings us back again to Bach. In 1716 Handel made a setting of the Passion text of Barthold Heinrich Brockes. Brockes' *Der für die Sünden der Welt gemarterte und sterbende Jesus* had been compiled in 1712 and was to be set by almost every German composer of note in the eighteenth century. Bach did not indeed set Brockes' libretto as it stood but he incorporated some parts of it in the *St. John Passion*.

I

THE PASSION SETTINGS OF HANDEL
AND BACH

In 1703 Handel was living in Hamburg and was persuaded to compose a setting of the Passion—the words from St. John's Gospel and with additional 'lyrics' by a local poet named Christian Postel. This is a slender, cantata-type work of no particular interest (the slightly later *Resurrezione* is a far more mature work and well worth occasional presentation). In 1716 came a setting of a Passion text made by Barthold Brockes of Hamburg. This is clearly written from without the authentic Passion tradition (cf. Schütz, Sebastiani, Bach to realize its unliturgical nature). In 1721 the oratorio-type Passion was performed in Leipzig for the first time.

Although the story of the Passion had been performed motet-wise since the Middle Ages the new style was late in asserting its right of entry. The 1721 setting at St. Thomas's Church was by Johann Kuhnau (better known for his 'Biblical' Sonatas), who was Bach's predecessor.

Bach's *St. John Passion* was performed in 1723. Thereafter Bach (*vide* his five cycles of church cantatas and his five Mass settings) would appear to have written four further settings of the Passion story. The scores of the two best-known *Passions*, *St. John* and *St. Matthew* (1729), are extant and Spitta presumed the *St. Luke Passion*—published (1898) in the authoritative *Bachgesellschaft*—to be authentic. The lost *Passions* are the one to Picander's libretto (1725) and the *St. Mark Passion* (1731). Lest it should seem that Bach was overgenerous in the time he devoted to this subject it should be noted that his fashionable contemporary Telemann was responsible for forty-six settings.

The liturgical setting of the Passion on Good Friday at the Leipzig churches (for performances alternated at St. Thomas' and St. Nicholas') was as follows:

Chorale: *Da Jesus an dem Kreuze stand*
Part I of the Passion Setting
Chorale: *O Lamm Gottes unschuldig*
Chorale: *Herr Jesu Christ, dich zu uns wend*
Sermon
Part II of the Passion Setting

Motet: *Ecce quomodo moritur justus*—Gallus (i.e. Handl)
Prayer: Passion Collect
Chorale: *Nun danket alle Gott*

This pattern was generally established all over Germany. The chorales had held their traditional place from the sixteenth century and the esteem in which Handl's motet was held is indicated by a note in a Passion setting of the Prussian composer Sebastiani showing when it should be sung. As has been shown the familiarity of the motet led to its quotation by Handel in his *Funeral Anthem*. What is notable about the liturgical arrangement is the vastness of the scheme. In Handel's *Passion* there is no feeling for the tradition: it is clear that by 1716 he had forgotten a good deal of his native experience. Especially is this clear in the perfunctory treatment of chorale. Handel's bare harmonizations are extremely dull. With Bach it is equally clear that tradition is all, that the whole Lutheran heritage is swept up within his great imagination. Nothing shows this to greater effect than the incorporation of 'O Lamm Gottes unschuldig' within the first chorus of the *St. Matthew Passion*. Above all, the whole of the *St. Matthew Passion* is a summing-up of the theology of a people. Sacrifice, suffering, expiation, redemption: these words have some limited meaning as words; but their full significance is revealed only in Albrecht Dürer and Matthias Grünewald, and Bach. Rochlitz referred to Bach as the Dürer of music; to Handel as its Rubens.

The long and sentencious libretto of Brockes, who was a government official, really suited neither Bach nor Handel. Bach used the text as a basis for the *St. John Passion* (which was hastily composed in ten weeks) but he amended the words very considerably, and added lyrics which are presumed to have been his own work. The text of the *St. Matthew Passion* was prepared by the Leipzig writer 'Picander' (the pen-name of Friedrich Henrici, a postal official), under Bach's supervision. Handel was hardly moved at all by Brockes' text and his

EX. 11

extension of it is merely formal—except on one or two occasions Handel's music comes to life only when he contemplates Christ as the hero of a plot: the music for the Last Supper and the Agony in the Garden (some of which Handel transferred to *Esther*) is both dramatically fine and musically direct. Thus the passing of the Sacramental Cup (Ex. 11) and thus the despair of Jesus (Ex. 12). Handel sees the vision but without a specific theological background.

Ex. 12

BACH'S 'ST. JOHN AND ST. MATTHEW PASSIONS'

The *St. John Passion* has much personal significance. The process of emotional-cum-intellectual appreciation of the theme is the process of Bach's inner feeling and thought, with more apparent stress on the former than in other and minor works. In the *St. Matthew Passion* the feeling is as of an universal deposition of awed love and faith. The *St. John Passion* is described as a lesser work. It is better defined as a different work. Possibly of the two it is the more original in that it is the more removed from convention. (By this it is not only musical convention that is implied.) It is true that the later work with its double choir (Bach had his best sixteen singers for chorus I and his less adept —eighteen strong—'Motet-choir' for chorus II) and more extensive orchestration makes greater demands, but it still can be felt as a great ecclesiastical monument just as, in simpler form, can the Passion settings of Sebastiani and Theile. The *St. John Passion* brings pain and suffering before the listener in terms which the normally pious would discountenance as alarming. This *Passion* is full of discomfort. In *St. Matthew* the idea of pain is engulfed in the larger idea of God's love. We are also made deeply aware of man's trust. The *St. Matthew Passion* may appear as the more musical work of the two because the 'real' is demonstrated as less than real, the symbol as but a symbol

The Scourging of Jesus in *St. John* is obsessive (Ex. 13). In *St.*

Ex. 13

Matthew the same action is absorbed into the wonderment of No. 60 where sorrow and pain are placed more distantly—though still with diminished sevenths, arranged in the generally accepted rhythmic palpitation of distress—in the strings. True the recitative 'Now Barabbas was a robber' and the air 'Behold Him: See!' in *St. John* are separated by the tranquillity of the bass arioso 'Come, ponder, O my soul', with its background of lute and viola d'amore: but this number was an afterthought and was added to the work after the first performance. We may also notice the contemplative quality which in *St. Matthew* surrounds the actual Crucifixion: the recitative 'Ah! Golgotha', almost ingratiatingly scored for oboe da caccia and *pizzicato* 'cello; the great aria, also for contralto, 'See the Saviour's outstretched Hands', which bears some resemblance in contour to Handel's 'As when the Sun' in *Samson*; the memorial 'Passion' chorale; the calm 'Truly this was the Son of God'; the extraordinary repose which characterizes the Descent from the Cross and the Burial. All this, in a sense, is too great to be sad, whereas in *St. John* sadness is the dominant message from after the Rending of the Veil of the Temple (see especially the affective 'O heart, melt in weeping'). The final choruses of the two *Passions* meet together in a sublime indication that sanctity is no confined province in music, for both choruses are in a dance measure and both are derived from secular sources—that of *St. Matthew* from a Sarabande of the Cöthen period, that of *St. John* from the Rondeau of the Suite in B Minor for flute and strings.

The respective opening choruses of the two works—vast applications of the concerto form to the choral-orchestral medium—are instructive. That of *St. John* is an enormous *da capo* movement, impregnate with anxiety and eagerness that Christ should demonstrate his power in some clear manner. The voice parts are strenuous, arresting and vital. The accompaniment is restless and discordant. In the *St.*

Matthew Passion the scene is sublimated by the chorale and while the discords are no less strong than in *St. John* they are subordinate to the whole of the scheme.

The chorales are generally more thoroughly incorporated within *St. Matthew*. In No. 1 'O Lamm Gottes unschuldig' is treated as a fantasia. 'Herzliebste Jesu' (see *St. John* No. 7) is introduced, as appendix to the announcement of the Passion, in No. 3; then it forms the lyrical expansion of the tenor aria 'O grief.' A monumental treatment of 'O Mensch, bewein dein' Sünde gross' ends Part I. In *St. John* there is the one extended chorale—in opposition to the bass air 'My Lord and Saviour'. And here we may quote Terry to suggest that this particular movement was—relatively—ill-placed. 'The situation is treated less movingly than in the *St. Matthew Passion*, where the simple chorale that follows the Saviour's death is charged with deeper realism.' This deeper emotion is surely also to be experienced in the arias.

Almost without exception the arias in *St. John* have an energetic quality; energetic, that is, in the textural balance. In 'Chains of bondage' the alto voice is co-equal with the two oboes and the contrapuntal development is at once fascinating and exacting. 'I follow, I follow in gladness' is an exquisite duo for soprano and flutes. Whether this is in any way relevant to the character of St. Peter is open to doubt. With the final aria of Part I—'Ah! my soul, what end awaiteth thee'—the case is far different. The accompaniment is of strings, against which the anguished leaps and ruminative remorse of the tenor voice stand out. In the preceding recitative Peter weeping is over-painted: the recollections of the denial at the end of the aria have associative force in the supposed realism of the melody: but the over-all musical idea and its realization are the enduring features (Ex. 14).

In the second part, after the episode of the Scourging, to the solo music of which reference has already been made, there are the not very distinguished 'Haste! haste, poor souls'—with the upper chorus voices interjecting interrogations; 'All is finished' for alto and with a viol da gamba countersubject, in which the broken phrasing and the masterly condensation of the *da capo* are profoundly moving but of which the central section is somewhat highly conventionalized and after the pattern of Vivaldi.

It is, I think, arguable that the *St. John Passion* achieves its unity primarily on account of the narrative—and it should be noted, how, as in the *St. Matthew Passion*, the recitative of the Evangelist reaches the

Ex. 14

Yea, the ser - vant hath de - nied

(Str.)

his Lord.

highest point in the tradition of recitative. Here indeed is the peak of heightened speech. The *St. Matthew Passion*, however, achieves an integrated unity of narrative, of the general Christian philosophy arising from traditional, Lutheran interpretation of the narrative, and of music. It is clear in almost every bar of Bach that the symbolic power of music meant a great deal to him personally. It is equally clear that many interpreters of Bach have allowed to Bach's symbolism a virtue which does not immediately belong to it.

It is not the likeness to something else which is the criterion of great music: indeed it is the unlikeness of music to anything visible or tangible which is its great distinction. No man can escape the habits of his time, but a great man can transcend the limitations of familiar practice. So in the solo music of *St. Matthew* we discover throughout a sublimity of thought which may touch dogma and may incorporate symbolic expression, but which is confined to neither. In many of the chorale preludes for organ this is equally apparent. The music reigns supreme, but within the music is a divinity which only the great artist can apprehend.

Consider 'Break in grief', 'Jesus, Saviour, I am Thine', 'Have mercy, Lord', 'For love my Saviour now is dying', 'If my tears be unavailing', 'Come healing Cross', 'See the Saviour's outstretched Hands', and 'Make Thee clean my breast'. In these great movements is the perfection of song as song, and in all cases, however intellectual may be the interplay between voice and accompaniment, there is an absolute propriety of balance; the purpose of the expression is affiliated with the verbal text, but, even without a specific understanding of the words, the music makes such impact on the understanding that none can fail to perceive the inner idea.

The whole of *St. Matthew* appears to flow from one source. The chorales are wonderfully chosen and skilfully distributed and they join up both with the choruses and the soloists as has been shown. Recitative is sometimes formal and *secco* ('dry'—i.e. accompanied only by harpsichord) but at other times is lyrically intensified as specially in the words of Christ. The choruses are 'dramatic' (they are more obviously and sometimes awkwardly 'dramatic' in *St. John*) but the dramatic content of that in which Christ is bound and in which lightning and thunder burst out, and the crowd choruses, serve principally to

display contrast with the lyrical flow of the whole work. They are not, however tempting it may seem to the singer or conductor, ends in themselves. The movement which shows 'Christ bound and led into the city' is a fine example of thesis and antithesis—of consistent phrase and conflicting percussion. As well as any other single movement it shows the range of Bach's counterpoint and harmony. After an instrumental preamble, of the same material as the non-choral part of the following, we have (Ex. 15). The 'binding with cords' gives this use of the Neapolitan sixth—an off-key chord frequently used in the eighteenth century for its element of surprise (Ex. 16); the two

choruses are then deployed in an elemental frenzy, which sweeps up treachery and cruelty into this cataclysmic coda of condemnation (Ex. 17).

This exploration of eternity with the capacity to see past, present and future as one is the mark of Bach. Edward Holmes put it that Bach lived in the futurity of art, by which he meant that Bach could carry thought, through music, from out of the eighteenth century. Handel also could do this, but not Georg Philipp Telemann, nor Johann

Mattheson, nor Reinhard Keiser, nor Gottfried Stölzel, nor any of the other once venerated writers of Passion music. Of the *St. Matthew Passion* each measure should be quoted. I must be allowed the epitome of tender love: the love of humanity for other humanity; the love that sees a divinity within the human, or a human in the divine. And I must be allowed to show the evocative power of so ordinary a vehicle of musical method as a dominant seventh. The last chorus begins (Ex. 18)

and it ends (Ex. 19). Here note the pedal (and compare with the first

chorus of the Passion), the chromatics, the discord, the delayed resolution of the leading-tone in the flutes.

MENDELSSOHN'S REVIVAL OF THE 'ST. MATTHEW PASSION'

Revival of the *St. Matthew Passion* was due to Mendelssohn, who conducted it in Berlin in 1829. His master Karl Friedrich Zelter did his best to appreciate Bach. He found for himself that in general 'the biggest obstacle is the atrocious German chorale texts which are full of the polemical earnestness of the Reformation and try to disturb the mind of the non-believer by smoking him out with the dense fumes of belief which is what no one really wants nowadays'.

Zelter's opinion is valid. In some works the dogma impedes. In the *St. Matthew Passion* this is transcended. Goethe, through Zelter and Mendelssohn, became aware of Bach and, perhaps, his appreciation of the spirit of Bach to Zelter is more relevant than the specialized reaction of any musician.

'It was there in Bach,' he once wrote 'when my mind was in a state of perfect composure and free from external distractions that I first obtained some idea of your grand master. I said to myself, it is as if the eternal harmony was conversing within itself as it may have done in the bosom of God just before the creation of the world. So likewise did it move in my inmost soul and it seemed as if I neither possessed nor needed ears, nor any other sense—least of all the eyes.'

The work of Mendelssohn as composer will be considered at a later point. Here it is proper to indicate the extent to which modern music is indebted to him for the faith which he displayed—at the age of twenty—in Bach's forgotten masterpiece. He was encouraged and assisted by Edward Devrient, the actor, who sang the part of Christ at the 1829 performance. 'Well,' said Mendelssohn, pointedly, 'it needs a stage-player and a Jew to reintroduce the greatest Christian music to the people.'

On March 22nd, 1829, Mendelssohn's sister Fanny wrote a long letter to Karl Klingemann. The account of the performance of the *St. Matthew Passion* at the Singakademie deserves complete reproduction, as showing not only the nature and effect of the presentation but also the feeling for its interpretation as experienced by Mendelssohn and the obstacles which he had to overcome. So is it always when unfamiliar music is concerned.

'We are,' wrote Fanny to Klingemann in London, 'soon going to send you Felix. He has left himself a beautiful memorial here by two crowded representations of the "Passion" for a benefit of the poor. What used to appear to us as a dream, to be realized in far-off future times, has now become real: the "Passion" has been given to the public, and is everybody's property. . . . Felix and Devrient had been talking for a long time of the possibility of a representation, but the plan had neither form nor shape until one evening at our house they settled the affair, and walked off the next morning in brand-new yellow kid gloves (very important in their eyes) to the managers of the academy. They very carefully minced the matter, and in all possible discreetness put the question whether they might be allowed the use of the concert-hall for a charitable purpose. In that case, and as the music they were going to perform

was likely to be very successful, they offered to give a second performance for the benefit of the academy. This the gentlemen
declined with thanks, and preferred to insist on a fixed payment of
fifty thalers, leaving the profits to the disposal of the concert-
givers. . . . Zelter made no objections, and the rehearsals began on
the Friday following.

'Felix went over the whole score, made a few judicious cuts, and
only instrumented the recitative "And the veil of the temple was
rent in twain". Everything else was left untouched. The people
were astonished, stared, admired; and when, after a few weeks, the
rehearsals in the academy itself commenced, their faces became *very*
long, with surprise at the existence of such a work, about which
they, the members of the Berlin Academy, knew nothing. After
having got over their astonishment, they began to study with true,
warm interest. The thing itself, the novelty and originality of the
form, took hold of them, the subject was universally compre-
hensible and engaging and Devrient sang the recitatives most
beautifully. The genial spirit and enthusiasm evinced by all the
singers during the very first rehearsals, and which each new
rehearsal kindled to ever-increasing love and ardour; the delight and
surprise created by each new element—the solo, the orchestra,
Felix's splendid interpretation and his accompanying the first
rehearsals at the piano from beginning to end *by heart*, all these were
moments never to be forgotten. Zelter, who had lent his help at the
first rehearsals, gradually retreated, and during the later rehearsals,
as well as at the concerts, with praiseworthy resignation took his
seat among the audience.

'And now the members of the academy themselves spread such a
favourable report about the music, and such a general and vivid
interest was created in all classes, that on the very day after the first
advertisement of the concert all the tickets were taken, and during
the latter days upwards of a thousand people applied in vain.

'On Wednesday, March 11th,[1] the first representation took
place, and excepting a few slight mistakes of the solo singers it
may be called a perfect success. We were the first in the orchestra.
As soon as the doors were opened, the people, who already had
been long waiting outside, rushed into the hall, which was quite
full in less than a quarter-of-an-hour. I sat at the corner, where I

[1] Fanny mistakenly wrote March 10th.

could see Felix very well, and had gathered the strongest alto-voices around me. The choruses were sung with a fire, a striking power, and also with a touching delicacy and softness the like of which I have never heard, except at the second concert, when they surpassed themselves.

'Taking for granted that you remember the dramatic form, I send you a textbook, just mentioning that the account of the Evangelist was sung by Stümer, the words of Jesus by Devrient, of Peter by Bader, the High-Priest and Pilate by Busolt, Judas by Weppler.

'Mmes. Schätzel, Milder and Türrschmiedt sang the soprano and alto parts exquisitely. The room was crowded and had all the air of a church: the deepest quiet and most solemn devotion pervaded the whole, only now and then involuntary utterances of intense emotion were heard. What is so often erroneously maintained of such like undertakings truly and fully applies to this one, that a peculiar spirit and general higher interest pervaded the concert, that everybody did his duty to the best of his powers, and many did more. Rietz, for instance, who with the help of his brother and brother-in-law had undertaken to copy the parts of all the different instruments, refused all pay for himself and the other two. Most singers declined accepting the tickets offered to them, or else paid for them; so that for the first concert only six free tickets were issued (of which Spontini[1] had two), and for the second none at all.

'Even before the first concert the many who had not been able to gain admission raised a loud cry for a repetition, and the industrial schools petitioned to subscribe; but by this time Spontini was on the alert, and—with the greatest amiability—tried to prevent a second performance. Felix and Devrient, however, took the straightest course, and procured an order from the Crown-Prince, who from the beginning had taken a lively interest in the enterprise, and so the concert was repeated on Saturday, March 21st, Bach's birthday; the same crowd, and a still greater audience, for the ante-room and the small rehearsal-room behind the audience were added, and all tickets sold. The choruses were still more exquisite than the first time, the instruments splendid; only one sad mistake

[1] Spontini, Intendant of the Opera and much favoured at the Prussian court, was very unpopular among German composers in a period which saw violent reaction against Italian music. In 1828 Spontini had given the first performance in Berlin of the 'Credo' from Bach's *Mass in B Minor*, which had just been published by Nägeli of Zürich.

of Milder's, and a few slight shortcomings in the solos, put a damp on Felix's spirits—but on the whole I may say that a better success could not be desired.'

THE BACH CULT

Although Mendelssohn adapted Bach's scoring to the taste of his day more than Fanny indicates, March 11th, 1829, deserves red-letter mention in the calendar of music. The *St. Matthew Passion* was performed both in Breslau and Königsberg shortly after the Berlin revival and it was published in 1830, the *St. John Passion* following a year later. The *Mass in B Minor* was published in full in 1845. Once started the Bach cult swept through the musical world with irresistible momentum. The *Bachgesellschaft* was founded in 1850 and Bach Choirs sprang up in many centres. The London Bach Choir was founded in 1875 through the interest of Arthur Coleridge, a barrister and a great-nephew of the poet: this under the direction of Otto Goldschmidt (husband of Jenny Lind), C. V. Stanford, Walford Davies, Hugh Allen, Ralph Vaughan Williams and Reginald Jacques has been a focal point of English concern for Bach. In America the Bethlehem Bach Choir in the Moravian centre at Bethlehem, Pennsylvania, was founded in 1900. The first conductor was John Frederick Wolle, who gave the first complete early performances of the *St. John Passion*, the *St. Matthew Passion* and the *Mass in B Minor*. The first American performance of the *St. Matthew Passion* was in 1879 by the Handel and Haydn Society of Boston.

'MASS IN B MINOR'

It has already been shown that Lutheranism retained the 'Kyrie' and 'Gloria' from the rites of the pre-Reformation Church and that many famous composers set these words in a German-inflected form of the ancient polyphonic style. (A work of some special interest in its attempts to unite two forms of expression—of mass and chorale—and two sets of references is a *Missa supra chorale: Christ lag in Todesbanden* attributed to Zachau.)[1]

[1] See *Denkmäler Deutscher Tonkunst*, Vol. XXII.

In 1733 Bach supplicated for the post of court composer to the Elector of Saxony. In support of his application and as evidence of his skill he sent what were to be the first two movements of the entire *Mass in B Minor*. Bach received from the Elector his appointment in 1736. It was an appointment which could be held conjointly with that in Leipzig and entailed only occasional visits to Dresden. He subsequently sent for use in Dresden four other settings of the Mass. These other Masses are relatively unimportant and consisted largely of the rearrangement of music which Bach had composed for other occasions. The *Mass in B Minor* was continued beyond its Lutheran limit to embrace the movements proper to the Roman service (the Elector of Saxony was a Roman Catholic), but the scale of the whole far transcends the possibility of any liturgical performance. In the later part of the work —after the passage 'Gratias agimus'—Bach followed normal eighteenth-century practice (cf. Handel) in adapting material from earlier works. The whole Mass was finally completed in 1738.

No one can be said to be educated who has not experienced this work. We must now defend our proposition. We may start with the material. There is no work within the eighteenth century (not even the *St. Matthew Passion*) which so clearly demonstrated the Platonic truth-within-beauty concept or the Shelleyan gloss that art (poetry) exists to show unfamiliar aspects of familiarity. Fugue is a familiar form and it was even more familiar in the days of Bach: but such treatment of fugue as distinguishes the first great movement of the *Mass* lies beyond the capacity of the eighteenth century. The eighteenth century appreciated the bizarre but hardly the titanic, and themes of this order (Ex. 20, Ex. 21) were considered too Gothic, too repelling for easy accept-

ance. The working-out of this material—note that only six words are sung—into a vast symphonic structure of 270 measures is an intellectual prodigy. But by intellectual endeavour and with hardly any recourse to obviously effective devices Bach determines an imaginative reaction. The reaction is of wonder, of awe, of humility. So we may react to Bach but, as he himself would have had it, through Bach to God. The first four measures of the 'Kyrie' are an index to this. They summon the spirit to awareness. And what follows is counterpoint. As reference to the 'Forty-eight' Preludes and Fugues will explain, intellectual clarity is the province of counterpoint—the dialectic method of musical expression with thesis and antithesis, subject and answer, analysis and synthesis of detail: but intellectual clarity incorporates beauty. The 'academic' contrapuntist is an obscurantist: Bach was no obscurantist. He may appear obscure, but that is generally our fault. Compare the fuguing friction of the 'Kyrie' with the serene 'Gratias' (which music forms also the material of 'Dona nobis pacem'). The contrast between these two is polar: the world lies between. And then see the vivacity of the spectacular concerto-style movements, particularly the 'Cum sancto spiritu'. No one but Bach could have encompassed the convention of 'glory' thus (Ex. 22). Vivaldi was a great

contemporary of Bach but his conception of 'glory' in the *Gloria* is miniscule in comparison. Vivaldi does what is (was) possible: Bach what is (was) impossible. In the end, however, human effort can reach up to Bach and achieve the miracle of execution. Think back from the concert hall and the trained artist to Leipzig and the Thomasschule—or Dresden and the court chapel: faith with Bach was more than a theological tenet.

The importance of the bass part was fundamental to eighteenth-century design. But the bass part of the 'Sanctus' is fundamental to an intellectual conception of the limitless universe. Handel, in *Samson*, calls us beneath the stars and halts us (with terrific suspense) at the sight of the stars: Bach in his 'Sanctus' presents a sort of symbol of an Hegelian Absolute. (As a matter of interest Hegel was present at the Berlin performance of the *St. Matthew Passion* in 1829 and was profoundly impressed.) Yet we are led to the heights from the familiar knowledge that D major (the convenient key for trumpets) was ordinarily associated with dignity, pageantry, high spirits and so on.

A hundred people before Bach had used the ground bass as design:

so with flutes as symptomatic of melancholy; with chromatically inflected polyphony to the same end. That merely serves to emphasize the superlative synthesis of these factors into the 'Crucifixus'. The end of this movement must be quoted to show the beginning of the next (Ex. 23).

Ex. 23

There is nothing in all these examples that could not have been achieved within the period; but nothing comparable (Handel must be excepted as deploying his genius in other fields) was achieved. In regard to the last excerpt it may be asked whether the words make any difference to the intellectual significance of the aesthetic and philosophic whole. The words, in fact, are not adequate to the music.

Which brings us back to the liturgy. In itself a set form of words is finite, even when it deals with the infinite. Music which is made ancillary will generally, thus, suffer as music. Music, as Mendelssohn once pointed out, is much less finite than words—and therefore potentially more exact. In respect of Bach we may feel to exist a Platonic 'reason'—a concern with pure ideas; whereas the words of the Mass are concerned with intuitions based on unprovable premises. Immediately Bach's music to 'Laudamus te' may be instanced as greater than a verbal clause, for it is so completely unlimited in ecstasy.

I have no doubt that the Pietist contemporary of Bach would have deplored this as 'secular'. Precisely because the Pietist and his successors (they are still with us) have encouraged a division in thought the present tendency is towards 'secularity'. Yet in this secular age Bach survives. He, like Handel, was catholic, and I have some idea that his spirit was in many ways akin to that of St. Augustine of Hippo.

K

'My soul,' said the saint, 'yearns to know this most entangled enigma.' That was at the heart of true Protestantism and St. Augustine held great influence at the time of the Reformation. The *Mass in B Minor* is Bach's *Civitas Dei*. Within his magnifical D major choruses 'Gloria', 'Cum Sancto Spiritu', 'Et resurrexit', the resolution of the confessional 'Confiteor' into expectation of the life to come, and 'Sanctus' and 'Osanna', Bach uses the fulness of his resources to celebrate, as St. Augustine at the end of his great work, the saint's vision of God in heaven and the felicity of the City of God.

We may lay out the detailed framework of the *Mass*, emphasizing that this is an 'oratorio' or 'sacred concert' pattern unrelated to, and indeed greater than, liturgical action.

TECHNICAL ANALYSIS OF 'MASS IN B MINOR'

KYRIE (LORD HAVE MERCY)

(1) B Minor, *Adagio* introduction of four bars, fugal development of the subject shown in Ex. 20; five-part chorus and orchestra (of strings, flutes, oboi d'amore, bassoons and organ).

(2) D major, 'Christe eleison' (Christ have mercy) duet for two sopranos, in which the conventional sequences of thirds familiar in Agustino Steffani and Handel soften the character of the music. A fluent counter-melody runs through unison violins. The supporting harmony—as in all such movements which have the character of chamber music—is entrusted to the harpsichord. As always in this period the keyboard bass is reinforced by 'cello.

(3) F sharp minor. The tripartite scheme—'Lord have mercy, Christ have mercy, Lord have mercy'—is completed by a new fugue (see Ex. 21), strict and intellectually severe,[1] set out with the same resources as (1). The concluding Picardy third (chord with a major third ending a movement otherwise in a minor key) makes the succeeding[2]

(4) GLORIA (GLORY TO GOD) burst into a D major setting which seems unconscionably radiant. Trumpets outpour and flutes add brightness to the scintillation of the strings. At 'in terra pax' greater

---

[1] The subject which Bach uses in this fugue was something of a contrapuntist's test piece. It will be met again in the 'Gloria' of Mozart's *Missa brevis* in G major (K. 49).

[2] Nos. 4, 7 and 11 of the *Mass* were extracted and used as a cantata for Christmas Day in 1740.

solemnity of utterance prevails and the passage should be compared
with Handel's 'and in earth peace' in the 'Glory to God' chorus in
Messiah. The motiv (Ex. 24) grows, however, into an extensive fugal

Ex. 24 ⌈1st statement   ⌈completion of fugue subject

et____   in__ ter - ra__ pax ho - mi - ni - bus bo-nae vol - un - ta - tis

coda in which the trumpets, silent during the middle section, return.
The end section is in D major.

(5) LAUDAMUS TE (WE PRAISE THEE) in A major, soprano solo with
violin solo (so marked by Bach in the Dresden parts).

(6) GRATIAS AGIMUS (WE GIVE THANKS TO THEE) in D major, chorus
and orchestra. The orchestra (in which the trumpets are reserved for
the climactic second part) double the voices in a fugue based on an
ancient subject and so worked as to evoke memories of the poly-
phonists. This music had been previously used by Bach, also to a text
of thanksgiving, in the opening chorus of Cantata 29—*Wir danken dir,
Gott*. This cantata was in honour of the Leipzig Town Council and was
performed on August 27th, 1731.

(7) DOMINE DEUS, REX COELESTIS (O LORD GOD, HEAVENLY KING) is
an enchanting, humanist, vision set out as a duet for soprano and tenor,
accompanied by flute and muted strings. The mood changes to the end
at mention of 'the Lamb of God' and the tonality is moved to B minor
in which key lies the four-part chorus.

(8) QUI TOLLIS. Here canonic behaviour in the voices and similar
contrivance, though in sixteenth-notes, in the flutes increases the
severity of a concentrated consideration of the idea of 'the sins of the
world'. Tonality is difficult and the individual lines, e.g. (Ex. 25 and Ex.
26) frequently conflict with the commonplace ease of expression which

Ex. 25

Qui   tol - lis   pec - ca - - -

Ex. 26

de - pre - ca - ti__   o - nem,__ de - pre-ca-ti - o-nem nos - tram.

singers 'enjoy' and listeners expect. Thus we are disturbed to an
awareness of the other-worldly. This chorus is taken from a movement
in Cantata 46—*Schauet doch und sehet*—where it is set to a text from

Lamentations 1, 12. Since there the words are 'Behold and see if there be any sorrow like unto my sorrow' we may again compare the Handelian outlook as expressed in *Messiah*. We may see the this-worldly sympathy and humanist instinct of Handel as against the more idealized philosophic conception of Bach.

(9) QUI SEDES (WHO SITS AT THE RIGHT HAND OF GOD) is still in B minor but the atmosphere is gradually changing. The spirit of 'Qui tollis' still overhangs but the more pointed rhythm and the sinuosity of the solo contralto, contrasted with the plangent voice of the solo oboe d'amore, tends towards the familiar.

(10) QUONIAM TU SOLUS SANCTUS (ONLY THOU ART HOLY)—for bass solo and in D major—restates the symbolic kingship which is in the air 'Grosse Herr' (Mighty Lord) in the *Christmas Oratorio*. Here, however, the corno da caccia ('hunting horn', i.e. French horn), instead of trumpet, tries conclusions with Bach's idea of what brass should be able to accomplish. It is a fine movement but respect for the music is sometimes affected by anxiety for the brass player.

(11) CUM SANCTO SPIRITU (WITH THE HOLY SPIRIT)—in D major—is complementary both to No. 10 and to the whole of the earlier sections of the 'Gloria'. Full chorus and orchestra are involved.

(12) CREDO (I BELIEVE). At this dogmatic point Bach returns to an academic seven-part fugal utterance (in A major) which shows the Fathers of the Church in the universal motiv (Ex. 27).

Ex. 27

(13) PATREM OMNIPOTENS (THE FATHER ALMIGHTY) (A major—D major). The attributes of the Creator are discussed in invigorating, but dignified, polyphony. It will be noticed that at the outset the declaration of belief—'Credo in unum deum' are given threefold utterance in the high voices. In this movement Bach incorporates material from Cantata 171.

(14) ET IN UNUM DEUM (AND IN ONE GOD) (G major) is largely canonic—the alto voice succeeding the soprano to symbolize, according to Albert Schweitzer, the proceeding of the Son from the Father. The two oboi d'amore enrich the background together with the full body of strings. As in 'Domine deus' the end-lighting is dimmed to prepare for the grave mystery of:

(15) ET INCARNATUS EST (AND WAS BORN) (B minor), in which the five-part chorus, accompanied only by strings (the violins being in unison), gravely pictures the descent from heaven to earth. Chromatic shifts add to the general awe-ful effectiveness of the movement. This, however, is but preparatory to the greater mystery of

(16) CRUCIFIXUS (CRUCIFIED) (E minor—G major). It is possible to draw attention to the introduction of funereal flutes, to the use of the old procedure of chromatic ground-bass, to the wayward tonality—note the entries (Ex. 28), to the suspensory effects of the rests, to the

Ex. 28

[instrumental bass, showing the 'ground']

magical transformation to the last cadence in G major within which is contained the hope of the resurrection and faith in the ultimate victory of the sacrificial Saviour: it is not possible to make observation on the inner character of this tremendous utterance. This music was taken from the first chorus of Cantata 12 (*Weinen, klagen, sorgen, zagen*).

(17) ET RESURREXIT (AND HE AROSE FROM THE DEAD). Everybody bursts out singing in D major. And how? Listen to the sopranos (see Ex. 23).

(18) ET IN SPIRITUM SANCTUM (AND IN THE HOLY SPIRIT) (A major) for bass solo and two oboi d'amore. This is purely musical and not theological grace. 'Bach's method is more definite than Palestrina's, and more decorous than Mozart's; but in essentials it agrees with both these masters. If doctrine is beyond musical illustration, let us illuminate it with musical decoration.' In any case the unity of Bach is beyond the mere word-conditioned emblem of priestly aspiration.

(19) CONFITEOR (I ACKNOWLEDGE). As in the 'Kyrie' and the 'Gloria' Bach rounds the scheme of his gigantic 'Credo' with a movement of fitting dimension which serves also as summary to the whole. The first 146 bars in F sharp minor are accompanied only by organ (so we notice the necessity for a not too large choir), although further instrumentation was added by Carl Philipp Emanuel Bach: the movement is strictly fugal, in solemn tread—though with a quicker persistent pattern against it in the instrumental bass, with severe display of

inversion and canon. At bar 69 there is a *stretto* above a dominant pedal. After three bars the ancient plain-chant appears in the bass, to be imitated in canon at the fifth, after one bar, in the alto. Next the theme is more strongly set in the texture, for it is given to the tenors in long notes. So the music looks backward to the highest medieval standards of esoteric, and scientific, skill. This is a passage which shows in what way, as Schoenberg noted, Bach enlarged the rules of the old Netherlands composers.

In magniloquent contrast in mode is the expectation of the resurrection of the dead. Bach explores futurity in every way. An abstract of the harmonic movement in his 'Adagio' passage will serve to indicate the richness of the symbols (Ex. 29). Then to the finality of D major, the

Ex. 29

exhilaration of percussive rhythm, of clear, if florid, contrapuntal *joie de vivre*, of trumpet fanfares, and much ecstatic high register work for the sopranos.

(20) SANCTUS (HOLY). The previous movement takes us across the river. Here we stand within the Celestial City. All the forces are in action, but the music is not merely impressive, nor merely cheerful, nor merely exciting: it is engulfing. Study the texture and the rhythm, particularly the latter. This is the vastest commentary ever conceived on the ideas which lie within the word 'Sanctus'. The 'Sanctus' has the quality of holiness: it gives way to a brilliant end piece—*Pleni sunt coeli et terra gloria* (The heavens and the earth are fully of glory). The music rings with brilliance—notice the wreaths of thirds in the soprano part —and with gaiety, being in Bach's cheerful triple-meter pattern: it is the sublimation of eighteenth-century kingship. Bach understood this world and the next; the latter the better for a wide appreciation of the former. The choral writing in this movement is in six parts.

(21) OSANNA (HOSANNA IN THE HIGHEST) carries on where the previous movement left off. But the field spreads out for double choir. The antecedents of this piece add point to our comment on Bach's worldliness. The 'Osanna' is the opening chorus of the *Cantata gratuloria: Preise dein Glücke, gesegnetes Sachsen*. This cantata celebrated the accession of Augustus III as Elector of Saxony. It has been noted that

both Bach and Handel freely adapted music from one occasion to another and often crossed secular with sacred, but the aptness of music to the context and the propriety of artistic form to spiritual or philosophical idea makes the reference to arbitrary standards of 'secular' and 'sacred' irrelevant.

(22) BENEDICTUS (BLESSED): a tenor aria in B minor with violin obbligato after which the Osanna is repeated.

(23) AGNUS DEI (LAMB OF GOD): a contralto aria in G minor with a counter-melody in the unison violins. This is an adaptation of a melancholy movement in the 'Ascension Oratorio' (Cantata 11). At an earlier point in the Mass Bach considered the symbol of the 'Lamb of God': here he expounds his reflection in passionate, dramatic and harmonic melody.

(24) DONA NOBIS PACEM (GIVE PEACE TO US): this is a repetition of the 'Gratias agimus'. Its point here may be appreciated by reference to Aristotle: 'an end . . . is that which itself naturally follows some other thing, either by necessity, or as a rule, but has nothing following it.'

'MAGNIFICAT'

The St. Matthew Passion is greater than any Lutheran conception of the Passion and the Mass in B Minor ranges further than any doctrinal act of exposition. Both project the particular into the universal so that both stand outside the limits of place. One further work which has this quality is the Magnificat.

The Magnificat, the song of the Blessed Virgin, is a hymn of joy and it is round the experience of joy that Bach creates. This music also arises from the Christmas tradition. There are in fact two versions. The Magnificat was sung (in Latin) at Vespers at Christmas, Easter and Whitsuntide. At Christmas the concerted movements of the canticle were separated by hymns designed to relate the story of the Nativity. Bach's first setting (1723?) included these movements. They were, however, omitted in his revision for the other Festivals and the whole was transposed from E flat to D major.

Within its 600 measures (the Mass in B Minor contains 2,300) the Magnificat has much variety: (1) MAGNIFICAT (MY SOUL MAGNIFIES THE LORD), chorus in five parts; (2) ET EXSULTAVIT SPIRITUS (AND MY SPIRIT HAS REJOICED), aria for soprano II; (3) QUIA RESPEXIT (FOR HE HAS

REGARDED), aria for soprano I; (4) OMNES GENERATIONES (ALL GENERA-
TIONS), chorus in five parts; (5) QUIA FECIT (FOR HE HAS MAGNIFIED ME),
aria for bass; (6) ET MISERICORDIA (AND HIS MERCY), duo for contralto
and tenor; (7) FECIT POTENTIAM (HE HAS SHOWN STRENGTH), chorus in
five parts; (8) DEPOSUIT POTENTES (HE HAS PUT DOWN THE MIGHTY),
aria for tenor; (9) ESURIENTES (THE HUNGRY), aria for contralto; (10)
SUSCEPIT ISRAEL (HE HAS HELPED ISRAEL), trio for two sopranos and
contralto; (11) SICUT LOCUTUS (AS WAS SPOKEN TO OUR ANCESTORS),
chorus in five parts; (12) GLORIA PATRI (GLORY TO THE FATHER), chorus
in five parts. The orchestration is as in the *Mass* and there is much
similarity in outlook between the two works. Particular attention may
be drawn to the sweeping triplets of the 'Gloria' which anticipate the
handling of the 'Sanctus' in the *Mass*. The emotional range is from the
sweetness of (Ex. 30) and the warm sympathy of (Ex. 31) to the dynamic

shock of (Ex. 32). The brilliance of this first movement, which is

repeated in shortened form as the final movement, is an Italian
brilliance and reflects the acquaintance with Italian music which Bach
enjoyed at Cöthen. But within this modern style Bach could incorporate the ancient: thus the *tonus peregrinus* of the medieval church,
the melody for the Psalm 'When Israel came out of Egypt', points in
oboes the reference to Israel in the trio 'Suscepit Israel'.

    In performance the *Magnificat* will be discovered to have a tender
quality. That it is too strong, too 'masculine' as protested by Hubert
Parry, is an unreal evaluation, though sometimes the vigour of the

choruses is improperly translated into pompousness by the multiplica-
tion of voices. The theme is joy not power.

CONTEMPORARIES OF BACH AND HANDEL

At no period is the difference in distinction between the great and the
lesser masters so marked as in the period under review. And in no
branch of composition is this difference so obvious as in choral music.
As has already been suggested the seventeenth century was a revolutionary period in scientific discovery and in the cultivation of a
scientifically controlled attitude of thought. The eighteenth century
rationalized what had gone before. In music, the theories of the seventeenth century promoted a new melodic and harmonic scheme, to be
noticed in almost every work of the lesser masters. And, of course, a
rationalized plan dominated opera and, to a certain extent, oratorio.
Bach and Handel stand out because, although appearing more
'romantic' than their contemporaries, they were more perceptive in
analysis and more capable in synthesis. They, in fact, were the composers who alone could fill a large space of time with commanding
musical thought. There were, as has been shown, reasons of environment which had much to do with this. But this is not all. Both Bach
and Handel believed sufficiently in their respective missions that they
could withstand, if need be, the climate of popular opinion.

There is a good deal of choral music other than that of Bach and
Handel and of the same period which merits some attention. Much is at
least readily performable and, therefore, accessible to the choral society
which seeks novelty while wishing to skirt the greater hazards which
lie in the path of the adventurous. Some will show good composers
doing their competent best—the English anthems of William Croft,[1]
who was a fine composer of hymn tunes; of Maurice Greene;[2] of
William Boyce;[3] the Catholic church music of Antonio Caldara,
Johann Ernst Eberlin, and Niccolo Jommelli, all of which assisted in
nourishing the Austrian tradition into which Mozart and Haydn
were to come; the sober Passion music of Johann Theile.[4] Other music,
including much from the Italians, will show composers seeking easy

[1] See H. A. M., No. 268, *Put me not to rebuke.*
[2] See ibid., No. 279, *Acquaint thyself with God.*
[3] See *I have surely built Thee an house* (Novello).
[4] See *Passionsmusiken* of Theile and Sebastiani (D.D.T., Vol. XVII).

effectiveness and writing beneath their ability. Compare Telemann's *Der Tag des Gerichts* (see chorus in *Historical Anthology of Music*, Vol. II, No. 272) with the Bach *Passions* written at the same time. Or notice the decadent ease of Karl Heinrich Graun's *Der Tod Jesu*, which conformed successfully to the fashion of the time. Or see the choral works of Vivaldi which, effective though they are, compare neither with Bach or Handel nor the more intellectually strenuous religious music of an earlier period in Italian musical history.

A few works may be extracted from the huge body of early eighteenth-century choral music: a cantata by Zachau, an oratorio and part of a mass by Vivaldi, and Pergolesi's *Stabat Mater*.

Zachau's '*Herr, wenn ich nur dich habe*' is a convenient yardstick by which to measure the Bachian church cantata. It is a setting of part of Psalm 73. It has a grave sinfonia of ten measures to introduce a fine serious chorus, over which the academic tradition begins to brood. Zachau knows his Italian models, but he adds a pensiveness to his style which may be regarded as characteristically 'German'. A soprano solo, in the main key of A minor, follows. Zachau like his illustrious pupil Handel and like Bach—but in style somewhere between the two —selects the significant words for intensification: thus (Ex. 33). The

Ex. 33

ver - trau - - - - - - .en

bass solo, in C major, is introduced by a *ritornello* for strings. This is a fine, simple act of faith. The tenor aria—'Der Erden Stolz'—is a variation on that previously sung by the soprano, and the final solo number—for contralto—is, likewise, a variant of the bass melody. The whole is rounded off by an abbreviated version of the opening chorus. This is a solemn, well-proportioned piece of music and excellently suited both to its text and to its environment. It is a worthy example of what was known as the *kapellmeisterlich* style—the staid, correct, academic style associated with routine-bound provincial musicians.

Antonio Vivaldi was a Venetian, the son of a violinist in St. Mark's Cathedral. For the last thirty years of his life he was as *maestro de' concerti* in charge of music at the Ospedale della Pietà in Venice. His main significance in musical history lies in his extraordinary cultivation of the concerto form. He composed a number of operas and some church music. Of this latter some, coming in on the crescent of his newly appreciated instrumental excellence, has gained a place in contemporary performance. The *Gloria* may be set beside that from Bach's *Mass in B Minor* to appreciate the vastness of the latter. Vivaldi's work is a conventional setting of a conventional text. Although Vivaldi was a priest there is nothing in the work to suggest an intense study of the words. They serve to accommodate a bright party piece, in which much that is jejune is disguised by the competence of the manipulation. Vivaldi was a master of *timbre*, of the individual qualities of voices and instruments and thus always a pleasure to hear.

Like many Italian pieces of the period this is a collection of *mots justes* and it is difficult to escape the conviction that they have been heard before: thus (Ex. 34) (Ex. 35). Together with his cultivation of

the cliché Vivaldi went outside the normal field to seek a higher degree of expressiveness (Ex. 36). This is sensuously affecting and comes

within the spiritual connotation of the text.

Juditha Triumphans is really an excellent opera, although designated 'Sacrum Militaire *Oratorium*' and composed in 1711 for the benefit of the Ospedale della Pietà (thus in its original form the parts of Holofernes, of Holofernes' servant and of the High Priest were given to female voices).

The story of Judith is recounted in the *Apocrypha*: it offers magnificent opportunities for more than Vivaldi's picturesqueness. Judith goes to the camp of Holofernes to intercede for the Israelites. Holofernes is carried away by the beauty of Judith, entertains her with royal generosity and (foolishly) falls into a vinous stupor while protesting his love. Judith cuts his head off, takes it home and receives the gratulations of her people. Out of this Vivaldi draws the character of Judith and invests it with a voluptuousness that is characteristic of the secular Italian operatic tradition. Comparison between Vivaldi and Handel shows how greatly Handel's conceptions were enlarged by his studious use of the chorus.

The *Stabat Mater* of Pergolesi is not far removed from this modest style. Pergolesi, however, adapts the style to one aspect of his subject and the Mother of Christ is enveloped in passionate love and sympathy. It is not the way of everyone so to address the Virgin Mother; but it is Pergolesi's. This is the manner in which Pergolesi invokes her (Ex. 37).

Ex. 37

San - cta   Ma - ter ˌ i - - - - stud a - gas - - - i - stud a - gas,

Here he implores her aid (Ex. 38). At an earlier moment she is seen

Ex. 38

In - flam - ma - tus___ et   ac - cen-sus   Per te,___ Vir-go___ sim de - fen-sus

viewing the agony of Jesus (Ex. 39). It is the ideal of beauty which

Ex. 39

Quae moe___ re - bat___ et do - le - bat,___ et do - le - bat,

extends throughout this work. Yet the brief choruses are compelling and epigrammatic. It is, perhaps, the economy of Pergolesi which is remarkable, for his fertility in melody is familiar from his other works. The first chorus holds out dissonant suspensions. The third chorus—'O quam tristis'—is a study in the effective disposition of rests and diminished seventh chords. The same technique is used again in 'Quando Corpus'. The two fugal choruses 'Fac ut ardeat' and the concluding 'Amen' are lithe examples of the form. The ultimate effect of the work, perhaps, is to encourage luxuriance in grief. The Calvary scene is, so to speak, publicized and we are tempted to gaze at rather than to feel with. Giovanni Paisiello complained that the *Stabat Mater* was written in the style of a comic opera. Without necessarily accepting Paisiello's opinion (which was shared by Giovanni Battista Martini) as absolute it is worth remembering, as also is the sentimentality which long surrounded Pergolesi, who died at the early age of twenty-six.

4

The Period of Haydn and Mozart

LOCAL CONDITIONS IN AUSTRIA

WHEN Bach died Haydn had already embarked on his career as composer, for by 1750 he had written his first extant Mass and string quartet. Handel overlapped Mozart, born in 1756, by three years and it was only three years after that that Mozart composed (under his father's ambitious direction) his earliest pieces. Yet there is little evident continuity between the great masters of the first half of the eighteenth century and those of the second. We have seen that Bach—though well aware of and indebted to the Italian tradition—made himself essentially a local, Leipzig composer, adapting his style and his genius to the needs of his environment; and that Handel, proceeding from the advanced Italian technique of the late seventeenth and early eighteenth century, conformed to the looser, but none the less distinguishable, expectations of the English.

The glory of Europe formerly was in the cultural independence of many regions—Venice, Florence, Rome, Dresden, Munich, Vienna, Mannheim, Salzburg, Paris. The reader should turn to the elegant enthusiasm of Dr. Burney's *Travels* (*The Present State of Music in France and Italy*, London, 1773, and *The Present State of Music in Germany, the Netherlands and United Provinces*, London, 1775) to appreciate the genius of each place that he visited. The Masses of Haydn and Mozart vary in manner and in point of view not only because of the exploratory character of each of these composers but because conditions at Esterház and Salzburg called forth different attributes. Similarities between the composers were due to a certain technical community of outlook, to a reliance on certain masters held in esteem in Austria and, therefore, by Haydn and Mozart, but subsequently largely forgotten.

We will, for the moment, leave aside such works as Haydn's oratorios and Mozart's Masonic music and examine the background to their main choral works, which were for the Catholic Church. And here is one reason (among many) for deviation from the Protestant

Bach and Handel, for Haydn and Mozart, in their ways, were devout members of the Catholic Church.

As a choirboy at St. Stephen's Cathedral Haydn was aware of the 'ancient style' of Palestrina and Lassus—composers who by 1738, or thereabouts, were reserved for the penitential seasons of the Church's year; of the Masses of Johann Fux, the great teacher of counterpoint; of Antonio Caldara, a pupil of Legrenzi who settled in Vienna; of the Bohemian Franz Tuma; and of Johann Reutter, Kapellmeister of St. Stephen's and Haydn's own teacher. Mozart, whose early career centred on the archiepiscopal music of Salzburg (where his father—Leopold —was second Kapellmeister (1763)) was brought up to the broad and sonorous sacred music of the local composers: Johann Eberlin, Anton Adlgasser, Michael Haydn and Leopold Mozart himself. Michael Haydn was brother of Josef, by whom he was regarded as a distinguished composer of church music. Certainly Michael was more conventional but whether he was 'better' or not leads directly to the crux of the difficulty which faced eighteenth-century Catholic composers.

There was the new, demonstrative, music of the age on the one hand; the old, unyielding liturgy, which demanded, as always, that music should be subordinate to the action and intention of the form of worship on the other. Outside the services of the Church were the blandishments of oratorio, more and more a thinly disguised form of entertainment. Beyond were the adventures of symphony and opera. Opportunities for composers were wider but the devout called a halt in the matter of a suitable 'church style'. Certain conventions obtained, in respect of imagery and in the use of counterpoint. But at best there was an unsatisfactory compromise and at worst considerable dulness. The conflict between the arbitrary standards set up during the seventeenth and eighteenth centuries and the natural flow of musical inventiveness has never finally been resolved, so that we still backwardly speak of 'sacred' and of 'secular' music while relying on false premises and misleading prejudices. Such premises and prejudices afflict our judgement of Haydn and Mozart. Haydn was too cheerful for church! As for the Masses of Mozart even so affectionate a Mozartian as Eric Blom finds himself obliged to apologize: 'In church music, for one thing'—he writes[1]—'it may fairly be said that Mozart was not specially interested.' And again: 'Many other composers of

[1] *Mozart*, E. Blom (pub. London 1935), p. 168.

the period wrote Masses artistically almost as good as Mozart's, if stylistically as inappropriate to their purpose. . . .' I would call attention to Alfred Einstein's spirited defence:[1]

'[Mozart's Catholic church music] surely cannot be called unliturgical. It always employs the full text of the Mass or liturgy; and only in individual cases does it encloud the understanding of the text by its use of "polytexture"—that is, by a simultaneous singing of different textual passages that according to liturgical precept should properly follow in succession. Mozart's church music, we repeat, is "Catholic" in a higher sense—namely, in the sense that it is pious as a work of art, and the piety of an artist can consist only in his desire to give his utmost. Otherwise the devout little pictures, the imitation Lourdes grottos, the besugared "Christ-childs" of the religious-goods industry would be more Catholic than Giotto's frescoes or Duccio's panels, and one of the boring "Nazarene" Masses or hymns by Ett or Aiblinger more Catholic than Mozart's *Misericordias* or *Ave Verum*. Furthermore, the Catholic quality of Mozart's church music, in the higher sense, consists not perhaps in any so-called and questionable dignity—a fitness for the interior of a Romanesque or Gothic church—but in its humanity, in its appeal to all devout and childlike hearts, in its directness. If one wishes to be "pure in style", one should certainly not perform it in a Gothic church and least of all in a nineteenth or twentieth century church; just as one should not perform the Organa of Pérotin or the Masses of Obrecht in a Rococo church. One can no more find fault with Mozart for writing Masses, vespers, offertories, motets, litanies and hymns in the spirit of his time than one can find fault with Giambattista Tiepolo for approaching his church pictures with the same artistic assumptions as those with which he approached his mythological or historical scenes. It was the ultra-cultured and Alexandrian nineteenth century that first cast this stone.'

The conclusions of the Church were issued in 1903 in a celebrated document—or *Motu Proprio*—issued by Pope Pius X.[2] The excellence of this document in many respects cannot be denied: but, like all such

---

[1] *Mozart, his Character, his Work*, A. Einstein (pub. London 1946), p. 321.
[2] See pp. 274. See also *Musical sacrae disciplina*, an Encyclical letter of Pius XII (1957).

'official' statements it is indifferent to exceptional circumstances. Only plainsong, music of the 'classical' era of Palestrina and 'approved' modern compositions untainted by theatricality were to be admitted into the service of the Church. Mozart and Haydn, therefore, came under the classification of theatrical and went out with the worst of the nineteenth century. (That is to say they should have gone out but the *Motu Proprio* has never attained its objectives, despite the benefits it has conferred on a revivification of plainsong.) I, for my part, would have welcomed an opinion from St. Francis, or St. Teresa or St. Philip Neri: I have an idea that they would have appreciated the church music of Mozart and Haydn, for they were saints of poetic perceptiveness.

SOME ITALIAN COMPOSERS

It must be admitted that the ill-repute into which eighteenth-century music fell among the ecclesiastical might be deserved in the case of many of the oratorios. These, as has been suggested, were but operas in disguise, without the epic quality which distinguishes the Handelian form, and without the choral element which was so important a factor therein. The more famous works—as has been noticed in the case of Vivaldi—were elegant display pieces and distinguished by brilliance of melody and scoring on the one hand and 'affecting' harmonic variety on the other. The complaint is not that the music is bad but that it had become stereotyped—exactly as in the characteristic Italian-style opera which provoked the reforms of Gluck. But there remains a great mass of liturgical music which should impress us and certainly impressed Mozart. Composers of the period who were noticed by Mozart were Antonio Caldara, Francesco Durante, Niccola Porpora (who had Haydn as disciple, servant and pupil), Leonardo Leo, Johann Hasse, Giovanni Battista Martini (the greatest teacher of his generation) and Niccolo Jommelli. These masters furnished the basis of the style on which the Austrians based theirs. Austria was the focal musical point of Europe in that these Italian and German traditions met and intermingled—as was noticeable even in the sixteenth century. Therefore the development of music in eighteenth-century Austria is of significance in appreciation of the great works of Beethoven and Schubert: the *Missa Solennis* is, one might say, the glorious justification of the years of endeavour to formulate a style which, while 'modern', was proper

L

to the philosophy of the liturgy. Of the Italians above-mentioned, the English scholar Vincent Novello has this to say in the introduction to his anthology *Fitzwilliam Music*:

> 'They lived when Sacred Music was much encouraged and studied, where it was performed with the greatest care and precision, and when its style though more elaborate, varied, and refined than that of the Ambrosian and Gregorian chants, had not exchanged much of its grandeur and solemnity for those ornaments which have been introduced in more recent times.'

Caldara was a pupil of Legrenzi, who was *maestro di cappella* at St. Mark's in Venice; Durante was a Neapolitan and teacher of Jommelli, Paisiello, Pergolesi, Vinci and others; Leo was organist of the royal chapel in Naples; Martini was *maestro di cappella* in the church of St. Francesca in Bologna; Jommelli was a church musician in Stuttgart; Hasse, an Italianized German, and Porpora (in opera, Hasse's deadly rival in Dresden) were world famous. The prevailing characteristic of the music produced by these men is clarity; this shows in the sharp definition of melody which while brilliant never becomes extravagant, in the ease and logic of modulation, in the relative directness with which words are set, and—above all—in the fine consistency of contrapuntal texture. We may instance Leonardo Leo's *Christus factus est* (Ex. 1) in which all the available harmonic resources are mobilized

to effect a mystical awareness; yet the two solo voices are not over-individualized. Or the opening of a 'Kyrie' by Clari to show (cf. 'Kyrie' of *Mass in B Minor*) how nearly Italian Bach often was in spirit, but also the growing simplification and codification of practice in respect of such movements (Ex. 2). Or a fine specimen of Durante

Ex. 2 Adagio (voice parts only)

at his most dignified (Ex. 3), in which neither plainsong nor Palestrina are forgotten.

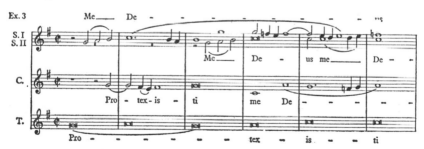

Ex. 3

On such models, which represent a great endeavour to preserve tradition without permitting it merely to ossify, the Austrians worked. It now remains to examine for whom and for what various purposes Haydn and Mozart wrote their great Catholic works. And here a third factor supervenes. We have already had the purely musical and the abstract ecclesiastical standards before us: but now a personal problem arises. That of the patron. One might serve God, but displease an Esterházy, a Schrattenbach, a Colloredo; and however well one pleased the former it paid no dividends if the Prince or the Archbishop decided (as in the case of Mozart at Salzburg) that resignation from service would be mutually beneficial.

LOCAL AUSTRIAN CUSTOMS

In general there were two types of Mass settings: those for the Mass for ordinary Sundays, and those for the High Mass of extraordinary occasions. In Austria the former (in which in general the 'Gloria' and 'Credo' were not divided sectionally with separate movements for the various clauses, and which often had no more than organ accompaniment) was designated *Missa brevis*. (The same term is applied to the Lutheran Mass, but in that case only the 'Kyrie' and 'Gloria' were employed.) There are some excellent examples of *Missa brevis* by Michael Haydn in particular, in which he combines plain utterance with much charm and some feeling (Ex. 4a and b), though his sim-

plicity can—see the trite *Te Deum* in D (1800)—descend to banality. He also introduces (from time to time) chorale tunes.[1] It is in his simple settings that one can realize his brother's respect for him as a church composer. Both Josef Haydn and Mozart were happier when the full resources of the festal Mass were available to them. The festal Masses in Salzburg were splendiferous, with the clergy in full canonicals, attended by the Archbishop's soldiery, with the ladies of the court

---

[1] cf. Josef Haydn's 'Heiligemesse'.

making (as is perhaps not to be wondered at) an opportunity for a dross parade, with the opera singers added to the normal choral resources of the Cathedral and with a full panoply of brass to augment the normal orchestra. In 1772 Hieronymus Colloredo succeeded Sigismund von Schrattenbach in the see of Salzburg. In more ways than one Colloredo caused trouble to the Mozart family. His character, as exhibited by Edward Holmes, makes it apparent that if there was a decline in spiritual standards in the eighteenth century musicians were by no means the cause but merely convenient scapegoats.

'In figure he was tall and commanding; much devoted to horses and field sports, and fond of being surrounded by a brilliant assemblage of ladies. He had not the least taste for music. . . . When it is added that with his irregular qualifications as an ecclesiastic he combined *hauteur* and moroseness of manner, the relation of the parties (Mozart being the other party) may easily be conceived; and although their acquaintance seems to have begun favourably, their good understanding was of short duration.'

Towards the end of 1776, and in a mood of disenchantment, Mozart wrote to Padre Martini (whom he had previously met in 1769) as follows:

'. . . a few days before my departure [from Munich] the Elector expressed a desire to hear some of my contrapuntal compositions. I was therefore obliged to write this motet [K.222, "Misericordias Domini"] in a great hurry, in order to have time to have the score copied for His Highness and to have the parts written out and thus enable it to be performed during the Offertory at the High Mass on the following Sunday. Most beloved and esteemed Signor Padre Maestro! I beg you most earnestly to tell me, frankly and without reserve, what you think of it. ["It has," replied Martini, "all the qualities which modern music demands, good harmony, rich modulation, etc. . . ."] . . . I live in a country where music leads a struggling existence, though indeed apart from those who have left us, we still have excellent teachers and particularly composers of great wisdom, learning and taste . . . I am amusing myself by writing chamber music and music for the church, in which branches of composition we have two other excellent masters of counterpoint, Signori Haydn [Michael] and Adlgasser. My father is in the service of the Cathedral and this gives me an opportunity of writing as much church music as I like. He has already served this court for thirty-six years and as he knows that the present Archbishop cannot and will not have anything to do with people who are getting on in years, he no longer puts his whole heart into his work. . . . Our church music is very different from that of Italy, since a Mass with the whole Kyrie, the Gloria, the Credo, the Epistle sonata,[1] the Offertory or Motet, the Sanctus and the Agnus Dei must not last longer than three-quarters of an hour. This applies even to the most solemn Mass said by the Archbishop himself. So you see that a special study is required for this kind of composition. At the same time, the Mass must have all the instruments—trumpets, drums and so forth. . . .'

Thus Mozart shows his serious intentions in regard to church music and, at the same time, the disabilities under which he laboured.

Haydn lived a less feverish and a more regular life at Esterház. It was in 1796 that the younger Prince Nicholas encouraged his Kapellmeister again to undertake the composition of Masses.

Haydn's Masses, however, were not all designed for Esterház. The 'S. Cecilia' Mass (c. 1773) which is long (too long) and ceremonial was written for a guild of musicians in Vienna. The 'Mariazell' Mass, so-called after the monastery of that name (1782) was commissioned by Anton Liebe von Kreutzner, as a thank-offering for his own ennoblement. Mozart's Masses were also for other occasions than the cathedral services. His 'Pater Dominicus' Mass (K.66) was composed for the ordination of Cajetan Hagenauer (in religion Pater Dominicus) and was first performed at his first Mass, celebrated in the Monastery of St. Peter on October 15th, 1769. For the same occasion Mozart wrote the 'Benedictus sit Deus' (K.117). The D minor Missa Brevis (K.65), which despite its accompaniment of two violins is a grave and conscientious work, was performed in the University Church in Salzburg, also in 1769, for the opening of a Forty Hour Prayer. In 1768 the C minor Mass (K.139) was for the consecration of Weisenhaus-Kirche am Rennweg, while the 'Veni Sancte Spiritus' of the same year was written for Father Parhammer's Orphanage. The 'Spaur' Mass of 1776

[1] Mozart had limited opportunities for writing chamber music for performance in church, for between the reading of the Epistle and Gospel a brief (sonata) instrumental movement was interpolated. This, though but one movement of a Sonata da chiesa, was called an 'Epistle sonata'. Mozart composed seventeen sonate all' epistola.

(K.258) was for another consecration—of Friedrich Franz Joseph Count von Spaur. The *Litaniae* (K.100 and K.125), in which is to be found some of Mozart's most mature writing, were not for public occasions, but private devotions. The '*Coronation*' Mass (K.317) of 1779 seems to be a more or less personal response to the coronation of the miraculous image of the Virgin, even though it was also designed for the Archbishop for Easter Day, 1779. The *Mass in C Minor* (K.427)— later to be turned into the oratorio *Davidde penitente*—was a thank-offering for Mozart's marriage to Constanze Weber in 1782. The last, most famous, most 'romantic' and most deeply felt and expressed of all Mozart's larger ecclesiastical compositions—the *Requiem*—was commissioned on behalf of Count Franz von Walsegg, who wished to pass it off as his own.

On other occasions we discover Mozart writing church music in Munich, in Padua (where Hasse acclaimed him as his own superior), in Milan (where the brilliant, 'operatic'—but how exhilarating and transcendently exultant concerto-style—'Exsultate, jubilate' was composed for the eminent contralto Rauzzini), in Paris; and always with an eye on local conditions and traditions.

'But thrown upon his own resources,' writes Holmes in praise of the Masses, 'for the style and form of his music, he seized upon every occasion that could be gained for the general advantage of the art. Thus accompaniment and modulation proceeded to the great improvement of dramatic music; towards which many of the masses may be considered as preliminary studies. The "Crucifixus", which is generally treated dramatically, often displays chromatic harmony, wrought up to the highest pitch of the awful and sublime; while the "Benedictus" exhibits those sweet cadences and "dying falls" which afterwards became so conspicuous in Mozart's operas. Nor were the interesting problems of counterpoint disregarded, as the frequent canons and brief fugues of those works evince.'

It is Mozart's abundant resourcefulness that first holds attention, so that any one department of his music appears to hold within it the character of all the others. Our immediate concern is with the masses. If we are reminded from time to time of concerto, of symphony, of opera, of chamber music, of the traditional polyphony, or in the case of Haydn, of folksong and even dance, then we may conclude that these composers proposed to serve the Church in no niggardly manner but with an abundance of their riches. Both composers were aware that music was attaining to a new degree of expressiveness, and that because the general imagination of the eighteenth century sought new spiritual ecstasies. Different approaches to 'expression'—particularly in so far as music inspired by words is concerned—are clear throughout the history of church music. Thus plainsong departed from its first severity and aspired towards the lyrical through *melismata*; the sixteenth century varied from the fifteenth in its greater flexibility and its more adroit handling of 'atmosphere'; the seventeenth expanded in musical colouring as well as in some special skills. Mozart and Haydn went both backwards and forwards: in some respects—handling of the chorus unit and verbal statement—they achieved a new simplicity; in others—musical structure and use of instruments—they pointed the way to the symphonic manner of Beethoven.

'MISSA BREVIS' (K.192)

Bearing in mind what has been said concerning the circumstances surrounding the composition of *Missae brevis*, we may examine more closely some representative works. First Mozart's *Missa brevis* in F (K.192) of 1774 as a characteristic production for a normal Sunday. The orchestration is simple—two violins, but no violas (for these were not always available), bass and organ with the vocal parts divided into solo and tutti. As far as the 'Sanctus' all the movements are in the tonic key. The 'Benedictus' as is not infrequent in this period (see also Beethoven's *Mass in C* and *Missa Solennis*) is in the subdominant. It is noticeable that the 'Benedictus' assumes an especial importance in eighteenth-century Masses and if it is set in apposition to the other sections as a slow movement to the remainder of a symphony that is one way of emphasizing an especial attribute of godhead: that of serenity and benediction. The 'Agnus Dei' is in the relative minor; the concluding 'Dona nobis pacem' in a brisk triple measure. Only twice in K.192 does the instrumental ensemble play independently, as a prelude to the 'Kyrie' and the 'Agnus Dei'. It will be noticed that gay or 'galant' phrases in the violins recur—as they do in *opera buffa* also—in the first three movements to tighten the musical structure. It is conceivable that (Ex. 5)—the motiv that rides behind the 'Kyrie' or (Ex. 6)

which is behind the 'Gloria' may be considered 'secular'; but is there not a particular significance in this contrast (Ex. 7), in which the

operative word expands momentously through harmonic energy? In this style of writing for the *Missa brevis* the text is delivered without instrumental intermission, relief from monotony being mostly achieved by antithesis of solo and tutti. The general search for design and proportion gives the opening choral theme (soprano only) of the 'Gloria' to the final 'Amen' in impressive octaves—(Ex. 8). In the 'Credo'

musical unity is achieved by the employment of this motiv—F G B flat A, a famous sequence for contrapuntal exercise in the sixteenth-century Roman school and apotheosized in the final movement of the *Jupiter* symphony. In this 'Credo' the phrase is inflected according to the text (Ex. 9) and subjected to various contrapuntal treatment (Ex. 10)

and at the end, when the strings have ceased, it is restated by the voices, simply, and as an embellishment of the final chord. Such fragments of melody as this are, so to speak, universal musical truths: here we find an eighteenth-century exposition. Just as old memories are stirred by this, so in the 'Sanctus' a descending and dominating scale passage in the bass puts us in mind of Bach's treatment of the same word.

'CORONATION' MASS (K. 317)

The Mass just discussed is a typical Mozartian *Missa brevis*. We may now turn to a more extensive work on a grander scale—the '*Coronation*' Mass of 1779. This work is in the popular Mass key—see the three Masses of 1776—the '*Credo*', the '*Spaur*' and the '*Organ-Solo*' Masses—of C major. It is opulently scored for strings, oboes, bassoons, horns, trumpets, trombones, drums and organ. In its use of solo movements the '*Coronation*' Mass has the character of a Cantata-Mass; but in the longer movements—'Gloria' and 'Credo'—we are aware of the far-reaching consequences of sonata-form. The 'Kyrie', the music of which is used again for the 'Dona nobis pacem', is an anticipation of Fiordiligi's 'Como scoglio' in *Cosi fan tutte*, while the melody of the 'Agnus Dei' is the Countess's 'Dove sono' in *Figaro*. It is, however, extremely doubtful whether the churchgoer would have been aware of such connections, for—as is so clear in both Bach and Handel—it is the context which gives significance.

The 'Kyrie' is a broad introduction to the 'Gloria' in three-part form. This develops symphonically round (Ex. 11) and (Ex. 12) and

the exchanges between voices, strings and woodwind are enchanting. The middle section of the 'Gloria' moves through a picturesque cycle of keys used for the sake of musical expression rather than for any pointed reference to the words. It is to be noticed, particularly in this and the next movement, that the charm and brilliance of the orchestration frequently makes the choral element subordinate. The same symphonic pattern as is found within the 'Gloria' fits the 'Credo', but here the words exert a powerful influence. Consider the originality, the beauty and the striking doctrinal force of the 'Et incarnatus' (Ex. 13) in which mystery and grace are spun through the muted

arabesques of the first violins, and then the gravity of the scoring at 'sepultus est', when the trombones, after two bars rest, re-enter *pianissimo*, while organ and strings remain silent and only the descending thirds of the oboes link what has gone before with what comes after. The cadence breaks into C major and the 'et resurrexit' is declaimed homophonically while the orchestra points the score with the conventional rising scale. The 'Sanctus' and the 'Benedictus', with (Ex. 14,) worked into a sonata rondo are still in C major and it is not until the 'Agnus Dei' that the key of the sub-dominant is reached. This no more than conventional soprana aria is touched with bitter-sweet harmonies at the words 'miserere nobis'.

'PATER DOMINICUS' MASS (K.66)

It is interesting to compare this Mass (K.317) with that of 1769 composed for the ordination of Cajetan Hagenauer. The later work takes less time in performance (of the former Pater Dominicus remarked 'Duravit Missa supra duo horas' ('The Mass lasted for more than two hours')) but sounds more impressive, and more spacious. In K.66 the music is more disparate—from (Ex. 15) to (Ex. 16), from the pretty subdivision

of the early part of the 'Gloria' to the magisterial fugue 'Cum sancto spiritu'. Archbishop Colloredo's insistence on half-hour Masses was by no means unhelpful to the composer. The antiphon 'Benedictus sit Deus' (K.117) which was the offertory for the *'Pater Dominicus'* Mass (a *sinfonia* in form) is again ecclesiastically interesting for the final section is constructed on this psalm tune (Ex. 17) against which is set an

instrumental figure of great vivacity—the usual practice of Mozart who might be thought thus to hint of two worlds, of the spiritual and the material.

It may, perhaps, be said that all composers who have written liturgical Masses have found fuller and more characteristic expression in church music which is not so intimately allied with sanctuary activity. Thus Mozart shows more of his own nature in the *Vesperae de Dominica* than in the '*Coronation*' Mass. Both works were composed during the same year. The exploratory character of the Vespers (and also of the *Vesperae solennes de confessore of* 1780) recalls the originality of Monteverdi's *Vespers*. In both sets of Mozart's *Vespers* there is more independence than in the Masses which have been discussed. The movements of the first set are in these keys: C major ('Dixit Dominus'), E minor ('Confiteor'), B flat major ('Beatus vir'), F major ('Laudate pueri'), A major (Laudate Dominum), C major ('Magnificat'); the movements of the second set in: C major ('Dixit Dominus'), E flat major ('Confiteor'), G major ('Beatus vir'), D minor ('Laudate pueri'), F major ('Laudate Dominum') and C major ('Magnificat'). The keys thus employed are more various than was generally the case in such music at that time. We are within sight of the Romantic period when the effect of widely contrasted tonalities was extensively explored. The way in which Mozart here chooses his keys may well appear to have some analogy with the choice of key of other late works. So we may compare with movements in the *Vesperae* the apparent darkness of D minor in the *Pianoforte Concerto* K.466, the warmth of E flat as in *Symphony* K.543, the pastoral sensibility in the A major *Violin Concerto* K.219 and the *Clarinet Concerto* K.622. But tonality is but one aspect. In the Vespers there is a wide emotional range explored in every possible way: the fugal movements in D minor are, again, reminders that Mozart—not fully aware of the significance of J. S. Bach until the last years of his life—was, in his own right, a magnificent master of strict contrapuntal expression. The 1779 'Laudate pueri' starts in strict canon; that of 1780 is based again on a conventional motiv (as used by almost every seventeenth- and eighteenth-century composer and by Mozart in the 'Kyrie' of the *Requiem*) which is worked out with the aid of such 'learned' devices as inversion and stretto. (One should compare the stiff exercises—K.85 and 86—which Mozart worked for Martini in Bologna to realize that even Mozart needed more than intuition and innate genius to accomplish his ends.) Of the Vespers Dr. Einstein writes 'Anyone who does not know such settings does not know Mozart.'

At this juncture we may turn, for the time being, to the Masses of Haydn. My own introduction to this branch of Haydn was by way of the 'St. Nicholas' Mass. Of this the 'Benedictus' is one of the most perfectly beautiful pieces of music ever written (Ex. 18a). The whole

Mass is an idyll and the character is outlined at once in the volutes of the 'Kyrie' (Ex. 18b). The 'St. Nicholas' Mass was composed for the

name-day of Prince Nicholas of Esterházy (December 8th) and it has associations with the Christmas season in two directions. Now the lyrical music of this work is enchanting; the movements which should otherwise be significant are not so. In his church music Haydn could easily run out of inspiration and appear at a loss. His defence of his deficiencies as an ecclesiastical composer (which were pointed out to him not infrequently) ran as follows: 'At the thought of God my heart leapt for joy, and I could not help my music's doing the same.'

The main differences between the early Masses of Haydn and those of Mozart are these: Haydn is, on the whole, nearer to contemporary south German/Austrian practice, so that it is only isolated movements which are at all personal in character; he was more interested in purely instrumental problems and not concerned more than superficially with the significance of the individual words of the text; his melodic material as supplied to the voices is frequently trite. Were it not for the instrumental layout much of this music would be dismissed as naive. It may, of course, be recalled that Haydn's peasant antecedents did not fit him for intellectual appreciation of the philosophic concepts expressed in the Mass, whereas Mozart, living in an atmosphere of knowledge and sophistication, was predisposed to such appreciation. It is noticeable, for instance, that Mozart avoids the practice (forbidden by the Church but indulged in rather generally as a time-saving device) of setting different clauses of the text simultaneously—so as, of course, to make more sense of the words. Haydn uses the device in the early F major *Missa brevis* (*c.* 1750) and in the *Missa Sancti Joannis de Deo* (the 'Little Organ Mass' of *c.* 1770).

The *Missa brevis* is, perhaps, the first extant work of Haydn and is scored for the minimum resources of string ensemble (without violas), organ, chorus and two solo sopranos. In general Haydn followed Austrian tradition in contrasting the two solo voices (often oscillating in rather pointless flurries of thirds) with the *tutti*, in a similar manner to the *concertino—concerto* antithesis of the instrumental concerto. The *Missa in honorem Beatissimae Virginis Mariae* (*c.* 1766) adds horn, bassoons (which normally played the bass part throughout) and two English horns to the score. But what distinguishes this work is the exciting, written-out, organ part which makes the Mass in effect an organ concerto. Except occasionally the text of this Mass might not be present at all, since the impressiveness of the work is almost entirely dependent on the exhilarating flourishes of the instruments.

The next Mass—*Missa Sanctae Caeciliae* (*c.* 1769–73)—is also on a large scale. Its festal character is underlined by the use of trumpets and its composition for a company of musicians encouraged Haydn to some fine, bold and extensive fugal writing, notably in the concluding section of the 'Kyrie' and in the 'Gratias agimus'. In this Mass Haydn has something of a field day with the solo voices and the athletic sixteenth notes which surround the name of Jesus in the 'Quoniam' may well be dismissed for their extravagance. The *Missa Sancti Nicolai* (1772) is oustanding among the earlier works because of its simplicity and its sincerity. The strings still preserve their brilliance, but this is softened and the scoring is beautifully radiant through the introduction of horns. The music of the 'Kyrie' is repeated for the 'Dona nobis pacem' and this repetition ensures that the conclusion of the work is free from the all-too-general frivolity in triple time which is the normal conclusion of a Haydn Mass.

In the 'Mariazell' Mass (or *Missa Cellensis*, 1782), with a fine opening movement and an impressive tenor solo for the 'Incarnatus est', with an extensive key range leading to the choral entry in C minor for the 'Crucifixus', Haydn borrows a movement from his opera *Il Mondo della Luna* (1777) and transforms it into the 'Benedictus'. This practice of self-quotation becomes less frequent as the eighteenth century progresses and in later works where Haydn falls back on the practice he does it—as in the *Heiligemesse*—with deliberation. The 'Mariazell' Mass is the last of the 'first period' of Masses. The next to appear—the *Missa in tempore belli* ('Paukenmesse')—is of a new age and shows the goal towards which Haydn was consistently aspiring.

We may turn aside for a moment to consider the *Applausus*, written in 1768, for the installation of a new prelate in the monastery of Gottweig. Haydn was not able to be present at the performance of this work. Therefore he sent a meticulous list of instructions for the Kapellmeister's information. Some salient points may be extracted (and their point may well be considered in contemporary performance):

'The composer asks that his indications of tempo be carefully observed and that, in accordance with the festive character of the text, the allegro be taken a little faster than usual.'

'The composer requires the dynamic signs to be strictly observed and points out that there is a great difference between piano and pianissimo, forte and fortissimo, crescendo and sforzando.'

'He requests a good and slow diction of the soloists, so that every syllable may be understood.'

'He hopes that at least three or four rehearsals be given to his composition.'

LATE MASSES OF HAYDN

The importance of the right tempo, of dynamics, of adequate rehearsal, was a new idea in the 1700's. In the later Masses (as, of course, in the symphonies) the importance of all these details becomes considerable and, perhaps, we may be allowed to mitigate the baldness of some of Haydn's earlier choral writing by understanding the effect of such music when 'interpreted' by the composer. The 'Paukenmesse' ('Kettledrum' Mass) is aware not only of the liturgy but of the events of the world outside the Church. This is a Mass which is both Revolutionary and revolutionary. The orchestra reaches a new independence in this last period, so that the dramatic use of trumpets and drums in the 'Agnus Dei' may be seen as anticipatory of Beethoven. Indeed the spaciousness of design, the confidence with which Haydn finally throws over the casual conventions which diminish the stature of his earlier church music in favour of dramatic effectiveness and symphonic architecture, the powerful mastery over the chorus so that they, too, are imbued with the restlessness, the dynamism, the exploratory sense of the 'Romantic' outlook, all become increasingly apparent. It is not only the fertility of Haydn that is remarkable, but also his genius for originality. The trumpets and drums of the 'Agnus Dei' of the 'Paukenmesse' have been noticed. Also to be noted is the intensification of the 'et' in 'et incarnatus est', which is expanded through a diminished seventh, sung *forte*, before the miracle of the Incarnation is stated *piano*. In this Mass as in the 'Heiligemesse' of the same year Haydn's lucid counterpoint is seen at its best. Indeed in these works—see the canonic writing in the 'Credo' of the 'Nelson Mass' and the 'Incarnatus' of the 'Heiligemesse'—polyphony becomes more important. The 'Heiligemesse' is so-called because the inner parts in the 'Sanctus' sing the melody of the Lutheran hymn 'Heilig, heilig'.

There is only one Mass by Haydn in a minor mode—the 'Nelson' Mass of 1798. It is said that the trumpet calls at the end of the 'Benedictus' celebrate Nelson's victory of the Battle of the Nile. (In commemoration of the same event Haydn also composed his aria— 'Lines from the Battle of the Nile'. It may also be mentioned that Nelson and Lady Hamilton, a great disciple of Haydn, paid a visit to Esterház in 1800.) The 'Nelson' Mass—*Missa in Augustiis*, or 'Imperial' Mass—has been a favoured work in England since the sacred music of Haydn was introduced into England by C. I. Latrobe, a Moravian minister and a great devotee of Haydn, and Vincent Novello at the beginning of the nineteenth century. It is, indeed, an impressive work, exemplifying Haydn's capacity in his later style for integration of solo and chorus. The 'Kyrie' is a noble, sombre movement in which the

M

dramatic feature (Ex. 19), later to be made immortal in the Ninth

Symphony, strikes an urgently humanistic note. In his later works Haydn was influenced by Mozart: this passage from the 'Kyrie', for instance, recalls the *Requiem* (Ex. 20). The opening movement of the

Ex. 20

'Gloria' has the manly affability of the cheerful choruses of *The Creation*. It was on hearing this sort of melody that the English composer James Hook accused Haydn of borrowing his ideas. The 'Qui tollis' section is a masterly piece of craftsmanship and conspicuous for the brief choral interjections in the broad line of the bass solo (Ex. 21)

Ex. 21

and for the felicity of the instrumentation. The remaining movements have grandeur but are too much designed to four-square rhythmic figures which choral singers often present in solidity and unconcern. The *Theresienmesse* was named (probably) after the Empress Maria Theresa—second wife of Francis II of Austria. The most notable movement here is the vast 'Kyrie' 'which can be roughly likened to (the shape of) a palindrome or reversible word of five letters, say, minim '[1] But the tremendous power of the 'Gloria' should also be considered. In 1801 Haydn linked two traditions in his 'Creation' Mass (*Schöpfungsmesse*), for from his oratorio music he borrowed the melody of the *allegro* of Adam and Eve's duet in *The Creation* for the 'Qui tollis'. An organ solo reappears in this Mass to add naturalistic symbolism to the 'Incarnatus'. One more Mass came in 1802—the *Harmoniemesse* or 'Wind-Band' Mass. Here again is a fine 'Kyrie'—a vast choral expression of first movement sonata form. The generally strong influence of instrumental forms is evident throughout the Masses of Haydn and the 'Benedictus' of the Wind-Band Mass is also an example of sonata form.

MISCELLANEOUS WORKS OF HAYDN

In the Masses one may be captivated by Haydn's orchestration, by his melodic happiness (which may sometimes derive from folksong), his striking and original dramatic gestures; impressed by the general scope of his large-scale movements and the imaginative changes of his vivid harmony; or entertained by the child-like diversions which, in triple measure, dance unselfconsciously heavenward. But this is not music of the highest order, despite that Beethoven would have been the poorer without its frequent example. Hardly ever does a Mass make a unity. We may, then, admit Edward Holmes' judgement to be sound, even though his generalities clearly admit of many exceptions.

'Haydn's Masses, though mostly written for more complete orchestras than Mozart's, and more equally finished, do not contain the same inspirations of genius. In the sublimity of the "Sanctus" and the angelical character of the "Benedictus" he falls short in comparison; nor are his "Kyries" generally so beautiful. The religious elevation expressed by Mozart in harmonies and modulation which raise the soul on wings is deficient in the genius of Haydn—or he so seldom reaches it that when he does it is an accident. He had little of melancholy in his nature; and he seldom attains to grandeur. His melodies, however, possess sweetness,

[1] See *Two Haydn Masses*, Rosemary Hughes, *Musical Times*, June 1950.

elegance and tenderness; his accompaniments abound in resources of fancy; and the charm and effect of his part writing is not to be excelled. As a fugue writer he was Mozart's equal. These composers of kindred soul on many points, appear to differ in the Mass thus— Mozart has the superiority in grandeur and in poetic sentiment, but his great movements are found at intervals; Haydn maintains excellence at a more uniform rate, and displays throughout a more careful finishing.'[1]

There are other Latin works of Haydn briefly to be considered. In 1775 he branched into Italian oratorio with *Il ritorno di Tobia*. This old-fashioned work—with its *da capo* arias—has good choruses, of which one—*Insanae et vanae curae*—is frequently revived. In 1785 Haydn was commissioned to compose seven orchestral adagios as interludes for the Three-Hour Service on Good Friday at Cadiz Cathedral. This sequence (which is more often performed in its string quartet version) is the most sublime example of Haydn's religious devotion, for within the limits of his wordless medium he strikes terror and awe and inspires pity and kindness in the most direct and economical manner. In fact, Haydn, relieved from the immediate necessity of considering texts which were so frequently taken for granted, is able to concentrate exclusively on the expression of his own personal feeling. 'We are able,' wrote the *Musikalische Realzeitung*, 'to guess in practically every note what the composer meant to convey by it.' In 1796 Haydn, in collaboration with Gottfried van Swieten, prepared an oratorio from the *Seven Last Words*. A work which always repays performance is the fine *Te Deum* of 1800. Mature but direct in cheerful adoration it exemplifies the nature of one who 'wherever he thought on God, could only conceive of him as a king infinitely great, and infinitely good . . . this last quality of the divine nature inspired him with such confidence and joy that he could have written even a *Miserere* in *tempo allegro*'.

'REQUIEM'—MOZART

Haydn sweeps forward into the Romantic movement. But, in the last resort it is Mozart who, seeing beyond the technical and entertaining

---

[1] See *Musical Times* between 1852 and 1858 for Holmes' essays on the masses of Mozart Haydn and Beethoven.

the metaphysical, reaches the heart of Romantic mystery in his unfinished *Requiem*. The circumstances surrounding this great work are not unfamiliar. They are recapitulated, for their strangeness provides an apt setting. In May 1791 Mozart, poor and also in poor health, was commissioned by Emanuel Schikaneder to compose music for an opera—*Die Zauberflöte* (*The Magic Flute*). While engaged on this work, in July or August,

'the composer was one day surprised by the entrance of a stranger, who brought him a letter without any signature, the purport of which was to inquire whether he would undertake the composition of a requiem, by what time he could be ready with it, and his price. . . . On the departure of the stranger (an emissary from Count Walsegg) he fell into a profound reverie, then, suddenly, calling for pen, ink and paper, began to write. He had not proceeded far, before his further progress was interrupted by the commission to compose the opera for the coronation of the Emperor Leopold, at Prague.' (Edward Holmes.)

This work, *La Clemenza di Tito*, was completed in quick time and the Mozarts, together with Wolfgang's pupil, Süssmayr, set out for Prague. Before their departure, however, Count Walsegg's messenger reappeared to enquire about the progress of the *Requiem*. Mozart had great success in Prague and in Vienna with *Die Zauberflöte*. But illness engendered dejection and melancholy provoked the idea that the *Requiem* was for himself. On December 5th, the *Requiem*, so far as it was completed, was performed in Mozart's sickroom—'himself taking the alto part. Schack[1] sang the soprano, Hofer,[2] his brother-in-law, the tenor, and Gal the bass. They had proceeded as far as the first bars of the 'Lacrymosa', when Mozart was seized with a violent fit of weeping, and the score was put aside.' Later in the day Süssmayr, who had been intimately associated with Mozart during these last few months during which the *Requiem* was taking shape, 'was standing by the bedside, and on the counterpane lay the "Requiem", concerning which Mozart was still speaking and giving directions. . . . As he looked over the pages of the "Requiem" for the last time, he said, with tears in his eyes, "Did

---

[1] Benedict Schack (1758–1826) was a Czech flautist and singer who created the part of Tamino in *Die Zauberflöte*.
[2] Franz de Paula Hofer (1755–1796), a violinist, was married to Constanze Mozart's elder sister Josefa.

I not tell you that I was writing this for myself?" ' A little more than two hours later Mozart died.

Two years after Mozart's death Count Walsegg conducted a performance of the work in memory of his wife. At Constanze Mozart's request Mozart's manuscript, which broke off after the eighth bar of the 'Lacrymosa', was completed by Süssmayr. After the 'Lacrymosa' (the voice parts of the 'Dies Irae' were complete and enough indication as to the scoring to make its implementation simple) Süssmayr had the voice parts and bass of the 'Domine Jesu' and 'Hostias'. For the conclusion of the 'Agnus Dei' Süssmayr followed adequate precedent in repeating music from the first movement. So far as documentary evidence is available Süssmayr alone was responsible for the 'Sanctus' and 'Osanna', the 'Benedictus' and the first part of the 'Agnus Dei'. It is impossible to believe that Mozart had not given reasonably firm oral instructions regarding the final form of his work. It may, on the other hand, be felt that two movements which lie well below the standard of the remainder of the Mass were hardly considered by him: they are the 'Sanctus' and the 'Osanna', the first an easy display of pompous effect, the second a jagged *fughetta* (a 'little fugue') in triple time. The work, as a whole, has affinities with *Die Zauberflöte*. In its metaphysical character the opera transcends opera and with its contemplation of the subject of death, from the Masonic aspect, is allied to the *Requiem*. Apart from certain thematic resemblances the principal other point of similarity lies in the dark-toned scoring, which includes two basset horns (a kind of alto-clarinet now obsolete), and three trombones, as well as two trumpets and the normal body of strings, bassoons and organ.

On June 21st, 1826, the remains of Carl Maria von Weber (himself a nephew of Mozart's wife Constanze) were buried in the Catholic Chapel of Moorfields, in London. For this occasion Mozart's *Requiem* was performed. Thomas Attwood, organist of St. Paul's Cathedral and a former pupil of Mozart, played the organ. An account of this funeral taken from *The Times* places the work in an appropriate setting and also impressively analyses the quality of the music:

'At half-past ten o'clock, the procession arrived. . . . Long before that time, those seats not appropriated to the subscribers had been gradually filling by persons attracted as visitors to so novel and interesting a ceremony, so that when the time arrived for its commencement, the whole of the interior, which it is said will

accommodate 2,000 individuals, was fully occupied. The pulpit
and the altar were covered with black cloth, and the gallery in
which the organ is placed was filled with vocal and instrumental
performers. On the altar and at the sides were large waxen tapers,
and lamps burning. The priest, the deacon, and sub-deacon, with
the acolytes (boys arrayed in the sacerdotal costume who assist on
such occasions), were waiting the approach of the body, and when
the coffin with the procession appeared at the grand entrance,
advanced to meet them. As the whole moved slowly through the
principal aisle, the band commenced the opening movement of
Mozart's *Requiem*. . . . The slow movement and fugue ("Requiem"
and "Kyrie"), which justly number among the masterpieces of
musical composition, were both sung in full chorus, and, deriving
an increased effect from the solemnity of the occasion, became
almost sublime. The mourners having taken their seats during this
performance, and the coffin being placed on a platform prepared
for its support, the priest chanted the introductory prayers pres-
cribed for the occasion under the Romish ritual, the responses being
made from the full choir in the gallery. The orchestra then commenced the celebrated *Dies irae, dies illa*, of the *Requiem*, which, with
the succeeding movements, is intended as a description of the day
of judgement. The appeals for mercy, the triumph of the just, and
the despair of the guilty, are depicted in glowing colours. The mind
of the composer was evidently absorbed by the awful nature of his
subject. As instances of musical power in this noble work, few
exceed the *Rex tremendae majestatis* and the dying away of the choir
into the passage *Salva me, fons pietatis*. But the *Recordare*, the movement *Confutatis maledictus* describing the punishment of the wicked,
and the *Lacrymosa dies illa* are characterized by the most original and
profound conceptions.

'After the last movement, the priest's functions, and those of his
assistants, were resumed, and at various intervals between other
portions of the *Requiem*, the burning of incense, the sprinkling with
holy water, and the elevation of the host, took place, attended with
various ceremonies and genuflexions, which when compared with
the noble simplicity of the Protestant form of worship, are viewed
with little complacency by one of that communion. After the
concluding pieces of the *Requiem*, the "Sanctus", the "Benedictus"
and the "Agnus Dei" had been performed, and the prayers brought

to a conclusion, the body was conveyed from the chapel into the vaults below, the orchestra playing the *Dead March in Saul*.'

The spectacle of the service of the Mass is impressive. It is intended to be impressive. The Church, rightly and wisely, has instructed the faithful, at all times, through the senses. In the highest significance of the word the performance of the liturgy is theatrical. In Mozart music reached such expressiveness that it could amply match the ritual pageantry. The argument against the so-called operatic style—provided always that the integrity of the style is maintained—is built on false, pedantic, narrowly Puritanical premises. The Requiem for Weber is a splendid example of the overwhelming character of this most solemn, splendid and awe-inspiring form of ceremony.

Considering the solemnity of the opening movement, lit by the homophonic passages—'et lux perpetua . . .', and finished by the stringent fugue set round an ancient fragment of melody; the frenzied alternations of timbre and the percussive battery of the 'Dies Irae'; the serenity of the 'Recordare'; the jagged dissonances of 'Confutatis' (but note the supreme atmosphere of resignation in which this movement concludes); the broken cries of the 'Lacrymosa' with the ineluctible *crescendi* which brings climaxes of the utmost poignancy; the chromatic evanescence (compare the exquisite motet *Ave Verum*) and the cadences of the 'Agnus Dei'; considering all these points of different tension within their dramatic and, therefore, religious context we must conclude that Mozart's genius is not to be confined to a liturgiologist's set of arbitrary rules, but that the latter should adapt his point of view. And the same must be said in respect of the masterpieces of Beethoven, Berlioz and Verdi; all of whose Mass music follows Mozart's lead in making such music not only particular but universal.

'THE CREATION' AND 'THE SEASONS'

It is not often that English music has affected that of Europe. In the case of Haydn, however, we should not have had two of his latest and greatest works but for the fairly established—at the end of the eighteenth century—cult of Handelian oratorio performance. It may be mentioned, in passing, that modern English oratorio—that is, oratorio performable by a choral society comprising women (in place of the boys who had drifted oratorio-wards from the choir stalls) and men—owed something to Thomas Arne for in his *Judith*[1] women first appeared in the chorus. Haydn was in London—whence he was invited by Salomon the concert promoter—in 1791 and in 1794. In 1791 he was present at a Handel Commemoration in Westminster Abbey which, if anything, was on a larger scale than that of 1784. Haydn was mightily impressed both by the prodigious tone of the 1077 performers and by the stature of the music. Grandeur, nobility, dignity: these qualities, perhaps, are not sought after by the contemporary composer unless for an occasion, but one attribute of the true Romantic of the late eighteenth century was the wish to encompass or at least to point with awe to vastness. Handel done up in a manner which was grandiose rather than grand (for Handel is 'grand' enough without a thousand performers) was an inspiration. 'This man,' said Haydn, 'is the father of us all.' And Beethoven not long afterwards said very much the same. The charm of Haydn's personality largely lies in his humility. He was, at all times, a learner. He was prepared to make use of what he had learned from Handel when the Baron van Swieten talked to him about oratorio. Haydn returned to Austria from London with a libretto, based on Milton's *Paradise Lost*. This libretto is said to have been given to him by one Lidley (who has no historically authenticated existence apart from this connection), who may have been, as Tovey recommended, Thomas Linley. Linley succeeded John Christopher Smith as co-director with John Stanley, of the oratorio performances at Drury Lane. There had, however, been[2] a libretto prepared for Handel, through Mrs. Delany's interest, on the same subject as *The Creation*, but Handel never set it. It may be, then, that this was the text which Haydn took back with him to Vienna, for van Swieten to translate, edit and augment.

And here we may consider van Swieten's part. He was a firm believer in the purpose of music to arouse feeling by representational method. In this he was, of course, not alone; for the eighteenth century, with the advantages of multi-toned orchestras, was continually looking for ways and means of conveying to music the naturalistic effects which were invading both painting and poetry. Van Swieten pointed out to Haydn 'that though some scattered passages of the descriptive genus were to be met within the works of the great masters, yet the harvest of this field remained on the whole untouched. He proposed

---

[1] This was in a revival at Covent Garden Theatre on February 26, 1773: the oratorio was composed in 1761.
[2] See *Handel*, Percy M. Young (pub. London 1947), p. 74.

to him to be the Delille[1] of music, and the invitation was accepted.'

Haydn spent two years over the composition of *The Creation*. When asked why he was taking so long he replied, 'I spend much time over it, because I intend it to last a long time.' The oratorio has fulfilled its composer's intention. It was completed in 1798 and during Lent it was performed for the first time at the Schwartzenburg Palace. Handel's *Messiah* and *Fireworks Music* gave the precedent for interruption of the normal traffic of a town for a musical occasion. *The Creation* followed precedent, for to allow easy approach to the Palace all the market stalls in the Neuer Markt had to be dismantled. Antonio Salieri played the pianoforte: the principal singers were Christine Gerardi, Matthias Rathmayr and Ignaz Sual: Haydn directed the performance with his hands—which was by then the normal way of controlling choral singers. The performance was vastly successful. The whole performance had been underwritten by the aristocratic friends of van Swieten at a personal cost of fifty ducats each. What *The Creation* meant to Haydn—as his 'greatest' work—is indicated by his after reference to his nervous condition at the performance: 'One moment I was cold as ice all over, the next I was on fire, more than once I was afraid I should have a stroke.'

The orchestral introduction to *The Creation* is a landmark in musical expression. It points the way to Schumann and Mahler and Schoenberg, for, in its 'Representation of Chaos', it is compounded of suggestions rather than statements, of feeling rather than form, of controlled (for Haydn could never lack control) lawlessness. Where do we go from here? (Ex. 22).

---

[1] Jacques Delille became famous by his translation of Virgil's *Georgics* (1769). As an original poet he was conspicuous in his appreciative description of the eighteenth-century cultivated landscape—see *Jardins* (1782), *L'Homme des Champs* (1800), etc.—and gained notoriety for his periphrastic style.

Eventually to C minor—for Haydn could not see even Chaos unending —but, for the time being, nowhere. When this music was 'contemporary music' the effect was thus analysed in the London *Monthly Magazine* of March 18th:

'Were it necessary to bring together farther illustrations of the superior powers of the new music, compared with that of the ancients, we might attempt a description of the Chaos, which opens this extraordinary composition.

It commences with all the known instruments, displayed in 23 distinct parts. After these are amalgamated in one tremendous note, a slight motion is made perceptible in the lower parts of the band, to represent the rude Masses of nature in a state of Chaos. Amidst this turbid modulation, the bassoon is the first that makes an effort to rise, and extricate itself from the cumbrous mass. The sort of motion with which it ascends, communicates a like disposition to the surrounding materials, but which is stifled by the falling of the double basses, and the *contra fagotto* [double bassoon].

In this mingled confusion, the clarinet struggles with more success, and the ethereal flutes escape into air. A disposition verging to order is seen and felt, and every resolution would intimate shape and adjustment, but not a concord ensues! After the volcanic eruptions of the *clarini* [trumpets] and *tromboni*, some arrangement is promised; a precipitation follows of the discordant sounds, and leaves a misty effect that happily expresses the "Spirit of God moving upon the force of the waters". At the first "Let there be light!" the instruments are unmuted, and the audience is lost in the refulgence of the harmony.'

The method in which Haydn was to compose *The Creation* was set down in a memorandum from van Swieten to the composer. In arranging the text van Swieten was influenced by the general manner of Handel's librettists and, wherever possible, he forsook the normal, contemporary German practice of weak paraphrase to employ the words of the Bible. In *The Creation* the character of the words directs, without dominating, that of the music. One instance of van Swieten's perception lies in his injunction regarding the first chorus: ' "Let there be light" must be sung only once.' The hammer-stroke method of dominant octaves, three times uttered by unaccompanied voices and resolving into a great choral-orchestral blaze of C major, is employed.

Thereafter Haydn, making his soloists and chorus collaborate rather than be set in antithesis, follows Handel's loose-limbed but plastic method of recitative and aria and arioso with laudatory and magnifical choruses of direct and economical texture furnishing the climaxes of splendour. It is these great choruses which have commanded the respectful affection of choralists for a century and a half. But affection has sometimes led to misconceptions. Take the matter of rhythms, for instance. Tovey[1] points out that most editions misprint $\frac{4}{4}$ for ₵ in the air-cum-chorus 'Now vanish before the holy beams', in 'The heavens are telling', and also in the air 'On mighty pens'. When Haydn is confined to a bar-by-bar squareness appropriate to a small-town brass band in the practice room his broad, sweeping phrases are lost. And it is in the wide range of the fluent patterns that his largeness of design is felt. Consider (Ex. 23), a wonderful, air-borne contrast to the harsh

Ex. 23

p A new cre - a - ted world, a___ new cre - a - ted world springs

up, springs up at___ God's com - mand

descents of (Ex. 24); or (Ex. 25), wherein is also Haydn's sense of

Ex. 24

f Des - pair - ing, curs - ing rage

Ex. 25

p

cresc.

The heav'ns and earth thy pow'r a - dore, the heav'ns and

earth thy pow'r a - dore, thy pow'r___ a - dore;

[1] See *Essays in Musical Analysis* (pub. London 1937), V, p. 124.

exploration and of endless mysteries; of the familiar lines of 'The heavens are telling', or of the brilliant trio and chorus 'Achieved is the glorious work'. We may compare such writing with the choral parts of *Il ritorno di Tobia*. In the early work there is brilliance in abundance— see the final quartet and chorus of Hebrews which stretches the chorus sopranos to top C twice on the one page—but there is not the fine balance between chorus and orchestra which distinguishes *The Creation*. In 'By thee with bliss', for example, the orchestra is used with dramatic —symphonic that is—power throughout and the vastness of the contrasts lead thought naturally towards the 'Choral Symphony' (a work of Beethoven which would hardly have taken the form it did take but for the choral-orchestral example of Haydn).

The orchestra employed in *The Creation*—double woodwind plus double bassoon; two horns, two trumpets, three trombones; timpani; and strings—was enormous for its period. (The orchestra for *The Seasons* was the same but without the double bassoon.) Haydn uses it to fullest effect. In the Introduction every instrument and every group is exploited. Muted strings enhance the strangeness of the opening; grouped woodwind Brahmsianly convey the mood from somewhere near E flat minor to D flat major in bars 20-21; fragments of bassoon, of oboe accompanied by rich lower-register or '*chalumeau*' arpeggios in the clarinets, of clarinet, and—most beautifully before the entry of Raphael's first recitative—of flute, show the gathering elements of creation; full brass emphasizes the sudden, flooding, 'light'. Then with the utmost felicity, for such passages possess their own independence and beauty apart from their delineatory aptness, flutes and clarinet may 'represent' lightning (No. 3); clarinet the song of the lark, bassoons that of the dove, or flute of the nightingale (No. 15); bassoon and double bassoon the 'heavy tread' of the dionysauri and ipthycauri or whatnot of No. 23, wherein also the brass makes brave display of the fullest glory of heaven. Or look at the 'blissfulness' of the pastoral oboe phrase, poised over string triplets, and the magnifical distant rumble of timpani in the duet and chorus 'By Thee with bliss'.

Alas! how often is the masterpiece of orchestration maltreated, because the whole work lies within the province of choral conductors. Of course Handel and Bach integrate their forces, so that chorus and orchestra become one (whereas the rank and file Italians of the eighteenth century frequently didn't) but Haydn brings to his work all the resources of the developed 'symphony' orchestra.

The Creation divides into three parts (compare the three 'Acts' of the Handel oratorio). The first deals with the first four days of Creation, the second with the fifth and sixth day, the third (with an orchestral prelude for 'Morning' in the Mendelssohnian key of E major) presents Adam and Eve. The narrative in the first two parts is given to Raphael (bass), Uriel (tenor) and Gabriel (soprano), all of whom have famous arias which balance between Italian effectiveness and Romantic sentiment.

From 1798 to 1801 Haydn was engaged, against the disabilities of age and increasing ill health, on a libretto based on a famous poem by James Thomson by the indefatigable van Swieten, who, as before, instructed the composer to pay due attention to all the opportunities for naturalist research. That Thomson in his *The Seasons* chose to depict Nature rather than comment philosophically, and that van Swieten made no alteration in this approach at least was fortunate: for it is the freshness of the objective method which stirred Haydn to his greatest resources of charm. Thomson's great poem was one of the most powerful influences towards a new Romantic approach in the eighteenth century. He was occupied on the poem and its revision for a matter of twenty years—from 1725 to 1744—and his intention was to counter the current idea that 'the proper study of mankind was man'. 'Where,' he wrote, 'can we meet with such variety, such beauty, such magnificence—all that enlarges and transports the soul? . . . But there is no thinking of these things without breaking out into poetry.' Haydn captured Thomson's attitude and his view of nature profoundly affected the out-of-door music of the nineteenth century—of Beethoven, Schubert, Schumann, Weber, Mendelssohn and even Wagner. The charm of Haydn lies in the fact that his music is of the eighteenth century. His scene painting is simple and naive, and in clarity of draughtsmanship recalls the attractive, formalized, engravers to be met with in students' drawing books of the period. To read Thomson, to see the model sketches of Bernard Lens, to hear Haydn: these are an insight into a new appreciation of the universe.

And yet:

'The oppression, the exhaustion of everything that breathes, and even of the plants, during the intense heat of a summer's day, is perfectly given. This very natural description concludes in a general silence. The clap of thunder, with which the storm commences, breaks this silence. Here, Haydn is in his element; all is fire, tumult, noise and terror. It is one of Michelangelo's pictures. At length the tempest ceases, the clouds disperse, the sun re-appears, the drops of water with which the leaves of the trees are charged, glitter in the forest; a charming evening succeeds to the storm, night comes on, and all is silent, except that, from time to time, the stillness is broken by the song of some nocturnal bird, or the sound of a distant bell. . . . The physical imitation is here carried to its height. But this tranquil scene forms, by no means, a striking conclusion of the summer, of the tremendous passage of the tempest.'[1]

In Haydn's lifetime there was a greater power in the music than we, now surfeited with stronger and greater volumes of sound, may appreciate. The passage which is described above is a magnificent example of Haydn's orchestral-choral mastery on the largest scale. The chorus is conceived as part of the total mass and should on no account be regarded by those who sing it as the dominant partner. This is a passage of scoring in which the extremes should be watched—the chordal fury of 'Hark! the deep tremendous voice', the country air contentment of the trio—'Now come the conflicts'; the use of the flute in the storm with fierce triplets dropping from the sky, and reflective clarinet which draws the evening scene to its end by metamorphosing the tremendous figure which at the outset of the storm had been sounded horrifically in the strings; the shudder of the chorus; the tonal range—from C minor to C major; to F major (for 'Now come the conflicts'), and, for the evening curfew, sounded by the horn, to a reposeful E flat.

Being considered as a sequel to *The Creation*, *The Seasons* not unnaturally has many affinities with the earlier work. For want of a better nomenclature it is called—or rather miscalled—an oratorio. It has, therefore, the same concessions to the Handelian norm in the big choruses—see the 'Endless praise' section of the great 'God of Light' chorus, a fine fugue in which the introductory rhythmic motiv is used with markedly instrumental effect and the final trio with double chorus—'Then comes the dawn'. (It may also be pointed out that Haydn's scene-painting, though not directly derived from Handel, bears some relation to the experiments of the earlier master, whose skill

<hr>

[1] *The Life of Haydn . . ., translated from the French of L. A. C. Bombet* (by William Gardiner) (pub. London 1817).

in this direction is frequently missed by those who look only for massiveness.) Haydn also had in the forefront of his mind the example of Mozart—in the airs in the instrumental interludes of the 'God of Light' which may be compared with the trombone utterances in *The Magic Flute*, in the subject of the fugue—'With power of produce' which is akin to that in the *Requiem* for the section 'Quam olim Abrahae'. From *The Creation* itself he borrowed the trio of soloists. The angels are changed, however, into Simon, a farmer (bass), Lucas, a countryman (tenor), and Jane, Simon's daughter (soprano). As in *The Creation* he makes enchanting use of solo and trio in apposition to and in conjunction with the chorus. It will have been noted that the storm lies in C minor—a symbol of turbulence with Beethoven also—and that this is the key of the 'Chaos' Introduction to the earlier oratorio. This key is the setting for the Introduction to the last part of *The Seasons*— 'Winter: the introduction paints the thick fogs at the beginning of Winter.'

There are, however, new devices in the choral structure. Haydn lightens the texture, by gay rhythms which ask for great flexibility of treatment—see 'Come, gentle spring' (the parent of many a nineteenth-century 'part-song') 'Hark! the mountains resound!' and 'Joyful, joyful, the liquor flows'; and by contrasts, as in each of these choruses, between high voices and low voices.

The Seasons was first performed at the Schwartzenburg Palace on April 24th, 1801. It was twice repeated during the following week. On May 24th it was performed at court, with the Empress singing the soprano solos. Five days later it had its first public performance in the Redoutensaal. The comment of the correspondent of the *Allgemeine Musikalische Zeitung* was 'Silent reverence, encouragement and loud enthusiasm alternated, for the powerful appearance of colossal visions, the immeasurable abundance of splendid ideas surprised and overwhelmed the boldest expectations.'

5

The Nineteenth Century 1

THE GROWTH OF CHORAL SOCIETIES

THE complete History of Music in Education still remains to be written. When it is written (provided the hand is competent and the mind discriminating) it should make fascinating reading. And no part of it will be more exciting than that which deals with the nineteenth century. For in the nineteenth century many tongues that were formerly dumb—in Britain, America, Germany and the Scandinavian countries—were unstopped and music became not merely a distant delight to, but an activity for, the many. In the main the greatest activity was choral. And, for the most part, choral music thrived most in industrial communities, in large cities, and (in Britain) among the members of the new nonconformist societies. English choral music, which had hitherto supported its reputation on a respectable rather than brilliant tradition of cathedral and parish choirs, achieved high technical excellence; German choral music developed prodigiously (and for this development the genius of Mendelssohn should be recognized); and in America the foundations of a whole new structure of music were laid. Choral music no longer was confined to the chancel, and great new halls were erected to accommodate the huge choirs that symbolized, in one way, the Revolutionary aspirations towards at least equality and fraternity. The symbol of the symbol surely was the 'Choral Symphony'.

Some material considerations assist in assessing the social setting of nineteenth-century choral music. Throughout the eighteenth century the great corpus of church music sung by church musicians represented two-thirds of the whole of choral music, and the remaining third, consisting of oratorio and various forms of occasional music, was eclectic in that its performance called only for a selected—and more often than not—professional corps of executants. Rather low down in the social scale were fraternities, stimulated to activity by coffee and mellowed by wine into easy acceptance of the merely convivial, which preserved something of the tradition of *a cappella* in anything but an *a cappella* atmosphere—by singing glees and catches and travestied madrigals—and classicized their function by promoting such glorious titles as the Society of Apollo. Let us, however, not regret the good cheer of our eighteenth-century choralists; for pleasure in companionship is one of the great contributions of music to national, and sometimes international, amity. Though in saying this we are perched precariously on the stairway that leads to the path of good intentions. Pleasure for the performers has wrecked many a promising composer's career: see Sterndale Bennett and Gade, Sullivan and Gounod, Spohr and Cornelius. The truth is that the choral societies of Europe and America have been responsible for much of the worst music of the nineteenth century;[1] while the greatest works of that age have tended to defy the lowest-common-denominator appreciation of so many committees of management. Yet the start to the nineteenth-century tradition was most propitious.

It has already been represented that Leipzig in the days of Bach enjoyed a virile—if not always contented—communal musical life in which the churches, the civic body and the University were interdependent. In 1743, and under the direction of Johann Friedrich Doles —himself a pupil of Bach—the Gewandhaus concerts (so-called because given in the Gewandhaus, the ancient market-hall of the Leipzig linen merchants) were established. These were early experiments in providing a more genteel musical appreciation by private and middle-class enterprise. Their perpetuation was due to the support and enthusiasm of the merchants and the professional classes as well as to the integrity and skill of a succession of enterprising directors. Chief among these was, of course, Felix Mendelssohn who made Leipzig in the first half of the nineteenth century a world-centre of music. But the chief concern was orchestral music and it was not until 1854, when the Riedel-Verein was formed with the laudable intention of 'popularizing' (if that is the right word) the *Mass in B Minor*, that choral music was really independent of the great churches of the city.

In Berlin, where culture developed from the time of Frederick the Great with some self-consciousness though with characteristic efficiency, our first concern is with the Singakademie. This, founded in 1791,

---

[1] cf. *A Short History of Cheap Music* (pub. London 1887), p. 27. 'The standard of taste not being very high among the people, the absence of discriminating power among audiences in general gave rise to careless and even to bad work in what were supposed to be high-class performances. Singers and performers who had been well trained, instead of persistently endeavouring to elevate the popular judgement, drifted into ways of indifference, and, counting upon the ignorance of those before whom they performed, made false taste serve as the true canon of art.'

became the pattern for many choral societies. The Singakademie was inaugurated by Carl Friedrich Fasch, a prolific if indifferent composer, whose principal aim was to ensure the performance of his own works. Fasch links two great epochs. He was a fellow harpischordist, in 1756, with C. P. E. Bach at the court of Frederick the Great. His successor as director of the Singakademie was Zelter, the teacher of Mendelssohn. Zelter was appointed to the Singakademie (which was not only a choral society but also a school of music) in 1810. In that year he gave a performance of Mozart's *Requiem*. Two years later the choir numbered 200 members. In 1817 *Judas Maccabaeus* was the principal work for performance; in 1815 *The Creation*; 1829 was the great year of the *St. Matthew Passion*; in 1834 Beethoven's *Ninth Symphony* and the 'Kyrie' and the 'Gloria' from the *Missa Solennis* (the whole of which was performed two years previously in a private house in London[1]) showed an awareness of what was then both formidable and contemporary. The two cathedrals in Berlin—the Lutheran Dom, and the Catholic Basilica of St. Hedwig—preserved high standards in the cultivation of traditional church music and from the choir of the former stemmed another Concert Society. A characteristic of Romanticism was its affection for antiquity. In this respect choral music outshone the other arts for there were many treasures to be revived and exposed to the community. In 1822 there was an *Akademie für Kirchenmusik* in Berlin, while forty-five years later another body was set up—the Caecilien-Verein, by which name many similar societies were called in Germany—as guardian of sacred music.

The careers of Mendelssohn and Schumann in which we range from the great Festivals at Düsseldorf[2] to the *Liedertafel* (male voice choir,

[1] That of Thomas Alsager (1779–1846), a proprietor of *The Times* and a friend of the literary and musical celebrities of London. The *Missa Solennis* was performed on Christmas Eve 1832, and conducted by Moscheles. The soloists were Clara Novello (soprano), Miss H. Cawse (contralto), E. Hawkins (tenor), Alfred Novello (bass). Vincent Novello played the organ, his daughter Mary sang among the altos, her husband, Charles Cowden Clarke—together with Edward Novello—being among the basses. Edward Holmes, the critic and a pupil of Novello, was one of the tenors. See *Musical Times*, Vol. 43, pp. 236–7, also *Life of Moscheles*, Charlotte Moscheles, ed. E. D. Coleridge (Pub. London 1873), Vol. 1, p. 279.

[2] Mendelssohn's taste and enthusiasm in his early days at Düsseldorf are reflected in his correspondence. Thus, on March 28th, 1834, he wrote to his father, 'Tomorrow evening (Good Friday) we are to sing in church the "Last Seven Words" of Palestrina, which I found in Cologne, and a composition of Lasso, and on Sunday we give Cherubini's Mass in C major'; on July 15th, 1834, to Schubring: 'This summer we executed in church a Mass of Beethoven, one of Cherubini, and cantatas of Sebastian Bach . . . and next month we are to give Handel's [Dettingen] "Te Deum".' Mendelssohn's passionate concern for choral music is extensively exhibited in a long letter to his father of March 10th, 1835. In this he discusses Bach and Handel and Haydn as well as the problems besetting a nineteenth-century composer. The chief problems arose 'when necessity of thought and noise in music are gradually being developed in inverse relation to each other'.

literally 'song-table') at Dresden[1] illustrate the vast expression of interest in choral music in Germany in general during the first half of the century.

Vienna was particularly prolific in choral societies. In 1812 the *Gesellschaft der Musikfreunde* was established under the patronage of Beethoven's friend and pupil the Archduke Rudolph. He occupied this position from 1814 to 1833. Vast numbers of singers participated in an annual *Musikfest*, of which the staple diet was oratorio. Somewhere about the middle of the century two other celebrated societies were started—the Singverein and the Wiener Singakademie. There followed associations with particular interests, and Palestrina, Haydn, Schubert and, later, Liszt and Bruckner had disciples thus to keep their memories alive. It may be noted that some of these societies with special interests were instrumental in reorientating the whole technique of musical composition in that those who wished to break the classical-academic hegemony were inspired to new ideas by a contemplation of the old. Wagner and Brahms, for instance, looked backward in order to look forward and knew their Palestrina and their Lassus. And in Paris the work of Choron and Niedermayer, and, surprisingly, Gounod, and the *Société de Musique Vocale Religieuse* (founded 1843) made possible the achievement in choral music of Saint-Saëns and Fauré.

In England the Three Choirs Festival (founded 1737) had long inculcated a love for the more sober forms of music in the West Country and may be allowed much credit for the eventual emergence of composers such as Hubert Parry, Edward Elgar, Gustav Holst, Ralph Vaughan Williams and Herbert Howells, all of whom were to have intimate connections with the Three Choirs Festival. London had its aristocratic Ancient Concerts[2] (1776–1848) and these maintained some of the finer choral works from the seventeenth and earlier eighteenth centuries. Many oratorio societies succeeded the great Handel Commemorations (the Caecilian Society, the Sacred Harmonic Society, the Choral Harmonists' Society, etc.), and in 1813 the Philharmonic Society was formed by Vincent Novello, Thomas Attwood, Sir George Smart,

---

[1] It is not generally realized that choral music (much of it not very inspiring) formed a considerable part of Schumann's output. He conducted, never very successfully, the Liedertafel in Dresden (in succession to Hiller) and subscription concerts in Düsseldorf. Schumann's part songs reflect his literary taste and judgement but he, like many other composers, found that lyrical verse and choral homophony do not mate happily.

[2] The last Director of the Ancient Concerts was the Duke of Wellington, whose father—the Earl of Mornington—was a minor composer of glees and part songs and the first Professor of Music in Trinity College, Dublin.

William Horsley, Sir Henry Bishop, the ageing Salomon, William Ayrton, a pioneer in musical journalism, John Cramer, Muzio Clementi, Domenico Corri and others.[1]

Handel and Haydn were the mainstays of the 'popular' choral societies and it was these two composers whose works began to inaugurate the music of the United States.

The first centre of music in the New World was Philadelphia and the earliest native American composer of any fame came from there. Francis Hopkinson, lawyer, politician, and amateur painter, poet, inventor and musician, was a friend of George Washington and one of the signatories of the Declaration of Independence. As a practising musician he introduced to his milieu the works of Handel, Pergolesi, Scarlatti, Corelli, Vivaldi, Arne and Purcell. As a composer he wrote songs and anthems and occasional choral pieces for the College of Philadelphia; his most interesting work (historically) was, however, his 'oratorial entertainment' *The Temple of Minerva* (possibly an opera disguised because of anti-stage laws) in which he extolled the merits of political alliance with France. William Billings of Boston, enjoying something of a modern revival, has received more attention than perhaps any other early American composer. Billings was a fascinating character, a fierce, deformed, single-minded tanner who gave up that odoriferous occupation for the profession of music, in which he died in poverty. Billings was musically uneducated and his compositions, mostly sacred, evidence his lack of a polished technique.[2] Yet (and the same applied to any one of the working-class composers who compiled or contributed to anthologies of Sunday-school and chapel music in England in the early years of the nineteenth century) his works have sometimes an elemental force or something of charm to make them individual. Apart from composition Billings was a powerful popular educator and the promoter of singing classes and choirs. He formed a singing class in Stoughton, Massachusetts, that in 1786 became the Stoughton Musical Society and has the honour of being the oldest musical organization in America still in continuous existence. On the practical side Billings may be commended for his distaste for out-of-tune singing which he rectified by reference either to the pitch-pipe or else to the 'cello, which he daringly introduced into the service of the Church.

[1] The history of English choral societies from the middle of the nineteenth century is admirably detailed in *The Mirror of Music*, P. A. Scholes (pub. London 1947), Vol. I.

[2] Many of the works of Billings are available in the edition published by Mercury Music Corporation, New York.

Oliver Holden, composer of the hymn-tune 'Coronation' (which is still used in American hymnody to 'All hail the power of Jesus' name') and a graduate to music *via* carpentry, deserves commemoration here for his pioneer work in the propagation of musical knowledge. Even though there was an icy response from the public (how often is this the case?) it was as early as 1793 that Holden announced *The Massachusetts Musical Magazine* which was intended 'to furnish Musical Societies and other Practitioners in that pleasing art, with a choice and valuable collection of odes, anthems, dirges and other favourite pieces of music'. At the end of the eighteenth century many compilations of hymns and psalms were published in America. But in a wider sphere there were the concerts of Selby in Boston in 1773, which promoted interest in Handel and Haydn and which helped to lead the way for the formation of a Handel and Haydn Society in that city in 1815. In Philadelphia Benjamin Carr built the Musical Fund Society on the wide popularity of these two masters of oratorio (Americans loved oratorio almost as much as the English and largely for the same reasons) and Thomas Hastings established yet another Handel and Haydn Society in Utica in 1828. In New York there had been a Philharmonic Society in the late eighteenth century which had been directed by the Englishman James Hewitt. The German community had their own Society, the Concordia, and at the very end of the century yet another choral body—the Euterpean Society—commenced. By 1831 there was a New York Sacred Music Society which in that year performed *Messiah* and seven years later Mendelssohn's *St. Paul*.

Now a choral society without music can hardly flourish and the spread of musical culture was in no small way due to the enterprise, courage and taste of a number of publishers. Three especially are of great importance. In Leipzig there was the firm of Breitkopf which had been established in 1719 as a general publishing house by Bernhardt Christoph Breitkopf and which developed music publishing as a major part of its activity in 1750, Johann Gottlob Immanuel Breitkopf then having succeeded his father and having a considerable personal interest in both music and in music-printing. A close friend of Breitkopf was Gottfried Christoph Härtel who joined the publishing house in 1795. At his death in 1800 Breitkopf left the business to Härtel with the understanding that it should be known as Breitkopf and Härtel. From Breitkopf and Härtel came the first large and popular editions of the music of Haydn, Mozart, Clementi and Dvořák. In Offenbach Johann

Anton André, son of Johann André—publisher and amateur musician —managed another firm of considerable importance for in 1799 he acquired all the musical remains of Mozart and published that composer's own thematic catalogue. A familiar English imprint in choral music—that of the house of Novello—established itself at the beginning of the nineteenth century in direct response to the growth of popular interest in choral music.

Vincent Novello[1] (1781–1861) was a remarkable figure in English music and his family made a huge contribution to English culture in the nineteenth century. His eldest daughter Mary, wife of Charles Cowden Clarke, was the author of a great *Shakespeare Concordance*, the translator of theoretical works by Cherubini, Berlioz and Catel, and sometime editor of the *Musical Times*. The fourth daughter was Clara, one of the greatest of English sopranos (in 1829 she studied under Choron at the Institution Royale de Musique Classique et Religieuse): her later career is not yet, perhaps, entirely forgotten;[2] it should be remembered again that in 1832 she took part in the famous performance of Beethoven's *Missa Solennis* at the house of Thomas Alsager, the proprietor of *The Times*. The sixth daughter, Mary Sabilla, although handicapped by ill-health, undertook useful work in singing classes in London or Dublin and also engaged in translations of musical textbooks. Vincent Novello's eldest son (Joseph) Alfred commenced as publisher in 1829 and through his business acumen and musical training (he was in the choir of Somers Town Catholic Chapel, choirmaster at the Lincoln's Inn Chapel and an excellent bass soloist in oratorio) brought the firm to its high standing in nineteenth-century musical affairs. Handel, Mendelssohn, Beethoven, Haydn, Mozart . . . all the major choral works of these and many other composers, and an infinite number of anthologies suitable for church, chapel and singing-class were made available through the Novellos.

'There were many hindrances, the chief being found in the firmly rooted prejudices of all classes, and the pertinacity with which they were retained, and their existence defended. However great might be the desire to create an "impulse" which should be useful in its effects, sufficient power had not accumulated, and difficulties increased as the days grew on. The popular love for music had never been denied, but

[1] See essay by the present writer in Grove's *Dictionary of Music and Musicians* (5th ed.).
[2] For instance a celebrated Welsh singer prefaced her homely Davies with Clara Novello and thus became known as Mme Clara Novello Davies. Her son left the Davies in Wales and made his own particular niche as Ivor Novello.

means for popular education did not exist. The people had little or no legislative power. Their wants were known only to themselves, for the higher classes took no interest in the desires of the poor. It is true that men's minds were shaken with the strong breeze of reform which was then blowing over the land. The hoped-for reform was chiefly to be relied upon to affect many existing abuses, and only indirectly to institute changes which might benefit the community. Music could never be thoroughly popular until it was within the reach of all. True art lingered in fretful captivity under mere fashionable patronage. The people longed to give it welcome in their own hearths. The restrictions which surrounded it kept it away from those who could value it for its own sake, and for the refining influence a better knowledge of it would bring. There were no cheap publications, and there were no cheap concerts. The taxes on knowledge[1] and the vexatious rules observed by the printing trade laid an embargo upon all attempts at reform in this direction.'[2]

Thus we are introduced not only to the devotion which went into music publishing but also to a realization of the fact that choral music in the nineteenth century was not entirely an end in itself but some expression of social aims and political sentiment as well as of religious fervour.

From this it seems a far cry to the great works of Beethoven but, even if Beethoven's Masses were a development of eighteenth-century practice, he would have been the first to subscribe to the disinterested concern for 'the masses' (in another sense) which inspired the Novellos.

CHERUBINI (1760–1842)

There are some unfortunate composers rather less than great whose qualities are obscured by their successors. Cherubini is a case in point. He is recalled as the composer of, say, the opera *The Water Carriers*— of which the estimable overture is still in the repertoire—and other operas which brought him, though a Florentine, considerable fame in Paris until the Napoleonic Wars disrupted his career. It is also noted that Beethoven and Haydn, in admiration of his meaningful melody,

---

[1] See *A Short History of Cheap Music*, p. 59. Novello petitioned the House of Commons, through Milner Gibson, requesting relief from taxation discriminating against musical publications.
[2] *A Short History of Cheap Music*, p. 22.

his expressive harmony, his orchestral felicity and his generally serious approach to the problems of operatic expression, regarded him as the most important composer of his time, while Mendelssohn thought so highly of him as to revive some of his greater ecclesiastical works for festival performance. With the approbation of these masters his influence in Germany was correspondingly great. But so far as we are concerned he exists by hearsay. Are his Masses any longer performed? Should they be, except as historical curiosities? The answer to the second question is possibly no. For, in general, Cherubini's choral music falls between two stools. It lacks the brilliance of Haydn and Mozart, while in seriousness and dramatic power it is not comparable with Beethoven. Cherubini was in search of a style: it was Beethoven who found what Cherubini sought.

Fétis wrote of Cherubini's Mass in F (1809):

'The prevailing idea in this effort has nothing in common with that which pervades all the music of the ancient Roman school; that was conceived as an emanation of pure sentiment, apart from all human passion; while Cherubini, on the contrary, chose that his music should express a dramatic sense of the words, and in the fulfilment of this idea, he gave proof of a talent so exalted as to leave him without rival in this particular.'

Again the problem was set before a composer: how to unite the conventions of spiritual exercise with the demands of changing philosophy and artistic expression. Having spent half a lifetime in pursuit of the dramatic Cherubini could not throw overboard all that he had acquired in that experience when concerned, as he was almost exclusively in his later life, with religious music. Cherubini was not only a serious-minded artist but a devout religious believer and his Masses are impregnated with high seriousness: but much of them is, alas, dull. Dull, that is, when sited between Mozart and Beethoven.

In 1816 Cherubini was appointed, together with Jean-François Lesueur, Superintendent of the Royal Chapel of Louis XVIII and his greater ecclesiastical music dates from this time. (The Mass of 1809 was an occasional work composed for the village choir and band of Chimay when, in disillusionment, Cherubini was there in retreat.) The work by which Cherubini is best known is the *Requiem* in C minor which was written at the end of 1816, in commemoration of the death of

Louis XVI, for performance in the Cathedral of St. Denis. This was not Cherubini's first *Requiem*—there was his vast setting in D minor of 1811, comprising 2563 measures and said to be the longest *Requiem* in existence; nor was it his last—for the three-part male-voice setting of 1836 was his swan-song; but it became the most familiar. In some degree its familiarity may be attributed to the enthusiasm of Berlioz, who wrote:

'The *Requiem* in C minor is on the whole the greatest work of its author. No other production of this grand master can bear any comparison with it for abundance of idea, fulness of form, and sustained sublimity of style. The "Agnus Dei" in *decrescendo* surpasses everything that has ever been written of the kind. The workmanship of this portion, too, has an inestimable value, the vocal style is sharp and clear, the instrumentation coloured and powerful, yet ever worthy of its object.'

I am not sure that the closing measures may not be quoted as a supreme moment in Romantic expression, for here is fulness of emotion expressed through the barest means (Ex. 1). A fine gravity attaches to the opening movement, in which Cherubini keeps his voices mostly in a low register (the D minor *Requiem* of 1836 was for male voices because the tone colour fitted the subject) and the 'Dies Irae' (notable for its demonstrative agony) is a tempestuous piece in C minor. Here Cherubini lies half way between Mozart of the *Requiem* and Beethoven; but the movement is too long and the long series of solos at the 'Recordare' section become perfunctory. In the 'Offertorium', despite some impressive fugal writing at 'Quam olim Abrahae promisisti', the rhythmic impulse now appears somewhat threadbare. (Here is met a criticism which is valid in respect of much nineteenth-century choral music, where the energy of verbal stress is forgotten and the over-all squareness of contemporary instrumental patterns is imposed.) In 'Pie Jesu' Cherubini is deliberate, and academic; but sentiment is not far distant (Ex. 2).

The *Mass in D Minor* (1811) is a far more impressive work, albeit uncomfortably long either for liturgical or non-liturgical use. The criticisms put against the *Requiem* concerning rhythmic monotony (see 'Gloria') and incipient sentimentality (see 'Qui tollis') will probably be discovered as apt also to this work. But, on the other hand, there are

Ex. 1

Ex. 2

many passages which show Cherubini's appreciation of the classical Italian church style—out of which developed his contrapuntal mastery. The last section of the 'Kyrie' is darkly impressive, and while retaining the impersonality of the ancient style, benefits, especially in its orchestration and in characteristic octave passages in the final utterance of the voices, from the dramatic infection of the period in which the Mass was written. Attention may also be directed to the 'Cum Sancto Spiritu' which is a vigorous double fugue—a fugue, that is, on two themes or subjects; to the wonderful 'Crucifixus est' episode of the 'Credo' where octave E's are intoned by the voices for fifty measures against a changing harmonic background of orchestral texture which finally dissolves among the low strings, in anticipation of Schumann, (Ex. 3), before the horns and the trumpets burst into the opening bars

Ex. 3

of 'Et Resurrexit': and here the voices build up finely, by way of B minor tonality, to a great climax. One further point: Cherubini was masterly in his disposition of voices. In this we may compare Mendelssohn, whose enthusiasm for Cherubini is betrayed in *Elijah*, *St. Paul* and *Lauda Sion*. The 'Gloria' and 'Credo' of the C major Mass are especially distinguished in this technical respect.

Cherubini's influence was through his attitude towards church music rather than through the music itself. He was antipathetic to the style of deposed *galanterie*, reaching its nadir in the facile flippancies of Rossini's *Stabat Mater*. He sought to re-establish the dignity, while adding to the splendour of the colour, of the nearly forgotten Carissimi,

Palestrina, Leo, Durante, Jommelli. . . . These composers Cherubini had known for a lifetime, for his early teacher Sarti had instructed his pupil to form a style by copying the best among the ancients. In his turn as teacher Cherubini became Inspector of the Paris Conservatoire in 1795 and Director in 1822—Cherubini also made his pupils copy the best of the traditional styles.

BEETHOVEN

While it is possible to applaud Cherubini's intentions and his craftsmanship and to be struck by the occasional emanations of genius it must be confessed that his ecclesiastical music can bear no comparison with the greater, contemporary instrumental music of the opening years of the nineteenth century. It is to Beethoven that we must look in order to see the complete emancipation of the choral element. The *Missa Solennis* is among the first dozen of all musical works. It is of its age, yet it transcends its age; it was written for an especial occasion, yet it fits no occasion, being rejected by the Church for which it was composed and finding no adequate home in the unsympathetic atmosphere of the concert hall where, perforce, it must be performed. Being exceptional it is often taken to indicate that Beethoven was exceptional in employing voices. On the contrary he was a considerable choral composer, even if he expressed at times his impatience at the limitation of the medium. Beethoven was a pupil of the great Viennese contrapuntist Albrechtsberger and also of Haydn. In later years he expressed the opinion that without their teaching his music would have been less good. Certainly without them his two Masses would have suffered. Moreover since the commission for the *Mass in C* (1807) came from the Esterházy household it is improbable that the first would have come to existence but for the intervention of Haydn. There is a moving anecdote of Haydn's last year. At a festival performance of *The Creation* at the University of Vienna in 1808 a great press of people came to congratulate the composer: among them was Beethoven, who stooped to kiss his master's forehead and hand. Reverence for this work and its composer is paralleled by Beethoven's late devotion to Handel. 'I would,' he said after hearing *Messiah*, 'uncover my head and kneel down at his tomb.' 'Everyone of us was moved,' writes Schulz of the incident which he recorded.

The way to the *Missa Solennis* was the way of the eighteenth-century composer.

In 1790 Beethoven composed cantatas on the death of Joseph II and for the accession of Leopold II. The former was highly thought of by Brahms, and Beethoven himself borrowed from it for the episode in the second part of Act II of *Fidelio*, where Leonora liberates Florestan from his shackles. In experiments with high-placed chords in voices and orchestra in the second Beethoven anticipated a striking effect used in the 'Choral' Symphony. Other occasional pieces were the cantata *Der glorreiche Augenblick* (1814), a celebration of Napoleon's defeat, the elegiac *Sanft wie du lebtest*, for four voices and string quartet, in memory of Eleonora Pasqualati, and the *Cantata campestre*, for four voices and pianoforte, for Dr. Bertolini. In 1815 Beethoven set two pieces by Goethe as *Meeresstille und glückliche Fahrt* (which title stimulated Mendelssohn to one of his most familiar and spectacular overtures). This work should be remarked not only for its word painting—how irresistible is the scene: 'calm sea and a prosperous voyage'—but also for its consideration of the psychological background to the words—the quality most to be noticed in the *Missa Solennis*. The choral society in search of a *pièce d'occasion* should become acquainted with the *Choral Fantasia* (1808) in which—although they do little more than repeat the chord of C major while piano and orchestra sun themselves after the accomplishment of a tricky set of variations—singers always seem to enjoy themselves.

Between the years 1799 and 1801—the period of the first symphony, the early pianoforte sonatas, the Op. 18 quartets, the ballet music *Die Geschöpfe des Prometheus* among other works—Beethoven was occupied in *Christus am Oelberge* (*Christ on the Mount of Olives*), his solitary oratorio. The text of this work was based on the scene of the Garden of Gethsemane and was produced by the Viennese popular poet and theatre writer Franz Xavier Huber. The music was based on theatrical models. Thus the Seraph diverts by cadenzas and over-athletic scales; the trio for the Seraph with Peter and Jesus is an entertaining opera ensemble; the part of Jesus (which Beethoven himself deplored in later life) is often melodramatic. The incongruity of such sections is emphasized by the sterner writing of the final chorus (in the *Choral Fantasia* key of C major) and by the moving orchestral introduction. The presentation of the story of the oratorio was judged by English taste as too secular and a new libretto was fabricated by Dr. Henry

Hudson and if English-speaking choirs wish to perform the work they must sing a doggerel version of the 'facts of Saul's persecution of David'.

The *Mass in C Major* was composed, in 1807, at the request of Prince Nicholas Esterházy. It was intended for liturgical use, though planned for a quartet of soloists, chorus and full orchestra. The reception of the work was discouraging: the Esterházys could make nothing of it, nor could Johann Hummel who, as Kapellmeister to Prince Esterházy, was present, and Breitkopf and Härtel declined publication. For Beethoven it was a work of importance—a first essay in the expression of his deepest personal convictions, which derived from the Catholic Church of which he was a member, but also from a Revolutionary sympathy with mankind in general, of which particular officers of the Roman Church, at that time, appeared not to approve. Beethoven explained to his publisher why he wished the Mass to be published: 'chiefly because it is dearer to my heart and in spite of the coldness of our age to such works'.

Holmes diagnoses both the importance of the Mass and the cause of its ill reception. 'The chief importance of this remarkable Mass consists in showing how far sacred music may be freed from formulas, and placed under the dominion of imagination.'[1] The Mass now being set under the 'domination of the imagination' with all that that represented to the furthest reaching mind of modern music lost something of its liturgical power. The point of view of the Church may (insofar as we can read it from without) arouse sympathy. Beethoven in neither of his settings of the Mass leaves time or energy for contemplation of any other considerations than those which arise from the music itself. Nor can one escape from it. Beethoven then becomes the sole interpreter of the divine. Whether he is competent or incompetent as such must be for the individual: for the Church, however, such a role is impossible. Since Beethoven wrote for the Church he must be subject to the Church's philosophy. (The argument about Beethoven differs from that previously concerning Haydn and Mozart, for they in their liturgical music never monopolized attention, whether willing or unwilling, to the same extent.)

We may now admit that, as music, Beethoven's two major works are of immense significance: that they are the most complete works of their order since the *Mass in B Minor*—which also, it will be recalled, was greater than the liturgical framework could allow. It is something of

[1] See essays by Holmes in *Musical Times* between 1852 and 1858.

a truism to observe that had not the *Missa Solennis* been written the *Mass* of 1807 would appear greater than it does. But it is as well to mark out the actual as well as the potential greatness of the earlier work. The weaknesses of the *Mass in C Major* lie in observance of earlier musical conventions—the dependence on a mere flood of sound to announce the 'Gloria' and some rather desultory writing from 'Quoniam tu solus', through the hearty clamour of the fugal 'Cum Sancto Spiritu', to the end of the movement—and in incomplete fusion between the old and dignified and the new and dramatic, as in the commencement of the 'Credo'. But these are points in the text which had more often than not, in the eighteenth century, been perfunctorily dismissed. The 'Sanctus' settings of Haydn and Mozart rarely, if ever, reveal 'the beauty of holiness'. Thus Beethoven, leaving his voices unaccompanied, achieves a renascence of wonder (Ex. 4)—whence back to A major. It

is in such transitions of tonality that Beethoven first strikes the imagination. The *Mass in C Major* is full of episodes in which a particular exegesis comes through sudden, though inevitable, alterations.

The 'Kyrie' begins, almost demurely, in C major. Before long, however, the music has moved to the key of E major—a favourite shift with both Haydn and Beethoven. The return-home embraces such enharmonic behaviour as (Ex. 5). In the 'Gloria' a sixteenth-

century contrast, much used also by Handel, surrounds the word 'adoramus' with reverence (Ex. 6a), wherein there may be seen

Beethoven's opinion of Pontius Pilate (Ex. 6b).

The second factor to be noted is the intensity of the rhythmic structure in the moments of highest passion. The previous example is a case in point. We may feel in the pulsation of the 'Agnus Dei', in the placing of the chords, a human 'cry from the heart' (Ex. 7), after which

the 'Dona nobis pacem' patterned on the cheerful conclusions of the eighteenth century, is an anticlimax.

Cherubini looked backward in order to attain propriety of style but he too often forgot that form alone is insufficient, that matter and form must be fused. The *Mass in C Major* of Beethoven recalls the 'gothic' (Ex. 8), but he tempers the severities of antiquity to the needs of mood

and time—though 'without such a resource Beethoven probably would have thought his work deficient in religious severity' and admits this particular passage to a predominantly lyrical movement. In the 'Benedictus', with due regard to the spacious division between soloists and chorus and the flow of orchestral movement, we see the empyrean quality of Beethoven's slow movements. Insofar as this is a choral work it is Beethoven's most rewarding work for performance. The more particularly instrumental quality which defeats most singers in the Ninth Symphony and the *Missa Solennis* has not yet appeared in all its

boldness of operation. Even so there are symptoms of impatience with
the limitations of the human voice. The 'Hosanna' keeps the sopranos
hard at work on a high A; the end of the 'Credo' makes fairly severe
demands on breath control as does the 'Agnus Dei' section of the
'Gloria'; to picture the 'world' in the final movement the basses
are taken far down in their register; but none of these are im-
probabilities.

The last, but not at all the least, significant feature of the score is the
orchestration. In the eighteenth century instrumental music in new-
found freedom developed away from vocal music. In the Romantic
period composers aspired to instrumental symbolism so that instruments
might appear to have, as it were, the gift of tongues. In the end, that is
in the next work to be considered, as in Mendelssohn and Berlioz and
Verdi, voices are used as part of the orchestral ensemble, while the
particular atmosphere of philosophy or drama which the voices
contain is transmitted to the orchestral accompaniment. We have, in
fact, no longer choral works with accompaniment but choral-and-
orchestral works in which the two units are co-equal. We are back to
the age of Buxtehude and Bach; but with a difference. The difference
is in the emotional emphasis. Here we may refer to the rich simplicity
of the woodwind and horn chords in the 'Sanctus' and to the generally
beautiful use of woodwind throughout the work.

There is a passage in Cardinal Newman which, echoing Plato and
Sir Thomas Browne and Shakespeare, may be deemed apposite to the
Mass in D:

> 'Can it be that those mysterious stirrings of heart, and keen
> emotions, and strange yearnings after we know not what, and
> awful impressions from we know not whence, should be wrought
> in us by what is unsubstantial, and comes and goes, and begins
> and ends in itself? It is not so; it cannot be. No; they have escaped
> from some higher sphere; they are the outpourings of eternal
> harmony in the medium of created sound; they are echoes from our
> Home; they are the voice of Angels, or the Magnificat of Saints, or
> the living laws of Divine Governance, or the Divine Attributes;
> something they are beside themselves, which we cannot compass,
> which we cannot utter—though moral man, and he perhaps not
> otherwise distinguished above his fellows, has the gift of eliciting
> them.'

Consider (Ex. 9). Here at once is the titanic Beethoven, taking his

human agency beyond any reasonable expectation of capability and loosing the thunders of a mighty orchestra which added to the normal 'classical' ensemble a double bassoon, trombones and organ; but in affirmation of a religious faith. What, perhaps, is the most shattering realization from this passage, and from the whole work, is its intellectual simplicity. Marion Scott[1] might well write:

'Where the belief in immortality . . . lies at the heart of Bach's B Minor Mass, a sure knowledge of God as the all-loving Father (Pater Omnipotens) lies at the heart of Beethoven's *Missa Solennis* in D major'. In passage after passage Beethoven leaves the great statements of Christian belief in awe-ful simplicity. From the

[1] *Beethoven*, Marion Scott (pub. London 1934), p. 78.

'Credo' we may extract (Ex. 10), which the orchestra completes

as a transition to a major chord of A and above which the flute shines like a star in the East: and this (Ex. 11), when again the

austerities of the 'gothic' are employed without accompaniment. Or there is the sublime 'Benedictus', where the Gregorian contour of the opening basses is enhanced by a *pastorale* allusiveness in the surround. Before this is set a *Praeludium* for the lower strings, for flutes (in the low register), bassoons, clarinets and, finally, double bassoon and organ pedal. The theme is D E A G, descended from that of Mozart's C Major Mass and the 'Jupiter' Symphony. This *Praeludium* is at that point of the mass when the Host is elevated and underlines the fact that, although he was well aware that his Mass was for the ideal and not the actual, Beethoven was setting his music within the over-all pattern of the Church service.

'. . . It is far too long for liturgical use, and the treatment of the words sometimes departs from Catholic dogma and the oratorio. But Beethoven had in view a ceremony of exceptional grandeur, in which a prince of the imperial house[1] was to be enthroned as a prince of the Church, while above all was the thought of God the

[1] The Archduke Rudolph as Archbishop of Olmütz.

King and Father, before whose Throne those earthly and spiritual splendours were no more than the drift of star-dust. For such purposes the Mass in D was not unsuitable—it was only too great for average human beings, a fault of which few composers are guilty.'[1]

The enthronement of the Archduke Rudolph was in 1820: Beethoven started work on the Mass in 1818 and completed it in 1823. On May 7th, 1824, the 'Kyrie', 'Credo' and 'Agnus Dei', announced as 'three hymns' and sung to German words, were performed, together with the first production of the Ninth Symphony at the Kärntnertor Theatre, Vienna. The work was published in 1827 and the first complete performance was at Warnsdorf, Bohemia, on June 29th, 1830. From that time, and for reasons which are obvious, performances have been infrequent and invariably in concert hall rather than in church. This is not always satisfactory because the music calls for the mystery of the added resonance that comes from within a great ecclesiastical building. Consider, for instance, the chords which end the middle, contrapuntal, section of the 'Kyrie' with the last part—in itself a recapitulation, though with an unexpected succession of keys. Or consider the end of the 'Kyrie' where voices and woodwind (with horns) sustain the tonic chord after the strings have left their evanescent pizzicato chord.

The 'Gloria' sweeps through one key after another—D major, G major, E minor, B minor. From a low-voiced Picardy third chord within the key which enfolds the words 'adoramus te' a sudden, off-the-beat, minor seventh transfers the music to the original, jubilant D major for 'glorificamus te, laudamus te' and a homophonic half-cadence in G major differentiates the expression of 'benedicimus te'. A further contrapuntal treatment of the 'glorificamus' phrase carries to C major: an orchestral interlude substitutes C minor for C major and that, in turn, moves, inevitably as it seems, to a *cantabile* section in B flat major in which 'gratias agimus tibi propter magnam gloriam tuam' is lyrically considered, first by the solo quartet and then more ecstatically by the chorus. The brief rising scale motiv which commenced the movement is then delivered triumphantly by the orchestra. The voices comment 'Domine Deus' and, after a brief allusion to D major—a wonderful semitonal shift to underline 'coelestis'—the tremendous climax of Ex. 9 above is wrought. Thence through a rapid succession

[1] Marion Scott, op. cit. p. 223.

of G minor, F major, D minor, C major to an impassioned prayer centred on the idea of 'miserere', in which remote keys (as far away as D flat), shuddering orchestral chording, and sweeping cries from the solo voices create an intensity that is unbearable. 'Miserere' is one of the key words in Beethoven's conception of the Mass and with its treatment in the 'Gloria' should be compared its setting in the 'Agnus Dei', where the male voices at first give to it deep utterance. The final section of the 'Gloria' commences with a typical thunderbolt: a kettledrum roll *pianissimo*, a great, rhythmic unison phrase for the full orchestra— (Ex. 12), repeated cries from the various choral groups 'Quoniam tu

Ex. 12

solus sanctus'; finally a gigantic fugue—(Ex. 13). A brilliant coda

Ex. 13

succeeds the fugue and, having reached top B in the soprano part, the composer seems reluctant ever to leave the single word 'gloria', which again is left with the voices after the instruments have stopped.

The 'Credo' has similar vastness to the 'Gloria'. Of the details not previously mentioned we may select (Ex. 14), where the climactic

words descend in overpowering octaves; the Dorian mode setting of 'Et incarnatus'; the vision of the Day of Judgement, the noble fugal writing of the concluding section, and the final immersion of the 'Amen' into eternity. All this was in B flat major. The 'Sanctus' commences with these four sounds (Ex. 15). That is sufficient to show

the dominance of Beethoven's imagination. But before we reach the vivacity of 'Pleni sunt coeli' this breathless passage is interposed: the holiness of God is beyond expression. The third part of this movement — Osanna', presto, runs straight into the *Praeludium* to the 'Benedictus'. The last movement of the Mass is in two parts: 'Agnus Dei' in B minor and 'Dona nobis pacem' in a pastoral D major—'a prayer', noted the composer, 'for inward and outward peace.' A great working-up of the material of this movement leads to a martial, though distant, irruption from drums and trumpets, followed by agonized phrases of recitative from the three high soloists and 'miserere nobis' from the chorus. In this, and the two succeeding movements of allusion to the reality of war, Beethoven recalls the special treatment of the 'Agnus Dei' in Haydn's 'In tempore belli' Mass. Thus at the end the original mood is re-established and there is a triumphant and secure conclusion.

Eduard Hanslick writing after a memorable performance of the work in Vienna in 1861 thus summarizes his conclusions:

'All his music was to him religious; in art he always felt himself to be in a church, and that is why, in this particular case, it did not occur to him to don specifically churchly raiment. "With devotion," he wrote at the beginning of the "Kyrie" and the "Sanctus"; and, indeed, what music has the character of devotion if not this? The imposing and austere spirituality of this holy office strikes one as significantly more religious than the brighter spirit of the Haydn Masses, although the latter may be incomparably more valuable and useful to the church. Comparison of the respective treatment of the text of the Mass by Beethoven and Haydn reminds us of an analogous contrast in the respective interpretation of the Bible by Klopstock and Goethe. While the devout bard of *The Messiah* simply opened the Bible in unquestioning faith, we see the young Goethe, surrounded by a maze of learned commentaries, examining the Book of Books with respectful scepticism. The unthinking, childish credulity of Klopstock was lost upon Goethe and his time. We see the same contrast repeated in the field of sacred music with Beethoven and his predecessors.'

SCHUBERT

We see, also, something of the same contrast between the religious music of Beethoven and that of Schubert, and, in relation to the literary analogy, it may be noted that Klopstock provided Schubert with the texts of the *Stabat Mater*[1], the Easter hymn '*Ueberwunden hat der Herr den Tod*', *Das grosse Halleluja*, for female voices, all composed during 1816. Of these works the first is the most important. The *Stabat Mater* was, traditionally, a non-liturgical piece and intended for private use. Pergolesi's setting (see p. 154 above) was widely sung during the eighteenth century and Klopstock's free translation of the Latin text, which he intended to be set to music, was sometimes employed for the benefit of non-latinists during performances of Pergolesi's work. Schubert's *Stabat Mater* shows its debt to Pergolesi in fugal interpolations at the same places and in the choice of key. In the non-fugal sections Schubert is concise, harmonically enchanting, and melodically as inventive as ever.

If Schubert inherited much from Klopstock and the movement towards 'sentiment' he inherited more from his immediate environment. The nineteenth-century English writer H. Heathcote Statham had these severe strictures on Romanticism in the period of Schubert: '[It was] of that somewhat heavy, melancholy, semi-mystical type . . . which would gaze with sentimental tears at the splendours of sunset, and sing passionate serenades to *die Treue*, with its long hair blowing wildly in the evening breeze, and then indulge itself with an orgy of beer and tobacco; which could be amused with schoolboy pranks . . .' Schubert had a habit of gazing with sentimental tears at the symbols of the Holy Mysteries and, while he would be offensive about the 'Bonzes', or priests, we can discover in the majority of his liturgical works the naive subjection of will and feeling to both fear and love of the traditional deity that distinguishes the simple, impressionable mind. For the Liechtental parish church, of his native part of Vienna, Schubert wrote numerous works, including the *Masses* in F (1814), G, B flat (1815) and C (1816), in none of which is there any lack of ingenousness.

In the *Mass in A Flat* (1822) Schubert achieved his most personal expression of the text of the Mass. It is a forward-looking work. The richness and poetic sensibility of its key ranges—between the poles of the tonic key and that of E major, wherein the 'Gloria' is set—are enchantingly beautiful. In the 'Credo' Schubert returns to the ancient style which Beethoven, having completed his *Missa Solennis*, approved as the true style for church music. In the 'Sanctus' (always a testing

---

[1] Schubert composed an incomplete *Stabat Mater* in 1815. In this work, which is without soloists, he set only the first two stanzas.

point for the imagination) he achieves one of his greatest strokes of
genius, in the heaven-splitting choral outburst of F sharp minor
(approached from F major) and its eventual resolution in the tonic key
of the movement.

In 1825 Schubert composed his greatest piece of church music—the
Mass in E Flat. During the last years of his life Schubert envinced a deep
interest in church music. There were many occasional pieces, but, in
addition to the *Mass in E Flat*, two works stand out as of special interest.
One was the so-called *Deutsche Messe*, in which the text was not in
Latin, but in German. This represented a particular, Austrian tradition,
for there was precedent in the work of Michael Haydn, to 'popularize'
the Mass by a text in the vernacular. The author of Schubert's text was
Professor Johann Philipp Neumann, a Viennese scientist and scholar.
Schubert set the simple stanzas of the text with simplicity if not
ingenuousness 'in homophonic song-form for mixed voices and wind
instruments'. In 1828 Schubert set the Hebrew text of Psalm 92, for the
chief Cantor of Vienna, Salomon Sulzer, who, in endeavouring to
reform the liturgical music of his faith, had the good sense to engage
the best available composers to second his efforts.

The *Mass in E Flat* was composed in the summer of 1828, between
the C major Symphony and the string quartet. It is possible that
Schubert was inspired to this composition by one, at least, of the
motives which drove Bach to the *Mass in B Minor*. It seems that he may
have written it in search of more lucrative occupation. Thus he tried
to conform to some of the conventional tenets more than in the *Mass
in A Flat*, observing the usual proprieties so far as the relation of one
movement to another was concerned and putting contrapuntal
episodes in the traditional places. On the other hand the work, which
perplexed the critics,[1] was new in the sense that it was a choral Mass in
which soloists, although allowed their place, are not permitted to
abuse it. But it was new, and perplexing in other ways; and one may
sympathize with those who did not immediately approve.

The main substance of this Mass lies in the orchestral texture and
the words tend to have a commentary function in respect of the
unfolding of the imagination through instrumental scoring which is

---

[1] The Vienna music critic of the *Berliner Allgemeine Musikzeitung* wrote (on March 20th, 1830)
after the commemorative performance of November 15th, 1829: 'Even though the actual
performance cannot be described as having been successful, it is none-the-less just possible that
an absolutely perfect rendering of the work might produce a lasting impression. It almost seems
as if the prospect of death lay heavy on the late master's heart and mind, while he was engaged
upon this Mass.'

often unexpected and strangely beautiful. The most considerable quality is of warmth, in which the comforting style of Bruckner is foreshadowed. Warmth comes from extensive exploitation of—to be truthful—commonplaces of Romantic harmonic diction through the woodwind chorus (with no flutes included) and the trombones. Although the general effect is, therefore, genial there are passages which over-leap the easy manner: the vaulting octaves in the bass which give especial intensity to the great D major climax (how characteristically far away from the home key) of the 'Kyrie'; the brilliant triplet figure with which the strings summon attention in the 'Gloria'; the horrific trombones and shuddering strings of the 'Domine Deus' section of the same movement; the prodigiously terrifying triple forte expression of 'Crucifixus'. In such moments the energy and sincerity of the creative spirit of Schubert is manifest.

There are many surprises in the general harmonic scheme: sometimes so many that they cease to surprise. On occasion, as in the opening of the 'Gloria', the 'Credo' and the 'Benedictus', the sequences are too aromatic. But there are magical transitions. In 'adoramus' ('Gloria') we are now within D flat major; in 'benedictus' within D minor. In the 'Crucifixus' episode F sharp minor is used (cf. 'Sanctus' of *Mass in A flat*). The 'Sanctus' proceeds thus at the outset—E flat major, B minor, G minor, E flat minor, and thence to B flat major.

Melodic invention is not conspicuous in this Mass, unless in the flowing 'Et incarnatus' which might have sprung from Francesco Durante. But fugal writing abounds. Most of it lacks genuine contrapuntal impulse as must all counterpoint which is without the tensions of dissonance: but visions of an earlier master are evoked by the 'Saints in glory' subject (see E major fugue of 'Forty-Eight', Book II) of 'Cum Sancto Spiritu' and the 'Agnus Dei' figure, which is that of the C sharp minor fugue in Book I of the 'Forty-Eight'.

Among Schubert's last works there is the *Song of Miriam*, a not-too-difficult piece for chorus and pianoforte (though the pianist is inclined to feel his contribution wasted effort). Here Schubert shows the inevitable Handelian influence; but a ghostly canonic passage which takes leave of the Egyptian hosts submerged beneath the Red Sea is starkly impressive: a stern counter to the sweetness which all too often infects Schubert's religious music and which, in dilution, is to be found in many minor composers of the nineteenth century who followed the perfumed way of chromatic harmony and enharmonic change. The words of the great hymn *Pange Lingua* were composed by St. Thomas Aquinas. A very late piece of Schubert sets the two last stanzas of this hymn as 'Tantum Ergo'. It ends thus: (Ex. 16).

Ex. 16 (voice parts only)

ge - ni - to - ri   ge - ni - to - que   laus   et   ju - bi — la — ti - o.

Nothing here recalls the 'Angelic Doctor': all that we have is a reminder of the tawdry imagery and feeble reproductions with which Romantic Catholicism often went to work.

SPOHR AND GOUNOD

The two great masters of odorous devotion were Spohr and Gounod, who flooded the world with such piety and lachrymosity that their effluence is hardly yet spent. Parts (if not the whole) of *The Last Judgement* and *The Redemption* may crop up round the next corner but one if the choirmaster is improbably moved to change from the accepted norm of oratorio and cantatas by some strange recurrence of bourgeois whim.

Spohr, in his way, was a great man. He was personally charming and tolerant (except towards the music of Beethoven), a considerable experimentalist in respect of instrumental combinations,[1] a quite brilliant technician, a fine and generous conductor, a fervent Mozartian (indeed his style, like the worst of Schubert, is a debasement of that of Mozart), but a sentimentalist. Those who sought after 'feeling' in the eighteenth century could never have foreseen that 'feeling' would have resulted in *The Last Judgement* (1825), *Calvary* (1833) and the *Fall of Babylon* (1842), epic subjects not fit for those who wear rosy-tinted spectacles. In mitigation it may be said that Spohr received great encouragement from the English middle classes. *Calvary* and *The Fall of Babylon* were sensational successes among oratorio-goers and the libretto of the second was prepared for Spohr—for production at the Norwich Festival of 1842—by one Professor Edward Taylor. Lest, however, it should be thought that Victorian England had a particular

---

[1] In choral music see Op. 54—a Mass for five solo voices and two five-part choirs.

prerogative to indulge in easeful contemplation of spiritual and physical calamity let it at once be said that Spohr enjoyed no less success in Germany. On the practical side he was a great director of Musical Festivals—indeed the first to be held in Germany, in 1809, at Frankenhausen in Thuringia, was under his control. Unfortunately he took his own music with him. Like Schubert—and others—Spohr sometimes felt that certain rigours should be suffered. Thus, when commissioned by the French Governor to compose an oratorio for the Fête Napoléon in Erfurt in 1812 he hastily studied counterpoint and fugue, through Marpurg, for the better fashioning of appropriate polyphony. This oratorio—*Das jüngste Gericht*—did not in the end please Spohr, although it was performed twice in Vienna in the year following its composition, and he renounced it.

LITERARY INFLUENCES

The wide popularity of choral music had its influence on almost every composer. Oratorios and masses were all very well—and their production increased mightily to keep pace with demand[1]—but since the concert hall was now the general home of the choral body there was no reason (apart from the remarkable lip-service paid to religion by the *soi-disant* musical of the period) why sacred words should monopolize the attention of the composer. Romantic ardour stimulated dreams of olden times, of open-air life, of national greatness or national independence. So that Cantata (nineteenth-century model) came to birth; as an extension of Romantic literature and of the German *Lied* on the one hand and as a medium wherein the new symbolism of colourful orchestral music might be exploited.

Between the years 1803 and 1817 the principal architects of nineteenth-century music were born. In 1803 Berlioz and Glinka; in 1809 Mendelssohn; in 1810 Chopin and Schumann; in 1811 Liszt; in 1813 Dargomizhsky, Verdi and Wagner; in 1817 Niels Gade. Of these Berlioz, Schumann, Liszt, Verdi and Gade qualify for discussion as choral composers; since, however, their greater achievements in this sphere came later in the century Liszt and Verdi will be discussed in the following chapter.

Looking at the first roll of names it is significant that no fewer than

[1] There are long lists of such works in Scholes, op. cit.

seven of these composers were educated for and, in some cases, followed careers other than that of music. Berlioz was intended for medicine, Glinka and Dargomizhsky were civil servants; Mendelssohn, Schumann, Liszt and Wagner were all competent in faculties other than that of music: in every case there was a mutual love of, and often skill in, literature and drama. The names which occur most frequently in the reading of these composers are those of Thomas Moore, Lord Byron, Goethe, the mock-Gaelic 'Ossian', Shakespeare, Dante, Tasso; among the Germans their own Romantic poets—Eichendorff, Uhland, Rückert, Hebbel, Geibel and so on: Hugo and Pushkin attracted Dargomizhsky especially; and folk poetry was widely studied. Above all, however, was the mighty influence of Goethe. Among the composers above mentioned (settings of, incidental music to, and programmatic interpretations of Goethe continue to appear) we discover the heroic Faust[1] in choral works by Berlioz and Schumann, in a symphonic work by Liszt and an overture by Wagner; Faust stimulated the setting of the *Erste Walpurgisnacht* by Mendelssohn; the *Meeresstille* overture by Mendelssohn was due to Goethe, and, of course, there are many Schumann song settings of that poet. The only composer really to parallel the achievement of Goethe in music was Beethoven (whom Goethe did not especially approve): the composer whose genius most attracted Goethe was Mendelssohn, whose temperament was too equable at a too early age fully to be able to express the conflicts of Goethe. Schumann, perhaps, had the best intellectual understanding of Goethe—he indeed had created counterparts to *Götz von Berlichingen* and *Werther* in *Eusebius* and *Florestan*; but he had not the equipment to express Goethe in choral music.

'His powers,' said Alan Pryce-Jones of Goethe, 'alone are a kind of transmuted diary. Both seen through his eyes and through those of his friends, he existed in a tumult—a tumult from which he never wholly emerged, but which the combination of administrative tasks and a growing and rigorous devotion to scientific studies to a large extent assuaged. It is at this point that the image of Goethe as the full-grown Western man begins to emerge. He was having to impose on a temperament which naturally operated in successive fields and by fits and starts his own classical concept of *ruhige*

---

[1] There have been operas on Faust by Spohr (1816), Bertin (1832), Gounod (1859), Boïto (1868), Zöllner (1887), Busoni (1925); while Berlioz's *La Damnation de Faust* was staged in 1893 and subsequent years.

Bildung. He was preparing the part which has most impressed posterity: the imposing of an unusual order on a mind by instinct not less unusually dispersed.'[1]

'FAUST' IN MENDELSSOHN, SCHUMANN AND BERLIOZ

The Faust music of Mendelssohn (for the *Erste Walpurgisnacht*, although an independent poem, expands an episode from the greater work), Schumann and Berlioz all holds much interest. Each composer trying in his own way to appear (musically at any rate) as 'the full-grown Western man' catches some of Goethe's inspiration. Mendelssohn was early in the field of secular cantata and in his avoidance of an 'ecclesiastical' style and his cultivation of an unnatural wildness showed himself, as in so many ways, a pioneer. With this work—about diabolic festivities on the Eve of May Day—at one extreme, *Lauda Sion* at the other, and *Elijah* and *St. Paul* between it is possible to appreciate more properly the range of Mendelssohn's skill and imagination. The orchestral introduction to *Walpurgisnacht* is as felicitously scored as all Mendelssohn's overtures and has the clarity that is generally associated with his style. In its A minor—A major progress and also in melodic shape it recalls the *Scotch Symphony*. In such works it is not difficult to see the opera composer that Mendelssohn always hoped to be and the choral writing throughout suggests the spectacular. The great central chorus is quite the most terrifying piece ever written by Mendelssohn. His interchange of $\frac{6}{8}$ time and $\frac{2}{4}$ time, his austerity of texture, his percussive ferocity, his skirlings of first inversion chords, his scarifying octaves (Ex. 17),

Ex. 17

[1] Goethe—*the Legend and the man,* in *Johann Wolfgang von Goethe: A Radio Commemoration* (B.B.C., London 1949).

his unvocal intervals, and the bizarre character of his orchestration make this a remarkable point of departure in choral music. It is small wonder that Mendelssohn's old master Zelter found it impossible to set this text. Whether Goethe approved the style, although for Mendelssohn he had both the highest regard as a musician and affection as man, may be doubted: in the séances which he held with Mendelssohn he relaxed with Mozart and Bach.

When Mendelssohn was at work on *Walpurgisnacht* he was travelling in Switzerland and Italy. In one of his letters to Goethe— from Lucerne and dated August 28th, 1831—he describes a storm in the Alps. From storm to fair weather is detailed with the finest precision and the literary description is a fitting complement to the musical one of the introduction to *Walpurgisnacht*. In both mediums he demonstrates his strength and his weakness: the former in the integrity of his style; the latter, despite all his output of energy, in an almost complete appearance of detachment.

In their different ways Schumann and Berlioz lose themselves more readily within their subject. But neither achieved the realistic super-finality of Mendelssohn, who aimed, as he wrote to his mother, at a symphony-cantata (cf. *Lobgesang*, 1840). Berlioz composed a series of flashing episodes: Schumann composed a wonderful third part in the fulness of his power and then set before it two other parts—to accomplish a full-scale oratorio[1]—when his genius was in decline. Schumann, as Goethe and Berlioz, occupied himself with the subject of Faust for many years. He actually commenced the composition of Part III in 1844. Four years later he completed this section. Parts I and II were not finished until 1853. The first complete performance of *Scenes from Faust* took place in 1862 at Cologne under Ferdinand Hiller.

[1] See *Schumann*, ed. G. Abraham (London 1952), p. 266.

Schumann confessed to Mendelssohn that it was the 'sublime poetry' which led him to attempt the work. After the first private performance of Part III at Dresden in 1848 he wrote to Brendel that what pleased him most was to hear from many 'that the music made the poem intelligible to them for the first time'.

In 1827 Goethe's *Faust* was published in a French translation by Gérard de Nerval. A year later Berlioz sent his *Huit Scénes de Faust*, which he had engraved at his own expense, to Goethe. Goethe sought an opinion on the score from Zelter, who, conservative as he was, could find nothing good to say of it. In 1846 the *Huit Scénes* were absorbed into *La Damnation de Faust*. In December of that year this work was first performed in Paris; on each of two evenings the audience was both meagre and hostile.

By comparing Berlioz and Schumann we may conclude that, were it possible for composers of such genius to collaborate, a combined operation might have achieved a fitting musical counterpart to the drama, the picturesqueness, the poetry and the philosophy of Goethe. Berlioz was more than competent in expressing the dramatic and the picturesque, Schumann's province was the poetic and the philosophic.

The eight sections of Berlioz's 1828 work were the Easter hymn; a Peasants' chorus; the Dream chorus; the Rat song; the Flea song; the King of Thule ballad; Margaret's romance; and the Soldier's chorus. The *Damnation* of 1846 consisted of four parts. The words were still based on the translation of Gérard de Nerval, but with additions by Gandonnière and by Berlioz himself. Part I finds Faust approximately where the composer was when at work on this section, for in the early part of 1846 Berlioz was in Budapest and it was in anticipation of this visit that he wrote the Rakoczy March.[1] Part I has country music and martial music, the former centred on an engaging chorus based on droning fifths in the bass, the latter culminating in the March. In Part II Faust is back in Germany, alone in his study. Across his restless soliloquy breaks the Easter hymn. Then Mephistopheles comes to tempt Faust away from his books and to urge him towards his pre-destined end. A merry Drinking Chorus in Auerbach's cellar in Leipzig leads to Brander's song and to a satirical fugue for male voices, on the theme of this song which serves to show how far Berlioz removed

---

[1] He was advised: 'If you wish to please the Hungarians compose a piece on one of their national themes.' See *Historical Notes* to vocal score (Novello) of *Faust* by F. G. Edwards (1903). The Rakoczy March was named after Prince Ferencz Rákóczi, who led a revolt against the Austrians in 1703–11.

choral music from its traditions of sobriety and godly living. To the same scene belongs the Flea song. Scene VII is another pastoral episode set in 'wooded meadows on the banks of the Elbe'. A long and lovely Dream chorus, in which voices and instruments unite to effect a flutter of anaesthetic lullaby, sends Faust into beguiled sleep and the orchestra to the familiar and masterly Dance of Sylphs. Faust dreams of Margaret and Mephistopheles promises to lead him to her. A Soldiers' chorus and a Students' chorus, and then both at once, end this part. In Part III we are introduced to Margaret and to some of the most ecstatic music in the whole work. We may instance the archaic (Berlioz called it 'Gothic') charm of (Ex. 18)—Berlioz uses this sort of bass with almost

Ex. 18

twentieth-century frequency in *Faust*, and this fusion of souls in chromatic commingling (Ex. 19). Midway between these movements

Ex. 19

P

lies the *Dance of Will-o'-the-Wisps*, another engaging (and well-known) example of Berlioz's most delicate orchestration. After the wonderful Romance with which Margaret—introduced by the English horn—commences Part IV Berlioz is seized by a melodramatic fit and Faust and Mephistopheles, mounted on black horses, gallop to the Abyss to this music and movement figure ♩ ♫. While on their journey the easy contrast afforded by evocative religious sentiment (a great stand-by of opera composers of the period) brings a chorus of peasants hymning the Virgin Mary. Faust and Mephistopheles fall into the Abyss, are picked up amid a pandemonium in which Berlioz tested all his theories relating to brass and percussion, and are taken to Hell by a squad of Devils who sound more drunk than diabolic. There follows an Epilogue on Earth, and (one floor higher) a brief passage in Heaven where angels sing, as tritely as angels are often supposed to sing (see Elgar's Devils and Angelicals, blood-relations of those of Berlioz), while Margaret is apotheosized.

There is much music in the *Damnation of Faust* that is both original and great. The pastoral music, the spirit music, the true-to-life soldiers' and students' songs, the most moving love music: all of these are remarkable. But the work as a whole is Berlioz rather than Goethe. Possibly that is inevitable; but where Berlioz and Goethe overlap the result is impressive in the extreme.

The difficulty, of course, is to bring off this sort of work in the concert hall, where stall-holders occupy the abyss and organ pipes most of heaven and where Mephistopheles must appear in a white shirt. 'Well,' wrote Bernard Shaw[1] after a performance, in 1893, by the Royal Choral Society in the Albert Hall, 'the sole criticism I have to make . . . is that the damnation has been lifted from the work. It has been "saved",

---

[1] *Music in London*, Vol. III, pp. 80–2.

so to speak, and jogs along in a most respectable manner'. It may be mentioned that the first complete English performance was in the Free Trade Hall in Manchester, under Sir Charles Hallé, on February 5th, 1880. Hallé had been friendly with Berlioz while a student in Paris and that was the start of a lively Berlioz tradition in Manchester.

The difference between Berlioz and Schumann is apparent from their respective selections from *Faust*. Schumann's work comprised much less of the spectacular. Part I commences with the Garden Scene of Faust and Margaret: then follow Margaret before the Mater Dolorosa and the Cathedral Scene, in all of which the music lies sombrely in the minor mode around the key centre of D. Part II begins in the same key of B flat as the composer's 'Spring' Symphony (No. 1), while at sunrise spirits hover round the restlessly sleeping Faust. Next there is the midnight scene with four grey hags. Finally the death of Faust. All of this is taken from Goethe's Part II. The best part of this music lies not in the choral writing, which is pedestrian, nor in the solo music, which is often tedious, but in the orchestral development, which is effective in its intellectual progress yet texturally interesting. In Part III Schumann accomplishes a great spiritual climax, both in his own music and in the music of the nineteenth century. Here he reaches a profundity of which Berlioz was incapable. The first section shows a mountain gorge (taken by Goethe from a description of Montserrat, by Barcelona), on which are to be found holy anchorites. We may notice this subdued piece of illustration (Ex. 20) which has characteristic

Ex. 20

Voice parts only

(S. & C.) Li - ons with qui - et tread,

Ca - verns give shel - ter near;

(Bass 8va lower)

harmonic dénouement. There follows a tenor solo from Pater Seraphimus against this recurring, Bachian figure (Ex. 21). From D minor

Ex. 21 Cello Solo

the music moves to B flat major and to a bass air from Pater Profundus, a baritone solo from Pater Seraphicus and a concluding chorus of 'happy spirits of boys' in which the naive nursery-tune opening dissolves into a gentle, ethereal, cross-rhythm. A long chorus of Angelicals —first the whole company in A flat; then the younger angels again in a more flexible interplay of rhythmic patterns in C sharp minor; the spirits of boys in G flat major; last in eight parts and in B flat—receives the immortal part of Faust. The vision becomes more intense. Dr. Marianus reveals the holiness of the upper regions and the chorus hymn the spirit of holiness: the Mater Gloriosa floats onwards and female penitents implore her. Here among Magna Peccatrix, Mulier Samaritana and Maria Aegyptiaca is to be found Una Poenitentium (formerly known as Gretchen = Margaret). The whole work concludes with the Chorus Mysticus (of which there are two versions), in which traditional polyphony (a double choir as well as four soloists is used) unites with the intellectual beauty of Schumann's harmonic method (Ex. 22). This

Ex. 22

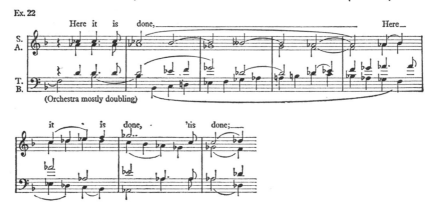

style was not unnoticed by Brahms, who is nowhere more Schumann-esque than in his *Requiem*.

One notable feature of Schumann's *Faust*, which stands out against the insouciance of Berlioz, is his devotion to Goethe's text, which is unaltered and barely cut. Previous to the great German Romantics words and poets had generally received less than courtesy. In the nineteenth century it is, increasingly, a matter of 'word over all'. Apart from *Faust* the choral work of most significance in the development of Schumann was *Paradise and the Peri* (Op. 50). This 'Oratorio, but for cheerful people', as Schumann called it, based on a translation of Thomas Moore's *Lalla Rookh*, was composed in 1843. In Leipzig, where it was produced in that year, under Schumann's direction, *Paradise and the Peri* appeared as a striking specimen of 'modern music'. It contained most of the ingredients which have subsequently been re-sorted and blended into musico-pictorial mixtures for the millions. There are choruses for Houris, for Nile Spirits, for the followers of

Mahomet; suitably wayward music to describe the Peri's wanderings in Egypt and India; and many allurive episodes in the orchestra. The orchestral writing is more effective than the choral (which medium nearly always found Schumann at a disadvantage) and must have seemed stimulating and adventurous a century ago. But even then there were critics who complained that the work was unsatisfactory. That critics will often make that observation on new music is, alas! true; but in respect of *Paradise and the Peri* at least one of them hit the nail on the head. 'There is,' said one of them, 'too much music in it.'

'SACRED' MUSIC OF BERLIOZ AND MENDELSSOHN

That, of course, is a change from those works which have too little music. It is possible that among these must be placed two major works by Berlioz: the *Mass for the Dead* (better known as the *Requiem*) and the *Te Deum*. These were spectacular works. The first was commissioned by the Minister of the Interior, in 1836, for a memorial service to the victims of Fieschi, the Corsican assassin. In the end, after intrigues against Berlioz (so he suspected) from Halévy, Cherubini, Habeneck and others, the work was performed in the Church of the Invalides in December 1837, at a service of commemoration for those French soldiers who had lost their lives during the Algerian campaign. The *Te Deum* was composed in 1849 and first performed in 1855 in the church of Saint Eustache as preliminary to the opening of the Palace of Industry. It was dedicated to Prince Albert, the Consort of Queen Victoria and the great patron of all industry.

The *Requiem* required a chorus of anything from 300–900 singers; fifty violins, twenty violas, twenty 'cellos, eighteen double basses, four flutes, two oboes, two English horns, eight bassoons, four clarinets, twelve horns, four cornets, twelve trumpets, sixteen trombones, six ophicleides or tubas, sixteen timpani, two bass drums, four gongs and five pairs of cymbals. The brass was to be divided into four groups to be disposed as flanking forces to the main body. The *Te Deum* asked for an orchestra a little less immense than that of the *Requiem*: the singers, however, were divided into two choirs, each of 100 voices, with a further group of 600 children. To enhance the impressiveness of all these timbres—among which the organ had an important part—the two adult choirs were to be at the far end of the church from the organ and the children placed elsewhere on a raised platform. Berlioz had predecessors in large-scale choralism. There was, for instance, Gossec, with two orchestras in his *Requiem* (1760); and, of course, the Venetian displays of the seventeenth century were designed impressively. In respect of Berlioz, however, it should be emphasized that he was too good a musician to use all his resources all the time.

Berlioz lived in a febrile period in the history of France. He was a child of his age—as, in their differently colourful ways, were Dumas, de Musset, Mérimée, Hugo, Balzac, Géricault and Delacroix—and, being a prey to intense emotions, self-centred. He was susceptible to atmosphere and especially the horrific. He was brought up in the Catholic Church, in which he appreciated at least the colour and poetry of the ritual. The *Requiem* and the *Te Deum* are as religious as *La Damnation de Faust*. The texts, which Berlioz treated with as much freedom as he required, stimulated the composer's vision but touched no philosophic conviction. We accept the *Requiem* and the *Te Deum*, then, as expressions of an extreme sensibility but not as contributions, in any sense, to ordered ritual; as passionate revolt against the conventional and statuesque in choral style; as protestation of the greatness of the individual imagination. Much of Berlioz is, in the figurative sense, vulgar: vulgarity, nonetheless, is a part of art. If Berlioz and Liszt, who shared many points of view, stress this element too forcefully it is because others among their contemporaries were either afraid of it (as Mendelssohn, and most of his pupils, especially the English) or misapplied it (as Rossini and many of the pianoforte hacks). In a letter to the *Gazette Musicale* in 1834 Liszt defined religious music as, at that time, it appeared to Berlioz and himself: 'For want of a better term we may well call the new music Humanitarian. It must be devotional, strong, and drastic, uniting—on a colossal scale—the theatre and the Church, dramatic and sacred, superb and simple, fiery and free, strong and calm, translucent and emotional.' Berlioz does not fall short of these objectives. His aim, perhaps, is too deliberate. For what is devotional say in the *Requiem* and the 'Sanctus', may seem either self-piteous or sanctimonious; the strong, the drastic, as in 'Tuba Mirum' or 'Rex tremendae', or the final chorus of the *Te Deum*, either merely noisy or hysterical; freedom—freedom from old associations—imposes its own bondage for deprived of the emancipating flow of contrapuntal texture Berlioz is forced into habits which are not essentially vocal. In

the end, as with other Romantics—Tchaikovsky and Elgar in particular
—it is in the quiet passages that the greatest significance emerges; in the
quasi-recitative ending of the *Requiem*, in the spacious simplicity of the
unaccompanied 'Quaerens me'; in the bare (Ex. 23) pattern which runs

Ex. 23

Do - - mi - ne,

throughout the Offertoire and which so forcibly impressed Wagner; in
the paradisal 'Sanctus' chords and the widely expanded 'Dignare,
Domine' of the *Te Deum*.

Berlioz would have sacrificed all his works but the *Requiem*. Present
opinion would retain, of the choral works, the oratorio *L'Enfance du
Christ*,[1] and this for the middle section 'La Fuite en Egypte'. The reason
for this rises directly from the conclusion of the last paragraph. 'La
Fuite en Egypte', which captivated Brahms, is Berlioz at his gentlest, his
most poetical, and his most self-effacing. Altogether this is an extended
pastorale with a dedicated purpose. Berlioz matches Haydn and Handel
and Domenico Scarlatti and Corelli in charm and affection. Here, in
music, is the sweetness of Fra Angelico. And it should be noticed how
perfectly idea and expression (in which the light-weight orchestra is
again emblematic of Berlioz's mastery of sound) are fused.

'La Fuite en Egypte' was written in 1850. The surrounding movements—the uneven, but extremely descriptive and operatic *Le Songe
d'Hérode* and *L'Arrivée à Säis*, with its reflective, wistful end-chorus—
were completed by 1854, when the complete trilogy was first performed.

Of Berlioz Ferdinand Hiller wrote: 'He does not belong to our
musical solar system; he does not belong to the planets, neither to the
large nor to the small. He was a comet, shining out, somewhat eerie to
look at, soon again disappearing; but this appearance will remain
unforgotten.'

Thus any performance of almost any work—and certainly any
choral work—by Berlioz is an occasion. Mendelssohn we take for

[1] Berlioz's note on the disposition of his singers may be quoted to show his consciousness of
the colour-potential of sung music: 'During the whole of the first part, the male choristers are
to stand alone on one side of the stage in sight of the public, soprani and contralti behind the stage
around the chorus-leader at the harmonium or organ. At the beginning of the second part, they
are to take their places on the stage opposite the men, with the exception of four of each of the
two voices, which are to remain behind the stage to the end, to sing the Alleluja and Amen.
Should the conductor of the orchestra not have an electric metronome at his disposal, the chorus-
master is to conduct behind the stage the invisible chorus, and the conductor to follow him
by ear.'

granted. And in taking him for granted we underestimate. Is the 'Italian' a less great symphony than the 'Fantastic'? Are Mendelssohn's sprites less *féerique* than those of Berlioz? Is *Elijah* inferior to the *Requiem*? Berlioz, who had much regard for Mendelssohn, happened on the characteristic difference. Fanny Hensel, Mendelssohn's sister, wrote in her diary on February 21st, 1843:

> 'Berlioz was at Leipzig at the same time with us, and his odd manners gave so much offence that Felix was continually being called upon to smooth somebody's ruffled feathers. When the parting came, Berlioz offered to exchange batons, "as the ancient warriors exchanged their armour", and in return for Felix's pretty light stick of whalebone covered with white leather sent an enormous cudgel of lime-tree with the bark on, and an open letter, beginning "Le mien est grossier, le tien est simple". A friend of Berlioz who brought the two translated this sentence "I am coarse and you are simple", and was in great perplexity how to conceal the apparent rudeness from Felix.'

The 'pretty light stick and the white leather' symbolize grace and courtesy of style: the whalebone a hidden strength of purpose.

Mendelssohn's purpose in life may be defined by some of his actions and some of his attitudes. His *stature* as a composer is not at the moment under scrutiny. But it may safely be observed that he was (and possibly still is) the most widely *popular* of nineteenth-century composers, and in achieving popularity he mirrored many of the facets of his age. He was in fact the 'modern man'—precisely, not adventurously nor dangerously modern. He disliked fanaticism and, having enjoyed it himself, preached the virtues of a general education: the humanities, but also the sciences. In religious matters he was tolerant and apparently well disposed to all who professed a Faith. Into his musical enthusiasm he allowed many of his contemporaries, but with Haydn, Mozart, Leonardo Leo, Antonio Lotti, Francesco Durante, Palestrina, Lassus. He had three main antipathies: excessive noise, formlessness, irrelevant display. By adding together Mendelssohn's characteristics we may arrive with some accuracy at the kind of music he ought to have written. The surprise is that, on the whole, it was the sort of music he *did* write. And the oratorios he wrote are model oratorios. Because they were model oratorios—in point of subject, technique and, with some reservations, expression—they were accepted with gratitude. In case it seems easy to achieve this ideal of the 'model' conceive the problem as today: one or two composers in America and Britain are not far from this particular ideal and are popular. Are they, however, 'great'; and if so, more than Mendelssohn?

The oratorio *St. Paul* was commissioned by the St. Cecilia Society or Caecilienverein of Frankfurt in 1831. Mendelssohn's acceptance of this commission was urged by his father. The text was prepared by his friends Fürst and Schubring, but Mendelssohn took—as might have been expected—a very keen interest in the selection and arrangement of the libretto. It may be noted that there was, perhaps, an unconscious sympathy with the subject, for a special reason. The Mendelssohns were Jews but also German citizens, and Moses Mendelssohn (Felix's grand-father) was insistent in his writings that such citizenship conferred both honour and responsibility. *St. Paul* should have been performed at Frankfurt but was in fact first performed at the Lower Rhine Festival, at Düsseldorf, on May 22nd, 1836.

'His mother and his sisters and brother came from Berlin to attend it; and, probably, never has this work been given to the ear in such perfection as on that occasion, during the first impetus of fervent enthusiasm for the composer and his creation. "St. Paul", indeed, had attained its full growth directly under the eyes of those who now took part in it. Each performer thought that he had a certain share in this wonderful production. One trifling passage alone did not go steadily; one of the "false witnesses" made a mistake. Fanny Hensel, who was seated with the *contralti*, became as pale as death, bent forwards, and, holding up the sheet of music, sang the right notes so steadily and firm that the culprit soon got right again. At the close of the performance, in the midst of all the jubilations, Felix tenderly clasped the hand of his helper in need, saying, with his sunny smile, "I am glad it was one of the false witnesses." '[1]

Mendelssohn was a master of the apt phrase. *St. Paul* was altogether gratifying, for, even before its performance, excited and privileged listeners punctuated rehearsals with applause.

---

[1] *Reminiscences of Felix Mendelssohn-Bartholdy*, Elise Polko, trans. Lady Wallace (pub. London 1869), see pp. 43–5.

In 1840 the *Lobgesang* (Hymn of Praise), in honour of the fourth centenary of the birth of printing, was performed in the Thomaskirche in Leipzig. This is an extremely dull work (it was intended as an improvement on Beethoven's choral symphonic manner in that the voices should be allowed more scope)—but read Lampadius, who was present at the first performance on June 25th:

> 'The work called out the greatest enthusiasm, which could hardly be repressed within bounds even by the fact that the audience were seated within the walls of a church. After the first duet a subdued whisper of applause ran through the edifice and betrayed the suppressed delight of the listeners. On one of the evenings following a torchlight procession was made in honour of the great composer. Mendelssohn . . . appeared at the window, his face lighted up with joy. "Gentlemen," he said in his neat, quiet way, with a sensible trembling of the voice, "you know that it is not my manner to make many words; but I heartily thank you." A loud "Hoch" three times shouted, was our reply.'

The second performance of *Lobgesang* was at Birmingham, which city has its own close associations with the composer and particularly on account of *Elijah*. This oratorio had begun to take some shape in the composer's mind in 1837. This year was, so far as oratorio was concerned, an important year. It was then that Mendelssohn was deep in his Bach studies (he played a great many organ works by Bach in London that year) from which significant works—notably the fine set of *Preludes and Fugues* (Op. 25) for piano and the three *Preludes and Fugues* for organ (dedicated to Thomas Attwood)—resulted. In 1837 Mendelssohn was considering a companion work to *St. Paul—St. Peter*. On this subject he wrote to Pastor Schubring: but before long the idea of *Elijah* takes precedence. In his correspondence with Schubring Mendelssohn is at pains to be theologically sound: this is especially the case in the St. Peter project. At the end of 1838 the person of Elijah has crystallized in the composer's mind: 'I figured to myself Elijah as a thorough prophet, such as we might again require in our own day, energetic and zealous, but also stern, wrathful, and gloomy; a striking contrast to the court rabble and popular rabble—in fact, in apposition to the whole world, and yet borne on angels' wings.'[1] In

[1] Letter dated November 2nd, 1838.

1840 and again in 1842 we hear of the detailed growth of the oratorio and learn of the immense pains which Mendelssohn took over this work. When in 1844 he received the invitation to conduct the Birmingham Festival of 1846 he determined that *Elijah* should be ready for that occasion.

'Had you only been there!' [Felix wrote to his brother Paul on August 26th, 1846, after the first performance.] 'During the whole two hours and a half that it lasted, the two thousand people in the large hall, and the large orchestra, were all so fully intent on the one object in question that not the slightest sound was to be heard among the whole audience, so that I could sway at pleasure the enormous orchestra and choir, and also the organ accompaniments. How often I thought of you during the time! More especially, however, when the "sound of abundance of rain" came, and when they sang and played the final chorus with *furore*, and when, after the close of the first part, we were obliged to repeat the whole movement. Not less than four choruses and four arias were encored, and not one single mistake occurred in the whole of the first part; there were some afterwards in the second part, but even these were but trifling. A young English tenor sang the last air with such wonderful sweetness, that I was obliged to collect all my energies not to be affected, and to continue beating time steadily. As I said before, had you only been there!'

Incidentally, the young English tenor, Charles Lockey (who did not die until 1902), passed on information regarding Mendelssohn's interpretation which might be generally noted: he grew very angry with those who showed a tendency to drag in the slow movements.

It is clear that Mendelssohn's oratorio music was enjoyed. I am in mind of the riposte of the priest to the lady who complained that she could no longer enjoy her church-going: 'You don't go to church to enjoy yourself!' So we see the weakness not only of Mendelssohn but also of many other composers of the nineteenth century. And we find the major works of Mendelssohn collapsing into the easy pleasure of 'I waited for the Lord', 'How lovely are Thy messengers', and 'Cast the burden upon the Lord', and the complacent bonhomie of the first 'Baal' chorus, of 'Thanks be to God', and of 'All that hath life and breath'.

St. Paul has gone out of fashion. It lacks the great dramatic qualities of *Elijah*, but it has a fine dignity in its choruses—note the echo of ancient polyphony in 'But our God abideth in Heaven' and the tragic impact of 'This Jehovah's Temple', a striking effect of timbre to etherealize the words of Christ in the Conversion Scene and a wonderful sequence of keys from this point to the F major of 'O great is the depth'.

Elijah is a greater work than *St. Paul* because it stirs the attentive imagination to greater surprise. Immediately, *Elijah* commands: for the first, wind-accompanied, recitative exhibits all that Mendelssohn had expressed in his earlier correspondence about the 'dramatic'. As a small point attention should be drawn to the superb placing of the drum rolls in this recitative. A half-cadence leads into the fugal overture and this goes, without a break, into the first great chorus. Here is a people, pictured Handelianly, impassioned in prayer. The coda of the chorus is a communal recitative—a fine piece of allusive delineation. In 'Lord bow Thine ear to our prayers' Mendelssohn evokes some ancient feeling by touching—as he does also in *Lauda Sion*—modal tonality. In this case there is a strong Phrygian flavour. There are magnificent choral moments, and it is in the choral writing of this work that Mendelssohn reaches great heights. Much of the solo writing is beautiful—note the scoring of Nos. 8, 13 and 33—and always grateful to the voice. But in the choruses there is great originality of treatment. Much of the style is after Handel—see 'Yet doth the Lord see it not' (in which the threatening phrase (Ex. 24) reappears from Elijah's first recitative),

Ex. 24

Tau   noch Re - gen   kom - men,

'Thanks be to God', 'Be not afraid' and fugues and double fugues abound. On the other hand there are movements in which a plasticity —effected in the general shape of the oratorio by avoidance of too many end-stopped numbers—of timbre is achieved by a new synthesis of voices and orchestra. In fact chorus and orchestra become one. This, hinted at in *Die erste Walpurgisnacht* and in the fragmentary *Loreley*, was an important contribution of Mendelssohn to nineteenth-century technique. Notice the use of C major in 'His mercies on thousands fall' and the symbolic spread of the musical material; the graciousness of the undulating background in 'Blessed are the men who fear Him';

the serenity of 'He watching over Israel', the transference of mood from E minor to E major in 'Behold! God the Lord passed by', and the brazen fury of the Baal music and the interjections in 'Be not afraid'.

The design of *Elijah* has lent itself to dramatic presentation and a stage version was for a number of years one of the annual highlights of the Royal Albert Hall in London. The oratorio is laid out thus: 1–5 the Thirsty People; 8–9 the Widow; 10–17 the Priests of Baal; 19–20 the Miracle of Rain. The second part of the Oratorio is more lyrical but Elijah's return from his sojourn in the desert and his disappearance in the fiery chariot balance the earlier dramatic fervour. It is not Mendelssohn's dramatic capacity, however, which is important; but his fusion of the dramatic and the musical, so that, in the end, it is the music which conducts its own logical case.

6

The Nineteenth Century II

MEDIOCRITY IN SPATE

THERE has rarely been a period of fifty years in the whole history of music when so much deplorable music by so many experienced composers was written as in the last half of the nineteenth century. There is no need to look beyond the great heaps of discarded choral compositions which represent almost the total output in this medium of practically every composer whether major or minor. It is recognized that much choral music of all periods is neglected. But in the seventeenth and eighteenth centuries and in the earlier part of the nineteenth century such neglect is a misfortune. We are reminded that while there are picture galleries, each with its fund of masterpieces, all over the world, we are limited to the meagre resources of our own provincial collection.

The unknown choral works of Handel and Bach, and their Italian contemporaries, of Haydn and Mozart and Beethoven and (within the limitations already defined) Berlioz and Schumann are significant works in the development of their composers and have all the vitality and variety which is to be found in purely instrumental music. When, however, we reach Wagner, Liszt, Grieg, Cui, Mussorgsky, Tchaikovsky, Smetana, Dvořák, Gounod, Franck, Sullivan, Sibelius, Reger, Wolf, Strauss (to take only the more celebrated of the period) we are aware of imaginative indifference, technical disability and a general reluctance to forsake the enchantments of symphony and symphonic poems, of opera and ballet, of chamber music and song unless for immediate and easy profit. Liszt and Dvořák stand somewhat apart from the others of the group, for both contributed much that was either original or beautiful to choral music. Still further away are those composers who have not been named: Brahms, Bruckner, Verdi, Gabriel Fauré, Edward Elgar and—perhaps—Hubert Parry and Charles Villiers Stanford.

There remains still another group: Frederick Gore Ouseley,

Michael Costa, William Sterndale Bennett, Alfred Gaul, Joseph Barnby, Julius Benedict, Frederick Cowen, Henry Hugh Pierson, John Barnett, Alexander Mackenzie, John Stainer (the British were nothing if not industrious); Josef Schachner, Niels Gade, Peter Cornelius, Max Bruch; and the Americans (who were mostly busy in transferring European musical habits across the Atlantic)—J. C. D. Parker, J. K. Paine, W. W. Gilchrist, Dudley Buck, G. W. Chadwick, A. W. Foote and H. W. Parker. These represent that great body of composers, some untrained and intuitive, some highly (and generally Teutonically) educated, but all obedient to 'academic' rectitude on the one hand and the principle that the customer is always right on the other. To look at any music by any of these composers is to appreciate the shock which Elgar's *Dream of Gerontius* caused.

Many nineteenth-century choral works were written to order. This, of course, is true of much music of earlier times; but since commissioned works of the nineteenth century were generally intended for the 'masses' rather than for a specialized community attuned to a special purpose and tradition (as in the Lutheran church in Leipzig and in the Catholic churches of Austria) or for an eclectic and often critically appreciative minority, such works were bound to aim at a rather low common denominator of knowledge and feeling. Now the 'popular' facet could have been absorbed but for the prevalent opinion that 'good taste' should distinguish choral music. We have already discovered that Spohr met with some opposition over the too-bracing climate of the text of *Calvary*; in 1886 Dvořák's *St. Ludmilla*, so far as the libretto was concerned, was criticized at Leeds as having 'no sense in it, while a great deal of it is irreverent'; the *Dream of Gerontius* was offensive to many Christians because of Newman rather than Elgar.

The wise composer therefore limited himself to safe, if sometimes obscure, subjects: to the story of *Hezekiah* (Pierson), of *Eli* and *Naaman* (Costa), of *St. Polycarp* and *Hagar* (Gore Ouseley), of *St. Kevin, or the Gate of Kathleen*—a more interesting choice (Ioseph Smith of Dublin), of *Israel's Return from Babylon* (Schachner), of *The Prodigal Son* (Sullivan), of *The Rose of Sharon*—which gave scope for much prettiness to a composer of talent in effective orchestration (Mackenzie). All these were Festival works, each of which enjoyed its own *succès d'estime* and was the occasion of much pious pleasure. But in the great age of town halls and concert halls (built with respectful obeisance to Classical or, less frequently, Gothic principles) secular works were required which should match the style of the buildings in which they were given, or better the esteem of the committee men who combined good works with oleaginous grandiosity. Many composers dabbled their fingers in the washing-up water of the Romantic revolution. Thus J. F. Barnett set Coleridge (*The Ancient Mariner*) and Moore (*Paradise and the Peri*); Sterndale Bennett set Tennyson—edited by Chorley (*The May Queen*), and, again, Moore; Benedict, who, conducting the Norwich Festival from 1845–78, had a great influence on choral music, essayed heroics in *Richard Coeur de Lion*; Dudley Buck and Sullivan found the happy-ending story of Prince Henry of Hoheneck (and Elsie) an inspiration, each for his *Golden Legend*. The Americans particularly found congenial company with Longfellow and the *Hesperus* was frequently wrecked and *Hiawatha* as often married or taken leave of. Some romantic poets—Shelley and Byron—were too immoral to be allowed into British Town Halls and were banished for the use of Continental composers. The Germans stuck to Goethe and Uhland and Geibel and Herder . . . while an expanding education embraced Norse mythology and Greek drama. National themes inspired the smaller European countries intent on emancipation and on the necessity—for composers who saw themselves as prophets—of influencing public taste.

The greater number of composers of the period learned their craft in Germany, excepting, of course, the French and Italians who, in any case, were less implicated in choral music. Sterndale Bennett, Cowen, Pierson, Barnett, Sullivan and Stanford among the British, and Dudley Buck and G. W. Chadwick among the Americans acquired at least part of their musical technique in Leipzig (where also were to be found all the Scandinavians), while Mackenzie, Parry, J. K. Paine and H. W. Parker underwent training in other German cities. The German academic tradition is evident in fields other than that of choral music. Much competent instrumental music was composed throughout Europe and America; precise, competent, thoroughly Germanic—and often entirely innocent of any genuine poetic suggestion, but herein language was not affected. In choral music (and, for that matter, in song), however, German teaching on melodic structure and phrase-balance, vocal lay-out, rhythmic method and harmonic development destroyed the delicate relationship which should exist between music and language; particularly at a time of literary fertility. It was possible until not so long ago to graduate as a Doctor of Music by practising the same principles.

Barnett's Ancient Mariner[1] (1867) was once highly esteemed. As the sopranos are invited to a high C sharp in the last few bars it might still win some esteem. Whether this form of expression (Ex. 1) would

Ex. 1   Andante religioso ... The souls did from their bo - dies fly, They

fled to bliss or woe

prove so attractive as used to be the case is more doubtful. But in this sort of petrified romanticism repose most of the emotional excitements of the later nineteenth-century choralists. It will be noted, time after time, that such passages have a domestic-interior flavour and neatly match the *bric-à-brac* which we ought to, but daren't (or for which we have a secret passion or a sentimental regard), shake out. Maybe the oratorios and cantatas and part-songs will be resuscitated by scholarly excavators one day; but many of them are past even that. The reason: nine-tenths of such music was spiritually born in Germany and German standards in that respect were in decline. At least among those who taught.

We may, then, examine the state of German choral composition.

GERMANY AND AUSTRIA: THE WORKS OF BRAHMS AND BRUCKNER

There is an interesting passage in Wagner's autobiography[2] which details the circumstances leading up to his composition of the *Liebesmahl der Apostel* for Dresden.

'As I was obliged at all costs to finish it within a limited time, I do not mind including this in the list of my uninspired com-

---

[1] Performed first at the Birmingham Triennial Festival of 1867.
[2] *My Life*, Eng. translation (pub. London 1911), pp. 310 *et seq.*

positions. . . . When . . . twelve hundred singers from all parts of
Saxony gathered around me in the Frauenkirche,[1] where the performance took place, I was astonished at the comparatively feeble
effect produced upon my ear by this colossal human tangle of
sounds. The conclusion which I arrived at was that these enormous
choral undertakings are folly, and I never again felt inclined to
repeat the experiment. The members of the Dresden Glee Club
were merchants, government officials and other professional men
[it sounds very like a Rotary Club] who displayed a not unfamiliar
blend of charm and philistinism: [they] had more taste for any kind
of convivial entertainment than for music.'

And so they were well satisfied, as also the smaller mixed voice
choirs, with the clichés offered by Weber and Mendelssohn and Hiller
and Schumann. Their successors continued to enjoy the same sort of
sentiments—love of woman, hearth, fatherland, ghosts, sprites, trees
—treated in much the same sort of four-square way by Brahms (see
Op. 41 and 93b), Cornelius, Wolf, Reger and Strauss. Many of these
pieces sprang from the same source of inspiration as the *Lieder* (as is
equally true of Wagnerian music drama), but the medium lacked the
poetic possibilities afforded by the more subtle combination of voice
and pianoforte. The heavy gait of the German part-song (see Cornelius's
egregious 'Beethoven-lied', Op. 10, with its quotations from the
'Eroica'), the muddied intellectualism of the harmonic movement (see
Cornelius's *Requiem* in commemoration of Hebbel), or the barren
tonic-dominant see-saw to a $\frac{4}{4}$ time signature (see Brahms' *Marienlieder*)
which expose superficial cheerfulness, or the earnest contrapuntal
junketings of Reger (see *Palm Sunday Morning*) all make this a tiresome
field; which in this particular enfolds Sibelius (despite the $\frac{5}{4}$ of his Op.18
No. 7), Tchaikovsky (see the well-known *Legend*), Mussorgsky (see
The Destruction of Sennacherib),[2] Taneiev (see *Die Alpen*), and almost
everyone else! No doubt this music is serviceable at competitive
festivals, for the adjudicator is relieved from the distraction of considering music as well as its performance; but it is stagnant. Yet out of this
style arose the great *Deutsches Requiem* by Brahms—a work which, it
may be said, clearly shows its origins.

---

[1] For the reinterment in Germany of the body of Weber.
[2] '. . . essentially orchestral music with vocal *obbligati*; the choral parts are seldom independent
and . . . might almost be dispensed with.' See *Mussorgsky*, M. D. Calvocoressi, p. 180.

I remember how once an experienced musician detected in me—
then a student—a growing reverence for Brahms, and, in particular, for
the *Requiem*. 'Ah,' he said with mild disapproval, 'but it isn't in the same
street as the *Mass in B Minor*.' The everlasting touchstone—Bach! I
suppose I have fought against the odious comparison for more than
twenty years. Brahms, truly, is not Bach. Nor is Shakespeare Milton.
And I sense there an analogy. Bach is lofty, intellectual, profound and
poetical after the Miltonic manner. Brahms has an affinity with
Shakespeare, whose poetry, and the actions which made the poetry,
sprang from common speech and, more significantly, common
thought. It was the commonplace philosophy of everyday life that
inspired the Shakespeare canon. And in Brahms, despite technical skill
and apparent profundity, it is the intensification of what is commonplace that is durable. It is admirable to admire Brahms on account of
his contrapuntal excellence: it is more admirable to recognize that (in
the *Requiem*) fugal form gave him a particular opportunity to achieve a
rare exaltation of an abiding hope: that 'redeemed souls are in the hand
of God' and that the Lord 'is worthy of praise and glory, honour and
power'. It will appear that all the masterly moments of the *Requiem* are
obvious in conception and often in execution: the same may be said of
Bruckner. Insofar as other writers of choral music of the period were
concerned what was obvious (emotionally and imaginatively) was by-
passed in favour of what was proper. Propriety is a poor guide.

Brahms is, above all, a balanced musician. On this account he has
been especially respected in England and America. In England, indeed,
through the devotion of Parry and Stanford his influence has been
more profound than in most other countries (particularly is this true
in the matter of chamber music). Brahms is (despite Schoenbergian
emphasis on his pioneering)[1] regarded as thoroughly 'classical'. We
note, of course, that he was a great architectural stylist; and that he was
one of the three or four notable exponents of *Lied*. Perhaps we less often
notice that it was in the synthesis of his several abilities that originality
lay. The *Requiem* is a symphony; but it is also a vast *Lied*.

Of the 'greater' composers of the late nineteenth century Brahms
was the most prolific and various in respect of choral music. When he
was employed at the little court of Detmold, from 1857 to 1859, he
conducted a Ladies' Chorus. That he enjoyed the experience is con-
firmed by his foundation of a similar chorus in Hamburg. For these

[1] See *Style and Idea*.

groups he composed a good deal of music that is mostly notable for an easy Mendelssohnian grace, which sometimes, as in the songs (Op. 17) for female voices, 2 horns and harp, dwindles into negligibility and at others rises to the interrogatory plane where Brahms is frequently to be found frowning at philosophic discontent. The last cadence of the *Ave Maria* (Op. 12) dropping down in the reflective manner of a consolatory phrase in the first movement of the *Requiem* runs into unexpected harmonic anxiety and in the not otherwise remarkable setting of Psalm XIII (Op. 27) the prospect of death finds Brahms with the fog in his throat and a stiffening of both harmonic and rhythmic method. This contemplation of mortality led Brahms to see the possibilities of the choral medium in relation to his own seriousness of outlook. He saw also the limitations of the homophonic practice—in which he would readily engage for the easy arrangement of folksongs or agreeable settings of von Arnim and Rückert, of Eichendorff, Müller, von Chamisso and Brentano for any choral body—of his period and sought a sharpening of choral expression by reference to the Bach motets. In texture Brahms learned greatly from Bach as also from Handel—see the motets (Op. 29, 74, 109,[1] 110) and, even more notably, the chorale preludes (Op. 122) for the organ. Mendelssohn had also learned from Bach, but Brahms was able to add to high competence in canonic and fugal presentation resources of harmonic expression that belonged to his generation.

Between 1867 and 1872 Brahms was much less engaged in instrumental than in vocal music. To this period the *Requiem* (1868), the cantata *Rinaldo*, to Goethe's text (1868), the *Rhapsodie*, for alto voice and male voice choir and orchestra—also to a text of Goethe (1869), *Schicksalslied* (1870), the poem being by Hölderlin (1871), the *Triumphlied*, a patriotic piece occasioned by Prussian successes in the Franco-Prussian War.

It has been suggested that the *Requiem* was occasioned by the death of Schumann, by the death of Brahms' mother (1865—in the following year Brahms commenced the composition of the work), or by both. It is probable there was such direct stimulus. Indeed the beautiful fifth movement—added after the remainder of the *Requiem* had, for the first time, been performed in Bremen Cathedral (Good Friday, April 10th, 1868)—was acknowledged by the composer as a particular tribute to

---

[1] Entitled *Fest-und Gedenksprüche*: in these more ceremonious pieces the Handelian influence is strong.

his mother's memory. But in one sense such a work as the *Requiem* was inevitable, for the idea of death is a persistent motive in the thought of Brahms.

The *Requiem* title as applied by Brahms generally and not particularly, for this is no liturgical work. The words were selected from the Lutheran Bible. The range of Brahms' study of the Bible is shown by his selection and arrangement of texts for the *Requiem*. The whole sequence so exquisitely planned to make an anthology of consolation, with a climax of sublimity in the paradisal joys of the fourth and the apotheosis of mother love in the fifth movement. (Despite Brahms' protestations of unorthodoxy in theology it must be felt that in his fifth movement he comes within the universal chivalry and devotion symbolized in other creeds in the mother cult.) And the words for each section are planned so that the symphonic musical structure does in fact arise naturally from contemplation of the words.

The plan of the words is as follows:
I Matthew v, 4; Psalm cxxvi, 5–6. II 1 Peter, 24–5; James v, 7; Isaiah xxxv, 10. III Psalm xxxix, 4–8; Wisdom iii, 1. IV Psalm lxxxiv, 1–2, 4. V John xvi, 22; Ecclesiasticus li, 27; Isaiah lxvi, 13. VI Hebrews xiii, 14 1 Corinthians xv, 51–55; Revelation iv, 11. VII Revelation xiv, 13.

It may be noted that Brahms appears not only to interpret the words as they stand, but also to interpret their biblical context so that in the fifth movement, for instance, while setting John xvi, 22, he also appears to incorporate the sensibility of verse 21. The *Requiem* had some great personal significance for Brahms, but like the poet Gray 'he never spoke out', so the purely personal is absorbed into a consideration of humanity in general. It is this attitude, together with an inability to accept facile interpretations and points of view, which relieves Brahms of any suspicion of sentimentality. It is not difficult to be didactic. Nor is it difficult to utter platitudes in token of sympathy. It is extremely difficult to be gracious and comforting, yet just and rigorous. This is what Brahms achieves.

Musically this works out thus. The design of the *Requiem* is firm. The first movement is in three-part form—F major, D-flat major and, recapitulating, F major. The second movement, a great Funeral March which may have originated in earlier symphonic sketches,[1] rises in B flat minor from the preceding F major, quickens into a gentle

---

[1] According to Max Kalbeck this movement was first conceived as a slow movement for a two-piano sonata which became the Concerto in D minor (op. 15).

pastoral episode in which patience sits on no monument but pulses with
the eager expectation of a child (how beautifully Brahms could read
the child mind is shown in other works): then the inexorable trend of
the first part returns to subside into a cadence ending with a Picardy
third. Out of this an eight-measure prelude bursts to lead into a
triumphant fugue in B flat major, wherein the German four-squareness
of the subject is offset by cross-rhythmic figures, by augmentation, by
stretto and by judicious textural contrasts. The end of this fugue is in
quiet ecstasy. In the third movement the state of man and the expectation of common mortality are cast in a solemn kind of cantata movement—with choral homophony interspersed severely and dramatically
in the questioning reaches of the baritone solo. This section, cast in
D minor, borrows from Lutheran hymnology in spirit at least (there is
the ghost of the chorale melody 'Vater unser' in the melodic germ and
in the tonality), but uncertainly conveys itself to the rhythmic structure,
which crosses $\frac{2}{2}$ and $\frac{3}{2}$ patterns. All of this resolves into a passage which
is the inevitable musical link with the succeeding fugue of 'the souls
redeemed'. For the interrogatory triplets suddenly become rhapsodic,
the key is established as D major, and polyphony is shown as
emancipation.

Above all Brahms is lyrical and this work is unique among those in
the oratorio-cantata-Mass field in its expression of the pre-eminent
quality of the German–Austrian *Lied*. However much we may discover, as in the fourth and fifth movements, such technical devices as
we have met in earlier music, of inversion, augmentation, fugato and
double counterpoint we are carried up into the soaring melodic virtue of
the music. The fourth movement, in $\frac{3}{4}$ time is in E flat major; the fifth,
with solo soprano, first alone and then poised above the chorus, is in
G major which, following the general feeling of tonal expression
hereabouts, steps up another third into B major. The sixth movement,
despite an opening which explores tonal unrest in accord with the
vagrant sense of the words is the tonic (C minor/major) to the
dominant of the fifth movement. The scheme is similar to that of the
third movement and the end-piece is again a fugue: this time a more
magisterial fugue, built on a more or less strict subject which allows no
great play of imagination. This, perhaps, is the section of the work
which has least interest. Having established C major Brahms rounds off
his tonal structure by returning to F major. In his last movement he
develops melodic material from the first movement. While in general

the last movement is in complement to the first it is not mere repetition and shows new lyrical growth. The middle section differs from that of the first movement in reaching *up* a third to the brighter quality of A major. (In the first movement the central portion, it will be recalled, was in D flat major.)

Emphasis on the structure of music is evident in the other major choral works. Both the *Schicksalslied* (Song of Destiny) and the beautiful, nostalgic *Nänie* mark their limits by a final return to first thoughts—even though such action is not called for by the immediate character of the words.

In harmonic and rhythmic development Brahms was to grow beyond the material nature of the *Requiem*, but in appositeness he never surpassed this achievement. Notice the keyless introduction to the sixth movement, and the pictorial detail of the melodic line also: the transition to F sharp minor ('We shall not all sleep') with the restless movement of the bass against the almost motionless voices: the enharmonic movement towards C minor and the prodigious exertions (in *vivace* ¾ time) of the resurrected at the sound of the last trumpet— which requires no imitative fanfares. Somewhere behind all this lies the great central section of the 'Confiteor' of the *Mass in B Minor*. In almost every measure it is possible to point to reflection of verbal atmosphere, but the listener will perceive for himself how unnecessary such demonstration of the obvious is. For the picturesque detail is never allowed to impede the lyrical flow of the whole. The suppression of violins in the first movement is a *locus classicus*: but this had precedents in earlier German Passion music, and also in Brahms' own second orchestral serenade.

It would equally be possible to point to melodic beauty in every measure. It must here suffice to draw the reader's attention to the fifth movement. This is the characteristic Brahms, inspired in melodic invention, in harmonic underwriting, in contrapuntal gloss and sympathetic orchestration.

The *Deutsches Requiem* was slow in attracting either respect or affection. When the first three movements were performed in Vienna, under Johann Herbeck, on December 1st, 1867, the audience audibly expressed its disapproval. Since rehearsals had been inadequate it was, no doubt, a strange experience; particularly since the long kettle-drum roll of the final fugue of the third movement was—either by accident or design—played *sempre fortissimo* to the ruination of everything else.

The Bremen performance was carefully considered by Karl Martin Rheinthaler, organist of the Cathedral. At Bremen the work was well received, but not at Leipzig in the following year, nor in London when the first performances took place in 1873. There was, however (cf. the first introduction of Beethoven's *Missa Solennis* into England) a private performance of the *Requiem* at the home of Lady Henry Thompson,[1] wife of a distinguished surgeon, as early as 1871: this was notable in that it was directed by Julius Stockhausen, who had sung the baritone solos at Bremen. The accompaniment [and here is a hint to indigent societies unable to afford a complete orchestra] was for two pianos and Lady Thompson shared it with Cipriani Potter, the first Principal of the Royal Academy of Music in London. The *Requiem* was introduced into America in 1883 by Theodore Thomas, a notable pioneer, at the Cincinatti Festival.

The *Schicksalslied* and the *Rhapsodie* are choral ballads, but once again Brahms fuses the lyrical with the symphonic. (In its contrasts between the turmoil of earth and the tranquillity of some heavenly hereafter, between the smooth $\frac{4}{4}$ opening, the tumultuous cataract of the central $\frac{3}{4}$ section, and the concluding recollection of the opening, Brahms gives in the *Schicksalslied* an abstract of the *Requiem*.) But this, to Hölderlin's text, is devoid of religious significance. The *Rhapsodie*, a setting of stanzas from Goethe's *Harzreise im Winter*, is notable for the strange and strong accents of the solo voice and for the skill with which Brahms exploits his vocal timbres. The characteristic of the hymn-like answer (in C major) to the familiar tumultuous heart-rending of C minor is the sonorous effect of the texture; this depth of tone is to be found throughout Brahms' choral writing.

Anton Bruckner has two attributes in common with Brahms: seriousness and competence in vocal writing. Bruckner, however, derives from southern, Austrian antecedents and his great church music springs from the same warm culture that generated Mozart, Haydn and Schubert: the intellectualism of the North is absent; in its place a colourful devotion to the tenets of provincial Catholicism. For a time Bruckner was organist in Linz, where his first symphony (unpublished) and his great Masses in F minor and E minor were composed and first performed. In 1868 Bruckner went to Vienna to teach at the Conservatory. In Vienna, where he gained the dislike of Hanslick who

---

[1] Before her marriage Kate Loder, a celebrated pianist. For details of this performance see *Musical Times*, January 1906; also *Proceedings of the Royal Musical Association*, 1883–4.

treated all who admired Wagner with contumely, he wrote the last eight of his symphonies and also the rich settings of the *Te Deum* and *Psalm* 150.

It is generally emphasized that Bruckner (like Franck, but in an even higher degree) was remarkable for spiritual zeal and for singleness of purpose in matters ecclesiastical. It is, of course, no bad thing to believe in the texts which you set. It is also no bad, nor extraordinary, attitude to have some pride in national traditions. Bruckner's church music is effective because of its emphasis on liturgical propriety and Austrian conventions on the one hand and the absorption of contemporary habits of technique on the other. It has been said[1] that 'the best church music, like the best stage music, loses much of its point when it is divorced from its original surroundings'. This may not invariably be true, but it often is, and it must be suggested that both church and stage music to be ideal should not be so close-packed with detail that there is no room for the other attributes of liturgy and drama. In Bruckner's Masses the liturgical background is strongly felt, which makes them not ideal for the concert hall. On the technical side Bruckner's choral writing is grateful to the singer and set on the firm bases of fluent polyphony and impressive homophony: his orchestration, like his use of chromatic harmony (he was a devoted disciple of Wagner), is warm if not demonstrative and his employment of the brass (see especially the E Minor Mass) is hieratic: he has a fine sense of occasion. This is excitingly shown in the great festal works—the *Te Deum* and *Psalm 150*. Both are in C major (as are the 'Gloria' and 'Credo' of the F Minor Mass) and it would be difficult to find two other works of the period which so effectively extend the exhilarating associations of a tonality much used by Handel and Beethoven in similar contexts. There is an admirable succinctness in the design and masculinity in the rhythmic pulse, while busy strings glitter behind the clear-cut statements of the chorus, often in octaves and in Mozartian brilliance. This contrasts with the revelation of the deeper spiritual qualities of a single violin—as displayed in the 'Salvum fac' of the *Te Deum* and also in the 'Et incarnatus est' section of the *Mass in F minor*. It is in the slow section that impatience with Bruckner's chromatic colouring may be forgiven. The voluptuous shifts of harmony in the 'Et incarnatus est' section of the *Mass in F minor* is a particular case in point. Much more beautiful is the motet-style presentation of the same

[1] By H. C. Colles in *Oxford History of Music*, Vol. VII. p. 436.

clause in the *Mass in E Minor*, where, obviously, the instrumentation cannot behave so seductively (Ex. 2). Indeed the *Mass in E Minor*

Ex. 2

throughout is a finer work, more rigorous and less prone to irrelevancies, than the larger work in F minor. And, in the 'Sanctus' especially it can rise to such heights as should keep it among the great works and certainly worthy of Dr. Hermann Kretzschmar's comment—'Eine vokale Komposition nach dem Prinzip der Renaissance-Musik.' ('A vocal work according to the principles of Renaissance music.')

'REQUIEM'—VERDI

Seven years after the *Deutsches Requiem* of Brahms was first performed in Vienna a different type of *Requiem* was presented: that of Verdi. In 1874 this work was condemned by von Bülow (who afterwards retracted his hostile opinion). One effect of von Bülow's opinion was to stimulate Brahms to a study of the score. And Brahms, for all his dislike of many aspects of contemporary music, declared it to be a work of genius. One suspects that Brahms saw in it precisely that form of genius which he himself lacked. What Brahms admired is set out in one of Hanslick's notable essays, in which may be seen his own critical perception and the atmosphere of nineteenth-century Viennese musical appreciation with all its currents and cross-currents of opinion and prejudice.

'In June of 1875, Verdi directed four performances of his Requiem in Vienna, scoring a series of triumphs over a hostile combination of summer heat and high admission prices. The public received the work with unwonted enthusiasm; our best connoisseurs and laymen, among them many a sworn anti-Verdian, participated unreservedly in the applause. Verdi, already so ill-considered as an opera composer in German countries, must have been prepared for the bitterest opposition as a church composer, the more so since it is one of the delights of the German critic to dampen the public's pleasure by merciless fault-finding in trivial and superficial matters. . . .

Verdi's Requiem is a sound and beautiful work, above all a milestone in the history of his development as a composer . . . it is unmistakably Verdi, wholly and completely. The study of old Roman church music shines through it, but only as a glimmer, not as a model.

To be sure—and this must be stated at the outset—the theatre has greater need of Verdi than has the church. If he has shown in the Requiem what he can do on foreign soil, he remains, nevertheless, far stronger on his home ground. Not even in the Requiem can he deny the dramatic composer. Mourning and supplication, awe and faith; they speak here in language more passionate and individual than we are accustomed to hear in the church.

. . . Verdi, following the better Neapolitan church music, had denied neither the rich artistic means of his time nor the lively fervour of his nature. He has, like many a pious painter, placed his own portrait on his sacred canvas. Religious devotion, too, varies in its expression; it has its countries and its times. What may appear so passionate, so sensuous in Verdi's Requiem is derived from the emotional habits of his people, and the Italian has a perfect right to enquire whether he may not talk to the dear Lord in the Italian language!'

(It may sometimes appear that Verdi not only talks but even shouts at the dear Lord in the strongest accents of Italian volubility!)

It should at once be said that this *Requiem* is first a highly personal work and secondly not intended for exclusive ecclesiastical use. It may also be said that Verdi, for his sympathies with Italian liberalism, was by no means in favour in conservative Italian church circles at this period of his career. Death is invariably affecting and no man will regard it with indifference. In the case of an artist grief will often go so far beneath the surface that to escape it and, at the same time, to placate it he must create; for creation is the answer to dissolution. I remember the German composer Sigfried Karg-Elert once, with tears in his eyes, pointing out to me a chorale prelude which he had written on the day his mother died. In 1867 and 1868 Verdi, himself in poor health, suffered the loss first of his father-in-law Antonio Barezzi and next of Rossini, whom he both liked and admired. The correspondence of Verdi shows his gratitude to his friends and benefactors; his impulsiveness; and his own generosity. The death of Rossini, he said, should not lack its proper memorial and he proposed that the leading composers of Italy should collaborate in a *Requiem* which he hoped might be performed in Bologna. But no one else displayed very much interest and the scheme foundered. There survived, however, Verdi's setting of the great and solemn responsorium 'Libera me'. At once let it be stated that Verdi's intention was to have this work sung by the company of the Teatro Communale and that if the whole is adjudged theatrical that is, in these circumstances, as should be.

In 1873 the writer Alessandro Manzoni (whose novel *I Promessi Sposi* in reissue after many years has lately stimulated a new respect for Manzoni's genius) died. Manzoni was a close personal friend of Verdi, and the composer greatly admired his gifts. After his death Verdi wrote to the municipal authorities in Milan, of which city Manzoni was a native, and offered a commemorative work which, he said, sprang from 'impulse or, rather, from a heartfelt necessity'. The *Requiem* was performed for the first time on May 22nd, 1874, in St. Mark's Church, Milan. Verdi directed a specially chosen choir of 120 singers and an orchestra of 110 players, and the soloists were Teresa Stoltz (the first *Aïda* of 1872), Maria Waldmann (a personal friend of the Verdis who also took part in *Aïda*), Giuseppe Capponi, and Ormondo Marini. The reception of the *Requiem* was tumultuous in Milan. In the following year it was performed in Vienna—with results which have already been described, in Paris—where there was more enthusiasm, and in London, where it was inevitable that such admiration as was shown should be tempered by Protestant suspicions.

Italian Catholics of Verdi's generation mostly accepted the suggestions and pictorial definitions of the text of the *Requiem*. As Verdi wrote so they felt. The classical restraint of the Palestrina period (which, from a distance, Verdi esteemed)[1] was unknown to the great majority in 1874 and religious feeling was dominated by a complete surrender to all that was pictorial. The greatness of the work lies precisely in its intelligibility to those for whom it was written. Dr. Vaughan Williams on one occasion made a spirited defence of cultural nationalism as essential to true internationalism. 'Our own community, language, customs, religion, are essential to our spiritual health.' Dr. Vaughan Williams would have been the last to deny an equal right to Italians as to the English to mature their art within their own environment. And so we must approach Verdi's *Requiem*.

The first movement—'Requiem aeternam dona eis, Domine'—is at once evocative. There is sadness, mystery, the sense of vast distances; there is penitence and humility. The key is A minor and this is announced by the muted cellos in a downward arpeggio and a scale phrase which reaches down from one dominant to another. The violins, supported by the remaining strings (but without double-bass), repeat the arpeggio, at the end of which the chorus tenors and basses enter in bare fifths and these are echoed in the upper voices. 'Rest eternal', set to a complete major chord, has great tranquillity. Then four sopranos, missing out the first beat of each bar, turn to contrite prayer: 'Grant them, Lord, Thy rest.' To lighten the darkness of mood a Schubertian change to A major brings the idea of the 'light eternal'. A further change—to F major—shows Verdi in emulation of the classical methods of polyphonic music. Unaccompanied, and in four parts, the chorus treat imitatively this figure (Ex. 3). The opening section is

Ex. 3

Te   de - cet   hym - nus,

repeated and leads to the 'Kyrie', again in A major. The contrapuntal idea is sustained and this—delivered by tenor solo—(Ex. 4) undergoes

[1] See his letter to Boïto, quoted in Hussey (p. 213) in which he replies to an enquiry regarding the proper curriculum for a State School of Choral Music. In the same letter Verdi faults Monteverdi for poor part-writing.

Ky - ri - e   e - le -   -   -   - i - son

impassioned treatment. The orchestra is without brass for the time being and, apart from some delicate filigree of sixteenth notes in string and flutes, functions mostly as an enhancement of the vocal parts. The vocal parts are full of variety and the effect of solo voices, and small groups, first of high and then of low voices, repeating the crucial word 'eleison' (have mercy), in suggestion of a vast concourse of prayerful souls. The movement ends *pianissimo*. The three concluding chords— of F major, B flat major and (after a dominant seventh) A major—are as striking as they are simple.

The 'Dies Irae' brings all resources into play. This is a vast movement in every way. There are 701 bars of music: the dynamic range is from *fff* to *pppp*: the tempo has *allegro agitato* at one extreme (for 'Dies Irae') and *adagio* (for 'Quid sum miser') at the other: as for key we are taken through almost all the major and minor keys. Every opportunity is taken to achieve precision in pictorial detail. All the diminished sevenths, compulsions of rhythm, chromatic descents, torrents of sixteenth notes, angry outbursts of brass (note Verdi's close writing of trombone parts (bar 78 *et seq.*), punctuations of bass drum ('Mors stupebit'), and vocal contrasts that we might expect are present. And for the 'Tuba mirum' there is the additional brass chorus—but here, out of sight, in *lontanza ed invisibili*—to put us in mind of Berlioz. The *picture* is as complete as a picture can be. The music is visually commanding. But then there is the musical architecture: the immense vocal sweep of every singing part; the ineluctable musical climaxes, whether of melody (see the treatment of 'Salva me') or harmony (see the consecutive triads of 'Ora supplex et acclinis' and, especially, the final juxtaposition of G and B flat tonalities). And amid all the complexities of technical virtuosity there stands out the abiding simplicity of the composer's personal faith in the concluding prayer— 'Pie Jesu'.

The 'Offertorio' ('Domine Jesu Christe') is set as a solo quartet and in the key of A flat. This is a movement of great beauty—perhaps too great beauty unless therein lies the true consolation of too deep grief; but its musical purpose is plain as it succeeds the 'Dies Irae'. Deliver the souls of the departed from darkness and the forms of darkness, the words of this most terrifying poem say; let the holy Michael take them into the light. This is Verdi's inspiration at that point (Ex. 5). The

violin melody is the main melody of the movement. The contrast to the lyrical fluency of the main part of the piece is in the more or less pedestrian setting of 'Quam olim Abrahae promisisti'. Verdi sets out along the road of convention to write a fugue; but this is no more than a gesture.

The relatively brief 'Sanctus' is laid out in F major with brilliant ease but, despite the apparatus of a double fugue, an engaging simplicity. Just as in the 'Requiem' the appropriate colouring comes from an arpeggio so it is here: but this time the figure surges upward against another rising theme.

The 'Agnus Dei' is in C major. It opens, unexpectedly, with the solo soprano and contralto in octaves but without accompaniment: a long, flowing, solemn extension of prayer (Ex. 6) which is repeated by the choir, an octave lower, and with clarinets, bassoons and strings reinforcing, but not harmonizing, the voices. A minor variant of the theme, with pensive counterpoint in flute and clarinet, follows. Next

Ex. 6 Andante dolciss.

S. (M.S. 8va lower)

Ag - nus De - i, — Ag - nus De - i, qui —

tol - lis · pec-ca - ta mun - di, do - na, — do - na,

e - is, do - - - na e - is re - qui-em;

a fully harmonized statement in the original major by choir and a fuller orchestra. The soloists yet again announce the theme and round it three flutes weave a pattern of quarter notes. The chorus end the movement with another slight variant, and expand into a tiny coda.

In the 'Lux aeterna', set as a solo trio, Verdi seizes on the immediate vision of supernal brightness. Against the shimmer of tremolo strings— at first the divided violins only—the sopranos give out a melody which has its roots in the traditional chant of the church (Ex. 7). (The F sharp

Ex. 7 ppp

Lux ae - ter - na lu - ce - at e - is, Do - mi - ne, ·

eventually turns into F natural so that at the end the movement may come safely home into the key of B flat major.) This is a poetic move-ment, infused with quiet beauties (note the trombone chords, the floating strings, the piccolo and flute illuminations) and much serenity.

The conclusion of the whole work is the 'Libera me' which, in whole or in part, survived from the project for a memorial Mass for Rossini. The necessity of a musical work to achieve a convincing musical form acceptable to the conventions of its own period is shown here as effectively as by Brahms in his *Requiem*. Verdi introduces into 'Libera me' a recapitulation both of the introductory 'Requiem aeternam' and the 'Dies Irae'.[1] Before the chorus reintroduce the 'Dies Irae' the solo soprano, hitherto not heard but with other voices, makes the concept of the Last Judgement intensely personal in a form of recitative that reaches out both to church and theatre. The recapitulated

[1] Although the verbal recollection of the 'Dies irae' is not exact, here being non-metrical. Cf. 'Dies irae, dies illa calamitatis et miseriae, dies magna et amara valde' with the previous metrical

Dies irae, dies illa
Solvet saeclum in favilla,
Teste David cum Sibylla.

'Requiem' gives to the voices that material which at first belonged to the orchestra and this key is now B flat minor—major, And over all is the dominating voice of the solo soprano. The final section 'Libera me' is a fugue (note the dramatic orchestral strokes which penetrate the exposition) which, with its *picturesquely* moving use of augmentation and stretto, resolves into a final utterance of the solo sopranos—above a sustained *ppp* chord of C major in the voices alone: 'Libera me, Domine, de morte aeterna, in die illa tremenda' to a monotoned C. The choir take up the monotone and dissolve from view: 'Libera me, libera me'. The drum rolls beneath and two deep chords of C major from the full orchestra (*ppp* and *morendo*) underline 'me'.

In 1898, the composer then being eighty-five, four sacred works of widely differing nature were published. Of these one—an *Ave Maria* for four voices *a cappella*—had been composed at an earlier period (*c.* 1889) and was somewhat adventurous in point of harmony.[1] The others were a *Laudi alla Vergine Maria* for unaccompanied women's voices; a moving *Stabat Mater*, with a penetrating, painful opening and a great final *crescendo* to indicate the certain hope of paradisal joys in eternity, for chorus and orchestra; and the *Te Deum* for double chorus and orchestra. The last work is related to the *Requiem* in its humanism, its endeavour to bridge the gap between the ancient traditions of church music and nineteenth-century sensibility. Thus two versions of the same motiv illustrate (Ex. 8 (a) and (b).) This second form develops freely

Ex. 8

(a)   Te De - um   lau - da - mus

(b)   *dolcissimo*

through the work. In the *Requiem* it was, on the whole, the poetic quality which prevailed: and so here. The mystical chords which enshrine 'Sanctus' and the *come in lontananza* triad of G flat major which extends the word infinitely: the apotheosis of another Gregorian tune in the unison setting of 'Tu, Rex gloriae'; the contrast of major and minor and of high voices and low in 'Miserere'; the reminiscence of the solo soprano of the last movement of the *Requiem* in the closing bars of the

[1] Boïto had drawn Verdi's attention to an 'enigmatic scale' published in the *Gazzetta musicale*, consisting of C, D flat, E, F sharp, G sharp, A sharp, B (F natural descending). This stimulated the composer to experiment.

R

Te Deum. These things Verdi did because he trusted his own powers and believed in his own vision.

These *Pezzi Sacri*, except the *Ave Maria*, were first performed in Paris in 1899. The first Italian performance was in the same year, in Milan, and under the direction of Arturo Toscanini.

ELGAR'S 'DREAM OF GERONTIUS'

It is, perhaps, about half true that works of art mirror the life of the times in which they are created. Some do. But equally others reflect not what is but what is not. Elgar is a case in point. It is convenient often to dub him 'Edwardian'. But his two most durable works—the *'Enigma' Variations* and the *Dream of Gerontius*—were composed at the end of the reign of Queen Victoria: but in no way do they conform to any concepts of 'Victorianism'. While the one does not concern us here it is to be remembered that both share a quality in orchestration not previously understood by English composers. Elgar educating himself (in contrast to the general run of 'successful' English composers) was better taught than those of his contemporaries who worked for the eye rather than for the ear. Elgar was the first nineteenth-century English composer to allow his imagination full freedom in large works. On a small scale both Samuel and Samuel Sebastian Wesley (who were confined to church music) produced admirably and often poetically: the motets of the one and the anthems of the other (*In Exitu Israel* and *The Wilderness* being the most familiar) ranging over key contrasts which, for mid-nineteenth century England, were distinctly stimulating. Sullivan was brilliant in one sense but deplorable when it came to 'serious' music. *The Prodigal Son* and *The Golden Legend* are profoundly depressing. Nothing, perhaps, is more depressing than Sullivan's attempts at the horrific: or, perhaps, it is that we know of terrors that fly by night which are more effectual than a Victorian's imaginary portrait of Lucifer. As early as 1868 we find mention of a new West of England composer at the Gloucester Meeting of the Three Choirs: Hubert Parry. He was then twenty years of age. In 1880 he made a more lasting impression with his *Prometheus Unbound*. *The Times* commended Parry for his meticulous care in handling a text, in the choice of which he was also commended. Parry continued a distinguished career in the field of choral music. Parry, however, is remembered now as an administrative and academic influence on the late rebirth of English composition rather than as a composer His spacious setting of Milton's *Blest Pair of Sirens* and his late *Songs of Farewell* merit performance; some of his songs are scrupulous and charming: but, on the whole, he refuses really to come to life in his music. It holds back. And his orchestral scoring is often ponderous.

Usually linked with him is the Irishman, Charles Villiers Stanford (also a very great influence on later composers). Stanford began to appear at the Three Choirs Festivals in 1877 and thereafter he turned out oratorios, cantatas, part songs and what-not for all the great choral festivals. Stanford often achieved effects of rare beauty: the last pages of the oratorio *Eden*, the truly exquisite miniature part song 'The Blue Bird'; and of picturesqueness—as in the cantata *The Revenge* or the set of *Songs of the Sea* for baritone, chorus and orchestra. His talent bordered on genius but his admirable technique was, in general, too neat, too precise, too foreign. Especially were Parry and Stanford immune from any taint of vulgarity.

Now vulgarity was the virtue which Elgar, provincial, unacademic, and uninfluenced by the prevailing fashions, possessed and which they didn't. Vulgarity, of course, is a condition of life and none have realized its presence, its power, its quality in fusing the artistic mind with the inartistic, more than Shakespeare, Defoe, Fielding, Dickens. It is, perhaps, Dickens whose art comes very near to that of Elgar; for both move us to tears when reason suggests that they are merely plucking the strings of sentiment.

I have often set out deliberately to refuse to allow *Gerontius* to overpower me. Yet invariably it does.

At the time of the first performance of *Gerontius* Elgar was forty-three. He had become known—though in no way well-known—through a series of works which had received performance first in the West Country festivals and then in London: works which were boldly conceived, exciting in tonal variety and harmonic colour. *The Black Knight* (based on Longfellow's translation of Uhland's poem) anglicizes the German heroic cantata: the *Songs from the Bavarian Highlands* blend song and dance not much less effectively than Brahms: *King Olaf* and *Caractacus* have fine climactic moments and pages of tranquil beauty: the oratorio *Lux Christi*, if very uneven, has material which grows more significantly in the later works in this form. 'Elgar,' said Ernest

Newman[1] of *Lux Christi*, 'has done almost all that could be done with this deadly form of British art, the day for which has long gone by.'

The Dream of Gerontius 'composed expressly for the Birmingham Musical Festival 1900' is, of course, no *oratorio* with set recitatives, arias and choruses in the accepted manner. Rather is it a work after the nineteenth-century German dramatic cantata manner: and the text is not selected from the Bible, but is taken from Cardinal Newman's poem of 1865. (The subject of *Gerontius* was proposed by the Birmingham Festival committee to Dvořák in 1886, but he rejected the proposal.)

Elgar was, by birth and upbringing, Catholic. Thus he was enabled to see the eschatological significance of Newman's poem from within. Further, the normal priggish habits of 'cathedral settings' (of that period) were as alien to him as the mystical effects of colour and ritual were familiar. It was Vincent Novello, at the beginning of the century, who saw more beauty in music both old and new than many of his contemporaries. He too was Catholic. In infusing English music from this source Elgar, unconsciously, was doing as much to restore the true traditions of English art as those who, contemporaneously, laboured in the field of folk music. Elgar was in communion with the tradition of feeling, just as the folk-song collectors were concerned (insofar as music may be factual) with a tradition of fact. Elgar's tradition was one of warmth; theirs, in no pejorative sense, of coldness. It is significant that nowhere does Elgar show serious interest in folk music.

The Dream of Gerontius survives because the music and the text effect an inescapable unity. This is not a matter of 'accentuation' (for Elgar was no pedant in this respect), not of 'word-painting', nor, indeed, of achieving complete textual clarity (which is practically impossible anyway); but of giving to the music the attitude and the atmosphere of the poetry. The theme of the poem briefly is this:— Gerontius, a Christian soul, is passing from this life to the eternal life. As he is dying he is fearful of his future state. He leaves this world fortified by the rites of the Church. In the second part he is taken by the guardian angel towards the Judgement Seat. He passes the demons of Hell. He hears the angelical choir, as also the souls in Purgatory, who chant the opening verses of Psalm 90. He is left awaiting Judgement, but within the hope of salvation as is suggested by the murmurous voices of the angelical choir.

[1] *Elgar*, E. Newman, p. 55.

Elgar is masterly in his realization of the disembodiment of so much of the narrative. Shifting harmonies—which may have been influenced by Wagner but which do not sound merely Wagnerian, spacious orchestration—which includes his handling of the voices, and a characteristic hesitancy in quiet melody give a sense of spiritual movement. We may instance the 'Fear' motiv[1] (Ex. 9) the serene

music that begins the second part (Ex. 10); the melody of the 'Angel's

Farewell' (Ex. 11).

Against the general backcloth are set the participants in the drama. Gerontius, whose impassioned visions, supplication for divine aid, awareness of a new life and final preparation for Judgement are all defined with sureness and succinctness: the priest, whose dignity of office is matched by the great march-like progress of the final section of Part I—'Proficiscere, anima Christiana': the guardian angel, whose graciousness lies in melodic colour as much as in the words: the groups —of priestly assistants, demons, angels, souls in purgatory. Elgar places his chorus units superbly well (notice the first appearance of 'Praise to

[1] Elgar was a thorough-going exponent of the *Leit-motiv* principle. The importance of *motiv* recognition on the part of the listener can easily be overestimated.

the Holiest') and relies—as does Verdi in the *Requiem*, and Wagner in *Parsifal*—on the situation of the chorus parts as much as on the actual notes that are sung. So the Angelical hymn—*on paper*—is poor: to the ear it is, within the limits of this text, ineffable.

The first performance of *Gerontius* in Birmingham, under Richter, was very nearly disastrous. The chorus, happiest in *Elijah*, found it beyond them: not only was it beyond them but they had no intention of trying to bridge the gap. So it was left to a German audience, at Düsseldorf in 1901, to acclaim it without hesitation. In 1902 Richard Strauss rose to the composer with 'I drink to the success and welfare of the first English progressive musician, Meister Elgar'.

Besides *Gerontius* Elgar busied himself with a project that had been with him since youth—a trilogy of oratorios. *The Apostles*, a lengthy, didactic work which, according to the composer, was to 'embody the Calling of the Apostles, their Teaching (schooling), and their Mission, culminating in the establishment of the Church among the Gentiles', was produced in 1903: *The Kingdom* in 1906. The third part of the trilogy—yet another *Last Judgement*—was never written. Both *The Apostles* and *The Kingdom*—and for that matter the curious pastiche of Elgarian quotations which comprise the ode *The Music-Makers* (1912) —have many incidental felicities, but their episodic structure which extensive use of *Leit-motiven* does nothing to mitigate—becomes wearisome. I am certain that were audiences not hypnotized by orchestral technique the same criticism would be found to apply to much late Romantic symphonic music: moreover, in respect of Elgar one should remember Ernest Newman's dictum: 'Time after time we feel that we are in the presence of a musical gift of the first order; and when all is said, *The Apostles* remains a work that no one but a great musician, and a man with an unusual power of synthesis, could have put together.'

SOME FRENCH WORKS

At the time when Charles Gounod, César Franck and Camille Saint-Saëns were all launched on the high seas of composition France, having forgotten its own particular musical traditions and being infected with all sorts of external influences, was a sorry place for choral music. These three composers possessed good intentions and much skill but they were for ever finding themselves in compromising musical situations. Particularly since almost any kind of simple homophony could pass itself off as 'good' choral music [1] It was left for Gabriel Fauré to reassert some of the basic principles of French art insofar as choral music was concerned.

However dim the present reputation of the earlier trio of composers may be it must be acknowledged that they were striving towards some ideal. And linking all their efforts was the behind-the-scenes exploration of Gregorian music and the modal system by Louis Niedermeyer;[2] and the fact that they were all organists. Gounod, with a profound respect for the style of Palestrina, brought back the idea, at least, of vocal polyphony; César Franck, with a more original gift of harmonic colour, imposed a sense of mysticism that is at times impressive, at others oppressive; Saint-Saëns was forward-looking in his excellence in linear clarity.

Gounod is often an embarrassment. His two notable works (for so they were regarded) *The Redemption* and *Mors et Vita* were first performed at Festivals in Birmingham—the one in 1882, the other in 1885. (Gounod, escaping from France at the outbreak of the Franco-Prussian War, lived in England until 1875.) They were intended in emulation—in melodic simplicity, harmonic delicacy and orchestral allusion—of Berlioz's *L'Enfance du Christ* and Massenet's *Marie Magdeleine*. The first was dedicated to Queen Victoria, the second to Pope Leo XIII. No more need be said of these works, except that they earned the composer a substantial fortune, that they swept the world, that the only immediate dissentient critics were in Germany and Italy; but that within two years it could be written:[3]

'Here necessarily arises the question whether Gounod's mind and soul were really subject to religious conviction. It is quite possible for a man to deceive himself, and believe that he has within him "the root of the matter", when merely revelling in an emotion the like of which, *au fond* and in a degree, might be excited by other means.'

[1] In a sense, of course, simple homophonic choruses were a French tradition: but the light-weight, and often charming, choral numbers in the operas of Lully and his school, or in Gounod and Saint-Saëns, are not susceptible of inclusion within the *magnum opus* type of choral work.

[2] We do not often consider modal influence in Gounod, but he uses *Vexilla Regis* in the 'March to Calvary' in *The Redemption*. In Saint-Saëns we may note the motets O *Salutaris*—a plainsong hymn harmonized—and *Veni Creator* (dedicated to Liszt), which is in Palestrinan style.

[3] Joseph Bennett, music critic of the *Daily Telegraph* a librettist to Barnett, Cowen Mackenzie, Sullivan and others, in *Musical Times*, December 1893.

Something of the same suspicion has fallen on César Franck, whose 'Biblical Eclogue' *Ruth* (1846), oratorio *La Tour de Babel* (1865), 'Poem-symphony' *Rédemption* (1871 and 4; the text was offered to but refused by Massenet) and *Les Béatitudes* (1879) are conspicuous for their poor choral texture, but also for their harmonic colour and occasional glimpses of real originality and beauty. The main objection against Franck's choral music is the flaccidity of its rhythm. It is recorded that Franck found Handel dull!

After the cosseting warmth of Gounod and Franck it is a relief to turn to the more invigorating atmosphere of Saint-Saëns. Saint-Saëns was a more polished composer than either Gounod or Franck and a good deal more professional in his attitudes. He would not (like Gounod) have considered writing a Mass in Rheims Cathedral while kneeling on the stone on which Joan of Arc once stood. Saint-Saëns' ambition was to reinstate French music in its proper dignities and with this aim he helped (in 1871) to found the Société Nationale de Musique. He will always be remembered for his devoted interest in the music of Bach. His interests were primarily instrumental—he was, of course, a virtuoso pianist. It is because his instincts were prompted by the sound of instruments rather than religious convictions (these may have the worst effect on *technique* whether in poetry or music) that his choral writing often left that of his contemporaries in France far behind. Liszt particularly admired the *Messe Solennelle* (1878) which he compared to 'a magnificent Gothic cathedral, in which Bach would conduct his orchestra'. In 1879 Saint-Saëns enrolled himself among those who had composed works for the Birmingham Festival. *La lyre et la Harpe* (poem by Victor Hugo) lies between Gounod and Fauré, having the charm of the former's *Philémon et Baucis* (an enchanting little opera) and the directness of musical vision in the *Requiem* of the latter. Attention must be drawn to the striking succession of common chords which introduce the first chorus; the deft interplay between soloists, chorus and orchestra in the fifth movement, which ends— more or less—with *Omphale's Spinning Wheel* and a nice mixture of C sharp major and E major chords; and to the flowing nature of the rhythm.

However congenial all these works may have been to the taste of the late nineteenth century there is only one French choral work which still commends itself generally: the *Requiem* by Fauré.

Gabriel Fauré is an unobtrusive figure in modern music. Perhaps that is inevitable, for his qualities—of limpidity, sensitivity, grace—are not those of the market place. He has, unjustly, according to his principal champions—Charles Koechlin and Norman Suckling—been overshadowed by Debussy. He has been condemned as 'too damned polite'. On the other hand he was 'in the musical language of our own time, a civilized artist of the age of Pericles'. In respect of his *Requiem* Nadia Boulanger once interpreted this quality of being civilized in another way. 'It might be said that he understood religion more after the fashion of the tender passages in the Gospel according to St. John, following Francis of Assisi rather than St. Bernard or Bossuet. His voice seems to interpose itself between heaven and men; usually peaceful, quiet and fervent, sometimes grave and sad, but never menacing or dramatic.' (Quoted by Charles Koechlin in *Gabriel Fauré*, pub. London 1946.)

Fauré was educated at the Ecole Niedermeyer, where he met and was befriended by Saint-Saëns. After various organistships he succeeded Théodore Dubois as chief organist at the Church of the Madeleine, in Paris, and in 1905, at the age of sixty, he became—also in succession to Dubois—Director of the Conservatoire. Besides the *Requiem* he wrote other church music. Some of his pieces for women's voices—the *Low Mass*, the *Ave Verum* and the *Tantum ergo* for example—are masterly in simplicity and clarity. Simplicity came naturally to Fauré: he had no need to cultivate it. But it was, said Koechlin,[1] 'from Bach that he derived that beautiful contrapuntal writing, compact, pure, and free in comparison with the narrowness of scholasticism; from Gounod, a delicate expression whose sincerity never avoided the use of simple chords, or naively expressive melodies'. One may look back at, say, the episode of 'The Holy Women at the Sepulchre' in Gounod's *Redemption* to discover one source of Fauré's exquisiteness and tact. Now a *Requiem* couched in these terms is unexpected. Yet precisely because grief can be assuaged by calm, Fauré's *Requiem* is outstanding: it is also outstanding in its period as being practicable for liturgical use.

In composing this work Fauré was moved by personal feelings, for it was in the year after the death of his father, in 1885, that he wrote it. In 1888 it was first performed at the Church of the Madeleine.

The restraint of the *Requiem* recalls the austere, but beneficent proportions and influence of the churches built by the Cistercians. Fauré shows his affinities with the older traditions of the church by

[1] *Gabriel Fauré*, Charles Koechlin, p. 39.

inflecting his melodies with Gregorian accent—thus the concluding
measures of the soprano solo 'Pie Jesu' (Ex. 12). Gounod has shown

Ex. 12   *poco ritenuto*

Sem - pi - ter - nam re - qui-em   sem - pi - ter - nam   re - qui - em.

previously the effectiveness of keeping a voice—for this sort of music
—within a normal range; but Fauré added relevance in his harmoniza-
tion. Yet when more *douceur* was needed he could give that too. The
chords which accompany the baritone solo in the 'Offertoire' are conventional enough—except in their colouring and their resolution, while
the final modulation of this same movement to B major is in no way
remarkable except (a) for its unexpectedness after the monochrome of
the rest of the movement and (b) for its brevity. The 'Sanctus' (which
is raised to a quiet ecstasy by the solo violin) is another movement in
contrast to the more generally powerful treatment of other composers: for the most part this phrase floats above harp figuration (Ex.
13) and the parts of the chorus echo one another, as might separate

Ex. 13

Sanc - tus____   Sanc - tus____

groups of angelicals from different parts of the heavens. The only time
in this movement when the voices sing together is during the final
'Sanctus'. Even when, in the 'Libera me', Fauré wishes to penetrate the
depths of fearful anticipation he achieves his purpose by handing a
single line of melody to the chorus to sing in octaves. Fauré omits
the terrifying picture of the 'Dies Irae'—the medieval concept of the
Day of Judgement as a day of anger seeming too crudely realistic—
from his *Requiem*. In so doing he defines the limits of his art.

The 'Agnus Dei', with its lovely canon melody, is emblematic of
Fauré's so-called 'Hellenic' approach. To suggest that this (Ex. 14) is
Platonic is to underline the critical attitude which enabled Fauré,
almost alone among composers of such works, to see the Lamb of God
as an idea rather than an anthropomorphic fact. The same spirit is in
the final 'In Paradisum' when, as in the 'Sanctus', the voices float above
the harp: 'It concludes the *Requiem* on a note of calm—not (even) of
hope—which impelled P. Tinel to suggest that it should rather be
headed *In Elysium*.'[1]

[1] *Fauré*, Norman Suckling, p. 175.

Tous les
Tlmm

Ag - nus De - i qui tol - lis pec -

- ca - ta mun - - - - di

The *Requiem* is scored for cellos and violas, each divided into two groups—there being no violin except for the solo in the 'Sanctus'—horns, trumpets, trombones, oboes, flutes, clarinets, bassoons, drums; organ and harp. The harp is used in three movements: the wind instruments have no more than a few measures in the whole work: the organ supplies a grave harmonic background. Yet such economy achieves the most moving and apt colouring and a convincing homogeneity.

OTHER SCHOOLS

At the heart of Romanticism is self-interest. The faculty of seeing oneself is not always to be deplored, for in following the teaching of the most familiar of Greek epigrams some otherwise hidden aspect of truth may be discovered. Nor is introspection confined to a particular period of time which happens to be labelled 'Romantic'. In such a period, however, the practice tends to appear to excess. Then the lesser artist is inclined to discover not what is present, but what might, or what ought to be present. Goodness; piety; love and so on; all to be wrapped up in the merest commonplaces of expression. Such is the route to sentimentality. Group-interest, community-interest, nation-interest are an extension of self-interest. Thus it is—since common-places of expression were thought proper—that many of the nineteenth-century 'nationalist' pieces wear badly. Particularly is this the case where words are attached; for significant words when superficially set mercilessly expose the musical cliché.

Gade and Grieg, the one Danish and the other Norwegian, were pioneers in a distinctively Scandinavian school of composition; but their choral works display singularly little trace of the accents which characterize their instrumental music. *The Crusaders*[1] or *The Erl-King's Daughter* of the one or *Landerkennung* of the other depart in no way from the moribund homophonic practice of the lesser Germans (cf. Rheinberger and Bruch who were prodigiously heavy-handed in their treatment of choral music). From Hungary and Bohemia came Liszt and Dvořák. Both these composers were nationalist—though Liszt's nationalism was less fundamental than Dvořák's—but again it must be recorded that their choral music hardly represents their most convincing work; even though their outlook was refreshing and their feeling for colour irrepressible.

Liszt, perhaps, is the more interesting. His *Hungarian Mass*, for the coronation of Franz Joseph as Apostolic King of Hungary, which was composed in three weeks in 1867, was the first of his experimental choral works, being based on what then passed as Hungarian rhythms[2] and containing a fiery 'Hungarian' March. This followed the oratorio *The Legend of the Holy Elizabeth* (daughter of King Andreas II of Hungary), which had been performed at Budapest in 1865. This large work, Wagnerian in manner, contains much that is striking: the Song of the Crusaders at the opening of the third scene; the Crusaders' march—the trio of which is an ancient melody, the death-scene of Elizabeth with the final threnode of the semichorus and the throb of the harps; the introduction to the last scene, with its quotation of the principal motiv (some of which again were from Hungarian 'art-music'), and its orchestration. *St. Elizabeth* has been dismissed as vulgar. The other great oratorio of Liszt, *Christus*, taking more than four hours in performance, has simply been ignored. Yet when it came to church music Liszt spoke with great authority—within the circumstances of the Catholic church as it carried out its ritual in Hungary in that period—and, as he himself said of the *Thirteenth Psalm*, he wrote 'with tears of blood'. In the last twenty-five years of his life Liszt turned increasingly to the consolations of religion (in humility and charity he practised ardently the precepts of Christianity) and to the proper mode

---

[1] Performed at the Birmingham Festival of 1876.

[2] Regarding the authentic Hungarian tradition see *Folk Music of Hungary*, Zoltan Kodály (London 1960).

of expressing religious faith in terms of music. Liszt the Romantic protested at the enervating atmosphere of dull propriety which conventional religious music exuded: in protest against dulness and in extension of his personal sense of adoration then he produced, towards the end of his life, a number of small works of exceptional interest. The large-scale works, as has been indicated, were too unconventional to commend them either to his own church or to the normal run of festival organizers. In certain unpublished works of his last period he departed even further from the conventional: in the motet *Ossa arida* we meet (Ex. 15), which no longer belongs to the fantasies of the

Ex. 15

nineteenth century but to the less euphemistic, realistic manner of the twentieth, while the *Via Crucis*, to a text composed of Biblical quotations and excerpts from Latin hymns and German chorales is a consistent study in a harmonic scheme largely based on the whole-tonescale.[1]

By the intensity of Liszt the warmth of Dvořák appears too comfortable. The *Stabat Mater* (1877) and the *Requiem* (1890) are inspired with Dvořák's inevitable sense of beauty of sound; but there is not overmuch reverence either for text or liturgy. One may note in the *Requiem* the prominence of a theme symbolic (Ex. 16) from Bach

Ex. 16

to Vaughan Williams, which, however, loses its painful contrasts in the enharmonic riches of Dvořák. The Bohemian *St. Ludmilla* and the secular *Spectre's Bride* were highly successful Festival pieces but—probably on account of their texts[2]—have failed to stay the course.

[1] See *Liszt's Final Period*, Humphrey Searle: *Proceedings of the Royal Musical Association*, Vol. LXXVIII.

[2] Mr. A. C. Peake suggested at a meeting of the Leeds Festival Committee in 1886 that the libretto of *St. Ludmilla* 'has no sense in it, while a great deal of it is irreverent'.

St. Ludmilla, which has been staged, looks back to Handel but its episodic nature calls for the unifying influence of the theatre. From 1892 to 1895 Dvořák was in America. In anticipation of his work at the National Conservatory in New York and the fourth centenary celebrations in honour of Columbus' discovery of America he wrote a *Te Deum* and also began to sketch *The American Flag*. The *Te Deum* is among Dvořák's happiest inventions. Symphonic in form and pastoral in inner feeling and in instrumentation it was a new interpretation of this great hymn.

PROGRESS IN AMERICA

Dvořák's sojourn in America gives opportunity to underline the manner in which, by the third quarter of the nineteenth century, American composers had caught up with the rank-and-file composers of Europe; and we become aware of two factors which, when worked into the nature of music, have produced striking and original work within the last two generations. These factors were—cosmopolitanism and enthusiasm.

When Dvořák arrived in New York on September 27th, 1892, he and his party[1] were welcomed by representatives of the Czech colony in the city. At Spillville, Iowa, where he summered, there was an almost exclusively Bohemian society. At the Chicago World's Fair in 1893 there was a Czech Day for which Dvořák journeyed to the city to conduct some of his works. The Welsh music at the iron town of Danville, Pennsylvania, is described in Jack Jones's *Off to Philadelphia in the Morning*. There were numerous German societies and many Germans took a leading part in the development of musical organizations in America. The first Cincinnati Festival of 1873 was the climax of much choral activity by the German choral societies of the Midwest cities. Chicago was indebted particularly to Hans Balatka, formerly a choral conductor in Vienna who made Chicago audiences aware of the classics, and to Theodore Thomas, a native of Essen, whose impetuous personality and limitless industry stabilized the place of the modern orchestra and of the native composer in American musical life. For the Chicago Fair of 1893 Thomas invited works from such

---

[1] His wife, two of his sons and a young protégé from Prague—Joseph Kovařík, whose father was organist at Spillville.

established composers as Paine, Chadwick, Foote and Dudley Buck and organized a competition for lesser-known composers. Thomas was all for the American composer, but he always said that he would never play anything merely because it was American. It must be good music.[1]

Enthusiasm made the great sequence of expositions, fairs, centennials and festivals for which a vast amount of music—much of it, to be truthful, of no more than passing interest—was composed; and enthusiasm made for generous provision for music, teaching in conservatories and universities.

A great sense of nationhood produced a number of agreeably written works which are of historic importance, even though the general technical habits show too many evidences of the all-too-familiar German students of correct deportment. Dudley Buck's *Don Munio* (1874) was based on a story from Washington Irving's *Spanish Papers*; his *Centennial Meditation of Columbia*[2] on an Ode by Sydney Lanier of Georgia; his *Golden Legend* and various settings from the *Saga of King Olaf* from Longfellow—a poet who inspired Arthur Foote to three picturesque cantatas; J. K. Paine, whose *Mass in D* was performed at the Singakademie in Berlin in 1867 and thus established American composition in a European centre,[3] seems conspicuous for the imaginative fancy of his orchestral music but with his *Centennial Hymn* to Whittier's words (Philadelphia 1876),[4] *Columbus March and Hymn* (Chicago World's Fair), *Hymn to the West* (St. Louis World's Fair 1904), his incidental music to *Oedipus Tyrannus* for Harvard University, and other occasional music he broadened the musical structure of his community and made his compatriots aware of the public importance of a natively inspired music. As Professor of Music at Harvard Paine influenced the greater part of the American school of composers of the first two decades of the twentieth century.

H. W. Parker, a Bostonian and from 1894 until his death in 1919 Professor of Music at Yale, was the most distinguished choral writer of the late Romantic American school. He had been a pupil of Rheinberger and taught for a short time under Dvořák's direction. He composed prolifically—more than forty works—for chorus, and

---

[1] *Our American Music*, John Tasker Howard, p. 289.
[2] Philadelphia, 1876: Wagner's very inferior *Centennial March* was written for the same event.
[3] Paine's symphonies were also played in Germany.
[4] Commissioned by Theodore Thomas.

achieved almost as much fame in England as in his native country. His *Hora Novissima*,[1] in which Parker blends his own, somewhat austere, feeling for the choral unit with an up-to-date, courtesy reference to the Wagnerian system of *Leit-motiv*, was performed at the Three Choirs Festival at Worcester in 1899. So successful was this that he was asked to compose the *Wanderer's Psalm* for the Hereford Festival of the next year. In 1902 he was made a Doctor of Music (honoris causa) at Cambridge and in the same year performances of his works took place at Chester, Bristol and Worcester. The larger works of Parker, like those of his contemporaries (except for the instrumental music of MacDowell) have passed into oblivion together with the larger number of all choral works of the same period. Yet there are numerous slender pieces which have freshness and individuality. See, for instance, the *Seven Greek Pastoral Scenes* (Op. 74)—a happy treatment of poems by Meleager and Argentarius for women's voices, oboe, harp and strings. These, written for his Monday afternoon Eurydice Society of Philadelphia, have a cool charm and appreciation of varied sonorities which contrasts with the heavy atmosphere of the conventional oratorio or cantata. But this—in point of time—belongs to the twentieth century. And as we turn to the twentieth century we discover a new influence striking English composers—that of Walt Whitman. In the end it may be fair, if paradoxical, to suggest that, in fact, Whitman was the greatest American musical influence of the nineteenth century. In America, as in England, much that in other countries finds outlet in musical form is expressed through the medium of words: Hence, of course, the safe anchorage which American and British composers discover in choral music.

[1] See *Musical Times*, October 1893.

7

The Twentieth Century

NEW POINTS OF VIEW

IF IT is assumed that the nineteenth century saw the hey-day of large-scale choral music it should not also be assumed that the present century is indifferent to the medium. In fact—as reference to the catalogue of any publishing house will show—there is no end to choral prolificacy. A combination of new ideals, ideas and technical methods, however, creates new circumstances both for performance and appreciation and, as choral singers in Britain and the often special type of audience (with less interest in other forms of music) which attends concerts of choral music are cautious in judgement and enthusiasm, it may be that some special pleading may become apparent in what follows. There is something of an impasse in present musical affairs. There is any number of technically gifted composers. There is a vast demand for music to hear. There are more societies of music-makers than heretofore. Yet contemporary music as a whole remains a province apart—for specialists and eclectics—and the contemporary composer is torn between his private interests and the economics of his calling. The 'established' choral society, meanwhile, stays resolute in devotion to a handful of familiar pieces.

I have a strong feeling that choral music is one means whereby many questions relating to the nature and purpose of modern music may be answered. For the medium lies midway between 'art' and 'life', between aesthetics and reality. Words and their selection and treatment reveal the attitude of the composer, the poet and the community to which both belong, towards the philosophic problems of the age. It was Mendelssohn, in a characteristically critical mood one day, who postulated that in contrast to music words are imprecise. Consideration of the music which is dealt with throughout this book will, possibly, underline the essential truth of his thesis. For Palestrina and Victoria are as indisputably Catholic as Bach is Lutheran, or Handel humanist; but their various interpretations of Catholicism, Lutheranism and humanism are more compelling than most other outward appearances of the ideals by which they were inspired. The inner nature of a philosophy is a matter for individual examination, but the composer who directs inwardly to the heart of philosophy occupies a position of high responsibility.

Insofar as many late nineteenth-century composers abdicated from their philosophic responsibilities and, under conditions which offer some mitigation, sought prestige in an abstract formula of popular commonplaces they have deserved the neglect into which they have fallen. With, of course, a few notable exceptions.

It will be recalled that at the end of the sixteenth century there was a not dissimilar state of affairs. The old style, which from a distance we idealize, possibly to excess, became *démodé*. The new style (for our purpose epitomized in Monteverdi) was not always acceptable, nor was it always certain. But its direction was towards a conscientious appreciation of new facets of truth. In the welter of modern music there are analogies, and the fascination of studying modern scores lies in appreciating not so much the ill-defined abstraction of that form of beauty which is merely attractive as that which may be considered to approximate to some potent element of truth in perception and in expression. The notable work is that which combines idea and formal presentation of that idea in an irrefragable unity. This is where the classics assist us. They are, as Matthew Arnold wrote, the criterion. But their validity only obtains when approach to them is critical rather than conventional. And one of the remarkable features of the modern approach is the influence of scientific and scholarly method. Thus there are opportunities for the contemporary performer and conductor to present music from the fifteenth to the eighteenth centuries with due consideration of the essential character of such music rather than with obedience to the drab conventions of Romantic optimism.

Now a new point of view does not immediately become established nor does the old suddenly and finally disappear. So the choral music of the twentieth century exhibits many, if isolated, points of resistance to new ideas and new techniques (except for occasional hints of superficial 'modernity'); numerous works extend the elements of sensuous impressiveness, and romantic escape, and apotheosize 'largeness'. The English school has been conspicuous, as might be expected, in caution, and the outstanding works of Vaughan Williams, Walton and Britten, if impregnate with the evolutionary ideal. are indifferent to the principles of violent revolution; while composers of the quality of John Ireland, [1a] Walford Davies, [1b] Dyson [1c] and Howells [1d] show no signs of even having noticed that we have been and are living in the middle of one. The same also applies to such important figures in twentieth-century American music as Converse, Hadley and Hanson. A characteristic and popular 'conservative' work is Hanson's *Lament of Beowulf* (1925) which, since early Festival performances at Ann Arbor and Worcester (Mass.) has established itself in the general repertoire. Yet to conclude that all such music is without significance is error. For sometimes there is a deeper inward quality which shows the adaptability of tradition to poetic sensibility. While there is the essential character of the choral medium always to be considered: of all mediums the most dangerous for the unwary.

Leaving the obvious traditionalists for the moment we may define some of the evidence of 'modernity' in twentieth-century choral music. There is intrinsic nature on the one hand and form on the other. We may first consider the prime influences on the former.

By long tradition (the Hindemithian theory of *Gebrauchsmusik* is no new thing in relation to church music) a large part of choral music has been specifically Christian. Its Christian values have been accepted in succeeding ages and its forms of expression have palpably accommodated themselves to general tendencies in religious thought. It is sometimes urged that the twentieth century is irreligious and that standards of thought are antipathetic to Christianity. Some part of this generalization is true; but a very large and influential minority is fervent, critical and eager. The search for truth within the tradition still goes on. The twentieth-century oratorio at its best is penetrating, uncompromising, fierce in protestation, more often than not concerned with the philosophic idea or the reality of the chosen text than with the personal comfort of the conventional pew-holder. Thus Walton's *Belshazzar's Feast* exhibits the splendid, barbarous beauty of the Old Testament:[2] Kodály's *Psalmus Hungaricus* emphasizes the essential continuity of folk art and unites the aspirations of ancient Israel and modern Hungary (through a sixteenth-century Hungarian paraphrase of Psalm LV): Janáček in his *Festliche Messe* makes religious

[1] (a) See *These things shall be* (pub. Boosey);
    (b)   *Everyman* (pub. Novello);
    (c)   *The Canterbury Pilgrims* (pub. O.U.P.);
    (d)   *Hymnus Paradisi* (pub. Novello).
[2] *Belshazzar's Feast* shocked the conventional in 1931 and its performance at a Cathedral Festival was disallowed.

art significant to the 'popular' mind, in a medieval manner, by denuding it of false piety: Frank Martin's *Golgotha* is a severely sculpted work of devout pity, as free from 'attractiveness' as a statue by Jakob Epstein: Szymanowski's *Stabat Mater*, rare in performance, is even colder in musical atmosphere but deliberate in its circumscription of all the emotions which a humanist, rather than a theologian, experiences at the Foot of the Cross: Vaughan Williams and Holst penetrate the mysticism peculiar to the ardently poetical in such works as *Sancta Civitas* and the *Hymn of Jesus*: and Britten recreates the charm and insouciance of the ingenuous attitude of the Middle Ages in his *Ceremony of Carols* and *St. Nicolas*. So, in a series of representative works of our time, we see a general and engaging capacity on the part of composers to see in religious thought the 'thing as it is', rather than as it should be, or others would have it. In a very general way—in no sense technical for the moment—this may be represented as a going-back to Bach—and to Handel; in that the attitude of the composer to his subject is honest.

THE 'MOTU PROPRIO' OF 1903

Oratorio is one side of religious music. Another is the more purely functional and liturgical and is specially attached to the Catholic Church. From time to time, notably in the seventh, fourteenth, sixteenth and twentieth centuries, the Church has made pronouncements which have had effect (not always as much as they were intended to have) on church music in particular but also on the art of music in general. Most of these pronouncements have formulated ideals which careful minds had long considered and which appeared as worthy ideals to the supreme Councils of the Church. The *Motu Proprio* of Pope Pius X (dated St. Cecilia's Day, November 22nd, 1903) is no exception. This document, at once precise and authoritative but stimulating, deserves the closest attention of all those to whom it is particularly addressed. (It is, alas, still honoured more in the breach rather than the observance.)

The *Motu Proprio* stresses the special *liturgical* virtues of the Gregorian chant and of the classical polyphony of the age of Palestrina. Thus it respects the pioneers of nineteenth-century musical research and approves their aspirations. It condemns irrelevant *conventionalism*—as particularly of the Italian operatic style—on account of unfitness to purpose. It requires directness and clarity in the setting of the 'liturgical text'. It forbids 'frivolous' instruments but—within limitations— accords a special place to 'wind instruments, limited, judicious and proportioned to the size of the place'—provided the composition and accompaniment to be executed be written in a grave and suitable style. In paraphrase we deduce, simplicity, economy of means, aptness of music to words, and philosophic integrity as necessary to a state of artistic grace. No composer, other than a Catholic composer writing for the Offices of the Church, is bound to regulate his behaviour to the letter of a papal instruction, but he may well consider the general significance of these observations. In the 'General Principles' of the *Motu Proprio* will be discovered encouragement and freedom and a due regard for the special value of art.

'Sacred music should . . . possess, in the highest degree, the qualities proper to the liturgy, and precisely *sanctity* and *goodness of form*, from which its other character of *universality* spontaneously springs.

It must be true art for otherwise it will be impossible for it to exercise on the minds of those who listen to it that efficacy which the Church aims at obtaining in admitting into her liturgy the art of musical sounds.

But it must, at the same time, be universal in the sense that while every nation is permitted to admit into its ecclesiastical compositions those special forms which may be said to constitute its native music, still these forms must be subordinated in such a manner to the general characteristics of sacred music that nobody of any nation may receive an impression other than good on hearing them.'

Under the influence of this document some notable works have been written and a great expansion in the appreciation and application of principles and practices therein defined has taken place. Such works as Ildebrando Pizzetti's *Missa di Requiem*, Francis Poulenc's *Mass in G*, Vaughan Williams' *Mass in G Minor* (although Vaughan Williams was a member of the Established Church of England), Kodály's *Missa Brevis*, Stravinsky's *Mass* (1948) and motets—*Ave Maria* and *Pater Noster*, the later works of Poulenc, compositions of the Olivier

Messaien group in France are noteworthy examples of large-scale acceptance of the intention of the *Motu Proprio*. It may well be that such works may appear to some as 'reactionary'. If so, it may be represented that progress (if it may be said to exist at all) is not necessarily a forward movement: Bach, for instance, by some is correctly interpreted as—in some ways—among the medievals.

On the whole the twentieth century has shown much zeal in analysing, in terms of music, the tenets of traditional faith; with a fairly strong inclination towards the dogmatic.

THE INFLUENCE OF NIETZSCHE AND WHITMAN

'It is only natural,' writes Neville Cardus, 'that Delius is not in favour at the moment; the spirit of the age is at the extreme of his Epicenean sensibility.' This is reasonable comment upon a certain point. Insofar as the choral works of Delius are concerned, however, it may well be doubted whether they ever were in favour. That they contained 'manifold effects of great beauty and originality' has never been denied; but since choral music is an amalgam of words and music, they have appeared strongly irrelevant. In general if purpose may be attributed to music in any moral sense that of the Delius works is negative and they symbolize a vague atheism and 'rationalism'. But as records of a phase of thought such works as the *Requiem* and *A Mass of Life* have historical and psychological significance. Delius' own exposition of his beliefs prefaced a performance of the *Requiem*[1] given in the Queen's Hall, London, at a Royal Philharmonic Society concert in 1922:

'It is not a religious work. Its underlying belief is that of a pantheism that insists on the reality of life. It preaches that human life is like a day in the existence of the world, subject to the great laws of All-Being. The weakling is weighed down thereby and revels in magic pictures of a cheerful existence hereafter. The storm of reality destroys the golden dream-palaces, and the inexorable cry resounds "You are the creature of the day and must perish". The world tries to soothe the fear of death; "the highways

[1] The *Requiem* was initially defined by the composer as a 'pagan Requiem'.

of the world give birth to gods and idols". The proud spirit casts off the yoke of superstition, for it knows that death puts an end to all life, and therefore fulfilment can be sought and found only in life itself. No judgment as to doing and not doing and evil can be found in any ordinance from without, but only in the conscience of man himself. Often a man is judged worthless to the world and its laws, who should be exalted by praise for his human goodness, and the love of which he freely gives. Thus independence and self-reliance are the marks of a man who is great and free. He will look forward to his death with high courage in his soul, in proud solitude, in harmony with nature and the ever-recurrent, sonorous rhythm of birth and death.'

It may, of course, be argued that the music of Delius is 'about' nothing. Yet if this is so why did he study Nietzsche (from whose *Also sprach Zarathusa* the *Mass of Life* is taken) to the exclusion of almost every other author and philosopher? And why did he attempt to define the 'meaning' of his *Mass*?

It is clear that the aspiration of Delius was towards a state of ideal— or rather idealized—beauty and in search of this disembodied condition he achieved some beautiful choral effects, notably without words as in the *Song of the High Hills* and in the third movement of the *Mass of Life*. We shall return to this matter of tonal beauty in choral music, but in searching for new modes of expression numerous composers at the beginning of the century found the relaxed accents of impressionist poetry, or of poetry which appeared to exist for its own poetic purpose, stimulating. Thus Granville Bantock, a highly popular composer of the first quarter of the century, put Whitman and Swinburne and (prodigious feat) the *Rubaiyat of Omar Khayyam*, and other exotic verse into fascinating, difficult, but time-bound settings which suited the skilful, if uncritical British choirs of that period; while Schoenberg was composing his *Gurre-Lieder*, in Ernest Newman's view 'the finest love-poem since *Tristan*'—an opinion now only shared by discophiles and/or ardent Romantics who combine with enthusiasm an exceptional skill in score-reading. For *Gurre-Lieder*, costing perhaps 6,000 dollars a performance, is now, despite revival in Britain in 1961, a fixture on the library shelf.

To revert to Delius. He first achieved notice as a highly individual composer at Essen in 1906.

'Mr. Delius's "Sea-Drift' was generally acknowledged to be (with the exception of Mahler's Sixth Symphony) the most important work of the festival. It is a striking piece of musical impressionism, marvellously coloured, and, in spite of many extravagancies, harmonically fascinating. There is no thematic material to speak of; chords and modulations, sound-experiments and mood-picturing alone produce such an astonishing effect, and express the composer's poetic idea in such a convincing manner that the listener feels persuaded almost against his inclination that he has heard a masterpiece of a very individual and novel kind.'

Sea-Drift is a setting of parts of Walt Whitman's first poem in his sequence. Delius is concerned with love of life, love of love; with the sadness of ended love, with the beauty of language and symbol and nature; with 'the mystic play of shadows twining and twisting as if they were alive'. For his emancipatory genius Whitman was congenial to some composers: for his liberal, world-brotherly optimism he was congenial to others. So that Whitman has occupied a powerful position in modern choral music: those who have set his poems include Stanford, Charles Wood, Coleridge-Taylor, F. L. Ritter, Cyril Scott, Roy Harris, John Alden Carpenter, Harvey Gaul, Charles Martin Loeffler, Normand Lockwood, G. W. Chadwick, Rutland Boughton, Frank Bridge, Holst, Hamilton Harty, Charles T. Griffes, Vaughan Williams, Arthur Bliss, William Schuman and many others. In a subtle way Whitman, through English music, has contrived to influence the Old World with the enthusiasm and new modes of untrammelled pioneering thought of the New.

The 'ethical' cantata came into being partly under the Whitman cult. It has shown a later tendency towards the 'ideological', which may or may not have some connection with nationalism. In the case of Tippett's *A Child of Our Time* we are led to the crux of contemporary problems of living: the text, written by the compiler, is impassioned in castigation of the immorality of authority just as is, in an even more specific way, Schoenberg's *A Survivor from Warsaw* describes the pitiless consequences of such authority. Elsewhere the theory that contemporary music should, in some way or another, deal with contemporary affairs is illustrated by William Grant Still's impressive *And They Lynched Him on a Tree*, by Vaughan Williams' *Dona Nobis Pacem* and by any amount of contemporary music from eastern

Europe. In communist countries ideological considerations (the answer to the thesis of the *Motu Proprio*) may be found profoundly to affect the nature as well as the outlook of music. Music, it is argued (as the Fathers of the Church argued), should serve a didactic purpose. Under this belief such composers as Prokofiev, Shostakovich, Eisler, Meyer, Ruth Zechlin and Kurt Schwaen have produced some excellent works. Others have produced less excellent works.

NATIONALISM AND ROMANTICISM

As for nationalism we may often find ourselves by the side of Mr. Desmond Shawe Taylor. 'Nationalism,' he writes,[1] 'which began by adding fascinating new flavours to the international musical diet, soon produced a new phenomenon: the good composer whose works won't travel.' He quotes especially Albert Roussel in France, Carl Nielsen in Denmark, Elgar in England and Janáček in Czechoslovakia. Choral music has notable examples (clearly folk song and the accentuation of language have a particular effect): Janáček's *Festliche Messe*; Roy Harris's *Folk Song Symphony*; Szymanowski's *Stabat Mater*; and, although not entirely localized, Bloch's *Sacred Service*—to quote only works which are not, perhaps, entirely unfamiliar to a few concert-goers.

In reaction against more and more ecclesiasticism or more and more internationalism, or liberalism, or authoritarianism, or nihilism, or experimentalism we discover occasional works which stand out merely by reason of their artistic value, or their entertainment content. Choral music has for so long been dominated by extra-musical associations and by false conceptions as to the proper character of the medium that works in this medium which are both qualitative and lighthearted have been rare. The classic of popular masterpieces is undoubtedly Constant Lambert's *Rio Grande*, which borrows but transmutes the jazzy idiom of the 1930's: but some of Britten's works —see the *Spring Symphony* and the *Cantata Academica*—bid fair to rival Lambert's *chef d'œuvre* in attractiveness. The American composer Randall Thompson, a master of choral technique, has effectively explored satire in such works as *Americana* and *Rosemary*.

[1] *The Record Guide*, Edward Sackville West and Desmond Shawe Taylor (London 1951), p. 317.

TECHNIQUE

These works are technically brilliant and we may next turn to the matter of technique to discover to what extent musical thought has devised technical method or to what alternative extent technique has controlled the development of choral music.

We may refer to an early work of Schoenberg and a late work of Stravinsky: the *Gurre-Lieder* of the one, the *Cantata* (1952) of the other. Schoenberg's work is scored for five soloists and a speaker; three male-voice choirs and eight-part mixed choir; for four piccolos, four flutes, three oboes, two English horns, three clarinets, two clarinets in E flat, two bass clarinets, three bassoons, and two contra-bassoons—at times the English horn players exchange for oboes (and the lateral clarinettists for A clarinets); for ten horns (out of which four 'Wagner-tubas' are taken), six trumpets, one bass trumpet, six trombones, contrabass trombone, contra-tuba; for a miscellany of drums and usual percussion with additional glockenspiel, zylophone, tam-tam, chains; for four harps and celesta; and strings. Such, Mr. Salazar[1] wryly observes, 'relegates Wagner to the position of a mere beginner'. Stravinsky, in his *Cantata*, employs but soprano and tenor soloists, female chorus, two flutes, oboe, cor anglais and 'cello. Schoenberg's work lasts four times as long as Stravinsky's. The former is expansive, woefully beautiful after Wagner and Mahler; the latter dryly attractive, laconic, intellectual. The *Gurre-Lieder* were composed for nobody in particular and everyone in general; the *Cantata* for the Los Angeles Symphony Society.

The material differences between these two works signify vast changes in thought. The Schoenberg work is in the end of the final, expansive and Mahlerian phase of Romantic other-worldliness, expressive of the pagan idealization of love, affiliated in feeling if not form to the great Delius works of the same period. Stravinsky is within the new field of what may be termed 'applied music'—to an intellectual rather than an emotional idea, to an occasion, to the principle of economy. In point of time it will be noted that, by and large, opulence of expression disappeared during the First World War and that the stringent years that followed not only encouraged but demanded a new mode of calculation of resources: so that, in general, a composer at the present time considers the minimum forces he can do

---

[1] *Music in our time*, Adolfo Salazar (London 1948), p. 204.

with rather than the maximum. So Britten, with boys' schools in mind, conceives *St. Nicolas* for voices, string, percussion and a pair of pianoforte ducttists. Frank Martin writes the pellucid score of *Le vin herbé* for twelve singers and twelve instrumentalists.

Whereas formerly the choral composer looked forward with some optimism to acceptance of a reasonably competent work by at least one of many choral societies the contemporary places his faith more often than not in high school or university choruses, or in one of the countless groups of women singers. Changed conditions have made it essential for the composer to examine the matter of what we may call group music anew. Choral music is singularly sensitive to social change for the obvious reason that in general it is the province of the amateur musician. Therefore it is also (so far as the nineteenth and twentieth centuries are concerned) one index to the condition of society in more ways than one.

Despite social change, however, a new valuation of the function of choral music was due at the turn of the century, if only because the massive, chordal style of the Romantics had gone as far as it could. And it was realized, by some sooner than others, that choral music has its limitations. Choral music is not happily chromatic. A chromatic style is instrumental and its musical complexity will (as in Delius or Elgar) obscure the words which generate choral song and, unless security is furnished in the accompanying orchestration, make intonation problematic. This is where dodecaphony, to say the least of it, shows its weakness.

The possibility of dispensing with words has been attempted: notably by Delius; by Howard Hanson in his *Heroic Elegy*; by Vaughan Williams, in *Flos Campi* and the *Sinfonia Antartica*. The effect is not perhaps entirely satisfactory, for the listener may feel mentally obliged to substitute for the indeterminate the definitiveness of words. There is, of course, no good reason why voices should not be appreciated for their own distinctive colour; but verbal associations are very strong. (In the *Sinfonia Antartica* voices appear only for two brief periods and are used as orchestral instruments: the colour effect here is remarkable, but this is a special kind of work.) Chorus singers have been made to shout (*Gurre-Lieder* and Delius' *Eventyr*[1]), to speak

---

[1] 'This is the only orchestral work I have ever come across in which male voices are used—not to sing, but to give a wild shout, behind the orchestra and out of sight. We had thirty men to do it, and they did it remarkably well; but in subsequent performances this novel and exciting effect has been omitted.' Sir Henry Wood on first performance of *Eventyr* (January 11th, 1919) in *My Life of Music* (London 1938), p. 307.

(Holst's *Hymn of Jesus*), to clap (Roy Harris's *Folk Song Symphony*), to whistle (Britten's *Spring Symphony*). No doubt many chorus singers are more adept at these activities than at singing. But their main purpose is to sing. Therefore mere bizarreness, which is inevitable in a period of transition, offers no firm future for the composer who wishes to turn his back on the standards of his immediate precursors.

The inner character of music has been radically changed by the influence of revived Gregorianism, by energy in cultivating first the polyphonic, then the medieval, then the baroque. Folksong has had a profound effect and especially in respect of rhythmic values. A fascination in tonal values, in timbres, in sonorities has established the independence of the element which these terms cover. All music has been affected, but the magnitude of the alteration to the structure has certainly not been readily accepted by the generality of choral singers: perhaps because—with their relatively limited opportunities—they can rarely experience more than a handful of contemporary works. And that is a sanguine expectation.

Modality began to come back into music in the nineteenth century: sometimes almost accidentally (as in Mendelssohn's *Lauda Sion*), sometimes self-consciously as in earlier references to Berlioz, Liszt and Gounod, sometimes inevitably as in Fauré and Debussy. The modal attitude of Vaughan Williams' *Sea Symphony*, first performed in 1910, is still self-conscious; but this does not apply to the works of this composer as from those of the *Sancta Civitas* (first performed in 1925) period. Modal inflection of choral music is effective in three ways. It is evocative—stimulating a particular area of associations. Thus Szymanowski in his *Stabat Mater* writes (Ex. 1)

Ex. 1

and deliberately recalls a sort of Byzantine deliberation. The effect is romantic, in that it is emotionally rather than intellectually disturbing, but it is the reverse of the familiar romanticism of the nineteenth-century tradition. The melodic structure of a modal-type melody clearly provokes a new attitude towards 'harmony'. The nineteenth-century practice (*vide* Gounod, or even Fauré) was to regulate the melody by the *a priori* behaviour of conventional harmonic movement. The twentieth-century is more empirical, but these processes are common—harmony, as in Vaughan Williams or Holst, may arrive through the vertical or horizontal exploitation of characteristic mode intervals. Therein lies the great beauty of such works as the *Magnificat* of the one and the *Hymn of Jesus* of the other. But harmony may also be derived, as was the case with Debussy, from medieval habits. Then we have a new simplification brought about by an approximation to organum. So the chorus parts in the Szymanowski excerpt run in consecutive triads: at first in root position, then in second inversion. Szymanowski integrates the medieval with the modern in remarkable fashion. Where mere fashion prevails, as in Orff's *Carmina Burana*, the result is as dull as the dullness it sets out to obliterate. It should be noted that Szymanowski throws against his main material a bass ostinato which, tonally remote but rhythmically strong, underlines the conflict implicit in 'tristis' and 'afflicta'. This example may be simplified in a linear way: by treating the chorus as one line, intensified by the parallelism of the triad formation, we discover new possibilities of logical structure.

While mode offers a whole field for development in respect of melody and harmony it also suggests rhythmic emancipation. Again to refer to Szymanowski it is notable that the musical rhythm, at least

partly, is decreed by verbal rhythm. Frank Martin's *Golgotha* shows
effectively the application of free speech-rhythm to choral observation
and the manner in which he crosses the principles of plainchant and
recitative in the narrative statements of his oratorio is immediately
impressive; particularly since Martin is masterly in his varying of vocal
sonorities. We may adduce the plainest statement from *Golgotha* (Ex.
2). The hard contrapuntal edge of this music is not calculated to give

Ex. 2

pleasure: but by its priestly strictness to draw attention to the essentials
of the subject. In short the music exists not so much in its own right as
ancillary to and expressive of the text.

Plain-chant is, of course, not one tradition but many and the
ecstatic contours of the laudes and alleluias of the thirteenth century
range freely without being earth-bound by metrical regularity. Here
we come, especially, to the renewal of religious ecstasy through this
method in Stravinsky's *Mass*. And in particular the 'Gloria' and the
'Sanctus'. In fact this loosening of rhythm is the only way in which
this powerful, compressed setting of the Mass forsakes the words first
principle for some feeling of human warmth. In his *Cantata* Stravinsky
continues this exploration of the dogmatic by a return to the binding
scholasticism of the medieval in strict canonic writing and even in the
merely visually effective 'cancrizans' process. ('Cancrizans' or 'crab-
wise' refers to music which reads the same form back to front.)

Closely allied to the return to medievalism is the frequent recourse to an authentic folk idiom. As in the nineteenth century the main influence here is from the east. Although the Negro spiritual has its own place in the music of William Grant Still and, more surprisingly, in Tippett's *A Child of Our Time*. The impress of Hungarian idiom is most strong in the works of Bartók. In his music, however, the folk impulse has mainly affected his instrumental writing and, despite the topicalities of the *Cantata Profana* (an entertaining but sophisticated work), a few arrangements of folksongs.

We must return to Kodály. *Psalmus Hungaricus* was first heard in England at Cambridge in 1927 and shortly afterwards at the Three Choirs Festival. This, as well as some of Kodály's smaller choral works for unaccompanied voices, was hailed as a work of striking originality. Its originality lies in the vitality of the rhythmic structure, in the high colours of choral tone (note how Kodály will leave the chorus wordless but only because the word-shape is implicit in the rhythmic idea) and of orchestration. In some ways Kodály is continuing established tradition, for his general harmonic scheme is romantic enough in its associations. But this conservatism is not to be written down as reactionary. For Kodály can put familiar terms into new settings. This we may discover in the Schubert–Bruckner flavour of the *Pange Lingua*.

Kodály's music is evidently exportable. While we are nearer to the native fount of inspiration than in, say, Liszt, the setting is still conscious of the west. In Janáček, however, we are aware of a peculiarly parochial atmosphere. (This obtains in other Czech choral music, as, for instance, the 'republican' music of Novák.) The *Festival Mass* may be listened to and appreciated for its wealth of colour and its simplicity and its patent sincerity it can only be understood in the light of purely local experience. The *Mass* is, in the Catholic view, no Mass. Its form is taken from a primitive rite—the Glagolitic (hence the actual title *Glagolská mše*) —practised in Croatia and Dalmatia in the tenth century, in the time of St. Wenceslaus. The fact that the millennium of the patron saint of Bohemia was to be celebrated in 1929 may have moved Janáček towards this particular composition; although he was also stirred by the participation of the Archbishop of Olomouc in the ceremony of placing a commemorative tablet on Janáček's birthplace in Hukvaldy in 1926. The Mass was intended to be simple, popular and joyful. Janáček was a pioneer in the musical education of the working classes and his Mass-style is derived not so much from a preconception of what people ought to know, but what in fact was within their everyday experience. Hence the fragmentary melody, the homophonic choral phrasing, the lack of 'thematic development', the flamboyance of the instrumental colouring, the instrumental introductions,

'In bygone years', writes Rosa Newmarch, 'and in country churches, the Mass was often preceded on festal days by an *intrada* which bore little or no musical relation to the Mass itself. It was simply a somewhat showy and dignified accompaniment to the entry of the officiating clergy. Janáček in his popular Mass has preserved this usage. The Intrada has a secular character and might have been designed as a movement of the composer's "Military" Sinfonietta.'

By an attitude such as that of Janáček new life comes into music, but the fate of the particular work is uncertain. Since the sixteenth century, and especially in the field of opera, the dangerous attraction of the temporal has caused many composers to seek topicality and to make music exclusively contemporary. Janáček appeared 'real' enough in 1928 (just as Puccini and Mascagni and Bizet in their own times); but after twenty years he appears, perhaps, more curious than relevant, more romantic than realistic. Whereas a composer such as Kaminski may very well seem to date less.

Heinrich Kaminski, who studied in Heidelberg and Berlin, emigrated to the U.S.A. in 1939, and died in Europe in 1946, has based his style on eighteenth-century method. In this he is by no means alone— Hindemith and Honegger among his contemporaries being particularly conspicuous in the back-to-Bach movement—and at the present time every other composer practises some part of his craft in a Baroque retreat. Kaminski, however, has sedulously applied his formal predilections to a seriousness of purpose shown in such works as *Psalm LXIX, Introitus and Hymnus, Passion, Magnificat, Drei geistliche Lieder* and a number of organ works which, like the choral compositions, are generally centred on chorale melodies. The principal effect of latter-day study of the seventeenth and eighteenth centuries has been a realization of the fact, which (probably because of academic insistence in the main teaching seminaries on 'exercises' written for the normal forces of the nineteenth century) escaped notice for a long time, that there is virtue in the imaginative handling of a small variety of tone values. Not only is there much scope for imaginative exploration but also—as has aready been suggested—more probability of performance. Thus Bax's *Of a Rose I sing* for voices, harp, 'cello and double bass; Britten's *Ceremony of Carols* in which the accompaniment is entrusted to a solitary harp or the same composer's engaging setting of Christopher Smart's *Rejoice in the Lamb* where the organ part is conceived picturesquely, and without too much regard to its figural conventions; Martin's *Le vin herbé* where the instrumental ensemble consists of two violins, two violas, two 'cellos, double bass and pianoforte: Bliss's suave *Pastorale* where the coolness of the lyrical verses is reflected in a characteristically temperate accompaniment of strings and flute; Kaminski's lightness of instrumentation in the *Magnificat* and the *Passion*; Burkhard's cantata *Genug ist nicht genug*, with strings, two trumpets and chorus; Boris Blacher's chamber-oratorio *Romeo und Julia*, with flute, bassoon, trumpet, piano and string quintet. Occasionally the affection for the past carries the harpsichord into the score. If, however, the pianoforte is used it is used (as in Britten's operas) not to 'fill in' but to point rhythm. That the pianoforte is now regarded generally as a percussion instrument is not so much due to the public activities of famous performers but to a zest for sharp edges both to tone and to rhythm. Return to the baroque suits us very well; for renewal of the attitude of the baroque composer creates eagerness and a fresh sense of the importance of the sound of music.

Even when large forces are deployed (as for the 'Festival') orchestration is various and exciting. Rhythmic vitality (sometimes music becomes so consciously vital that its movement appears neurotic or false) finds outlet in an apparent extravagance of percussion. There are the exuberant works—Orff's *Carmina Burana* and Britten's *Spring Symphony* with their mixture of drums, triangles, cymbals, castanets, jingles, gongs (one big and one small), bells, glockenspiels, xylophones and so on—with effects to have delighted the most naive among the percussive angels of antiquity. There are the spectacular works—Walton's *Belshazzar's Feast*, the passionate works—the *Symphonie de Psaumes*. All are bound together by tremendous rhythmic emphasis.

It used formerly to be said that 'advanced' composers treated their voices instrumentally. To a point when voices are intermingled with instruments that is inevitable: and sometimes, of course, the practice works in reverse with composers—Edward Rubbra and Samuel Barber serving as examples—writing vocally for instruments. The extent to

T

which voices may legitimately be used instrumentally may be considered.

Voices may be used simply for their tonal value and associations—as in Vaughan Williams' *Sinfonia Antartica*, where the wash of female voices gives a strange unearthliness to the beginning and to the end of the work, or in almost any other contemporary (so-called) choral symphony, such as Milhaud's third, which is symphony rather than (in the case of Holst's *Choral Symphony*) a cantata. Particular timbres may be desired for particular purposes. Many of the Germans and Stravinsky in his major works—in rebellion against the alleged *affetuoso* quality in women's voices—call for boys' voices. These are also intended to suggest, by a sort of Victorian regard for idealized choristers in paint rather than the real things in life, innocence and purity and so on. Distant choirs (who chant rather endless *Amens* and *Alleluias*) are also in vogue. The *Chansons françaises* of Poulenc—quite enchanting miniatures, fresh and witty—are entirely effective exploitation of seemingly meaningless 'las' and 'clic clacs', which, however, are properly gay and colourful in the setting. Vaughan Williams encourages 'humming' and other wordless effects in almost every work. Roy Harris makes magnificent point in the sixth movement of his *Folk Song Symphony* of resonant reiteration of 'Lawd' and 'Oh Lawd'. No one who has heard it will forget the choral shout at the announcement of the death of (Walton's) Belshazzar. All in all, then, the voice is exploited in two contrasting directions: either to encourage the belief that music is realistic or else to move the mind away from reality.

One feature of contemporary choral music to be noted is the relative impotence within this medium of the dodecaphonalists. Berg and Webern have done little in this field. Schoenberg, on the other hand, has, since *Gurre-Lieder* (which is not dodecaphonic), made several significant contributions: significant not so much for their own musical sake as for the conclusions to be drawn from them. *A Survivor from Warsaw* (1947) is a 'tonal work'. *A Survivor from Warsaw* is 'an essay in the evocation of nightmare': at the end, however, it finds relief in quotation of the Jewish prayer 'Shema Israel'. This was one of Schoenberg's last works. *Kol Nidre* (1938), which was commissioned by a Jewish organization, also makes use of a Jewish liturgical theme and thus drives back to one of the first impulses of choral music. *Kol Nidre* is, in a sense, a focal work for, in addition to its thematic foundation in tradition, it fuses the atonal (for the tone-row principles are evident) with the tonal. In

1925 Schoenberg composed two choral testaments to the new principles of atonality: *Vier Stücke* (Op. 27) and *Drei Satiren* (Op. 28). We have hitherto suggested that a 'return to' certain medieval conceptions is one characteristic of some contemporary music. Schoenberg goes back entirely to scholastic first principles. Thus in Op. 27 we have, successively, a strict four-part canon in contrary motion; a free canon; an exposition of quadruple invertible counterpoint; in Op. 28 an endless canon in four parts; a 'retrograde' canon; a 'little cantata' which concludes with a fugue. To Op. 28 is added an appendix containing three industrious, complex, fascinating essays in canon. The third, to be worked out in six parts, has some historic significance (Ex. 3). Bernard

Ex. 3

S' A S''
Wer Ehr er - weist, muss selbst da - von be - sit - zen;

T' T'
Sonst ist sie zu ge - ring. Drum huld- gen dem Ka - non

Mu - si - ker um Ehr: zu zei - gen; dass sie sie ha - ben durch ihn.

Shaw, devoted to Wagner and Elgar, has, so far as I know, left no comment on this birthday offering.

In a lengthy introduction to Op. 28 Schoenberg exposes the reasons for this particular set of compositions. A number of epigrams have point.

'For more than one who has reason to fear the light may think that he can hide behind the seeming obscurity of words and music. . . .'

'I was aiming at all those who seek their personal safety in the "middle way" '—those who 'grab at dissonances hoping thus to pass for "modernists"; the "pseudo-tonalists", who think that they can do everything to smash tonality just as long as they profess their faith in it by sticking in a triad from time to time, whether it fits or not.'

'I am aiming at those who work for a "return to ——". Let none of them try to convince us that he is capable of deciding how many years behind the times he will soon be, or that he can ally himself with some great master of the past (whose every effort was in the direction of the future).'

'I also enjoy taking a shot at the folk-lorists who try to treat the basically primitive ideas of popular music with a technique which is appropriate only to more highly evolved forms of musical thought. . . .'

'And, finally, I refer to all the "—ists", in whom I can see only "mannerists" whose music satisfies principally those to whose minds it constantly suggests a "label" that conveniently obviates the necessity for further thought.'

These may serve the reader as a somewhat convenient yardstick of criticism. But some of the criticism may turn back on Schoenberg himself. It is by no means clear whether in fact these particular works are 'new' rather than 'old'. And as for the '—ists' none have done more to provoke disrespect than Schoenberg's own disciples. René Leibowitz thus apotheosizes Op. 24 and Op. 27 (under the alarming subtitle—'The unfoldment of Schoenberg's twelve-tone activity'):

'[These works] solve, even more clearly, the problem of strict counterpoint. Now, thanks to the new technique, this counterpoint can give rise to laws as precise as those which governed earlier forms of counterpoint. In this sense, it must be said that an imitation could rarely be strict in the modal or tonal systems, while such strictness is obligatory here.'

But why? Music is to be heard and not seen. Choral music is to be sung. I have no doubts as to Schoenberg's great skill, nor indeed as to his genius in instrumental music; but I have considerable doubts concerning the performing potential of the works in question and a powerful suspicion that they are meant to pull rather than charm the listening ear. However, the reader is at liberty to gather a few acquaintances and to put these pieces to the test.

I notice that among my music-loving acquaintances there is a majority which refers to 'modern music' as though it were an easily defined commodity of one noxious consistency and to be avoided. Not being easily wearied in propaganda for the living as, sometimes, for the dead, I protest that Schoenberg, for instance, is but one among many. I would, therefore, turn from his Stücke and Satiren to a contrasting type

of choral music. In an inverted way Schoenberg, in avoiding popular
acclaim, is an exhibitionist, Honegger is an exhibitionist without
inversion. Thus we may notice, in particular, the spectacular music of
Le Roi David—originally intended as incidental music for the play by
René Morax and first produced at Mézières, in France, in 1921—
and of Jeanne d'Arc au bûcher (1939)—a setting of a poem by Claudel.
These works are magnificently spectacular and there is no necessity to
look either for inner meanings or digressions in technique. It is sufficient
to remark that the splendid visionary impulse of Morax and Claudel
are conveyed to the listener through a compelling musical style, conspicuous for its lyrical fluency on the one hand, its variety of colour and
sonority on the other. There is something owed to Berlioz; as in 'La
Danse devant l'Arche' and 'Le mort de David' which continue in their
way in Le Roi David the sensationalism of the Messe des Morts; and in
Scene IX of Jeanne d'Arc where the tenuous instrumentation and the
affective voices of children recall the character of L'Enfance du Christ.

In a general survey of twentieth-century choral music some mention
must be made of choral symphonies—of which there have been a great
many. Now the composer who employs voices in symphonic music is
liable to fall between two stools. Either his music concentrates on the
unfolding of an orchestral design and vocal parts are therefore relegated
to the subordinate position of the chorus in classical opera and some
eighteenth-century Masses; or it is too choral, too episodic and therefore
not symphonic at all. Among the choral symphonies there are a number
of works which should be more properly regarded as cantatas, except
for the fact that symphonic shape keeps the texts within limits which
words do not always appreciate. This applies to works as diverse as
Mahler's gigantic eighth symphony (1907)—the 'symphony of a
thousand voices', to Vaughan Williams's magnificently symbolic and
picturesque Sea Symphony, to Roy Harris's exhilarating and sometimes
beautiful Folk Song Symphony, to Britten's Spring Symphony, to Holst's
Choral Symphony (settings of Keats). This last work, now forgotten,
was included in a programme of the Royal Philharmonic Society,
London, in 1925, in commemoration of the centenary of the first
Philharmonic performance of Beethoven's Choral Symphony. In this
work, said one critic, 'cerebration tamed, and bridled inspiration'.

Here we discover the ultima Thule of choral music; for by reason of
its own nature it resists the impact of 'cerebration'. It is an extension of
natural function. It is by origin and tradition an enhancement of speech.

Both these points having been referred to in the introduction to this book it is not necessary here to enlarge on them. It may, however, be hinted to the composer that musical style exists not in itself but in its outward and audible manifestations. Therefore, while dodecaphony may be convincing in some contexts, style should be at one with the material which bears it rather than impressed on the material from without. In a sense a piece of sculpture creates itself from its own material. So it is with music. So it is that choral music has limitations which are not to be disguised by an overlay of orchestral virtuosity. But the limitations of a medium are the challenge to the artist. Accordingly we presume to look among the choral music of our age for some works in which singleness of purpose, originality of thought, and felicity of expression are conjoined and which may be upheld as models of their kind. It is clear that selection must be arbitrary. I have no intention of suggesting to posterity its duty in the preservation of twentieth-century masterpieces. Rather am I anxious to draw attention to a handful of varied works in the hope that their examination will reveal some method of approach to 'new music' and that my sceptical friends will realize that within the contemporary scene there is much diversity.

RALPH VAUGHAN WILLIAMS (1872–1958): 'MASS IN G MINOR' AND 'SANCTA CIVITAS'

Vaughan Williams has been represented at almost every English choral festival since 1907 when his setting of Whitman's *Toward the Unknown Region* was heard at Leeds. Three years after that memorable first performance came the suite of settings from Whitman's *Sea-Drift* and *Passage to India* which comprise the *Sea Symphony*: a mighty, oceanic utterance with all the imagery of the subject (the sea as a symbol is constant in Vaughan Williams right up to the last *Sinfonia Antartica* and the optimistic feeling for universal brotherhood which Whitman expresses. At Leeds they had 348 singers for this work. But that was in the spacious Edwardian days when such forces were obligatory and when geniality in expression, which is evident in the *Sea Symphony* as a relic from Parry and Stanford and the nineteenth-century Germans, was also expected. Two points stand out from an early notice of the *Sea Symphony* in the *Yorkshire Post* of October 13th, 1910. 'The composer's method is very modern in its elusive and tortuous harmonic progressions, but they leave the conviction that they are not affected for the sake of singularity, but are the genuine expression of the composer's ideas. Among the happy instances of his fancy is his use of a mystic semi-chorus. . . .' Genuineness and mysticism. From there we may progress to 1922. Then, after one great war in which the composer took his part, there was need for greater demonstrations of the two qualities by which the community might be stabilized and in which faith might descry some supernal purpose. A son of the English parsonage Vaughan Williams always kept close to the traditions of the English Church. But not too close. For his music is at all times blunt, spiritually critical, discomfiting; beyond the norm of Anglican decorum.

In 1922 Sir Richard Terry was in charge of music at the great Roman Catholic Cathedral at Westminster. There he did much to expose the wisdom of the *Motu Proprio* of 1903 by reviving the glories of the polyphonic period. Among modern works admitted to the Cathedral was a motet—*O vos omnes*—by Vaughan Williams. In this great piece for Holy Week there is reflection, stern yet commiserating, on the reality of sin. It is such a piece as Victoria might have conceived. A year later the *Mass in G Minor*, dedicated to Gustav Holst and his Whitsuntide Singers, was performed in Westminster Cathedral. It was performed liturgically.

The *Mass* is essentially a liturgical work. It is not a concert piece. It demands the associations of the liturgy, the acoustical aura of a great church, the impersonality of cathedral singers. It is austere. It plunges back into tradition and urges the universality of the Church and of the Faith by pointing out their expression in time. It was said when the *Mass* was performed in Westminster Abbey that 'not since the Abbey was a relatively new building can it have heard within half an hour so many consecutive fifths'.

The *Mass* owes much to the late medieval tradition: it is polyphonic; diatonic; spare; rhythmically fluid. But it is not an imitation of some other work. It is independently compounded. The archaisms become as much part of Vaughan Williams as the verbal recollections of the past in Whitman become part of Whitman. In this connection it will be noted that through his study of Whitman's philosophy Vaughan Williams comes to the religious formulation of the principal ideas of Whitman. But the brotherhood is within the idea of the Godhead.

To study the composer's approach to the word 'Sanctus' is to gain an immediate insight into his apperception of spiritual affairs. In Vaughan Williams we distinguish, in the dynamic marking, a vast distance towards the state of sanctification; beyond the distance clearness and a great depth of worship; a sense of awe

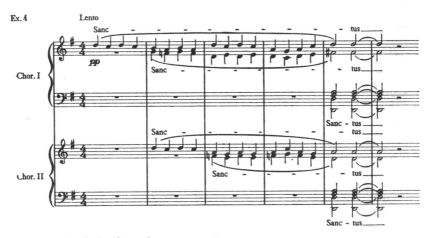

We may look back and see, in a characteristic choral sequence of this composer, an even greater sense of awe

In the secular way this Mass may not inspire. In the religious way it does. Consider the humility of the opening phrase of the 'Kyrie', the felt but not fully expressed anguish of the 'Agnus Dei', the graceful definition of 'Benedictus', the restrained melismata of the 'Gloria'. In every case the music searches the recesses of the verbal symbol and stimulates the worshipper to do likewise. While the *Mass* is unmistakably of Vaughan Williams it is without prejudice, without emotional over-emphasis. Thus, in showing the way to personal evaluation of the statements of the Church, it is Protestant: but at the same time truly Catholic. In such a paradox lies the hope of the present and the future.

In *Sancta Civitas* (1925) Vaughan Williams goes beyond the facts of religious belief—if so we may regard the Mass—to the apocalyptic vision of St. John. Here Vaughan Williams displays the mysticism—

the feeling that he is caught up within the flux of eternity—which is so remarkable in the sixth and seventh symphonies, particularly in the Epilogue of the Sixth. The theme of *Sancta Civitas* is the fulness of the spiritual life and the futility of the transient things which pass, as did Babylon the Great. It is in the contrast of the permanence of the beauty, the strength and the truth of honour with the decline of the earthly city that the musical ethos of this work springs.

Sancta Civitas is a sort of symphonic impression. It is symphonic because it is unified. But the unity lies in feeling much more than in form. In the period in which this work was written Vaughan Williams departed from, though in no sense relinquishing the right to employ it when the occasion demanded, the plain speech of 'modal' harmony and 'neo-Tudor' counterpoint. He expressed a more intangible form of harmonic colour. Thus the opening of *Sancta Civitas* (Ex. 6): the

heavenly alleluias (Ex. 7): the motiv which preludes the fall of

Babylon (Ex. 8). And here, too, we see the effect on the composer of

general experiments in bitonality (if not, indeed, atonality). This is a difficult work in execution. It is difficult in apprehension—unless prejudices are loosed and the imagination caught up within the poetic mystery of the text. Yet, Vaughan Williams being ever a moralist, the moral is clear: hope lies in spiritual regeneration.

GUSTAV HOLST (1872-1934): 'THE HYMN OF JESUS'

Gustav Holst just missed being a composer of the highest rank. He had great skill, high independence, absolute integrity; but remaining aloof from his contemporaries and from life in general he rarely achieved a convincing contact with his audience. On the whole his mind dwelt in a rarified atmosphere wherein music lost its corporeal qualities and became identical with the thought which it should interpret. This is notable in his songs, in his works in concerto form, in his chamber music, in the opera *Savitri* (1908) and in the *Choral Fantasia* (1930). When, however, he synthesized his personal qualities, his natural affection for people, and his artistry he could accomplish, on a small scale, the exultant miniature 'This have I done for my true love' or the *Two Psalms* for Chorus, string, orchestra and organ, and, of a larger scope, *The Planets* and *The Hymn of Jesus*.

Holst was a friend of, and a fellow student at the Royal College of Music with, Vaughan Williams. In outlook they had much in common. Both disliked coteries and artificiality. Both acted on the principle of saying things, when they needed to be said, in the most natural way. Both were ardent in revival of folk music, Tudor music and the forgotten works of Bach. Both were concerned with the artistic potential of the 'common man'.[1] The one conducted musical festivals, the other immersed himself in devoted work at Morley College (one outcome of the late nineteenth-century zeal for the further education of the 'working man'). Throughout his life Holst, although a composer by vocation, was compelled to follow his creative career at odd moments, at weekends.

Perhaps it is as much as any honest composer will hope for to leave one or two works which will remain after most other things have faded. *The Hymn of Jesus* is one of Holst's few permanencies. It is a highly personal work, being based, for instance, on words from the *Apocryphal Acts of St. John*; yet it touches the general. It was first performed at a Royal Philharmonic Society Concert in March, 1920. Its quality was thus perceived by Sir Donald Tovey:

'I have been reading *The Hymn of Jesus*. It completely bowls me over. Your presentation of it is the poem, the whole poem, and

[1] See Holst's *Walt Whitman Overture* (1899).

296

nothing but the poem. . . . I am thoroughly familiar with that kind
of enjoyment of a poem where one feels "ah—that's a clever way to
set this verse, not a way that would have occurred to me   perhaps
better, perhaps not quite so good as my idea of how to set it; ah, I
like this—eh, eh".

Well, your *Hymn of Jesus* doesn't occupy me in that way at all.
It is there, just as if neither you nor I had any say in the matter. It
couldn't have been done before . . . and it can't be done again. . . .
It's a blessed abiding fact; and not a matter of taste at all. If anybody
doesn't like it, he doesn't like life.'

I see no reason, after long experience of the work, to fault this
judgement, which is repeated in his essay on the work.

The words of *The Hymn* are instinct with a religious emotionalism
that is often felt but seldom admitted.

Thus:

> 'Fain would I be saved: And fain would I save.
> Fain would I be released: And fain would I release.
> Fain would I be pierced: And fain would I pierce.
> Fain would I be borne: Fain would I bear.
> Fain would I be eat: Fain would I be eaten.
>   . . . I am Mind of All!'

The text envisages the absorption of the sinner within the sinless, the
flesh within the spirit, the deed within the Word. And the Word is to be
found encircled by the dancing spheres. So Holst reads no passivity in
peace, but limitless motion. And the characteristic of the music is its
rhythmic vitality. In this we approach the province of Stravinsky: thus
Divine Grace is set moving (Ex. 9). The extract from the words already

Ex. 9

quoted shows a double choir as a necessity. Holst uses the two choirs
in apposition, he makes full use of the spacious effects of full homophony in moments of praise and of the extensive effectiveness of more
or less conventional imitative openings. But he goes beyond the
expected. So he drenches the spirit of the text with mystical rapture.

(Ex. 10). At an earlier point in the work the voices, one after another,

Ex. 10

speak the words 'Glory to Thee Holy Spirit', above a typical Holstian ostinato bass.

The Prelude to the Hymn contains two ancient church melodies 'Pange Lingua gloriosi' and 'Vexilla regis', which are also incorporated in the body of the Hymn. The scoring of this first section with its contrast of timbres, its keen brilliance (note the first *lento* passage), its premonitory pulsations of diatonic dignity, and the aspersive effect of the pianoforte and celesta, reveals not only the mystical sensibility but also the visual accuracy of the composer's mind. Floating over and around the music from beginning to end are the triads which carry the everlasting Amen of the semi-chorus and it is on this word in an 'O altitudo' of reverence that all the voices end, *morendo*, on a chord of C major. *The Hymn of Jesus* was dedicated to Vaughan Williams.

CONSTANT LAMBERT (1905–1951): 'THE RIO GRANDE'

At first sight there appears little in common between the music of Holst and that of Constant Lambert. *The Rio Grande*, indeed, appears as far away from *The Hymn of Jesus* as is possible. For this is, essentially, an entertainment, a diverting choral fantasia (like Beethoven's only in the importance of the solo pianoforte) on a languorous poem of Sacheverell Sitwell. Moreover the idiom is taken from the 'jazz' idiom of *circa* 1930. The score includes three timpani, side-drum, tenor-drum, bass-drum, cymbals, Turkish crash, tam-tam, tambourine, castanets, triangle, chinese tam-tams, cow-bell, Chinese block, xylophone, and glockenspiel in the percussion department.

Lambert, however, is not merely imitative. He catches the nature of dance—the contemporary dance—and idealizes it. So in his idealization he meets Holst whose music also led to idealism through the basic ritual movements of the body. Lambert, too, is intent on speaking his independence and if Holst protests the unique qualities of the tradition to which he belongs he, on the other hand, suggests the values of his own age and environment. Holst has something of the clarity of Ravel, Lambert the economy of the later French school of 'Les Six'.

Gaiety in choral music is the exception rather than the rule. It is in its expression of first, fine, careless rapture—Lambert was twenty-five when he wrote the work—that *The Rio Grande* is outstanding. 'It suggests', said one critic after the first performance by the Hallé Orchestra, 'a new fashion in music for choral societies, and a new fashion is badly needed.' In fact *The Rio Grande* has remained alone—the alpha and the omega of that style in choral music.

Sacheverell Sitwell's poem is romantic, evocative and rhythmic: its direction is poetic and artificial. By itself it appears mannered. But it suggests musical comment. And Lambert takes every opportunity to increase the allurements of the poetry by apt turns of melody and colourful switches of harmonic colour. The meticulousness of the poetic expression he places within a fairly formal structure which is marked by the repetition of (Ex. 11) and (Ex. 12). The instrumentation

Ex. 11 Allegro giocoso

ff (Str.)

Ex. 12 ff

By the Ri - o Grande___

glitters (note especially the use of brass, of percussion and of the piano which has two cadenzas, the first amusingly accompanied by percussion instruments) but there is great economy: no instrument is redundant. At the end of the work the solo contralto—accompanied by muted strings, by piano, by a semi-chorus which dissolves into the amorphous sweetness of wordless chords—recalls, nostalgically and as from a distance, the 'enchantment of the soft Brazilian air'.

This is an eminently quotable work. Consider (Ex. 13), wherein

one may catch a madrigalian flavour, at best in felicitous word painting; of (Ex. 14), which shows a largeness of conception that comes from the

main stream of choral tradition. One may be forgiven for feeling that this is the way in which a Weelkes or Morley would have responded if translated to the twentieth century. Appreciation of the sixteenth-century spirit does not necessarily lie in imitation of the sixteenth-century manner. Lambert further illustrates this in a longer choral work —*Summer's Last Will and Testament*. This setting of five poems by Thomas Nashe represents, in the most convincing manner, those sides of sixteenth-century life—plague, pestilence and famine—which do not lend themselves to idealization. Like such other outstanding British works as Vaughan Williams' *Five Tudor Portraits* and Dyson's *Canterbury Pilgrims* this is perhaps too local in significance for general appreciation.

IGOR STRAVINSKY (1882-): 'SYMPHONIE DE PSAUMES' (SYMPHONY OF PSALMS)

In the same year (1930) that Lambert produced *The Rio Grande* Stravinsky composed—in honour of the fiftieth anniversary of the

Boston Symphony Orchestra—his choral symphony, the *Symphonie de Psaumes*. This is, in this composer's development, a midway work, lying between the brilliance of the early ballets and the spareness of the *Symphony in C* and the *Mass* (1948), although the austerity of this had already been anticipated in the 'Opera-Oratorio' *Oedipus Rex*, which was first performed in Paris in 1927.

Early performances of the *Symphonie de Psaumes*[1] perplexed the first audience and Stravinsky felt obliged to explain his purpose in his autobiography. Some points (taken for this occasion out of their original order) are of material assistance not only in understanding Stravinsky's point of view, but also much other modern music. 'Most people like music because it gives them certain emotions, such as joy, grief, sadness, an image of nature, a subject for daydreams or—still better—oblivion from "everyday life". They want a drug—' "dope"....' Music would not be worth much if it were reduced to such an end.'

The listener should not have much difficulty in testing himself by this statement, nor in dividing the music he hears accordingly.

'Symphonic form as bequeathed to us by the nineteenth century held little attraction for me, inasmuch as it had flourished in a period the language and ideas of which were all the more foreign to us because it was the period from which we emerged.' [The problem of treating symphonic ideas symphonically had, of course, perplexed composers throughout the nineteenth century].

'My idea was that my symphony should be a work with great contrapuntal development, and for that it was necessary to increase the media at my disposal. Thus voices are employed not—as in the general "choral-symphony" manner to increase, to make more emotionally exciting, to "explain", or to add picturesqueness—but to interpret the essential and intrinsic musical idea. At the moment of commencement word symbols had not arrived.

I finally decided on a choral and instrumental *ensemble* in which the two elements should be on an equal footing, neither of them outweighing the other. In this instance my view-point as to the mutual relationship of the vocal and instrumental sections coincided with that of the masters of contrapuntal music, who . . . neither reduced the role of the choruses to that of a homophonous chant nor

At Palais des Beaux Arts, Brussels, under Ansermet, and Boston, under Koussevitzky.

the function of the instrumental ensemble to that of an accompaniment. This, as we have discovered, was the general fault under
which the Romantics—fresh from song and piano *accompaniment*—
laboured. And the fault persists in the minds of many who interpret
the great Bach works as though they were *accompanied* in the
nineteenth century sense.

I sought for my words, since they were to be sung, among
those which had been written for singing. And quite naturally my
first idea was to have recourse to the Psalms.'

The point is to be emphasized, for the acceptance of too literary
words intended to be read silently, leads to too much dissipation of
good intentions in musical digressions. This is a particular failing of the
English and the American composer, who has been too well educated
in a literary way. In the case of the Psalms they do, in fact, sing themselves. Stravinsky goes on to complain that many composers 'treat the
Holy Scriptures from the viewpoint of ethnography, history or
picturesqueness'. His intention is to let the words speak for themselves.
(Stravinsky clearly is over-rigorous here and would appear to exclude
many works—*Belshazzar's Feast* for example—which do make their
point picturesquely: but the contemporary attitude, in general, is
suspicious of 'picturesqueness' precisely because it can 'dope' or 'delude',
and in advising his contemporaries of the virtues of direct utterance he
was both timely and justified).

To what extent, then, do words matter? Stravinsky answers this in
respect of his use of Latin (a 'dead language') in *Oedipus Rex*. Thus he
urges that his musical style develops its own order from the discipline
of the restraining words; further such 'impersonal formulas of a remote
period' were suitable 'to the austere and solemn character to which they
specially lent themselves'.

Thus, independently, Stravinsky arrived at a point very near to that
contained in the *Motu Proprio*. At the time of writing the *Symphonie de
Psaumes* he was a member of the Russian Orthodox Church. Later he
became a member of the Roman Catholic communion. The *Symphonie*
gives a clue to his inner attitude for its dedication to the Boston
Symphony Orchestra begins thus: 'Cette symphonie composée à la
gloire de DIEU. . . .'

The words chosen for the *Symphonie* are (from the Vulgate) Psalm
XXXVIII, verses 13 and 14, which furnish the first movement; Psalm

XXXIX, verses 2, 3 and 4, on which the second movement is based; and finally the whole of Psalm CL. A large orchestra is employed but, with the intention of reducing the purely emotional temperature, without violins or violas. Again aiming at impersonality it is requested that the upper parts of the chorus should, wherever possible, be sung by children's voices. Harmony, as such, may be said to be almost non-existent; chords being mostly employed percussively to mark sectional endings.

The first movement has three elements: a perpetual motion of insistent eighth notes which are frequently arranged in this sequence of minor thirds (Ex. 15) a rising arpeggio of sixteenth notes, with which

Ex. 15

the pianos add much force to the climax of the movement at figure 12: a neutral, near plain-chant, motiv in the voices (Ex. 16). 'Four-part'

Ex. 16

E - xau - di___ o - ra - ti - o-nem me-am Do - mi - no - - - -

writing is at a minimum.

The second movement is as inexorable and as inevitable as the first. But whereas the first was in 2/4, 3/4 or 4/4 with crotchet = 92, the second is in slow 4/8, crotchet = 60. This allows clarity to the counter-point and power to the words—'He brought me up also out of an horrible pit, out of the miry clay . . .'—to be fully realized. There are two separate fugues, one for the instruments on this subject (Ex. 17)

Ex. 17

Ob.   mf

and one for the voices (Ex. 18). The contrapuntal movement (for

Ex. 18   mf Tranquillo

Ex - pec - tans ex-pec - ta - - vi Do-mi - num,___

there are *stretti* within this) leads to some compelling sounds at figure 14. The conclusion of the movement is a vocal monotone, against which the instruments disappear, to the words 'et sperabunt in Domino'.

U

A choral and instrumental prelude in which the exultant interval of the fourth is variously repeated and in which the tonality goes, in a general way, towards C major, introduces the final song of praise, in which the composer finds it impossible to escape either from his own heritage of instrumental-rhythmic virtuosity or from the infectious exuberance of the psalmist. The section from figure 21 to the end, where the prelude to the movement is repeated in abbreviation, deserves the closest attention: first for the simplicity of the idea, next for the manner in which all the elements are tuned, and lastly for the way in which Stravinsky's theories become modified by practice. For here (Ex. 19)

Ex. 19

we may be forgiven for seeing as well as hearing. As the apparently endless song continues above the pedal bass the orchestral forces, first with brass and woodwind in antiphon and then together, surround it with added light and vigour.

ERNEST BLOCH (1880–1959): 'AVODATH HAKODESH (SACRED SERVICE)'

Someone observed to Stravinsky that in his settings of the psalms he had 'missed' the essential Jewish character. By which the composer was stimulated to castigate all who contemplated such poetry from a particularist standpoint. Some point is added to his comment by consideration of such a work as Bloch's *Sacred Service*, by some acknowledged as his masterpiece and by others—for whom the English composer Edmund Rubbra speaks[1]—as the undoubted voice 'of the Jewish *Weltanschauung*'.

There is no doubt about Bloch's devotion to the cause of Jewry. His whole output has been distinguished by a poetic absorption in the spiritual heritage of his race. Signposts in his career at the *Trois Poèmes*

[1] See *Musical Times*, December 1949.

Juifs, the *Israel Symphony, Baal Shem* for violin and pianoforte, *Méditation hébraïque* and *From Jewish Life* for 'cello and pianoforte, *Voice in the Wilderness* and the *Schelomo* Rhapsody, both for 'cello and orchestra. It will be noticed that Bloch's use of the 'cello is both eloquent and personal and so experienced a critic as Lawrence Gilman considered *Schelomo* 'the finest work yet written by any composer, living or dead, for the 'cello'. Bloch is capable of the expression of deep anguish, in which he is often aided by quotation of traditional Jewish melody; he is distinguished in his orchestral texture. He is a convincing craftsman, of high integrity. For nearly forty years he lived in America and became an American citizen, although he was born in Geneva and educated in Brussels, Frankfurt and Munich.

The problem which confronted him was that which faces any composer with strong racial feelings. But there was this difference: Jewish music, apart from the Synagogue, has no definable tradition. Jewish composers have, generally, expressed themselves with varying degrees of success within the general terms of their times.[1] Bloch has also had to come to terms with the style which he inherited from Ivan Knorr in Frankfurt and Thuille in Munich. At best he has heightened romantic idiom and carried it in the general direction of his particular field of interest. In *Schelomo,* in particular, the result is convincing and the music stands (or falls) by its own merits.

The *Sacred Service,* however, is a different matter. For this is specially addressed to the members of the Jewish faith, being a complete setting of 'A Sabbath Morning Service according to the Union Prayer Book'. It is as liturgically proper as a polyphonic Mass, and set for Cantor (baritone), mixed choir and organ (or orchestra). The general pattern is of verse, delivered by the Cantor, answered by a choral response. The traditional, liturgical chant is strongly evident in the former, but in the latter is considerably modified. The Cantor, being free, is endowed with *melismata* and with characteristic intervals such as the augmented second. The unifying element is a general modality, which is, however, liable to disintegrate under the impact of chromatic fervour. The work is divided into five sections of which the last is musically the most compelling. (Elsewhere the episodic necessity laid on the composer by the liturgical design is distracting.) It is in this Epilogue that the music

---

[1] Cf. Milhaud's *Prières Journalières à l'ùsage des Juifs du Comtat Venaissin: Trois Chants de Rosch Haschanna:* and *Service Sacrée.* The last-named should be compared with Bloch's work: Milhaud is tersely French and lacking in the rhapsodic virtue which distinguishes Bloch.

fully integrates the elements of which it is compounded. The chorus departs from the restrictions which have hitherto retained it within a generally sacred, rather than especially Jewish, context and discovers a new sort of *seconda prattica* of Romantic expression (Ex. 20). This is a

powerful work, but within limits: it appears great or less than great according to the extra-musical sympathies of the listener. Since, however, it is in its own way 'occasional music' it must be judged by those to whom the occasion is significant.

HEINRICH KAMINSKI (1886–1946): 'MAGNIFICAT' AND 'PASSION'

Study of Hebrew religious observance in the *Old Testament* will indicate the importance of music in such observance. The reader will be struck by the (to us) bizarre assortment of brass and percussion associated with ancient song. We have grown accustomed to the conventions of a later piety and find in any expression of the sharper edge of Hebrew poetry a lack of propriety. The Magnificat is a case in point. This is either the exultant song of a primitive girl, or else it is a set piece in an Office Book. It has one significance to some, another to others. Two composers of our time have endeavoured to capture some of the essential physical impulse from the canticle—Vaughan Williams (in a wonderfully mystical realization for contralto solo, women's voices, orchestra) and Heinrich Kaminski

Kaminski has already been mentioned as a composer who has made much use of eighteenth-century principles. In the *Magnificat* he successfully shows the poise that can emerge from eclecticism. We discover, for instance, a soprano solo which requires for its execution much skill in Mozartian coloratura; a chorus which is polyphonic; an important violin solo; orchestration with the characteristic highlights of modern scoring; and a harmonic idiom which may be defined as extended Romanticism. It is, in short, a work in which several styles are blended. The result lies midway between the probable and the improbable: which, perhaps, is where we are balanced by a personal consideration of the poem. Kaminski takes us out of church, but does not forget the historical and ecclesiastical symbol which the *Magnificat* has become.

The sensibility of the composer is shown in an impressive *adagio* orchestral prelude which—in effect no more than an expression of dominant tonality—draws mystery and beauty down by the intermingling of percussion, celesta, harp, string harmonics and subtle and allusive hints from woodwind. Then the chorus commence with the

Ex. 21

angelic greeting 'Ave Maria'. This culminates in a resonant sequence of unaccompanied alleluias. Then the solo voice, against a background of sweeping scales on the harp, exclaims (Ex. 21). The remainder of the work derives from the rising motiv, rhythmically varied and with incidentally directive *melismata*—thus humility (Ex. 22). The chorus

Ex. 22

qui___ a re - spe - - xit hu - mi-li - ta___
___ tem an - cil - lae su - ae

part consist of interjections of 'Osianna', 'Sanctus', 'Gloria'.

The qualities apparent in the *Magnificat* are also to be seen in the brief, poignant Passion which Kaminski composed in 1925 to the text of a 'Mystery Play' by Arnoul and Simon Gredan: a tensely poignant sequence of scenes of the Passion, culminating in three finely illustrated choral epilogues—of the soul in Purgatory, of those in Hell and of those in Heaven. The latter welcome the Saviour with the opening words of the *Magnificat*, with Palm Sunday 'Hosannas', with 'Gloria in excelsis'. As in his *Magnificat* Kaminski centres this work on D tonality. He includes, allusively, movements based on the chorales 'Aus tiefer Not', 'O Haupt voll blut und wunden' and 'Herzliebster Jesu'.

THE CHORAL WORKS OF BENJAMIN BRITTEN
(b. 1913)

Benjamin Britten shares with only a few composers a complete certainty in aural perception so that his music appears—like Pallas Athene—to spring into being from the brain of its creator fully accoutred and ready for action. Britten has, perhaps, the most secure musical ear since Mendelssohn and (though his closest supporters will misconstrue this as pejorative) his style has its affinities with that master. Predominantly it is an attractive, athletic style so that even in such grave works as *Peter Grimes* and the *Sinfonia da Requiem* the solemnity of idea cannot escape grace in expression. And in works which are light-hearted we may appear to be deluded with trivialities. This is the crux of the critical problem. I recollect among my older mentors those who

(incredible though this may seem to present-day 'enlightment') preferred Bach to Mozart while ignoring Haydn altogether, or Bach to
Handel, because Bach was infinitely more 'serious'; while it is general
to esteem tragedy above comedy in oblivion of the indisputable fact
that comedy is sometimes more tragic than tragedy. In music the
quality which we like to construe as 'beauty'—using perhaps Mozart
as our criterion—is suspect because of its elusiveness. Britten is an
elusive composer. He is a popular composer. He is the victim of
adulation: Mendelssohn stood in something of the same relation to his
age. His position is still undefined. In either case we cannot determine
whether we are in the presence of a *grand maître* or a *petit maître*. But at
least it is of a *maître*. And there I acknowledge my tribute to Mr. Britten.

It is not for nothing that Britten's largest non-operatic work is a
Spring Symphony, for his entire output has the essence of spring. There
is no work which is devoid of eagerness, of freshness, of gaiety. Whatever future judgements may determine there is no doubt that these are
qualities which are required in contemporary music to steer it back to
its own waters. Music is a part of philosophy but forms of philosophic
interpretation which are alien to musical expression are not to be
imposed on music from without. Philosophic understanding grows
from within the texture of music.

There are certain early pointers to Britten's intrinsic seriousness of
purpose. In 1936 Britten was commissioned to compose a work for the
Norwich Triennial Festival. The outcome, which annoyed the conventional, was *Our Hunting Fathers*, a cycle for soprano and orchestra to a
libretto devised by W. H. Auden. The scintillating musical idiom
showed up the eccentricity of the text and whipped that part of the
audience which approved field-sports into self-defence, or stirred those
intolerant of such activity into approbation. An impish work—but
underlying it 'the sadness of the creatures'. In 1939 in conjunction with
Auden and Randall Swingler, he produced *Ballad of Heroes*. This is not
now performed, but it should be recollected for it had acridity in its
texture. It was dedicated to those of the British Battalion of the
International Brigade who died in the Spanish Civil War. In 1942 the
Hymn to St. Cecilia, again to a text by Auden, came in celebration of the
patron saint of music, in enchanting praise of the *beauty* and therapeutic
virtue of music, and—for he was born on St. Cecilia's Day—in honour
of the composer's own birthday. This work came after Britten's war-
time sojourn in America and represented an unexpected reversal of

form. Sophistication was diminished and satire eliminated. As an *a cappella* work this is outstanding for its freshness, its variety and its inevitability. It is, in fact, exquisitely practicable—even when the voices engage in melismatic imitation of musical instruments. In the same year as the *Hymn* the *Ceremony of Carols* was performed. With high voices and harp this little work moves artlessly with the engaging simplicity of the medieval carols which form the main part of its text. This is no very great work but it radiates light and (were the word above suspicion) innocence. Such subsequent works as the *Festival Te Deum, Rejoice in the Lamb* and *St. Nicolas* have been commissioned by the Church of England and have all served to display that religious faith should not be afraid of spiritual exhilaration. I discovered the peculiar rightness of *St. Nicolas* when by chance I came upon a set of medieval murals on the same subject in the ancient chapel of Haddon Hall, in Derbyshire.

The mastery of *St. Nicolas* lies in the wealth of colour extracted from a handful of instruments. The sea-picture (notice how much Britten, like Mendelssohn, is affected by water symbolism) of the voyage to Palestine is brought to a pitch of elemental fury through the aggressive arpeggio of the piano duet pointed by the percussion, through which the anxious melody of the tenors and basses moves uneasily. And then the flashes of lightning are brought down from above (literally) by a gallery choir of high voices, who also echo the overtones of the mariners' unease in anguished *vocalises*. After the prayer of St. Nicolas the storm is stilled: the tonality changes from minor to major and high strings emerge in serenity beneficently to illuminate the scene. The organ calls Nicolas to be Bishop and the voices move in impressive counterpoint to dignify his office. The whole narrative of this cantata is laid not in immediately effective and intelligible lines and colours. So easy is the manner and so disarming are such movements as the birth of Nicolas (with the celebrated bath-tub episode) and that which illustrates the 'pickled boys' that we may overlook the dramatic dénouement of the saint's death. Here Britten shows that capacity for succinctness which may be misunderstood as negligence. The death of St. Nicolas is, in fact, as strenuous as it is brief. We do not luxuriate in grief. We see the act of dying as grim and horrific but we see it in perspective and are carried forward to the final hymn (in which the audience or congregation must join) concerning the mysterious ways of God.

The *Spring Symphony* is dedicated (like Stravinsky's *Symphonie de Psaumes*) to Koussevitzky and the Boston Symphony Orchestra. It was first performed in 1949. It is a work which exposes almost the whole of Britten's musical personality and, while it may be regarded by some primarily as a suite of choral movements, this embrasive quality gives it symphonic stature. It is impressive first in exploration of sound; next in its appreciation of poetry; finally in its original point of view. Musically the work is unexpected for, while Britten is a thoroughly 'tonal' composer, the actual combinations of sound often have no apparent ancestry—Pallas Athene again. Thus the idiom of the introductory 'Shine out'.[1] Here (Ex. 23) we are reminded of an observation

of Lennox Berkeley[2] on the symphony: '. . . it is far removed from Wordsworth's appreciation of Nature's moral or religious significance, and it is equally distant from the serene classical landscapes of Claude and Poussin. To my mind it is more clearly akin to Brueghel . . .' After the introduction is a tiny fancy on the notes of the cuckoo given to three trumpets which are the background to the tenor solo.[3] The third

[1] Words anon, sixteenth century.
[2] See *Music and Letters*, Vol. XXXI, No. 3.
[3] Words by Spenser.

movement is a 3/4 presentation of Nashe's 'Spring, the sweet spring',
for chorus and full orchestra, interspersed with pretty bird noises. If the
previous musical quotation was unusual in one respect then so is this in
another (Ex. 24). 'The driving boy'[1] eliminates the lower strings and

Ex. 24

brings in the boys' choir who divert themselves and the audience with a
gamin-type tune and some exercise in whistling. The first part ends with
a pellucid setting of words by Milton—'The Morning Star'—for
chorus and brass.

The second part opens with a setting of Herrick's 'Welcome Maids
of Honour' which is followed by an exquisite piece of water imagery[2]
(Ex. 25) to which the only accompaniment is the two violins. The next

Ex. 25

section—'Out on the lawn I lie in bed' (W. H. Auden)—is a singular
example of Britten's dramatic genius. The centrepiece of this reflection
is the desire and the inability to be free from the distractions of cruel
life. We 'do not care to know, Where Poland draws her Eastern bow,
What violence is done . . .': but, with angry brass (as in the *Ballad of
Heroes*) we must know.

The third part of the symphony comprises the *scherzo* mood in
'When will my May come' (Barnfield) for tenor, strings and harps;
George Peele's 'Fair and finer' (in which the melodic contour is the
epitome of the words), for soprano and tenor duet with strings and

---

[1] Words by Clare and Peele.
[2] 'Waters above' (Vaughan).

woodwind; the choral 'Sound the Flute', wherein the instrumental groups are set first in apposition one against the other.

Finally comes the single, extensive 'London to thee I do present' (Beaumont and Fletcher) in which all the resources are employed and in the excitement of which is merged the ancient round 'Sumer is i-cumen in'.

All in all this work is sure in technique, as terse as can be and as various as spring. A masterpiece? Probably yes. But a merry masterpiece with its corner in the Forest of Arden. A later and equally lively contribution to the choral-orchestral repertoire is the *Cantata Academica* of 1960, commissioned by the University of Basel. In this work Britten alludes to fashionable techniques, but shows how they may be used when sententiousness is dismissed and musical values invoked.

THE AMERICAN TRADITION AND SOME SIGNIFICANT WORKS

It is a truism that each community has the music that it deserves. The dominant feature of the contemporary musical scene in the United States is generosity. So we note the entertainment of such distinguished immigrants as Schoenberg, Stravinsky, Hindemith, Honegger, Weinberger, Martinů, Bloch and many others who have sought refuge from the successive oppressions of twentieth-century Europe. A number of these composers have composed outstanding choral works (some of which have been discussed) for American audiences. In the course of time the effect of these works will be incorporated within the independent outlook and style of American music, just as—through the great teaching institutions of the New World—intellectual trends in composition in general are influencing the instrumental output of our younger and brilliant contemporaries.

There have been many recent instances of disinterested generosity to non-American composers, resident abroad, in the form of commissions. There is the case of Britten. And we may also notice the large-scale *Magnificat* composed by the English composer Gerald Finzi for Smith College, Massachusetts.

Then there are abundant sources of patronage for the native composer. Notable are the Pulitzer Travelling Scholarships, Guggenheim

Fellowships, Fellowships of the American Academy in Rome; there are Publication Awards of the Eastman School and the Juilliard Foundation; there have been prizes and commissions awarded by the N.B.C., the Columbia Broadcasting System, the American League of Composers. Yet despite this abundance of encouragement choral music has taken a back place in the representative works of modern America. The only Eastman award for choral music was to Eric Delamarter for his *Psalm CXLIV* and among those promoted by the League of Composers are relatively lesser works by Roy Harris, Virgil Thomson and Randall Thompson. To set against this, however, we must note the selection, in 1944, of Lukas Foss's *The Prairie* as the best American work of the year in the opinion of the New York Music Critic's Circle. Foss was born in Berlin, but came to the U.S.A. as a child and is a product of American training.

In 1942 Randall Thompson composed his *Testament of Freedom* in honour of the bicentenary of the birth of Thomas Jefferson: it is based on passages from Jefferson's writings, the first thus setting the ethical spirit in motion: 'The God who gave us life gave us liberty at the same time; the hand of force may destroy but cannot disjoin them'. So much for subject. As to treatment we discover Thompson 'with the hope of reaching large masses . . . (utilizing) the simplest possible resources for his musical setting. The chorus is often heard in unison; and when it is divided, the part-writing has the directness of an anthem. The orchestral background is subdued, built on conventional harmonic schemes to set off the voices. . . .' First performed at the University of Virginia, which was founded by Jefferson, the *Testament* was made more widely known when it was sung at Carnegie Hall in 1945 in memory of President Roosevelt.

This work symbolizes the three characteristics of the greater part of American choral music: it is patriotic, practicable and conceived as intelligible 'to the masses', or, more probably, to some of them. Thus the music is zestful (see also Thompson's *Alleluia* composed in 1940 for the opening of the Berkshire Music Centre), but rigorously harnessed. Certain conventions are to be observed in the cause of 'intelligibility'.

It will appear then that much choral music of the twentieth century has an indifference to theories of composition. Yet it is not merely static. There is a ruggedness and sense of purpose which has its place. We may recall, for instance, the fine swinging tunes of John Alden Carpenter's *Song of Faith* (a sort of aggregation of melodies which might be folk-songs but aren't), of Frederick Converse's *Flight of the Eagle* (the story of the settlement of Boston), Henry Hadley's *Admiral of the Seas*, and of Norman Dello Joio's *Psalm of David*. All of these works were conceived for high-school choirs and for that purpose are strikingly apt. Taken collectively there emerges from works of this type an *ethos*: just as is the case with music which belongs to the English 'cathedral tradition'. Reading between the lines some part of the American *zeitgeist* is evident. But the stolidity of the idiom would appear to be of local rather than general *musical* interest. In a sense, of course, this is so with a great deal of choral music. Eventually a work, or works, appears which transcends topical limitations.

Dello Joio's *Psalm of David* possesses something of the general idiom of the age; which is due in part to the composer's admiration and emulation of his teacher Hindemith, in part to a non-local text, and in part to the use of a motiv (running throughout the work) which was borrowed from des Prés's setting of the same psalm (No. L). Dello Joio is rhythmically convincing, impelling the poetry forward over hard-driving percussive figures to an inevitable and urgent final movement, which shows something of Stravinsky's clarity of vision in the *Symphonie de Psaumes*. There is much diatonic dissonance throughout which, however, suits the medium and reaches out to meet the text in a beauty devoid of sentimentality. So we may draw attention to the 'asperges me hyssopo' at the end of the first movement, to the balancing 'Benigne fac' of the third movement, and to this episode in Part I (Ex 26). The attractive feature of Dello Joio's style is his capacity for melody

Ex. 26

which, while neither sophisticated nor inaccessible, is original and yet in line with the American tradition of downrightness in this respect.

Then the line which carries gladness over the quiet excitement of a throbbing accompaniment (Ex. 27).

Ex. 27
S. & A.

Red - de   mi - hi   lae - ti - ti - am   sa - lu - ta - ris,   tu - i,   red - de

It is possible to distinguish between the 'indoor' and the 'open-air' music of America. The feeling for open spaces, for the contribution to the national character of Indians, cowboys, negroes, explorers . . . is responsible for a new form of Western Romanticism. Harder, more carefree, less sublimated than in the European tradition: but, none the less, romantic. In orchestral music there is the genius of Copland. In choral music there is Harris' *Folk Song* Symphony, which was intended for symphony orchestras desirous of collaborating with their local high school or college choruses.

In five of seven movements the *Folk Song Symphony* is choral and in these movements—'The girl I left behind me', 'Western Cowboy', 'Mountaineer Love Song', 'Negro Fantasy', 'Johnny Comes Marching Home'—are epitomized certain traditions of America. Yet Harris manages not only to recall the familiar to those within the traditions by the skilful deployment of familiar melodic material but also to convince the alien of the strength and beauty of his ideal. I can recall the impact made by this work on the occasion of its first English performance. The *Folk Song Symphony* was first performed (after which it was revised by the composer) by Dr. Howard Hanson, one of the most distinguished teachers, composers and interpreters of American music, by the Eastman-Rochester Symphony Orchestra in 1940. The definitive, final version was first done by the New York Philharmonic Symphony Orchestra under Mitropoulos in 1942.

The *Folk Song Symphony* differs from *The Prairie* by Lukas Foss in one respect in particular. Harris bases his work on the traditional melodies themselves. Foss (inspired by Copland's *Billy the Kid*) bases his cantata—to a text by Carl Sandburg—on the spirit rather than the letter of the melodies. *The Prairie* was introduced by the Collegiate Chorale, under Robert Shaw, on May 15th, 1944. The composer's own description of the work shall serve as epilogue to this section.

'The opening movement, which has the nature of a prologue,

speaks of the prairie, as we are accustomed to visualize it. The author, in a pastoral tenor solo, sings of open valleys and far horizons, and the music breathes fresh air. After this pastoral introduction, a fugue is heard in the orchestra, above which the chorus takes up a new theme in the manner of a chorale. This is the voice of the prairie. . . . As a complete contrast, a folk-like movement follows, but the melodies remain original throughout the work. . . . With the re-entry of the chorus, the prairie becomes "mother of men, waiting". Then the author reaches far back into the past and we see the cities rising on the prairie, out of the prairie, while the chorus chants of the years when the red and white men met. . . . In rugged . . . rhythms follows what may be styled the industrial section, ending with a fugue for male voices. A lyrical intermezzo brings us back to the prairie. This consists of a short a cappella chorus, a soprano song, and a scherzando duet . . . held together by a dreamy little shepherd's lay, a nostalgic woodwind refrain of the prairie. The tenor's voice introduces the seventh and last section, and every one joins in the final hymn to the future, expressing the healthy and sunny optimism unique to this country.'

There is, I think, something to be said in favour of optimism as an ideal and neither the art nor the singers of choral music will suffer from its pursuit at this juncture.

Bibliography

GENERAL

A Forgotten Psalter, and other essays: R. R. Terry (London 1929)
A General History of Music, 4 vols.: Charles Burney (London 1776–89)
Choral Conducting: A. T. Davison (Harvard 1940)
Essays in Musical Analysis, Vol. V (*Vocal Music*): D. F. Tovey (London 1937)
Handbook of Choral Technique: Percy M. Young (London 1953)
Historical Anthology of Music: A. T. Davison and W. Apel (Harvard 1946)
Hymns Ancient and Modern (Historical Edition), with Introduction by W. S. Frere (London 1912)
Music in the History of the Western Church: Edward Dickinson (New York 1902)
Music in Western Civilisation: P. H. Lang (New York 1941)
Oxford History of Music, 7 vols. (London 1905–34)
The Columbia History of Music through Ear and Eye: Percy A. Scholes (London 1930)
The Conductor Raises his Baton: William J. Finn (New York 1944)
The Technique of Choral Composition: A. T. Davison (Harvard 1945)

THE SIXTEENTH CENTURY

Contrapuntal Technique in the Sixteenth Century: R. O. Morris (London 1922)
English Madrigal Composers: E. H. Fellowes (London 1921)
Orlando di Lasso: C. van den Borren (Paris 1920)
Orlando Gibbons: E. H. Fellowes (London 1925)
Palestrina: Henry Coates (London 1938)
Sixteenth Century Polyphony: A. T. Merritt (Harvard 1939)
The English Madrigal: E. H. Fellowes (London 1925)
The Italian Madrigal, 3 vols.: A. Einstein (Princeton 1949)
The Style of Palestrina and the Dissonance: K. Jeppesen (2nd ed. London 1951)
Victoria: H. Collet (Paris 1914)
William Byrd: E. H. Fellowes (London 1936)

THE SEVENTEENTH CENTURY

Dietrich Buxtehude: A. Pirro (Paris 1913)
Monteverdi: H. Prunières (Eng. trans. London 1926)

Monteverdi: H. F. Redlich (London 1952)
Music in the Baroque Era: Manfred F. Bukofzer (New York 1947)
Purcell: J. A. Westrup (London 1937)
Schütz: A. Moser (Cassel 1936)
The Puritans and Music: P. A. Scholes (London 1934)

THE PERIOD OF BACH AND HANDEL

Alessandro Scarlatti: E. J. Dent (London 1905)
Bach: E. M. and S. Grew (London 1947)
Bach: Rutland Boughton (London 1927)
Bach: a biography: C. S. Terry (2nd ed. London 1933)
Bach: the Cantatas and Oratorios, 2 vols.: C. S. Terry (London 1925)
Bach: the Magnificat, Lutheran Masses and Motets: C. S. Terry (London 1929)
Bach: the Mass in B minor: C. S. Terry (London 1924)
Bach: the Passions, 2 vols.: C. S. Terry (London 1926)
Bach and Handel: A. T. Davison (Harvard 1951)
George Frideric Handel: his Personality and his Times: Newman Flower (2nd ed. London 1947)
Handel: H. Leichtentritt (Stuttgart 1924)
Handel: R. A. Streatfeild (London 1909)
Handel: Percy M. Young (London 1947)
Handel and his Orbit: P. Robinson (London 1908)
Handel's Messiah: a Touchstone of Taste: R. M. Myers (New York 1948)
Handel's Oratorio 'The Messiah': E. C. Bairstow (London 1928)
Johann Sebastian Bach: his Life, Art and Work: J. N. Forkel (Eng. trans. London 1920)
Johann Sebastian Bach: his Work and Influence on the Music of Germany: P. Spitta (Eng. trans. London 1899)
J. S. Bach: A. Pirro (Paris 1924)
J. S. Bach: A. Schweitzer (Eng. trans. London 1911)
Messiah: a Study in Interpretation: Percy M. Young (London 1951)
Music Book, Vol. VII of *Hinrichsen's Year Book* (London 1953)
Music in the Baroque Era: M. F. Bukofzer (New York 1947)
Notes on the Church Cantatas of Johann Sebastian Bach: W. S. Hannam (London 1928)
The Bach Reader: a life of J. S. Bach in letters and documents, ed. Hans T. David and Arthur Mendel (New York 1945)
The Interpretation of the Music of the XVIIth and XVIIIth Centuries: A. Dolmetsch (2nd ed. London 1946)
The Lost Tradition in Music: Rhythm and Tempo in J. S. Bach's Time: F. Rothschild (New York 1952)
The Music of Bach: an Introduction: C. S. Terry (London 1933)

The Oratorios of Handel: Percy M. Young (London 1950)
The St. Matthew Passion: its Preparation and Performance. Adrian C. Boult and Walter Emery (London 1949)
Two Centuries of Bach: F. Blume (Eng. trans. London 1950)

THE PERIOD OF HAYDN AND MOZART

Bekenntnis zu Mozart: ed. W. Reich (Lucerne 1945)
Die Messen von Joseph Haydn: C. M. Brand (Würzburg 1941)
Haydn: a Creative Life in Music: K. Geiringer (London 1947)
Haydn: R. Hughes (London 1950)
Michael Haydn: ein vergessener Meister: H. Jancik (Zürich 1952)
Mozart: E. Blom (London 1935)
Mozart: A. Einstein (London 1946)
Mozart: B. Paumgartner (Berlin 1927)
The Letters of Mozart and his Family: trans. and ed. by E. Anderson (London 1938)
The Life of Mozart: E. Holmes (London 1845)

THE NINETEENTH CENTURY I

A Short History of Cheap Music, with a Preface by Sir George Grove (London 1887)
À travers chants: H. Berlioz (Paris 1862)
Autobiography: L. Spohr (Eng. trans. London 1865)
Beethoven: E. Walker (London 1905)
Beethoven: Marion M. Scott (London 1934)
Beethoven's Missa Solemnis: W. Weber (Leipzig 1908)
Berlioz: J. H. Elliott (London 1938)
Clara Novello's Reminiscences, with a Memoir by Arthur D. Coleridge (London 1910)
La Damnation de Faust: J. Tiersot (Paris 1924)
Ludwig van Beethoven: Missa Solemnis: M. Chop (Leipzig 1921)
Maria Carlo Zenobi Salvatore Cherubini: F. J. Crowest (London 1890)
Memoirs: H. Berlioz (trans. E. Newman) (New York 1932)
Mendelssohn: Percy M. Young (London 1950)
Music in the Romantic Era: A. Einstein (New York 1947)
Our American Music: J. T. Howard (3rd ed. New York 1946)
Schubert: A. Einstein (London 1951)
Schubert: A. Hutchings (London 1945)
Schubert: the Documents of his Life and Works: O. E. Deutsch (Eng. trans. London 1945)
Schubert's Masses: (Monthly Musical Record 1871): E. Prout
Schumann: Joan Chissell (London 1948)

Schumann: a Symposium: ed. G. Abraham (London 1952)
The Mirror of Music 1844–1944, 2 vols.: Percy A. Scholes (London 1947)
Tragic Muse: the Life and Works of Schumann: Percy M. Young (London 1957, Leipzig 1962)
Vienna's Golden Years of Music: E. Hanslick, trs. and ed. H. Pleasants III (London 1951)

THE NINETEENTH CENTURY II

Annals of The Three Choirs: D. Lysons and others (Gloucester 1895)
Brahms: his life and works: K. Geiringer (London 1936)
Bruckner: F. Brunner (Linz 1895)
Camille Saint-Saëns: his Life and Art: Watson Lyle (London 1923)
César Franck: N. Demuth (London 1949)
César Franck: Léon Vallas, Eng. trans. by H. Foss (London 1952)
Dvořák: Alec Robertson (London 1945)
Elgar: E. Newman (London 1922)
Elgar: W. H. Reed (London 1939)
Fauré: Norman Suckling (London 1946)
From Mendelssohn to Wagner, Memoirs of J. W. Davison: compiled by Henry Davison (London 1912)
Gabriel Fauré: Charles Koechlin (Eng. trans. London 1946)
Giuseppe Verdi: his Life and Works: Francis Toye (London 1931)
Liszt: Sacheverell Sitwell (London 1934)
L'œuvre de Camille Saint-Saëns: Emile Baumann (Paris 1923)
Music and Society: W. Mellers (London 1946)
Musical England: W. J. Galloway (London 1910)
Mussorgsky: M. D. Calvocoressi (London 1946)
Our American Music: J. T. Howard (3rd ed. New York 1946)
Sibelius: Cecil Gray (London 1931)
Studies in Modern Music: W. H. Hadow (London 1895)
Tchaikovsky: ed. G. Abraham (London 1945)
The Apostles: Analytical and Descriptive Notes: A. J. Jaeger (London 1901)
The Dream of Gerontius: Analytical and Descriptive Notes: A. J. Jaeger (London 1903)
The Englishman Makes Music: R. Nettel (London 1952)
The Kingdom: Analytical and Descriptive Notes: A. J. Jaeger (London 1907)
The Life of Anton Bruckner: C. Engel (New York 1931)
The Mirror of Music 1844–1944, 2 vols.: Percy A. Scholes (London 1947)
The Music of Czecho-Slovakia: Rosa Newmarch (London 1942)
Verdi: Dyneley Hussey (London 1940)

THE TWENTIETH CENTURY

A Composer's World: Paul Hindemith (London 1952)

American Composers on American Composers: ed. Henry Cowell (Stanford University 1938)

Analysis of Schoenberg's 'Gurre-lieder': Alban Berg (Vienna 1913)

Benjamin Britten: a commentary on his works: ed. D. Mitchell and H. Keller (London 1953)

Catholic Church Music: The Legislation of Pius X, Benedict XV and Pius XI (Rome 1933)

Chronicle of my life: Igor Stravinsky (London 1936)

Delius: A. Hutchings (London 1948)

Delius as I knew him: Eric Fenby (London 1936)

Frederick Delius: Clare Delius (London 1935)

Frederick Delius: Peter Warlock, ed. H. Foss (London 1952)

Gustav Holst: Imogen Holst (London 1938)

Igor Stravinsky: A. Casella (Rome 1926)

Igor Stravinsky: ed. Merle Armitage (New York 1936)

Ildebrando Pizzetti—Guido M. Gatti (London 1951)

Introduction to the Music of Stravinsky: R. H. Myers (London 1950)

Music in our time: Adolfo Salazar (Buenos Aires 1944)

My Life of Music: Henry J. Wood (London 1938)

Notes without Music: Darius Milhaud (London 1952)

Our Contemporary Composers: John Tasker Howard (New York 1941)

Ralph Vaughan Williams: Hubert Foss (London 1950)

Schoenberg and his School: René Leibowitz (New York 1949)

Studies in Contemporary Music: Wilfrid Mellers (London 1947)

The Complete Book of 20th Century Music: David Ewen (New York 1961)

The Music of Czecho-Slovakia: Rosa Newmarch (London 1942)

The Music of Gustav Holst: Imogen Holst (London 1951)

Vaughan Williams: Percy M. Young (London 1953)

Westminster Retrospect: A Memoir of Sir Richard Terry: Hilda Andrews (London 1948)

Indices

Index of Principal Works

Works noted hereunder are discussed in some detail in the text, except for a few which are included because they are accepted in the repertoire. Works which receive passing notice in the text are to be found in the General Index. Those works marked by an asterisk are represented by musical examples.

I. THE SIXTEENTH CENTURY

Composer	Title of work	Forces required	Page reference
BYRD	An earthly tree	2 S soli/SATB/6 str.	20 (f.n.1)
	Ave verum*	SATB	45
	Cantiones sacrae (3 books)	In 5 or 6 parts, except 'Diliges Dominum' (1575) in 8	42, 46
	Civitas sancti tui*	SATTB	46
	Come tread the path	Solo S/str.	41
	From Virgin's womb	Solo S/str. SSAA	20 (f.n.1)
	Gradualia (2 books)	In from 3 to 6 parts, but 'Adoramus te' for S or T and strings	42, 43, 45
	La Virginella	SATTB	51
	Lullaby*	SSATB	46
	Mass à 3	SAB	42, 43
	Mass à 4*	SATB	42, 43, 44
	Mass à 5*	SATTB	42, 44-5
	O quam suavis*	SATB	46

Composer	Title of Work	Forces required	Page reference
BYRD	Psalmes, Sonets & Songs of Sadness & Piety (1588)	In 5 parts	21, 42, 46
	Senex puerum*	SATB	45
	Songs of Sundrie Natures	In 3–6 parts	42
GIBBONS (Orlando)	This is the record of John	T solo/SAATB/str. (and/or org.)	20 (f.n.1)
	What is our life?	SAA (or T) TB	52
HANDL	Adoramus te, Jesu Christe	Double chorus (SATB)	49
	Ecce, quomodo moritur justus*	SATB	49, 92 (f.n.1)
LASSUS	Christus resurgens*	SSATB	38
	Exspectans exspectavi*	SATB	37–8
	Magnificat*	SATB	37
	Salve Regina	SSATTB	38
	Scio enim quod Redemptor*	SATB	37–8
	Septem psalmi poenitentiales*	Varied no. of parts	39–40
MUNDY	Heigh ho! 'chill go to plough no more'*	SSAB	52
PALESTRINA	Alma Redemptoris	SATB	28
	Magnificats	Varied no. of parts	32
	Missa — Aeterna Christi munera	SATB	28, 32

328

Composer	Title of work	Forces required	Page reference
PALESTRINA	Missa — Ecce Sacerdos magna	SATB	29
	Missa — L'homme armé	SATTB	29
	Missa — Papae Marcelli*	SSATBB	29–31
	Missa — Ut, Re, Mi, Sol, La (Hexachord)	SSATTB	29
	O magnum Mysterium	SSATTB	28
	Stabat Mater*	Double choir (SATB)	28, 32–4
	Surge illuminare	Double choir (SATB)	28
	Tu es Petrus	SSATBB	28
PHILIPS	O virum mirabilem*	SSATB	50
SWEELINCK	Hodie, Christus natus est	SSATB	50
	O sacrum convivium	SATTB	50
TALLIS	Spem in alium nunquam habui	5 choirs	17
TAVERNER	'The Westron Wynde' Mass*	SATB	22, 24–6, 29
VICTORIA	Ave Maria*	SATB	48
	Duo Seraphim*	SSAA	49
	O vos omnes*	SATB	48
	Tenebrae	SATB	33
WARD	Weep forth your tears	SSATB	52

329

Composer	Title of work	Forces required	Page reference
WEELKES	As Vesta was from Latmos hill descending*	SSATTB	53-4
	Tan ta ra cries Mars	SSA (or T)	52
	Thule, the period of Cosmography	SSATTB	52
VARIOUS	Triumphs of Oriana	In 5 or 6 parts	19, 51-4

II. THE SEVENTEENTH CENTURY

Composer	Title of work	Forces required	Page reference
BLOW	Salvator mundi	SSATB/org.	84 (f.n.1)
BUXTEHUDE	Benedicam Dominum	Double chorus (SATB): 2 cornets, bassoon, 4 trumpets, bombard, 3 tbnes.: str., continuo and org.	
	In dulci jubilo	SSB/str./continuo	78
	Jesu meine Freude*	arr. for SATB/str./bassoon/org. (Hinrichsen ed.)	80
	Magnificat in D	SSATB/str./org.	79
	Missa brevis (Kyrie & Gloria)	SSATB (org.)	78
	O Jesu mi dulcissime*	SSB soli/str./org.	78
	Surrexit Christus hodie*	SSB soli/str./bassoon/org.	79
	Wachet auf	SSB soli/str./bassoon/org.	79

Composer	Title of work	Forces required	Page reference
CARISSIMI	Jephtha*	SSAT soli/SSSAITB/ str./continuo (org.)	58, 59-61
	Jonas	SATB soli/SATB (double choir)/str./continuo (org.)	58, 59
	Judicium Salomonis	SSTB soli/SATB/str./continuo (org.)	61, 81
HASSLER	Ave maris stella	SATB	68
LALANDE, de	Dixit Dominus*	S.MS.A.T.Bar.B.soli/SSATBB/2 fl., 2 ob., 3 bassoons/str./org.	82-84
MONTEVERDI	Laetatus sum*	SATB soli/SATB/bassoon, 2 tenor trombones/str./org.	66
	Lamento d'Arianna (Lasciate mi morire)*	SATTB	62
	Madrigals	Various no. parts.	61, 62, 63, 65
	Messa à 4 voci (1641)*	SATB (org.)	64-5
	Messa à 4 voci (1651)	SATB (org.)	64
	Vesperae*	2 S.A. 2 T.B. soli/SSAATTBB/3 ob. or cl. (2 bassoons), 2 tbnes./str./org.[1]	66-8
PURCELL	Beati omnes	SSAB	87
	Blessed is he that considereth the poor	SATB soli/SATB (org.)	86

[1] (a) An edition containing additional movements is that of C. F. Ghedini, pub. Zerboni (Milan); (b) ed. Denis Stevens, pub. Novello; this score includes an invaluable Preface.

Composer	Title of work	Forces required	Page reference
PURCELL	Dido and Aeneas	SAT soli/SATB/str./ continuo	85
	Hail, bright Cecilia (Ode to St. Cecilia, 1692)	SAATB soli/SSAATB/fl. ob. bass. tr. timp./ str./continuo	85
	Hear my prayer*	SSAATTBB	87
	Jehovah quam multi sunt hostes	SSATB	87
	Rejoice in the Lord ('Bell' anthem)	SATB soli/SATB/str./org.	87
SCHEIN	Die mit Tränen säen*	SSATB	76
	Vom Himmel hoch	SSATB	76
SCHÜTZ[1]	'Christmas' oratorio*	SSATTB soli/SSAATTB/2 fl. bassoon. 2 tr. 2 tbnes./str./org.	73–74
	Herr, unser Herrscher	SATB soli/SATB/2 tr. 3 tbnes./org.	70
	Passion acc. St. Luke*	SATB soli/SATB	74
	Passion acc. St. Matthew*	SATB soli/SATB	74
	'Resurrection' oratorio*	Double choir/soloists/str./org.	71
	Saul, was verfolgst du mich	Double choir/str./org./ continuo	71
	Seven last words*	SATTB soli/SATTB/str./org.	70, 72
	Was betrübst du dich, meine Seele	2 S or ST/str./org./ continuo	71

332

[1] In the works of Schütz there are numerous small solo parts best taken by singers from the chorus.

III. THE PERIOD OF BACH AND HANDEL

Composer	Title of work	Forces required	Page reference
BACH	*Cantatas (I) Sacred:*		
	Der Himmel lacht, die Erde jubiliret (No 31)	STB soli/SATB/3 ob. 2 bassoons. 3 tr./timp./str./org./continuo	99, 109
	Ein'feste Burg ist unser Gott (No. 80)	SATB/soli/SATB/2 ob. 2 ob. d'am. ob. da caccia bassoon 3 tr. timp./str./org./continuo	112
	Gleich wie der Regen und Schnee (No. 18)	SB soli/SATB/2 fl. bassoon/str. (viole divisi a 4, no vlns.)/org./continuo	99, 112
	Gottes Zeit ist die allerbeste Zeit (No. 106)	AB soli/SA─B/2 fl./ 2 viole da gamba/continuo (no vlns. or violas)	91, 99 (f.n.1)
	Herz und Mund und That und Leben (No. 147)	SATB soli/SATB/2 ob. ob. d'am. 2 ob. da caccia bassoon tr./str./org./ continuo	99
	Ich habe genug (No. 82)	B solo/ob./str./cont.	108
	Ich will den Kreutzstab gerne tragen (No. 56)	B solo/SATB/2 ob. bassoon/str./continuo	112
	Jesus schläf, was soll ich hoffen (No. 81)	ATB soli org./SATB/2 fl. 2 ob. 3 tr. timp./str./continuo	112
	Lobet Gott in seinen Reichen (No. 11—Ascension Oratorio)	SATB soli/SATB/2 fl. 2 ob. 3 tr. timp./str./org./continuo	149
	Man singet mit Freuden vom Sieg (No. 149)	SATB soli/SATB/3 ob. bassoon 3 tr. timp./str./org./continuo	109
	Meine Seele rühmt und preist (No. 189)	T solo/fl. ob./str. (no viola)/continuo	91

Composer	Title of work	Forces required	Page reference
BACH	Nun ist das Heil* (No. 50)	Double chorus/3 ob. 3 tr. timp./str./org.	108–9
	O Ewigkeit, du Donnerwort (No. 60)	ATB soli/SATB/2 ob. d'am. cor./str./org./ continuo	112
	Schauet doch und sehet, ob irgend ein Schmerz sei (No. 46)	ATB soli/SATB/2 fl. 2 ob. da caccia. tr. or cor./str./org./continuo	145
	Wachet auf, ruft uns die Stimme (No. 140)	STB soli/SATB/2 ob. bassoon cor./str./ continuo/org.	112
	Weinen, Klagen, Sorgen, Zagen (No. 12)	ATB/soli/SATB/ob. bassoon tr./str./org./ continuo	99, 147
	Wer nur den lieben Gott lässt walten (No. 93)*	SATB soli/SATB/2 ob./str./org./continuo	111
	Wir danken dir, Gott, wir danken dir (No. 29)	SATB soli/SATB/2 ob. 3 tr. timp./str./ org./continuo	145
	Cantatas (II) Secular: Der Streit zwischen Phoebus und Pan (No. 201)	SATB soli/SATB/2 fl. 2 ob. ob d'am. 3 tr. timp./str./continuo	102, 112
	Mer hahn en neue Oberkeet (No. 212—Peasant Cantata)	SB soli/fl. cor./str./ continuo	112
	Preise dei Glücke, gesegnetes Sachsen	STB soli/SATB/2 fl. 2 ob. d'am. 3 tr. timp./str./continuo	148
	Schweigt stille, plaudert nicht (No. 211—'Coffee Cantata')	STB soli/fl./str./continuo	112

Composer	Title of work	Forces required	Page reference
BACH	Magnificat*	SATB soli/SATB/2 fl. 2 ob. 2 ob. d'am. bassoon(s) 3 tr. timp./str./org./continuo	93, 119, 149–51
	Mass in B minor*	SATB soli/double chorus/2 fl. 3 ob. 2 ob. d'am. 2 bassoons cor. 3 tr. timp./str./org./continuo	67, 93, 102, 119, 139 (f.n.1), 140–9, 150, 153, 160, 192, 209, 215, 240, 245
	Motets:		
	Der Geist hilft unsrer Schwachheit auf	Double choir/org.[1]	112
	Jesu meine Freude	SSATB chorus org. (?)	93, 110
	Komm, Jesu, komm	Double choir/org. (?)	110
	Singet dem Herrn	Double choir/org. (?)	110, 111
	Oratorio:		
	'Christmas' Oratorio*	SATB soli/SATB/2 fl. 2 ob. 2 ob. d'am. 2 ob. da cacca (bassoons)/3 tr. timp./str./org./continuo	97, 112–16, 146
	Passions:		
	'St. John'*	SATB soli/SATB/2 fl. 2 ob. ob. d'am. 2 ob. da cacca (bassoons)/str./org./continuo	93, 127, 128–9, 140, 152
	'St. Matthew'*	SATB soli/SATB double chorus/2 orchestras: 4 fl. 4 ob. 2 ob. d'am. 2 ob. da caccia. vla. da gamba/str./org./continuo	71, 93, 123, 128, 136, 136–40, 142, 192, 193
BOYCE	I have surely built Thee an house	SATB/org.	151 (f.n.3)
CROFT	Put me not to rebuke	SATB/org.	151 (f.n.1)

[1] Accompaniment desirable in the motets, although original parts are not extant (see pp. 12, 110) except in the case of *Der Geist hilft unsrer Schwachheit auf*.

Composer	Title of work	Forces required	Page reference
GREENE	Acquaint thyself with God	T solo/org.	151 (f.n.2)
HANDEL	[Except where it is otherwise indicated, the following works of Handel employ a chorus mostly in four parts but sometimes increasing to eight; and an orchestra of 2 ob. 2 bassoons, 2 trumpets, (drums), strings, organ and continuo; accordingly, only solo requirements and exceptional instruments are indicated below.]		
	Acis and Galatea	S. 2 T.B soli/	92, 96
	Anthems:		
	Chandos	} Soloists from chorus	92
	Coronation		92
	Funeral		49, 92, 129
	Wedding		92
	Dixit Dominus	SSATB soli/	91
	Oratorios: (I) Sacred:		
	Alexander Balus*	2 S.T. 2 B soli/	95, 96, 126, 127
	Belshazzar	2 S.A. 2 T. 2 B soli/	86, 95
	Esther	2 S. 4 T. 2 B/3 tr. harp (also theorbo)	92, 104, 105
	Israel in Egypt*	2 S.A.T. 2 B soli/3 trombones	59, 95, 105, 125-6
	Jephtha	S. 2 A. 2 T.B soli/	95, 126
	Joseph	2 S. 3 A. 2T. 2B soli/	95
	Joshua	2 S. 2 T.B soli/	95, 96
	Judas Maccabaeus	SATB soli/	95, 96, 124-5, 193,
	La resurrezione	SSATB soli/	107, 128

336

Composer	Title of work	Forces required	Page reference
HANDEL	Messiah	SATB soli/	95, 96, 97, 98, 100 116–24, 184, 196, 203
	Occasional Oratorio	SSTB soli/3tr.	95, 100, 124
	Samson	2 S.A. 2 T. 2 B soli/	58, 61, 86, 95, 100, 126, 131
	Saul*	3 S. 2A. 3 T. 3 B soli/	95, 102, 122, 126
	Solomon	4 S. 2 A.T.B. soli/	86, 95, 126, 127
	Susanna	2 S.A. 2 T. 3 B soli/	86, 95, 126
	Theodora*	SATTBB soli/2 fl	52, 86, 95, 96, 12-, 127
	Oratorios (II) Secular:		
	Hercules	SATB soli/	95, 126
	Semele	2 S. 3 A. 2 T. 2B soli/	95
	Passions;		
	Brockes' (1716)*	SATB soli.	127, 129–30
	St. John (1704)	SSTB soli	107, 128
	Te Deum (Dettingen)	SATB soLI/	92, 193 (f.n.2')
	Te Deum (Utrecht)	SSATB soli/	91
PERGOLESI	Stabat Mater*	SA soli & chorus/str./continuo	154–5, 214
SCARLATTI (A)	'Christmas Cantata'	S.solo/str./continuo	108
	Exultate Deo	SATB (org.)	107

Composer	Title of work	Forces required	Page reference
VIVALDI	Gloria	S.S.C.soli & chorus/2 ob. 2 tr./str./org.	153
	Juditha triumphans	S.MS.T.Bar.B.soli/SATB chorus (see note on Handel orch.)	153–4
ZACHAU (OW)	*Cantatas:*		
	Herr, wenn ich nur dich habe*	SATB soli/SATB/str. (viole divisi)/harp/continuo	152
	Lobe den Herrn, meine Seele	SSATB soli/SSATB/2 ob. bassoon 2 cors (de chasse)/str./continuo	96
	Ruhe, Friede, Freude und Wonne	SAATTB soli/SAATTB/2 ob. 2 bassoons/str./org. (& continuo)	96

IV. THE PERIOD OF HAYDN AND MOZART

Composer	Title of work	Forces required	Page reference
CLARI	Kyrie*	SSATB chorus/str./org.	160
DURANTE	Protexisti me Deus*	SSATB chorus/org.	161
HAYDN, J.	*Masses:*		
	Brevis, in F	2 S soli/SATB/2 vl. celli. bass./org.	172
	'Harmoniemesse'	SATB soli/SATB/fl. 2 ob. 2 cl. 2 bassoons/ 2 cor. 2 tr. timp./ str./org.	177

Composer	Title of work	Forces required	Page reference
HAYDN, J.	'in honorem Beatissimae Virginis Mariae'	2 S soli/SATB.2 cor. anglais. 2 cor. bassoon (col bassi)/2 vl. celli. bassi/org.	173
	'Paukenmesse' ('in tempore belli')	SATB soli/SATB/fl. 2 ob. 2 cl. 2 bassoons/2 cor. 2 trs. timp./str./org.	174, 175, 213
	'Nelsonmesse' ('in Augustiis')*	SSATB soli/SATB /1 fl. 2 ob. 2 bassoons/3 tr. timp./str./org.	175–6
	Sanctae Caeciliae	S solo/SATB/2 ob. 2 bassoons (col bassi) 2 tr. timp./str./org.	164, 173
	Sancti Nicolai*	SATB soli/SATB/2 ob. 2 cor./str. (vle. in 8ve with bass)/org.	172, 173–4
	'Schöpfungsmesse'	SATB soli/SATB/2 ob. 2 cl. 2 bassoon/[2 tr. 2 cor. timb.]/org.[1]	177
	'Theresienmesse'	SATB soli/SATB/2 cl. 2 tr. timp./str./org.	176–7
	Oratorios: Die Worte des Erlesers am Kreuze[2]	SATB soli/SATB/2 fl. 2 ob. 2 cl. 2 bassoons/2 cor. 2 tr. 2 tbnes. timp./str.	178
	Il ritorno di Tobia	SSATB soli/SATB/2 fl. 2 ob. 2 cl. 2 bassoons/2 cor. 2 tr. 3 tbnes./str./pfte.	178, 187
	The Creation*	STB soli/SATB/2 fl. 2 ob. 2 cl. 2 bassoons contrabassoon/2 cor. 2 tr. 3 tbnes. timp./str.	176, 182–8, 189, 193, 203
	The Seasons	STB soli, SATB/orch. as for 'Creation' without contrabassoon	189–90

[1] See figured bass in fac-simile of autograph (G. Henle-Verlag, Munich, 1957).
[2] See Breitkopf und Härtel score of 1801 with Introduction by Haydn.

Composer	Title of work	Forces required	Page reference
HAYDN, J.	Te Deum (1800)	SATB chorus/fl. 2 ob. 2 bassoons/2 cor. 2 tr. timp./str./org.	178
HAYDN, M.	Missa brevis*	SATB. chorus/org.	162
LEO	Christus factus est*	2 S/org.	160
MOZART	Masses:		
	Brevis (K.49)	SATB soli/SATB/2 vl. vla. celli. bass/org.	144 (f.n.1)
	Brevis (K.65)	SATB soli/SATB/2 vl. celli. bass/org.	164
	Brevis (K.192)*	As K.65	166-8
	'Coronation' (K.317)*	SATB soli/SATB/2 ob. 2 cor. 2 tr. 3 tbnes. timp./str. (no vle.)/org.	165, 168-70, 210
	'Credo' (K.257)	as 'Coronation' without cor.	168
	in C minor (K.139)	SATB soli/SATB/2 ob. 4 tr. 3 tbnes. timp./str. (2 vle.)/org.	164
	in C minor (K.427)	SATB soli/SATB/2 ob. 2 bassoons 2 cor. 2 tr. 4 tbnes. timp./str./org.	165
	'Organ-solo' (K.259)	SATB soli/SATB/2 tr. timp./str. (no vle.)/org.	168
	'Pater Dominicus' (K.66)*	SATB soli/SATB/str. (no vle.)/org.	164, 170
	Requiem (K.626)	SATB soli/SATB/2 corni di bassetto 2 cor. 2 tr. 3 tbnes. timp./str./org.	165, 176, 178-82, 190, 193,
	'Spaur' (K.258)	SATB soli/SATB. 2 tr. timp./str. (no vle.)/org.	164, 168

Composer	Title of work	Forces required	Page reference
MOZART	*Motets and other Liturgical music:*		
	Benedictus sit Deus (K.117)	SATB soli/SATB/2 fl. 2 cor. 2 tr. timp./str. (2 vle.)/org.	164, 170
	Exsultate, jubilate (K. 165)	S. soli/2 ob. 2 cor./str./org.	165
	Litaniae (K.109)	SATB soli/SATB/str. (no vle.)/org.	165
	Litaniae (K.125)	SATB soli/SATB/2 ob. 2 cor. 2 tr./str./org.	165
	Veni Sancte Spiritus (K. 47)	SATB soli/SATB/2 ob. 2 cor. 2 tr. timp./str./org.	164
	Vesperae de Confessore (K.339)	SATB soli/SATB/ bassoon. 2 tr. 3 tbnes. timp./str. (no vle.)/org.	171
	Vesperae de Dominica (K.321)	SATB soli/SATB/2 tr. timp./str. (no vle.)/org.	171
	Oratorio:		
	Davidde penitente (K.469)	SST soli/SATB/2 ob. 2 bassoons. 2 cor. 2 tr. 4 tbnes. timp./str.	165

V. THE NINETEENTH CENTURY (I)

Composer	Title of work	Forces required	Page reference
BEETHOVEN	Cantata campestre	SATB/pte.	204
	Cantata for accession of Leopold II (Op. 196)	SATB soli/SATB/2222. 22. timp./str.	204
	Cantata for death of Joseph II (Op. 196)	SATB soli/SATB/2222. 2 cor.	204

341

Composer	Title of work	Forces required	Page reference
BEETHOVEN	Christus am Oelberge (Op. 85)	SATB soli/SATB 2 fl. 2 cl. 2 bassoons. 2 cor. 3 tr. 3 tbnes. timp./str.	204
	Der glorreiche Augenblick (Op. 136)	SATB soli/SATB/2222. 223/timp./str.	204
	Mass in C major (Op. 86)*	SATB soli/SATB/2222. 22/timp./str./org.	166, 203, 205, 206–8
	'Missa solennis' in D major (Op. 123)*	SATB soli/SATB/2222. contrabassoon 4 cor. 2 tr. 3 tbnes./timp./str./org.	159, 166, 193, 197, 203, 204, 206, 207, 208–13, 214, 246
	Meerestille und glückliche Fahrt (Op. 112)	SATB chor./2222.42/timp./str.	204
	Sanft wie du lebtest	SATB/str.	204
BERLIOZ	La damnation de Faust* (Op. 24)	MS.T.Bar or B.B.soli. SATB chor. children's choir. 3 fl. 2 ob. cor. ang. 2 cl. 4 bassoons. 2 tr. 2 cornets. 3 tbnes. tuba/ timp. perc./2 harps/str.	222–5, 228
	L'Enfance du Christ (Op. 25)	S. 2 T.Bar. 3 B soli/SATB/ 2 fl. 2 ob. cor ang. 2 cl. 2 bassoons/harp/str./org. (boys' voices and off-stage choir of women required)	229, 261, 291
	Grande messe des morts (Op. 5)*	SSAATTBB/422 cor. ang. 48/12 cor. 6 tr. 16 tbnes. 4 tubas/8 timps./perc./str.	227–9, 291
	Te Deum (Op. 22)	STB (chor. 1)	4444/4 (saxhorn) 262 STB (chor. 2)	(2 cornets)/perc. timp. SA (chor. of | 12 harps/str./org. children)	227

342

Composer	Title of work	Forces required	Page reference
CHERUBINI	Mass in D minor*	SSATTB soli/SATB/2222/2 cor. 2 tr. timp./str.	200–2
	Mass in F	STB soli/STB/fl. 2 cl. bassoon/2 cor. 2 tr. timp./str./org.	199
	Requiem Mass in C minor*	SATB chor./2 ob. 2 cl. 2ba ssoons/223/timp/gong/str.	199–200
MENDELSSOHN	Die erste Walpurgisnacht (Op 60)*	SATB chor./2 fl. 2 ob. 2 cl. 2 bassoons/2 cor. 2 tr. 3 tbnes./timp./str.	219, 220–1, 234
	Elijah (Op. 70)*	SATB soli/SATB/2 fl. 2 ob. 2 cl. 2 bassoons 4 cor. 2 tr. 3 tbnes. ophicleide/timp./str.	202, 221, 230, 2–2, 233–5
	Lauda Sion (Op. 73)	SATB soli/SATB/2222/2230 timp./str.	202, 221, 282
	Loreley (Op. 98)	S solo/SATB/3222/ 4230 timp. perc./str.	234
	St. Paul (Op. 36)	S.T. 2 B. soli/SATB/2223/4230 timp./str./org.	196, 202, 221, 231, 234
SCHUBERT	Mass in A flat	SATB soli/SATB/2 ob. 2 cl. 2 bassoons/2 cor./str./org.	214–15
	Mass in B flat	SATB soli/SATB/2 ob. 2 bassoons/2,tr./timp./str./org.	214
	Mass in C	SATB soli/SATB/2ob. (orcl.)/2 tr./timp./str.	214
	Mass in E flat	SATB soli/SATB/2 ob. 2 cl. 2 bassoons/2 cor. 3 tbnes./str./org.	215–16
	Mass in F	SATB soli/SATB/2 ob. 2 cl. 2 bassoons/2 cor./str./org.	214

343

Composer	Title of work	Forces required	Page reference
SCHUBERT	Mass in G	SATB soli/SATB/str./org.	214
	Psalm XCII	SATBarB soli/SATB chorus a cappella	215
	Song of Miriam (Op. 136)	SATB chorus/pfte.	216–17
	Stabat Mater	SATB chorus/2 ob. 2 cl. 2 bassoons/2 cor. 3 tbnes,/org.	214
SCHUMANN	Faust*	STB soli/SATB/3222/4231 timp. harp/str.	221, 225–6

VI. THE NINETEENTH CENTURY (II)

Composer	Title of work	Forces required	Page reference
BRAHMS	Ave Maria (Op. 12)	SSA chorus/pfte.	242
	Deutsches Requiem (Op. 45)	S.Bar.soli/SATB/2222.423/timp. harp/str.	226, 240, 241–6, 248, 254
	Marienlieder (Op. 22)	SATB (a cappella)	240
	Motets (Op. 29, 74, 109, 110)	4–8 parts (a cappella)	242
	Nänie (Op. 82)	SATB chorus/2222/203/timp./harp./str.	245
	4 Partsongs (Op. 17)	SSAA/2 cor./harp	242
	5 Partsongs (Op. 41)	TTBB (a cappella)	240
	Rhapsodie (Op. 53)	A solo/TTBB/2222/2 cor./str.	246
	Rinaldo (Op. 50)	T solo/TTBB/3222/223/timp/str.	242
	Schicksalslied (Op. 54)	SATB chorus/2222/223/timp./str.	242, 245
	Tafellied (Op. 93b)	TTBB/pfte.	240

Composer	Title of work	Forces required	Page reference
BRAHMS	Triumphlied (Op. 55)	Bar. solo/double choir/2222. contra-bassoon/4331/timp./str./org.	242
BRUCKNER	Mass in E minor*	SSAATTBB chorus/2 ob. 2 cl. 2 bassoons/4 cor. 2 tr. 3 tbnes. (or org.)	246, 247, 248
	Mass in F minor	SATB soli/SATB/2222/423/timp./str.	246, 247, 248
	Psalm CL	S solo/SATB/2222/4331/timp./str.	247
	Te Deum	SATB soli/SATB/2222/433. tuba/timp/str./org. ad lib.	247
CORNELIUS	Requiem (Hebbel)	SSATBB (a cappella)	240
DVOŘÁK	Requiem (Op 89)	soli/SATB/3333/4431/timp. harp perc./str./org.	000
	St. Ludmilla (Op. 71)	soli/SATB/2333/4331/timp. perc. harp/str./org.	237, 267, 268
	Stabat Mater (Op. 58)	soli/SATB/2222/4231/timp. perc./str.	33
	Te Deum (Op. 103)	SB soli/SAATTBB/2 2 cor angl. 22/423 tuba/timp. perc./str.	268
	The American Flag (Op. 102)	TB soli/SAATTBB/ orch. as below	268
	The Spectre's Bride (Op. 69)	soli/SATB/3332/4231/timp. perc. harp/str.	267
ELGAR	Caractacus (Op. 35)	S. 3 B soli/SATB/322 bass cl. 2 contra-bassoons/4431/timp. perc./harp/org./str.	257
	King Olaf (Op. 30)	STB soli/SATB/32 cor. ang. 2 bass/cl. 2 4331/timp. perc./harp/org./str.	257

Composer	Title of work	Forces required	Page reference
ELGAR	Lux Christi (Op. 29)	SATBar. soli/SATB/3222 contra-bassoon/4231/timp. perc./harp/org./str.	257
	The Apostles	SAT 3 B soli/SATB/ as 'Gerontius' with addition of 'shofar'[1]	260
	The Black Knight (Op. 25)	SATB chor./322 bass cl. 2/4231/timp. perc./str./org.	257
	The Dream of Gerontius (Op. 38)*	MS.TB soli/SATB/32 cor. ang. 2. bass cl. 2. contra-bassoon/4331/timp. perc./2 harps /str./org.	237, 256-60
	The Kingdom (Op. 51)	SATB soli/SATB/orchestra as for 'Gerontius'	260
	The Music-Makers (Op. 69)	SATB chorus/32 cor. ang. 2. bass cl. 2. contra-bassoon/4331/timp. perc./2 harps/org./str.	260
FAURÉ	Messe de Requiem (Op. 48)*	S.Bar soli/SATB/2 fl. 2 cl. 2 bassoons/423/timp./harp/str./org.	262-265
FRANCK	Les Béatitudes	SSATTB soli/2 choris/orch.	262
	Rédemption	S solo/SATB	262
GADE	The Crusaders	MS.TB soli/SATB/2222/4231/timp. perc./harp/str.	266
	The Erl-King's Daughter	S.MS.B soli/SATB/3222/420/timp./str.	266

[1] Ancient Jewish instrument, made of ram's horn and used for ritual purposes.

Composer	Title of work	Forces required	Page reference
LISZT	Christus	SATB soli/SATB/3222/4331/timp. perc./org./str.	266
	Coronation Mass	SATB soli/SATB (all div.)/2222/4231/timp/str./org.	266
	The Legend of the Holy Elizabeth	S.MS. 3 Bar. 2 B soli/SATB/4322/4331/timp./perc. harp/str./org.	266
MOUSSORGSKY	The destruction of Sennacherib	SATB chorus 2222/4231/timp. perc./str.	240
PARKER	Hora novissima	SATB soli/SATB double chorus/2222/4231/timp. perc./harp/str./org.	270
	Seven Greek Pastoral Scenes	SSAA/ob./harp/str.	270
PARRY	Blest pair of Sirens	Double chorus/2222. contra-bassoon/4231/timp./org./str.	257
	Prometheus unbound	SATB soli/SATB/2222. contra-bassoon/432/timp./harp/str.	256
	Songs of Farewell	4–8 parts (± cappella)	257
REGER	Palm-Sunday morning	SSATB (a cappella)	240
SAINT-SAËNS	La Lyre et la Harpe	SATB soli/SATB/3222. contra-bassoon/4231 (2 cornets)/timp. perc./2 harps/str./org.	262
	Messe Solennelle (Op. 4)	SATB soli/SATB/2 fl. 2 cor anglais/2 tr. 3 tbnes/org. 1 (solo), org. 2 (ripieno), harp/str.	262

Composer	Title of work	Forces required	Page reference
SIBELIUS	Songs from Kalevala (Op. 18)	TTBB (a cappella) 3. d. cor. ang. 2. b.cl. 2 contra-bassoon	240
STANFORD	Eden	2 SAT Bar.B soli/SATB/3. 2. cor. ang. 2 b.cl. 2. contra-bassoon/4341/timp. perc./2 harps/org./str.	257
	Songs of the Sea	Bar. solo/SATB/2222/422/timp. perc./str.	257
	The Blue Bird	SATB (a cappella)	257
	The Revenge	SATB chorus/3222/4431/timp. perc./str.	257
TANEIEV	Die Alpen	SATB (a cappella)	240
TCHAIKOVSKY	Legend	SATB (a cappella)	240
VERDI	Ave Maria	SATB (a cappella)	255, 256
	Laude alla Vergine Maria	SSAA (a cappella)	255, 256
	Messa da Requiem*	SATB soli/double chorus/piccolo 3224/4 cor. 8 tr. 3 tbnes. ophicleide/timp. perc./str.	248–255
	Stabat Mater	SATB chorus/3224/434/timp./harp/perc./str.	255
	Te Deum*	SATB double chorus/3. 2. cor. ang. 2. bass cl. 4/433/timp. perc./str.	255, 256
WESLEY (S)	In exitu Israel	SSAATTBB (a cappella)	256
WESLEY (S. S.)	The Wilderness	SATB soli/SATB/org.	256

VII. THE TWENTIETH CENTURY

Composer	Title of work	Forces required	Page reference
BAX	Mater ora filium	SSAATTBB (a cappella)	286
	Of a rose I sing a song (pub. Murdoch)	SATB chorus/harp/cello & double bass	287
BLACHER	Romeo and Julia (pub. Universal Ed.)	S. 2 A. 2 T.Bar.B soli/speaking parts/SATB/ fl. bassoon/tr. pfte./str.	287
BLOCH	Avodath Hakodesh* (Sacred Service) (pub. Summy-Birchard)	Bar. solo/SATB/org. or orch.—5.4.3.3. 2./str.	279, 304–6
BRITTEN	A Ceremony of Carols (Op. 28)	2 S soli/SSS chorus/harp	274, 286, 310
	Hymn to St. Cecilia (Op. 27)	SATB (a cappella)	309, 310
	Rejoice in the Lamb (Op. 30)	SATB/org.	286, 310
	St. Nicolas (Op. 42)	T solo/SATB/pfte. duet/org./timp. perc./ str.	274, 281, 310
	Spring Symphony (Op. 44)* (pub. Boosey & Hawkes)	SAT soli/boys' choir/SATB/3. 2. cor. ang. 2. bass d. 2. contra-bassoon/433/tuba/ cow-horn/timp. perc./str.	279, 282, 287 291, 309, 311–13
BURKHARD	Genug is nicht genug (pub. Universal Ed.)	SATB chorus/2 tr./timp./str.	287
CARPENTER	Song of Faith (pub. Schirmer)	Speaking part/SATB chorus/2.2.3.2./4.3. 3.1./perc./str./org.	314–15

349

Composer	Title of work	Forces required	Page reference
DELIUS	Appalachia	SATB chorus/3. 2. cor. ang. 3. 3. contra-bassoon/633 tuba/2 harps/timp./perc./str.	276, 277
	Mass of Life	SATB soli/SATB/3444/6431/2 harps/timp./str.	
	Requiem	S.Bar. soli/SATB/3444/6331/harp/celeste/timp./str.	276
	Sea-Drift	Bar. solo/SATB/3. 3. cor. ang. 3 bass cl. 3/633. tuba/2 harps/timp. perc./str.	278
	Song of the High Hills (pub. Universal Ed.)	SATB chorus/3344/6331/2 harps/celeste/timp./str.	277
DELLO JOIO	A Psalm of David* (pub. Carl Fischer)	SATB/4 cor. 4 tr. 3 tbnes. tuba/glockenspiel/perc./str.	315
HANSON, HOWARD	Lament for Beowulf (pub. Birchard)	SATB chor./str. (optional)	273
HARRIS, ROY	Folk Song Symphony (pub. Schirmer)	SATB chorus/32 cor. ang. 3 bass cl. 3/433 tuba/perc.	279, 282, 288, 291
	Symphony for voices	SSAATTBB (a cappella)	316
HOLST	Hymn of Jesus (Op. 37)* (pub. Stainer & Bell)	Double chorus SATB/Semi-chorus SSA/3. 2. cor. ang. 22/423/pfte./celeste/org./timp.perc./str.	274, 282, 296-8
	Two Psalms (pub. Stainer & Bell)	SATB chorus/str./org.	296
HONEGGER	Jeanne d'Arc au Bûcher (pub. Salabert)	2 S.A. 4 T. 3 B.soli/1 child/SATB/223. 3 sax. 3. contra-bassoon/44/2 pfte./celesta/perc./str.	291

351

Composer	Title of work	Forces required	Page reference
MARTIN	Golgotha*	SAT.Bar.B soli/SATB/2222/423/pfte./org./perc./str.	274, 284
	Le Vin herbé (pub. Universal Ed.)	12 voices (3333)/12 instrs. (2 vl. 2 vla. 2 celli. double bass/pfte.)	281, 286
MILHAUD	Service Sacré (pub. Salabert)	Bar. solo/SATB/org. (or orch.)	305
ORFF	Carmina Burana (pub. Schott)	ST.Bar soli/SATB/3333/4331/celesta/2 pfte./timp.perc./str.	283, 287
PIZZETTI	Messa di Requiem (pub. Ricordi)	4–12 parts (a cappella)	65, 275
POULENC	8 Chansons françaises (pub. Rouart, Lerolle)	SATB (a cappella)	288
SCHOENBERG	A Survivor from Warsaw (Op. 46) (pub Bomart)	Narrator/male chorus/ 3222/4331/harp/timp. perc./str.	278, 288
	Drei Satiren (Op. 28)	SATB chorus/cl. cello/ pfte. (for No. 3)	289, 290
	Gurre-Lieder	SAT.Tenor buffo. B soli/speaking part/12 part male chorus/SATB chorus/ 8575/10 1 tuba 6 tpts. (1 bass tr.) 7. 1/4 harps/celesta/timp. perc./str.	277, 280, 281, 288
	Vier Stücke (Op. 27)*	SATB chorus/mandoline/cl./vla. cello for No. 3	289, 290
STRAVINSKY	Ave Maria	SATB (a cappella)	275
	Cantata (1952)	ST soli/SSAA/2 fl. ob. cor. ang./cello	280, 284

Composer	Title of work	Forces required	Page reference
STRAVINSKY	Mass (1948)	SATB chorus/2 ob. cor. ang. 2 bassoons/2 tr. 3 tbnes.	275, 284, 301
	Pater noster	SATB (a cappella)	275
	Symphonie de Psaumes* (1948 revision) (pub. Boosey & Hawkes)	SATB chorus 5.4. cor ang. o. 3. contra-bassoon/453. tuba/2 pfte./timp. perc./celli. double bass	68, 287, 301-4, 311
SZYMANOWSKI	Stabat Mater* (pub. Universal Ed.)	SA.Bar.soli/SATB/2222/42/timp./harp/org./str.	274, 279, 282, 283
TIPPETT	A Child of our Time (pub. Schott)	SAB soli/SATB double choir/orch.	278, 285
VAUGHAN WILLIAMS	Mass in G minor* (pub. Curwen)	4-8 parts (a cappella)	275, 293-4
	O vos omnes (pub. Curwen)	SSAATTBB—(a cappella)	293
	Sancta Civitas* (pub. Curwen)	T.Bar. soli/SATB/semi-chorus and distant choir	274, 282, 294-5
WALTON	Belshazzar's Feast	BAR. solo/SATB double choir/323. sax. 2. contra-bassoon/4331/harp/pfte./org./timp. perc./2 brass bands/str.	68, 273, 287, 302

General Index

Only those works which receive passing notice in the text are referred to here: those which are more fully treated are indexed under their composer's name in the Index of Principal Works (p. 327). Dates of birth and death (where known) relate only to composers.